MOTOR CITY MOVIE CULTURE, 1916–1925

MOTOR CITY MOVIE CULTURE, 1916–1925

Richard Abel

INDIANA UNIVERSITY PRESS

This book is a publication of

Indiana University Press
Office of Scholarly Publishing
Herman B Wells Library 350
1320 East 10th Street
Bloomington, Indiana 47405 USA

iupress.indiana.edu

Manufactured in the United States of America

Library of Congress Cataloging-in-Publication Data

Names: Abel, Richard, 1941- author.
Title: Motor City movie culture, 1916-1925 / Richard Abel.
Description: Bloomington, Indiana : Indiana University Press, [2020] |
Includes bibliographical references and index.
Identifiers: LCCN 2019036664 (print) | LCCN 2019036665 (ebook) | ISBN
9780253046451 (hardback) | ISBN 9780253046468 (paperback) | ISBN
9780253046499 (ebook)
Subjects: LCSH: Motion picture theaters—Michigan—Detroit—History—20th century. |
Motion picture audiences—Michigan—Detroit—History—20th century. |
Motion pictures—Social aspects—Michigan—Detroit.
Classification: LCC PN1993.5.U752 A24 2020 (print) | LCC PN1993.5.U752
(ebook) | DDC 384.850977434—dc23
LC record available at https://lccn.loc.gov/2019036664
LC ebook record available at https://lccn.loc.gov/2019036665

1 2 3 4 5   25 24 23 22 21 20

For the "divine Ms. B"
Barbara C. Hodgdon
(1932–2018)
encore une fois

CONTENTS

ACKNOWLEDGMENTS

UCH LIKE MY PRIOR WORK, *Motor City Movie Culture, 1916–1925* is once again greatly indebted to a network of archives, libraries, colleagues, and friends for sustained support and encouragement.

Crucial support for the research on which this book relies came from the facilities and staff of the University of Michigan Hatcher Graduate Library, University of Michigan LSA Information Technology, Detroit Public Library, University of Michigan Bentley Historical Library, and University of Texas-Austin Ransom Center. That research also benefited from online databases of the Wayne State University Library, the *Detroit Free Press*, the Media History Digital Library, geneologybank.com, and newspapers.com.

I especially was grateful for the anonymous readers' reports that offered timely suggestions for revising the final version of the book. In different ways, each was helpful in making the introduction more precise in explaining the book's subject, what it is and is not primarily as a cultural history. Their suggestions also prodded me to reorganize and reduce the last chapter on Detroit's newspaper discourse, urged me to reposition the extensive list of picture theaters from an appendix to an early Entr'Acte, and confirmed my stress on certain lines of inquiry for further research in the afterword.

Special thanks go to Michael Hauser for permission to photocopy his personal collection of the *Weekly Film News* and to current and former University of Michigan doctoral students for their generous assistance. Ben Strassfeld found rare archive materials such as the *Michigan Film Review* as well as the digitized files of the *Detroit News Pictorial*, codesigned a graduate seminar that I taught on the history of Detroit, and created original maps of Detroit neighborhoods and many picture theater locations. Caitlin Dickinson deftly revised those into vector maps as required by the press. Ken Garner constructed a database of Detroit picture theaters, and Katy Peplin allowed me to draw on her research into Ford materials at the Ford Historical Museum and the National Archive. At one time or another, Garner, Strassfeld, Nathan Koob, and Jim Carter all scanned years of pages from the microfilm of surviving Detroit newspapers and offered useful contextual suggestions. Ginny Agnew photographed several fragments of early "house organ" programs that Koob found in research at the Ransom Center.

Many colleagues and friends graciously shared their own sources, helped locate new resources, posed pertinent questions, and led me to pursue those questions in unexpected ways. Paul S. Moore was especially helpful for his extensive knowledge of the early twentieth-century history of newspapers, film distribution, and film exhibition. Other support of one kind or another came from, in alphabetical order, Matthew Bernstein, Giorgio Bertellini, John Bukowczyk, Mark Garrett Cooper, Don Crafton, Leslie Midkiff DeBauche, Kathryn Fuller-Seeley, Doron Galili, Dan Herbert, Martin L. Johnson, Richard Koszarski, Stéphanie Salmon, Gregory Waller, and Mark Williams.

At Indiana University Press, Raina Polivka first expressed strong interest in the project. When she became acquisitions editor, Janice Frisch persuaded me to sign a contract with the press, and she smoothly kept the project on track, particularly when delays occurred in the later stages of writing. Allison Chaplin expertly eased the manuscript into production, despite some initial confusion over a few illustrations. David Hulsey directed the design team for the book's cover, and David Miller oversaw the processes of copyediting and proof review, which were handled so meticulously and efficiently by Jennifer Crane, Editorial Project Manager at Amnet. Garner helped edit the final version of the index.

Finally, finally, I am so deeply grateful to Barbara for the forty-two years we had together, often as Eeyore and Pooh, engaging in one "Expotition" after another "to discover what? . . . Oh, just something."[1] I would not have missed any of those for the world. Despite a lengthy illness, Barbara wrote another groundbreaking book, *Shakespeare, Performance and the Archive* (2016) and several essays, the last of which, "The Shakespeare Phonograph,"[2] announced a new research direction that has been cut short. Her keen intelligence, marvelously cadenced prose style, and mischievous wit certainly elevated my own writing. One of her typical marginal comments in reading most of the manuscript was "Punch up that last sentence."

But words sometimes do fail, now that "a great spirit is gone."

Parts of two chapters either draw on or are revised and much expanded versions of the following published essays:

- "'House Organs' and the Detroit *Weekly Film News* in the Late 1910s." *Film History* 27, no. 3 (2015): 137–179.
- "The Circulation of Local Newsreels in the Silent Period: The Case of Detroit." In *Rediscovering U.S. Newsfilm: Cinema, Television, and the Archive*, edited by Mark Garrett Cooper, Sarah Beth Levavy, Ross Melnick, and Mark Williams, 133–154. New York: Routledge, 2018.

Notes

1. A. A. Milne, *Winnie the Pooh* (New York: E. P. Dutton, 1926), 112.
2. Barbara Hodgdon, "The Shakespeare Phonograph," *Shakespeare Bulletin* 35, no.1 (Spring 2017): 1–14, doi:10.1353/shb.2017.0000.

LIST OF ABBREVIATIONS

For the purpose of space, the following abbreviations are used for frequently cited sources from the period.

Newspapers

BJ	*Brightmoor Journal*
CPD	*Cleveland Plain Dealer*
DFP	*Detroit Free Press*
DJ	*Detroit Journal*
DJC	*Detroit Jewish Chronicle*
DN	*Detroit News*
DNT	*Detroit News-Tribune*
DSFP	*Detroit Sunday Free Press*
DSN	*Detroit Sunday News*
DST	*Detroit Sunday Times*
DT	*Detroit Times*
FN	*Ferndale News*
HN	*Hamtramck News*
HP	*Highland Parker*

Industry Magazines

EFM	*Educational Film Magazine*
EH	*Exhibitors Herald*
ETR	*Exhibitors Trade Review*
FD	*Film Daily / Wid's Daily*
FT	*Ford Times*
M	*Motography*
MFR	*Michigan Film Review*
MPA	*Moving Picture Age*
MPM	*Motion Picture Magazine*

MPN	*Motion Picture News*
MPW	*Moving Picture World*
PM	*Photoplay Magazine*
R&S	*Reel and Slide*
V	*Variety*

Miscellaneous

E&P	*Editor & Publisher*
PW	*Photoplay Weekly*
WFN	*Weekly Film News*

MOTOR CITY MOVIE CULTURE, 1916–1925

INTRODUCTION

Michigan is in the midst of the greatest period of industrial expansion in its history.

"Made in Detroit USA," *Detroit Free Press* (November 5, 1917)

*M*OTOR *CITY MOVIE CULTURES* MAY SEEM TO NARROW my prior research on early twentieth-century American cinema, yet it also expands the subject of that research considerably. On the one hand, this book contributes to the study of local/regional cinema history by charting several paths through a specific historical site, a single city and its environs, Detroit, Michigan—with the caveat that "what defines the uniqueness of any place is by no means all included within that place itself [and] includes relations that stretch beyond."[1] Why Detroit? Although the fourth largest metropolis, according to the 1920 census, and "the most rapidly industrializing city in the country," it was relatively unique in being dominated by "a single heavy industry" dependent on a new mass of foreign-born, largely unskilled workers.[2] To date, the city has received almost no attention from cinema historians. I should add that acting as a devoted caregiver for six years put limits on the scope of my research that soon led to this project, which never failed to fascinate and provoked unexpected lines of inquiry. On the other hand, the book extends the temporal range of my research beyond 1916 to the years through early 1925. Why 1916–1925? Detroit's major newspapers did not begin devoting regular pages and columns to motion pictures until the fall of 1915 (somewhat later than many other cities), and smaller neighborhood papers carried only limited coverage until the period of 1922–1925. Moreover, most of the rare primary sources consulted do not run beyond 1925. Partly due to the Great War and its disastrous impact on Europe, this decade takes on added importance because, arguably, these were the initial boom years of Hollywood. In short, the book aims to become the first in-depth historical study of Detroit, primarily as a revealing example of the rich variety of American movie culture then emerging and secondarily as an important center of early twentieth-century motion picture distribution and exhibition and a more than minor site of production.

Among its objectives as a cultural history, then, *Motor City Movie Culture* argues for the significance of "movieland" culture in an unexamined metropolis during this crucial period of American cinema history. To that end, it offers "thick descriptions" and critical analyses of the defining features of that culture: the circulation of features as well as nonfiction films, the programming practices of palace cinemas as well as neighborhood theaters, and the moviegoing patterns of fans of all kinds. Rather than do a case study of Detroit's movie business (mainly restricted to chap. 1), it aims to construct a detailed understanding of the cultural network defined largely in terms of relations among rental exchanges, exhibitors, nonfiction producers, newspaper writers, and movie fans. To a degree, this cultural history aligns with Robert Allen's call for analyzing "the experience of cinema" and, more specifically, with Jeffrey Klenotic's focus on the "fixed-site experience for audiences."[3] The book also offers a model of how to deploy new primary sources—within the limits of their perspective lenses—to compile databases and create maps in order to analyze that cultural network. Those databases and maps highlight changes in space and time, especially in the context of demographics, transportation systems, commercial centers, and factory locations. That context sometimes plays an important role in studying the area's exhibition venues, and not only downtown palace cinemas but also theaters near ethnic/racial communities—that is, Polish, Italian, Jewish, Hungarian, and African American. Given the city's rapidly expanding population, due to a huge influx of immigrants and migrants (many of them actually refugees of one kind or another) drawn chiefly to the new automobile industry, the book argues that class, ethnic/racial, gender, and religious differences had particular pertinence in the development of Detroit's movie culture. A crucial arena for analyzing that development is the discourse—in newspapers, trade journals, theater programs, and spectator responses—devoted to the promotion and reception of motion pictures in the area. Finally, the book seeks, at least tentatively, to "stretch beyond" Detroit and compare its movie culture with existing studies of other cities and, ultimately, its implications for the broader conditions of American movie culture as a whole during this decade-long period.

Previous scholarship on local/regional cinema history in early twentieth-century America has tended to focus on metropolises such as New York, Chicago, Philadelphia, or Pittsburgh—for example, Ben Singer, Giorgio Bertellini, Doug Gomery, Moya Luckett, J. A. Lindstrom, Joel Frykholm, Michael Aronson—and on smaller cities and towns, including Los Angeles—for example, Jan Olsson, Greg Waller, Robert C. Allen, Kathryn Fuller-Seeley, Roy Rosenzweig. With the exception of the works by Gomery and Waller, those studies have not gone beyond the mid-1910s, when the Hollywood movie industry began its rise to dominance. My own prior work collected research on film distribution, exhibition, newspaper writing, and moviegoing in a wide range of specific cities, but closed off in the mid-1910s: (1) essays on Des Moines and Pawtucket; and (2) books on early American cinema encompassing Cleveland, Toledo, Youngstown, and Canton;

Pittsburgh; Buffalo and Rochester; Boston, Lynn, Lowell, and Lawrence; Philadelphia; Washington, DC; Atlanta; New Orleans; Chicago; St. Louis; Minneapolis, St. Paul; Salt Lake City; Seattle; and Portland, Oregon. Yet little of that involved Detroit, despite its proximity to my current location in Ann Arbor.

Motor City Movie Culture draws on original research material collected from a range of primary sources, most of which have never been examined by cinema historians. Those include

- pages, columns, ads, and stories in the city's major newspapers (*Detroit News, Detroit Free Press, Detroit Journal, Detroit Times*)[4] as well as neighborhood and ethnic/foreign language papers (e.g., *Hamtramck News, Highland Parker, Detroit Jewish Chronicle, Dearborn Press, Ferndale News, Brightmoor Journal, Dziennik Polski,* and *Tribuna Italiana d'America*);
- a rare surviving regional trade journal, the *Michigan Film Review* (1917–1918), held in the Bentley Historical Library at the University of Michigan;
- rare copies (more than fifty held by a private collector) of the *Weekly Film News* (1916–1919), a house organ of sixteen to twenty pages, given to its customers by the John Kunsky theater chain, the largest in Detroit and Southeast Michigan. Also, scattered programs of other large theaters (1917–1921), half a dozen copies of Kunsky's *Photoplay News* (1924–1925), and daily ads for seventy theaters in the *Detroit Times* (1922–1925);
- hundreds of digitized discrete film stories from a local newsreel, the *Detroit News Pictorial,* accessible on Wayne State University Library's website;
- spatiotemporal maps of Detroit, including "ethnic Detroit"; and
- city directories.

In order to better frame its analyses of the city's movie culture, the book also draws on existing scholarship on early American cinema history; early twentieth-century American urban history; and, specifically, early twentieth-century Detroit history—see the Bibliography. Why, then, is constructing that frame especially relevant?

In late 1917, the *Detroit Free Press* printed a column headlined "Made in Detroit USA" that congratulated the city for leading Michigan into its "greatest era of industrial activity."[5] Among the leading industries mentioned were railroads and factories producing industrial goods of all kinds.[6] The Detroit Terminal, for instance, encircled the city as far north as the middle of Highland Park; the Grand Trunk, Michigan Central, and Detroit Grand & Milwaukee intersected at Lake Shore Junction just southwest of Hamtramck. While many factories were

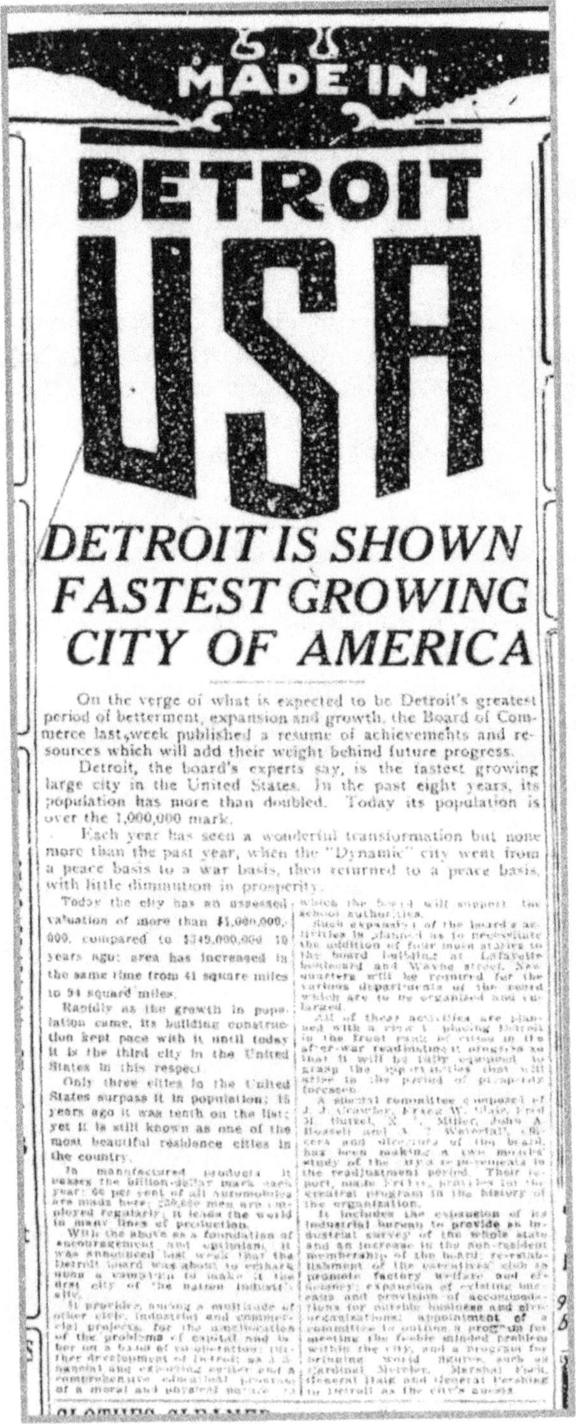

MADE IN DETROIT USA

DETROIT IS SHOWN FASTEST GROWING CITY OF AMERICA

On the verge of what is expected to be Detroit's greatest period of betterment, expansion and growth, the Board of Commerce last week published a resume of achievements and resources which will add their weight behind future progress.

Detroit, the board's experts say, is the fastest growing large city in the United States. In the past eight years, its population has more than doubled. Today its population is over the 1,000,000 mark.

Each year has seen a wonderful transformation but none more than the past year, when the "Dynamic" city went from a peace basis to a war basis, then returned to a peace basis, with little diminution in prosperity.

Today the city has an assessed valuation of more than $1,000,000,000, compared to $345,000,000 10 years ago; area has increased in the same time from 41 square miles to 54 square miles.

Rapidly as the growth in population came, its building construction kept pace with it until today it is the third city in the United States in this respect.

Only three cities in the United States surpass it in population; 15 years ago it was tenth on the list; yet it is still known as one of the most beautiful residence cities in the country.

Fig. 0.1. "Detroit USA" column logo, *Detroit Free Press* (January 13, 1919): 12.

located along the Detroit River, others clustered near Lake Shore Junction or in Hamtramck and near the intersection of the Michigan Central and Pere Marquette thirty blocks west of downtown. Yet automobile firms arguably constituted the most important industry. Lincoln had "1,500 men" building a new plant for making motors on the city's west side along the Pere Marquette line; and Packard Motor, on East Grand Boulevard along the Michigan Terminal line southeast of Hamtramck, was testing and assembling airplanes as part of the war effort. Topping them all was the Ford Motor Company. A few years earlier, Albert Kahn had designed Ford's three-story, 50,000-square-foot "Crystal Palace" factory for manufacturing the Model T in Highland Park next to the Detroit Terminal;[7] now the company was building even larger facilities at River Rouge (along another Pere Marquette branch line on the city's southwest edge) that eventually were expected to turn out "1,000,000 tractors annually," along with car bodies and rubber tires.[8] "The Michigan State Labor Department reported in 1919 that an overwhelming 45 percent of the 308,520 industrial employees . . . were in automobile and automobile accessory manufacturing."[9] Among the others were thousands of mostly Polish women in the city's fourth largest industry, making 5¢ cigars.[10] This industrial activity formed a favorable environment for entrepreneurs like John Kunsky, bent on developing the city's new motion picture industry. Yet that environment also was based on many other factors, all of which created a productive, yet complicated context shaping the Detroit area's film distribution, exhibition venues, and moviegoing practices from 1916 to 1925.

First of all, "analyzing a city," Olivier Zunz writes, "consists of understanding the spatial distribution of the population,"[11] and Detroit's spatial landscape changed considerably over the course of that decade. To accommodate its population of 993,678 by 1920—a stunning increase of 528,000 during the 1910s—the city "systematically annexed new territory on its periphery" until it had nearly tripled in size, reaching 79.6 square miles.[12] In the 1880s and 1890s, initial annexations had extended out from the central hub located around lower Third Street (where the new Union Depot was built near the Old City Hall),[13] west and east along the river (the latter, to the edge of Grosse Pointe Park), and north along Woodward Avenue (the crucial north–south artery)[14] to the adjacent areas of Hamtramck and Highland Park.[15] Between 1905 and 1917, an even larger land grab engulfed the mostly rural townships between the northwest (along Grand River Avenue), the north beyond Hamtramck and Highland Park, and the northeast along Gratiot Avenue (both major arteries radiating from the city's hub).[16] In the 1920s, further annexations added a swath of land in the northwest, another large area in the northeast, and a small section in the southwest next to Dearborn and River Rouge. In 1922, Henry Ford and the Dodge Brothers (the latter's auto factory was located on Hamtramck's southern border)[17] pressured elected officials in Highland Park and Hamtramck to rebuff annexation efforts and to incorporate

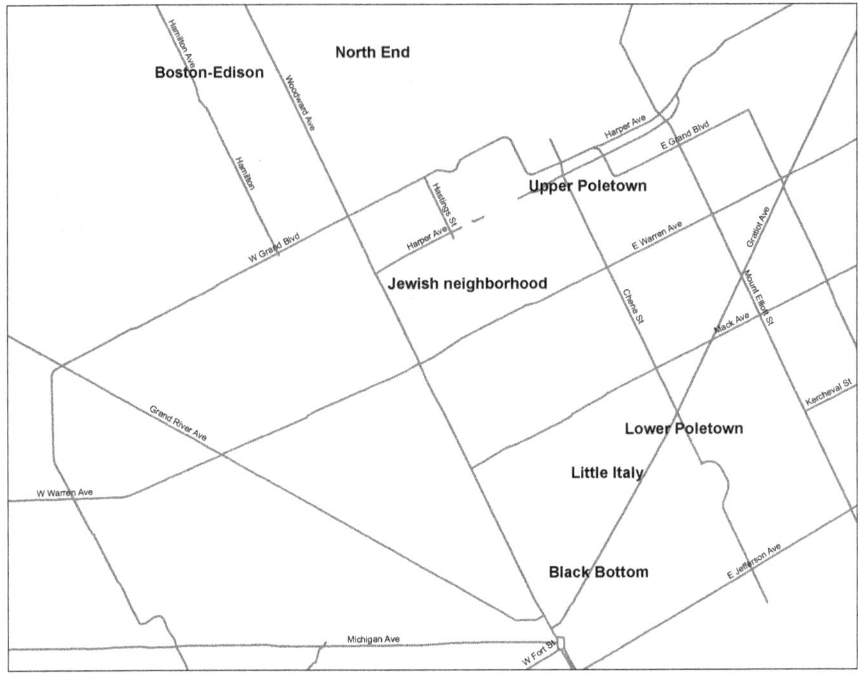

Fig. 0.2. 1917 Detroit map of neighborhoods.

as separate municipalities.[18] The result was that their factories escaped taxation from Detroit, and similar pressure from Ford kept the River Rouge facilities just outside the city. By then, Detroit's boundaries had reached their farthest extent. This huge land mass, not unlike Los Angeles, was sustainable until the late 1940s and early 1950s, when people (largely white) increasingly moved out into the suburbs;[19] by the late twentieth century, however, as the city's population declined precipitously and its property tax base shrank, those boundaries became a disastrous liability.

Among the city's burgeoning population during the 1910s, according to Olivier Zunz, "412,00 were migrants."[20] Most differed from those who had come to Detroit in earlier years—when foreign-born German, British, and Canadian residents dominated—but now resided on the city's west side (divided by Woodward), from close to downtown north to Highland Park, or on the east side, beyond any recent immigrant communities, and as far out as the residential suburbs of Grosse Pointe.[21] According to a 1914 *Collier's* article, their elite citizens formed "two fairly distinct social groups": "old families" in Grosse Pointe and a newer "North Woodward group" tagged the "Gasoline Aristocracy."[22] As the former immigrant population fell in proportional numbers, others increased: namely,

Poles, Italians, Hungarians, Slavs, and Russian Jews.[23] By 1920, 25.1 percent of the city's population was foreign-born, and another 3 percent were black migrants from the South.[24] Within five years, "the foreign-born constituted about one-half of Detroit's" total population, swelled by nearly 245,000 new immigrants.[25] These later immigrants and migrants (or refugees) tended to congregate in already established ethnic/racial neighborhoods. The black community, for instance, was restricted to a ghetto area called "Black Bottom" slightly east and north of downtown,[26] on the Jewish ghetto's southern edge; a more prominent Jewish community then developed in the "North End" near Central High School.[27] Slightly east of the initial Jewish ghetto was an Italian community and then a much larger Polish neighborhood known as "Lower Poletown" that stretched farther south and north.[28] Hungarians resided in Del Ray on the city's southwest edge, with small Polish, Italian, and Slavic neighborhoods nearby.[29] Generally, these immigrants were restricted to those areas not through zoning ordinances, "which were declared unconstitutional in 1917," but "through private real estate covenants."[30] The Polish were an exception, as many "Lower Poletown" residents and recent immigrants moved to a west side neighborhood along Michigan between 20th Street and 30th Street (near the railroad intersection) but mostly north to the east of Lake Shore Junction and especially into Hamtramck.[31]

Hamtramck and Highland Park, as "independent" cities within Detroit, were important for several reasons. Hamtramck had grown from a population of 3,559 in 1910 to 48,625 in 1920 and, when it was incorporated in 1922, had the largest concentration of Polish people outside Warsaw.[32] Consequently, it was a working-class community dominated by one ethnic group whose religious affiliation, like that of the Italians, was Catholic, and most Poles were employed as unskilled or semiskilled factory workers at either the Dodge Brothers plant (covering seventy-two acres) or other nearby companies, manufacturing automobiles or parts—for example, Packard Motor, Cadillac Motor, American Car, American Motor Castings, Detroit Steel Products, and Russell Wheel Foundry.[33] Similarly, Highland Park had grown from a few thousand people in 1910 to 46,615 in 1920.[34] Its demographic, however, was different. While "native white Americans" (a census category) were the primary residents, especially in the southwestern area near the wealthy Boston-Edison community, they were divided spatially into two classes: white-collar workers and skilled or semiskilled factory workers. Foreign immigrants tended to live either close to Ford's Crystal Palace, as did a small Syrian Muslim community,[35] or in the northern part of the city. Whatever their ethnicity, most were employed at the Ford plant; others, at Maxwell Motor.[36] Young, single men dominated the working class and resided as boarders relatively near the auto factories, so that in 1920 the ratio of men to women was unusually high: 133.1 to 100.[37]

As in many other American cities, recent immigrants and black migrants often found themselves the objects of prejudice and fear.[38] In 1912, the founder of

Cadillac, Henry Leland, had set up the Detroit Citizens League, an elite group of white Protestants aligned with the Republican Party's anti-Catholic, anti-immigrant, and temperance factions.[39] After a new charter was enacted in 1918 to mandate citywide elections for mayor and a smaller council, the league was chagrined to have the first mayor's election won by someone once considered a "friend": James Couzens, a Ford Motor vice president who actually managed the company until he had a fallout with Henry Ford in early 1914.[40] The former police commissioner, Couzens campaigned on a platform of Progressive "clean" government. Despite his efforts to reduce crime and corruption and to fund public works, a variety of conditions, including his own blunt style in working with other officials, conspired against him as one whom the *Saturday Evening Post* later called a "scab millionaire."[41] Among those conditions were insufficient tax monies; the Red Scare of 1919 that targeted "foreign workers";[42] the resurgence of the Ku Klux Klan, which had thirty-two thousand members in Detroit by late 1924;[43] the Eighteenth Amendment, which turned the city into a "wide-open booze town" and a center for bootlegging;[44] and a severe housing crisis, exacerbated by the 1920–1921 economic depression, that chiefly affected ethnic communities and the black ghetto[45] and was slow to gain the attention of city officials.[46] One of Couzens's pet projects (supported by only the *Detroit News*) was to convince city officials to purchase the often criticized private street car company; after years of fruitless negotiations, the purchase finally became a reality in early 1922.[47]

The auto industry developed its own plans to manage the flood of immigrants and migrants. After the first "boom and bust cycle,"[48] in 1915 the Detroit Board of Commerce[49] had begun to institute a paternalistic policy of dealing with fears of unrest among foreign workers. The policy, supported by the national Committee for Immigrants in America, was modeled on efforts by Ford and the YMCA to indoctrinate and transform immigrants.[50] This was the Americanization movement—led by Ford's Sociological department and a volunteer Committee on Education—which urged workers (and their families) to attend night classes in English and US citizenship, with the underlying aim of producing a more stable, efficient labor force by replacing ethnic ties with "school ties . . . sanctioned by the industrial order."[51] A Ford English School graduation ceremony in February 1916 staged a symbolic spectacle of that transformation for an audience that included prominent business leaders: against the backdrop of an ocean steamship, men dressed in foreign costumes and bearing signs naming their origin countries slowly descended a gangway into a huge "Ford English School Melting Pot" center stage and soon "emerged dressed in American clothes" and carrying small American flags, under a banner proclaiming "E Pluribus Unum."[52] In conjunction with this policy, Ford introduced the $5-a-day profit-sharing plan, but only for workers whose "thriftiness, good habits, good home conditions, and six-month residency" in the country made them eligible.[53] Unless they succeeded in "Americanization" classes, most foreign workers were excluded. The lack of strong unions in the city also allowed Ford and other companies to control their labor force more easily.[54] This was partly the result of the Employers' Association of Detroit (EAD), founded in 1902 to attract unskilled workers for the auto industry;[55] general manager Chester M. Culver (involved in the Americanization movement) made it perhaps the most "powerful political force in the city."[56]

At least one feature of the city's contextual landscape remains relevant: the range of available newspapers. Four dailies dominated the region during this period. The *Evening News* had long been one of James Scripps's working-class papers, addressed to "Mr. and Mrs. Common People."[57] A member of the Scripps-McRae chain in the Midwest, the *News* became part of the United Press wire service in 1907.[58] A progressive, "independent" paper that by the early 1910s—under publisher George G. Booth and managing editor Edwin G. Pipp—began to target a mass rather than a class readership,[59] the *News*, like other Scripps papers, remained often critical of industrialization, supported the city's 1918 charter reform,[60] and was a strong advocate of municipal ownership (such as the street railway system) and "public service."[61] Following the construction of an imposing new office-factory, celebrated in *Editor & Publisher*,[62] the *News* had the largest circulation in the city, with a daily edition of 218,500 copies in 1919[63] and a Sunday edition that exceeded 300,000 copies by 1925.[64] The next largest paper in circulation was the more conservative, "upscale" *Free Press*, a morning paper and, consequently, a member of the Associated Press wire service.[65] The publisher was Edward Douglas Stair, a major real estate owner and theater entrepreneur; Phil J. Reid was the managing editor.[66] The *Free Press* was closely aligned with the city's business interests, as evidenced, in March 1918, by other "Made in Detroit USA" stories and by scores of "Michigan Manufacturers" filling large block ads.[67] Four years later, the paper boasted of "more financial advertising" than all other papers combined.[68] In 1925, its offices moved into a new "14-story Albert Kahn designed building"; its daily circulation was close to 200,000 copies, the Sunday edition 275,000.[69]

The more important of the other two dailies was the *Detroit Times*, another evening paper, whose publisher James Schermerhorn, in 1919, tried to make the paper over into "the voice of a virile city"—"clean, complete, concise, constructive, conservative."[70] Despite his efforts, the *Times*'s circulation remained low until William Randolph Hearst, on a buying spree, made it part of his media empire in October 1921.[71] Within six months, its daily print run rose from a meager 26,000 to 100,000; by late 1923, the circulation of both the daily and Sunday editions reached 200,000; and its editorial positions hewed closer to Hearst's own oxymoronic promotion of "an unremitting fight for progressive Americanism."[72] Last was the *Detroit Journal*, an afternoon paper that Stair was publishing before investing in the *Free Press* in 1906.[73] The editorial policy of the *Journal*, not surprisingly, paralleled that of the *Free Press*, as in its opposition to any proposal for the city to purchase and renovate the streetcar system.[74] It claimed to offer "a remarkable daily double magazine page for women," with subjects—from "club news" and "society notes" to "menu ideas" and "shopping hints"—appealing to women of a certain class.[75] By 1922, the *Journal*'s circulation had reached 120,000; at that point, however, the paper was sold to its competitor, the *News*, which quickly closed it down.[76]

While there were a dozen or more neighborhood and foreign-language newspapers (with much smaller readerships), very few have survived. Fortunately for this study, the daily *Hamtramck News* and *Highland Parker* do—the *Hamtramck News* from the time the two cities were incorporated in 1922—as does the *Detroit Jewish Chronicle*.[77] Scattered copies of several weeklies on Detroit's western and northwestern outskirts also still exist: the *Dearborn Press*, the *Brightmoor Journal*, and the *Ferndale News*. Limited to just a few pages for each copy, the weekly *Tribune Italiana* and daily *Dziennik Polski* targeted readers restricted to, respectively, many first- and second-generation Italian and Polish immigrants.[78] Finally, among all the different trade magazines published in the city was the *Michigan Film Review*, one of only a few regional weeklies in the country devoted exclusively to the motion picture industry. Although this is unconfirmed, it may have had close ties with the *Free Press* and its business interests: each one's editorial office could be found in the same downtown building.

At various points, one or more elements of this framing summary inform this historical study of Detroit movie culture, which divides into four chapters and six entr'actes and concludes with an afterword.

Chapter 1 defines that culture from the perspective of film circulation, largely that of feature fiction films, and describes and analyzes the interrelations of distribution and exhibition over space and time. Although sketching the infrastructure of the city's movie business, it largely explores a complex nexus of circulation, especially attentive to the inclusion and exclusion of different ethnic neighborhoods, and it situates that nexus at points within one or more larger cultural, social, and/or economic contexts. Its analysis focuses on changes in film circulation, especially in terms of demographics, factory locations, transportation systems, and commercial centers. The chapter draws particularly on the following documents: surviving issues of the *Michigan Film Review*, Detroit's four main newspapers, extant issues of Kunsky's weekly house organs, the national trade press, and other local sources.

Chapter 2 looks at that culture from the perspective of programming practices: what the city's moviegoers would expect to find in their picture theaters. Although stars and their features usually were prominent on most programs, nearly all theaters essentially mounted variety shows, in which, as Richard Koszarski puts it, features were but one part of an "evening's entertainment."[79]

Within those variety shows, moreover, live performances and short films could be as attractive as features in luring customers to theaters. The chapter includes information that would have interested those establishing routines of attending certain theaters, on certain days, and at certain times: program starting times, seat ticket costs, promotions of upcoming films. The analysis of weekly and daily programs in individual theaters and categories of theaters in chapter 2 draws on the following documents: Kunsky's *Weekly Film News* and *Photoplay Weekly*, several other rare theater programs, and the city's four main newspapers—specifically, ads from a wide range of neighborhood theaters as well as palace cinemas.

Chapter 3 focuses on the circulation of short nonfiction films. That circulation includes weekly newsreels, "screen magazines," travelogues and "scenics," popular science films, and Hollywood "snapshots" of the stars, all from major producers or distributors. Yet its main concern is with "Detroit-Made" films, not only produced locally but also exhibited as local program attractions. One set of these films, produced by the Ford Motor Company, is relatively well known, but the others are not: the local newsreels produced by the Metropolitan Film Company in conjunction with the city's two main newspapers—the *Detroit Free Press Film Edition* (1918–1923) and the *Detroit News Pictorial* (1923–1925). The chapter examines these newsreels in particular for their choice of subjects, the implication of those choices, and their mode of representation (specifically in the surviving discrete stories of the *Pictorial*), as well as the range and extent of their exhibition.

Chapter 4 aims to analyze the movie pages and columns in the city's four main newspapers: the *Detroit Free Press*, *Detroit News*, *Detroit Journal*, and *Detroit Times*. Most generally, it addresses the question of how they shaped, often implicitly, their readers' sense of the movies as a more or less routine part of daily life. More specifically, if that shaping involved a regular diet of information and gossip that could change over time, whom did the newspapers assume their moviegoing readers to be, and how did their often quite different choices of menu items seem to address different kinds of movie fans? Finally, the chapter analyzes the "interactive" forums of selected responses from movie fans evidenced in a variety of newspaper contests as well as in material cut out of many *Weekly Film News* issues, likely for a scrapbook no longer extant.

Five of this volume's six Entr'Actes offer brief contextual profiles of the *Michigan Film Review*; major industry figures John Kunsky and George Trendle and their *Weekly Film News*; local film producers the Metropolitan Film Company and Detroit-Made Film Company; and the *Detroit News-Tribune*'s unique image of a "star-gazing" movie fan. To assist readers of chapters 1 and 2, the second Entr'Acte lists the names, addresses, and seating capacities of Detroit area theaters during this decade.

The afterword takes up several of the issues that arise in writing such a cultural history. Some of those issues depend on which sources are consulted in a region uniquely defined as an emerging hub for manufacturing automobiles and automotive parts, with an unusually large, predominantly male immigrant population. It also sketches several trajectories of further research suggested by this introduction that might recover primary sources that either have been difficult to locate or require much more time to find and access. Those include not only the career of John Kunsky, his enterprises in Detroit, and his relationship with Hollywood, but also the impact on the city's movie culture—brought about (1) by labor issues, particularly involving the automobile industry and not only the movie business; (2) by Detroit's unique ethnic and racial diversity, especially that of black migrants; and (3) by who actually were the fans who inhabited and played a crucial role in that culture.

A brief personal postscript: Although no one in my family ever had close connections to Detroit during this time, my father was a committed owner of Ford automobiles throughout his life. And I learned to drive by handling a 1951 Ford two-door coupe that enclosed me in the heavy metal shell that felt like a tank. I also recall a family vacation in the 1950s when my parents took all seven of us children on a tour of Greenfield Village in Dearborn, Michigan, the ersatz village that, in 1929, Henry Ford had constructed as a nostalgic reincarnation of turn-of-the-last-century America, with its huge collection of early automobiles and "imported" buildings such as his friend Thomas Edison's laboratory and adjacent boardinghouse from Menlo Park, New Jersey. Perhaps it's appropriate for such controversial pioneers of major twentieth-century industries as Ford and Edison to front this far-from-nostalgic reimagining of early movie culture in Detroit.

Notes

1. Doreen Massey, *Space, Place, and Gender* (Minneapolis: University of Minnesota Press, 1994), 5.

2. Melvin G. Holli, ed., *Detroit* (New York: New Viewpoints, 1976), 123; and Olivier Zunz, *The Changing Face of Inequality Urbanization, Industrial Development, and Immigration in Detroit, 1880–1920* (Chicago: University of Chicago Press, 1982), 5. See also "Made in Detroit USA: Detroit Is Shown Fastest Growing City in America," *DFP* (January 13, 1919): 12.

3. Robert C. Allen, "Getting to 'Going to the Show,'" and Jeffrey Klenotic, "Space, Place, and the Female Film Exhibitor," in *Locating the Moving Image: New Approaches to Film and Place*, ed. Julia Hallam and Les Roberts (Bloomington: Indiana University Press, 2014), 33 and 54, respectively.

4. Both the *News* and *Free Press* survive in nearly complete runs during this period: the *News* on microfilm (and just recently in digital form); the *Free Press* in digital files on the current newspaper's website. Although the *Journal* and *Times* survive on microfilm, neither is complete: the first is missing issues near the end of its existence in 1922; the second has scattered missing weeks from August 1923 through March 1924.

5. "Made in Detroit USA," *DFP* (November 5, 1917): 16. This column, embedded within dozens of ads, was centered in an "Industrial Doings" page that appeared on Mondays, from January 1917 at least through 1919.

6. Zunz, *The Changing Face of Inequality*, 298–303. These 1920 maps were drawn from G. William Baist, *Real Estate Atlas of Surveys of Detroit and Suburbs*, vols. 1–2 (Philadelphia: G. William Baist, 1918); C. M. Burton, *The City of Detroit, Michigan, 1701–1922* (Detroit: Clark Publishing, 1922); and R. L. Polk and Co., *Detroit City Directory*, 1920.

7. The name "Crystal Palace" aligned Ford's production site with an earlier icon of imperialist technology, London's famous 1851 "Great Exhibition of the Works of Industry in All Nations."

8. By 1926, the River Rouge facilities covered 1,115 acres and employed 7,500 people—David L. Lewis, *The Public Image of Henry Ford: An American Folk Hero and His Company* (Detroit: Wayne State University Press, 1978), 161.

9. Holli, *Detroit*, 119. Those accessory companies included manufacturers of steel and aluminum parts; African American men made up from 25 percent to 50 percent of the companies' work force, a higher percentage than in the automobile companies, despite the thousands employed by Ford.

10. Most cigar factories were nonunion, were located in or near Polish communities, and employed mainly young women. Patricia A. Cooper, *Once a Cigar Maker: Men, Women, and Work Culture in American Cigar Factories, 1900–1919* (Urbana: University of Illinois Press, 1987), 191–192. The 1910 US Census listed tobacco manufacturing as the fourth largest industry in Detroit—summarized in Sister Mary Remigia Napolska, *The Polish Immigrant in Detroit to 1914: Annuals of the Polish R.C. Union Archives and Museums*, vol. 10, 1945–1946 (Chicago: Polish Roman Catholic Union of America, 1946), 33.

11. Zunz, *The Changing Face of Inequality*, 9.

12. Zunz, *The Changing Face of Inequality*, 286–287.

13. Don Lochbiler, *Detroit's Coming of Age, 1873–1973* (Detroit: Wayne State University Press, 1973), 69.

14. The lumber baron David Whitney predicted the city's growth along Woodward, and his son erected a medical center in his honor at Grand Circus Park. See Lochbiler, *Detroit's Coming of Age*, 232–235.

15. Robert Conot, *American Odyssey* (New York: Morrow, 1974), frontispiece.

16. Zunz, *The Changing Face of Inequality*, 290.

17. For more information on the Dodge Brothers, see Charles K. Hyde, "The Dodge Brothers: The Automobile Industry, and Detroit Society in the Early Twentieth Century," *Michigan Historical Review* 22, no. 2 (Fall 1996): 49–82. For a 1915 layout of Dodge Main's assembly line design, see Hyde, "'Dodge Main' and Detroit's Automobile Industry, 1910–1980," *Detroit in Perspective* 6, no. 1 (Spring 1982): 7.

18. Conot, *American Odyssey*, 213.

19. See, for instance, Thomas J. Sugrue, *Origins of the Urban Crisis: Race and Inequality in Postwar Detroit* (Princeton, NJ: Princeton University Press, 1996); and David M. P. Freund, *Colored Property: State Policy and White Racial Politics in Suburban America* (Chicago: University of Chicago Press, 2007).

20. Zunz, *The Changing Face of Inequality*, 287.

21. Zunz, *The Changing Face of Inequality*, 291.

22. Julian Street, "Detroit the Dynamic," *Collier's* (July 4, 1914): 9.

23. Along with those from the Balkans, many Slavs came to the city's factories from copper mines and lumber camps in the Upper Peninsula or coalmines in Pennsylvania and

New York—see Richard W. Thomas, *Life for Us Is What We Make It: Building Black Community in Detroit, 1915–1945* (Bloomington: Indiana University Press, 1992), 25.

24. Clarence Hooker, *Life in the Shadows of the Crystal Palace, 1910–1927: Ford Workers in the Model T Era* (Bowling Green, OH: Bowling Green University Press, 1997), 44, 51; Zunz, *The Changing Face of Inequality*, 104, 287.

25. Holli, *Detroit*, 121.

26. Bounding the "Black Bottom" ghetto area were Beaubien and Hastings, respectively, on the west and east, and Brewster and Napoleon on the north and south. Hooker, *Life in the Shadows of the Crystal Palace*, 95; Elaine Latzman Moon, *Untold Tales, Unsung Heroes: An Oral History of Detroit's African-American Community, 1918–1967* (Detroit: Wayne State University Press, 1994), 37; and Kevin Boyle and Victoria Getis, eds., *Muddy Boots and Ragged Aprons: Images of Working-Class Detroit, 1900–1930* (Detroit: Wayne State University Press, 1997), 16. The first wave of 25,000–35,000 black migrants came in 1916–1917; these workers were lured by the labor shortages resulting from the United States' entry into World War I—see Thomas, *Life for Us Is What We Make It*, 26–27. Especially important to this crowded black ghetto were not only churches (there were thirty-nine by 1919) and the Columbia Community Center set up by the Detroit Urban League, but also the saloons of "Paradise Valley"—see Henri Florette, *Black Migration: Movement North, 1900–1920* (Garden City, NY: Anchor/Doubleday, 1975), 115; Boyle and Getis, 18; and Thomas, 69.

27. Bounding the initial Jewish ghetto were Watson and Monroe, respectively, on the north and south, and Brush and Orleans on the west and east. Central High School was located at Warren and Cass, and this later Jewish area stretched north of there and east for half a dozen blocks along Woodward up to Highland Park. Ernest Goodman recalled a "bloody battle" in the early 1920s between the "WASP students who politically ran the school" and the "roughhouse Jewish guys" who later joined the Purple Gang. Christopher H. Johnson, *Maurice Sugar: Law, Labor, and the Left in Detroit, 1912–1950* (Detroit: Wayne State University Press, 1988), 35. See also Moon, *Untold Tales, Unsung Heroes*, 61; and Zunz, *The Changing Face of Inequality*, 345.

28. The Italian and Polish neighborhoods inhabited the area along Orleans and St. Aubin from Gratiot on the south almost to Forest on the north. See Parker, 191; and Zunz, 345. "In 1914 the Polish population of Detroit numbered between 110,000 and 120,000," nearly one-quarter of the total population—Sister Mary Remigia Napolska, *The Polish Immigrant in Detroit to 1914*, 20.

29. Zunz, *The Changing Face of Inequality*, 327.

30. Zunz, *The Changing Face of Inequality*, 374. In 1924, the Detroit Real Estate Board codified these zoning restrictions—Beth Tompkins Bates, *The Making of Black Detroit in the Age of Henry Ford* (Chapel Hill: University of North Carolina Press, 2012), 105.

31. Cooper, *Once a Cigar Maker*, 191.

32. Greg Kowalski, *Hamtramck: The Driven City* (Chicago: Arcadia, 2002), 31; and Frank Serafino, *West of Warsaw* (Hamtramck, MI: Hamtramck Avenue Publishing, 1983), 39–40.

33. Zunz, *The Changing Face of Inequality*, 354.

34. Zunz, *The Changing Face of Inequality*, 291.

35. In the 1920s, the Syrian Muslim population in Highland Park ranged from 7,000 to 16,000. In 1921, the first mosque in the United States was constructed one block from the Crystal Palace. Sally Howell, *Old Islam in Detroit: Rediscovering the Muslim American Past* (New York: Oxford University Press, 2014), 34, 39, 44–50.

36. Hooker, *Life in the Shadow of the Crystal Palace*, 58; Zunz, *The Changing Face of Inequality*, 354.

37. Hooker, *Life in the Shadow of the Crystal Palace*, 60; and Kevin Boyle and Victoria Getis, eds., *Muddy Boots and Ragged Aprons: Images of Working-Class Detroit, 1900–1930* (Detroit: Wayne State University Press, 1997), 15.

38. Under the mistaken assumption that immigrants disproportionately were responsible for increases in urban crime across the country, Congress in 1907 had formed a commission to "investigate the problems of immigration." Despite four years of data (collected in forty volumes), which unexpectedly failed to support that belief, the commission nonetheless issued a report that completely contradicted its findings—see Conot, *American Odyssey*, 221–222.

39. Conot, *American Odyssey*, 186; Raymond R. Fragnolli, *The Transformation of Reform: Progressivism in Detroit—And After, 1912–1933* (New York: Garland, 1982), 24–117. During its first year, this organization was called the Detroit Citizens Uplift League.

40. Harry Barnard, *Independent Man: The Life of Senator James Couzens* (New York: Charles Scribner, 1958), 117–125. See also David Allan Levine, *Internal Combustion: The Races in Detroit, 1915–1926* (Westport, CT: Greenwood Press, 1976), 14–16; and Conot, *American Odyssey*, 197–198. John Kronk, a Pole, became the only non-Anglo councilman after the new nonpartisan at-large election—Fragnoli, *The Transformation of Reform*, 182.

41. Conot, *American Odyssey*, 213–215; Zunz, *The Changing Face of Inequality*, 323–324. "Scab millionaire" apparently came from "Who's Who—and Why—Serious and Frivolous Facts About the Great and Near Great," *Saturday Evening Post* (April 21, 1923): n.p.

42. Couzens tried to keep Detroit's police department from cooperating with US attorney general A. William Palmer's "red raids"—Harry Barnard, *Independent Man*, 124–125. Anti-German sentiment during the Great War framed initial attitudes toward the Soviet revolution, as evidenced in an early 1918 screening of *The German Intrigue in Russia*, paired with a reissue print of the French version of *Les Misérables*—Colonial ad, *DJC* (January 11, 1918): 8.

43. A Klan sympathizer, Charles Bowles, narrowly lost the race for mayor that year to John W. Smith, "whose primary support was among Catholics, Negroes, and recent immigrants." Bowles's support was especially strong in the white Protestant areas of the city's northwest, north, far west, and far east—Ken Jackson, *The Ku Klux Klan in the City, 1915–1930* (New York: Oxford University Press, 1967), 91, 134–139. While the *News* condemned the Klan and supposedly opposed Bowles, the *Free Press* may have given implicit support to Bowles, for it had accepted an ad for Klan membership in 1921—Jackson, *The Ku Klux Klan in the City*, 129. See also Frank Angelo, *On Guard: A History of the Detroit Free Press* (Detroit: Detroit Free Press, 1981), 146.

44. Paul R. Kavieff, *The Purple Gang: Organized Crime in Detroit 1910–1945* (Fort Lee, NJ: Barricade, 2000). The "Sugar House Gang" initially controlled bootlegging in the city, until younger men that the gang had mentored formed their own Purple Gang in the mid-1920s. The leaders of both gangs apparently were largely Jewish. "The Purples were reputedly named by a robbery victim who said they were bad like bad meat—purple"—William W. Lutz, *The News of Detroit: How a Newspaper and a City Grew Together* (Boston: Little, Brown, 1973), 94.

45. As early as the summer of 1916, the black ghetto was becoming crowded: "All acts playing at Detroit, Mich., will have a hard time in locating rooms, as the town is run over with people."—Singh Henry Jines, "Vaudette Theatre, Detroit, Mich.," *Indianapolis Freeman* (June 10, 1916): 5.

46. Levine, *Internal Combustion*, 37–45, 50–51; Thaddeus C. Radzialowski, "Ethnic Conflict and the Polish Americans of Detroit, 1921–1942," in *The Polish Presence in Canada and America*, ed. Frank Renkiewicz (Toronto: Multicultural Society of Ontario, 1982), 198. For a selection of photographs documenting the housing conditions, see the "Home" section in Boyle and Gettis, eds., *Muddy Boots and Ragged Aprons*, 27–73.

47. Lutz, *The News of Detroit*, 47–48. The *Free Press* "led the fight against public ownership of the street railway system"—Angelo, *On Guard*, 143.

48. Holli, *Detroit*, 125.

49. The Board of Commerce members included Horace Rackham (Ford's legal counsel), Oscar B. Marx (the city's current mayor), Frank D. Cody (the assistant school superintendent),

A. G. Studer (YMCA general secretary), and E. W. Scripps (director of the Scripps-McRae newspaper chain, which included the *Detroit News*). Marx was a political ally of the Dodge brothers and a frequent drinking buddy among the city's power brokers who gathered at the Pontchartrain Hotel—see Lochbiler, *Detroit's Coming of Age*, 215, 218.

50. That fear was driven by the 1914–1915 recession and the ensuing labor surplus—Anne Brophy, "'The Committee . . . has stood out against coercion': The Reinvention of Detroit Americanization, 1915–1931," *Michigan Historical Review* 29, no. 2 (Fall 2003): 2, 5–7. Brophy's essay (pp. 1–29) offers an excellent historical study of the Americanization movement in Detroit. A parallel strategy was the Detroit Urban League's "Dress Well Club," which aimed to transform black migrants from the South—Levine, *Internal Combustion*, 87–90.

51. Brophy, "The Committee," 8, 13. See also Conot, *American Odyssey*, 178; Zunz, *The Changing Face of Inequality*, 311–317; and Hooker, *Life in the Shadow of the Crystal Palace*, 115–117.

52. "A Motto Wrought into Education," *Ford Times* 9 (April 1916): 407–409. Of the "2,200 foreign born employees" enrolled, "519 pupils" graduated that day. A photo of the spectacle fills page 408. See also Levine, *Internal Combustion*, 25–26.

53. Zunz, *The Changing Face of Inequality*, 311–312; Hooker, *Life in the Shadow of the Crystal Palace*, 107–112; Levine, *Internal Combustion*, 21–24. It was James Couzens who most developed the Ford plan and announced it in early January 1914—Barnard, *Independent Man*, 87–93.

54. Despite leading several strikes in 1913, the Industrial Workers of the World (IWW) never played a strong role in the city; moreover, the Urban League, formed in 1916, actively recruited blacks from the South for the auto industry, in cooperation with the Employers' Association of Detroit (EAD). Conot, *American Odyssey*, 154; Hooker, *Life in the Shadow of the Crystal Palace*, 50, 116; Levine, *Internal Combustion*, 28–30, 81.

55. Levine, *Internal Combustion*, 28–29; Joyce Shaw Peterson, *American Automobile Workers, 1900–1933* (Albany: SUNY Press, 1987), 12–13. Henry Leland also was a member of the EAD; although he believed workers needed unions, he deplored strikes and thought employers needed advocacy groups even more—Mrs. Wilfred C. Leland and Minnie Dubbs Millbrook, *Master of Precision: Henry M. Leland* (Detroit: Wayne State University Press, 1966), 167–168.

56. A 1920 study "of the currents of opinion among workingmen and the prevailing conditions of labor in a progressive factory town" apparently supported the EAD—Myron Watkins, "The Labor Situation in Detroit," *Journal of Political Economy* 28 (December 1920): 840–852.

57. Gerald J. Baldasty, *E. W. Scripps and the Business of Newspapers* (Urbana: University of Illinois Press, 1999), 106–109, 146–148; Richard L. Kaplan, *Politics and the American Press: The Rise of Objectivity, 1865–1920* (Cambridge, UK: Cambridge University Press, 2002), 110–115.

58. Baldasty, *E. W. Scripps and the Business of Newspapers*, 21.

59. Lutz, *The News of Detroit*, 35, 57. The *Detroit Tribune*, a smaller "upscale" rival to the *Free Press*, which the *Evening News* had owned since the early 1890s, was closed down in 1915; but for several years the company's Sunday edition became the *Detroit News-Tribune*. Targeting a mass audience, the *News* may have been the first newspaper to launch a commercial radio station, WWJ, in the early 1920s—Lutz, *The News of Detroit*, 84–85.

60. For years, the *News* strongly criticized the city's ward system of governance (dominated by saloonkeepers and brewers), broke stories about aldermen taking bribes, and encouraged voters in 1918 to adopt the new charter of nonpartisan council governance—Lutz, *The News of Detroit*, 32–42.

61. Lutz, *The News of Detroit*, 21, 42–48; Baldasty, *E. W. Scripps and the Business of Newspapers*, 109–110; Kaplan, *Politics and the American Press*, 164–166. See also Conot,

American Odyssey, 155; Zunz, *The Changing Face of Inequality*, 313; and Jayne Morris-Crowther, *The Political Activities of Detroit Clubwomen in the 1920s* (Detroit: Wayne State University Press, 2013), 23–24. For an example of the paper's advocacy, see "Mayor Couzens Explains His Proposed Municipal Street Car Lines," *DSN* (February 1, 1920): 1.6–7. The *News*'s changing editorial position seems to have followed the decline of the Progressive movement, specifically, as William Leuchtenburg argued long ago, in the translation of progressive ideals into business boosterism—cited in Fragnoli, *The Transformation of Reform*, 182.

62. "Detroit News Published from New Home; $2,000,000 Plant Finest in United States," *E&P* (October 20, 1917): 2.1–16.

63. "Motion Picture News First Annual Newspaper and Theater Directory," *MPN* (December 27, 1919): 159. In January 1917, the "daily paid circulation" had been 188,000—Advertisement, *DN* (January 27, 1917): 9.

64. Advertisement, *DSN* (March 29, 1925): n.p. See also the *Detroit News* ad, *E&P* (December 8, 1923): 9.

65. Kaplan, *Politics and the American Press*, 117. Among all of the newspapers, only the *Free Press* has been digitized for access, not only on ProQuest but also at www.freep.newspapers.com.

66. Angelo, *On Guard*, 120, 129.

67. Advertisements, *DFP* (March 11, 1918): 14, and (March 14, 1918): 9.

68. Advertisement, *DFP* (June 6, 1922): 11.

69. Angelo, *On Guard*, 121, 126.

70. Advertisement, *DFP* (April 3, 1919): 9. Schermerhorn was well known for his after-dinner speeches and civic committee work.

71. "Hearst Buys Times, Report," *DFP* (October 7, 1921): 1, 3. Hearst already owned many evening newspapers, along with *Cosmopolitan* (acquired in 1905), *Good Housekeeping*, *Harper's Bazaar*, and other magazines; the *Detroit Times* was only one of eight papers that he bought or started up in 1921–1922—David Nasaw, *The Chief: The Life of William Randolph Hearst* (Boston: Houghton Mifflin, 2000), 190, 315.

72. Advertisement, *DFP* (June 14, 1922): 10; *Detroit Times* ad, *E&P* (October 13, 1923): 30.

73. Angelo, *On Guard*, 119–120. The *Detroit Journal* survives on rare microfilm reels at the Detroit Public Library.

74. Lutz, *The News of Detroit*, 46–47. See also the photo of a boy killed on the new trolley line—"Tiny Victim of City-Owned Trolley," *DJ* (October 28, 1921): 2.

75. Advertisement, *DJ* (September 25, 1919): n.p.

76. Angelo, *On Guard*, 120.

77. In 2019, the University of Michigan's Bentley Historical Library digitized surviving issues of the *Detroit Jewish Chronicle*, from 1916 on.

78. Robert Park's 1922 study strangely has hardly anything to say about the foreign-language press in Detroit—Robert Park, *The Immigrant Press and Its Control* (New York: Harper, 1922).

79. Richard Koszarski, *An Evening's Entertainment: The Age of the Silent Feature Picture, 1915–1928* (New York: Charles Scribner, 1990), 9.

ENTR'ACTE 1

The Michigan Film Review

THE *MICHIGAN FILM REVIEW*, ONE OF PERHAPS FEWER than ten regional trade journals in the country during the silent cinema period, first appeared in early November 1916 and ran at least through the 1920s. Fortunately, nearly all of the second volume, dated from November 6, 1917, to October 22, 1918, survives in the Bentley Historical Library at the University of Michigan. The *Review*'s publisher and editor was Jacob Smith,[1] who also contributed a few articles on the city to *Moving Picture World* at the time, and his initial office was located in the Free Press Building, suggesting the trade paper may have had links with that newspaper. "Published Weekly in the Interests of the Moving Picture Exhibitors and Exchanges of Michigan" (as the official organ of the American Exhibitors' Association in the state),[2] the *Review*'s sixteen pages offered not only a wealth of publicity but also a forum for exchanging information between the region's rental exchanges and its exhibitors as well as among exhibitors in this metropolis of nearly one million people.[3]

The *Michigan Film Review* advertised occasionally in *Variety* in the early 1920s,[4] and it celebrated its tenth anniversary in 1926 with a large ad in *Film Daily*, claiming that weekly issues were "mailed to 100 per cent of the exhibitors in Michigan."[5] A year later, it became one of seven regional trade journals that the publisher of *The Reel Journal* integrated into a single group, with an overall circulation of nine thousand, through Associated Publications in Kansas City.[6] In the 1930s, the seven combined journals became the basis for *Box Office Magazine*.

Notes

1. In 1929, Jacob Smith died at the young age of 45—"Illness Fatal to Publisher," *DFP* (September 23, 1929): 11.

2. Founded in July 1917, the American Exhibitors' Association (AEA) initially sought, without success, to become a member of the National Association of the Motion Picture Industry (NAMPI), which had been founded a year earlier, Within a month of gaining NAMPI membership, the AEA had hundreds of members in thirty-six states. By December 1917, it had 2,786 members in forty-six states and briefly coordinated its legislative activity with the NAMPI; negotiations between the two trade organizations broke down the following year, and the AEA aligned with the older Motion Picture Exhibitors' League of America (MPELA). See Kia Afra, *The Hollywood Trust: Trade Associations and the Rise of the Studio System* (Lanham, MD: Rowan & Littlefield, 2016), 53, 90–91, 95–96, 113.

Michigan Film Review

**Published Weekly in the Interests of·the Moving
Picture Exhibitors and Exchanges of Michigan**

VOL. II. NO. 5.   DETROIT, MICH., DECEMBER 4, 1917 $2.00 Per Year

Michigan Exhibitors Fraternize in Detroit

About 75 Michigan exhibitors met in Detroit last Tuesday, Nov. 27th, and discussed the various problems now confronting the motion picture industry, such as the film tax and the music tax. They also decided to continue as a permanent branch of the American Exhibitors' Association, and they ratified the action of the officers in engaging Ray J. Branch, as state organizer and manager.

A short meeting was held in the morning at the Tuller Hotel. At 2 o'clock in the afternoon another meeting was held, and it was attended by Detroit exhibitors, bringing the total attendance up to nearly 200. Permanent officers were elected as follows:

President, S. A. Moran, Ann Arbor.

First Vice-President, Herb Weil, Port Huron.

Second Vice-President, J. R. Denniston, Monroe.

Secretary, Claud E. Cady, Lansing.

Treasurer, W. S. McLaren, Jackson.

A good part of the meeting was given over to discussing the film tax. Many exhibitors present said they were paying the tax because of their desire to hold on to certain programs which would be immediately taken up by their competitors if dropped. However, there was also a goodly number who said they were not paying the tax and would not as long as others took the same stand.

It was decided to fight the music tax and not pay the license being demanded by certain music publishers. This is a matter of little worry to exhibitors now as there is plenty of music that can be secured on which there is no tax.

Charles C· Pettijohn, general manager of the American Exhibitors' Association, came over for the meeting and delivered one of his usual stirring addresses. This chap Pettijohn certainly speaks straight from the shoulder and does not hesitate to tell what he thinks. He even goes so far as to make certain allegations which he dares others to contradict. Mr. Pettijohn is unquestionably sincere in his fight for the exhibitor and in his fight to get them properly organized into one strong, gigantic, powerful association. He has a hard fight before

him, but he is apparently willing and game, judging from the fact that the American Exhibitors' Association has a membership of nearly 3,000. Michigan has nearly 250 memberships in the association, but will have a great deal more by the first of January.

"I am just back from Washington," he said. "We should all pay our just share of the war burden, and not do the cry-baby act, but we should not be called upon to pay a tax that is not our tax and which has been levied on the other fellow.

"You positively have the best state organization in the country right here in Michigan, and I want to congratulate you for it.

"Personally, I am opposed to the film tax and the big salaries paid the film stars· I believe they ought to get a good, big salary, if they make money for the producer and the exhibitor, but can you imagine some of these stars drawing salaries from $500,000 to $700,000 per year when a few years ago they could not earn more than $350 per week and even less.

"I sincerely hope you Michigan exhibitors will continue to keep organized and work together."

M. W. McGee, of the Majestic theatre, Detroit, spoke in favor of fighting the film tax, and urged exhibitors to "get together, stick together and stay together."

Charles W. Porter, of the Forest theatre; S. A. Moran, of Ann Arbor; Herb Weil, of Port Huron; King Perry, of Detroit, were among others who spoke during the meeting for the "greatest good of the association and the industry."

At Night

At 11 P. M. Tuesday night the exhibitors and exchange men, with the ladies, met on the eighth floor of the Temple building, 23 Monroe avenue, where they enjoyed a vaudeville show comprising 15 good acts, the feature attraction being Miss Myrtle Stedman, film star, who entertained the crowd for a few minutes by the rendition of several songs· She was encored so enthusiastically that she responded by a short address in which she heartily thanked the exhibitors and their ladies.

Charles C. Pettijohn and Mrs. Pettijohn thanked the exhibitors for the flowers sent to them at their hotel. (Mr. and Mrs. Pettijohn are newlyweds.)

Towards the wee hours of the morning space was cleared in the middle of the room for dancing.

It was 3:30 A. M. before the party broke up.

During the evening a fund of $57 was collected with which to buy tobacco and candy for the Michigan boys who are in service· You are welcome to increase the fund any amount you wish. Every penny will go to the boys who are serving their country in this great war.

King Perry, secretary of the Detroit branch of Exhibitors, was largely and mainly responsible for the entire entertainment, and King has proved beyond a doubt that he is a trojan for work in these affairs. And he is the ideal man, too, because King not only arranges the show, but "opens and closes the show" and acts as the bouncer while the show is on.

If there is a profit, it will go towards helping to finance the coming national convention of the American Exhibitors' Association in Detroit, July 3 to 6.

Fig. EA1.1. *Michigan Film Review* (December 4, 1917): 1.

3. "The Michigan Film Review is now the official trade paper of the Michigan and Detroit branches of the A.E.A.," *MFR* (December 11, 1917): 11.

4. *Michigan Film Review* ads, *V* (March 4, 1921): 54, and (September 3, 1924): 25.

5. *Michigan Film Review* ad, *FD* (1926): 790.

6. "Seven Midwestern Regional Papers Welded Together," *MPN* (August 26, 1927): 580; and "Regional Papers Combine: Gross Circulation, 9,000," *V* (August 31, 1927): 9.

1

MAPPING CIRCULATION IN DETROIT'S MOVIE MARKET

September Is Go-To-Theatre Month, with the Leading Motion Picture Theatres

Detroit Sunday Free Press (September 3, 1922)

Neighborhood theatres in Detroit have become almost as numerous as neighborhood groceries. People must have recreation and amusement just as they require food and drink.

Detroit Free Press (December 22, 1918)

IMAGINE YOU ARE THE MANAGER OF A NEW picture theater, such as the Farnum in Hamtramck, seeking reliable information about booking films in 1917. One source to consult, besides the industry trade press, personal contacts, and word of mouth, would have been the regional trade weekly, *Michigan Film Review*, which late that year began compiling a directory of downtown rental exchanges that distributed films throughout the city of Detroit and beyond.[1] This directory listed eleven exchanges that operated across North America: Paramount-Artcraft, Blue Bird, Fox, General, Goldwyn, George Kleine, Mutual, Metro, Pathé, Triangle, Universal, Vitagraph, and World. Most had offices, with their own screening rooms, on adjacent floors of the New Film Building (or Joseph Mack Building), but Metro and Triangle shared space with John Kunsky's Madison Film Exchange, while Universal and Paramount-Artcraft rented offices on the west edge and east edge of downtown, respectively. The other eleven local or regional exchanges, besides Madison Film, also were clustered downtown (many in the New Film Building as well), with some, like Strand Features and Standard Film Service, specializing in reissues or older short-reel comedies and cartoons. The downtown locations of this movie business hub allowed easy access to the main rail station, where film prints came in, were inspected, went out on trucks to picture theaters, returned in reverse order, and left for other cities and towns. The offices were close to major

Detroit Film Exchanges---Note Changes

Note: The address of the New Film Building is 63 East Elizabeth.

(To avoid confusion, DESTROY all other lists.)

Artcraft-Paramount	New Film Bldg.	Cad. 3917-3918.	H. A. Ross, Mgr.
Blue Bird	New Film Bldg.	Cadillac 5630.	C. S. Kingsley, Mgr.
Casino Feature Film Co.	Madison Theatre Bldg.	Main 6238.	C. C. Randolph, Mgr.
Dawn Masterplay Co.	501 Owen Bldg.	Cherry 866	A. S. Hyman, Mgr.
Fox	New Film Bldg.	Main 3101	Field Carmichael, Mgr.
General	New Film Bldg.	Main 1386	David Prince, Mgr.
Goldwyn	New Film Bldg.	Cherry 4655.	A. I. Shapiro, Mgr.
Harry I. Garson Productions	318 Woodward Ave.	Cherry 3169.	J. O. Kent, Mgr.
Hoffman Four-Square Pictures	New Film Bldg.	Main 2864.	Geo. W. Weeks, Mgr.
Jewell Productions	New Film Bldg.	Cadillac 5630	C. G. Kingsley, Mgr.
Jones Film Co.	New Film Bldg.	Cherry 3689.	Si Overpeck, Mgr.
George Kleine System	New Film Bldg.	Main 3721.	A. J. Reed, Mgr.
Mutual	New Film Bldg.	Cadillac 6400	George De Bute, Mgr.
Metro	75 Broadway	Main 3288.	G. N. Montgomery, Mgr.
Madison Film Exchange	75 Broadway	Main 3288.	G. N. Montgomery, Mgr.
Pathe	New Film Bldg.	Cadillac 92	Ed. Fontaine, Mgr.
Standard Film Service	New Film Bldg.	Main 6542.	J. C. Fishman, Mgr.
State Film Co.	New Film Bldg.	Cherry 3231.	Harry S. Lorch, Mgr.
Strand Features	94 Griswold St.	Main 5160.	Dave Mundstock, Mgr.
Select Features	New Film Bldg.	Cadillac 2659	W. D. Ward, Mgr.
Triangle	75 Broadway	Main 4677.	R. A. Perry, Mgr.
Universal	After Jan. 25 New Film Bldg.	Cadillac 2141.	Henry Fried, Mgr.
U. S. Exhibitors' Booking Corp.	New Film Bldg.	Main 2864	Geo. S. Trask, Mgr.
Vitagraph	New Film Bldg.	Cherry 4246.	J. M. Duncan, Mgr.
World	New Film Bldg.	Cadillac 2713.	Robert Cotton, Mgr.

SUPPLY HOUSES

United	New Film Bldg.	Cadillac 4908.	L. J. Gardiner, Mgr.
Michigan Motion Picture Supply Co.	New Film Bldg.	Cherry 5352.	Bert Weddige, Mgr.
M. S. Bailey	New Film Bldg.	Main 2864.	M. S. Bailey, Mgr.
Theatre Equipment Co.	New Film Bldg.	Cherry 5352.	J. George Fineberg, Mgr.

Fig. 1.1. Detroit Film Exchanges Directory, *Michigan Film Review* (January 22, 1918): 12.

hotels that could house industry representatives promoting their products in the branch offices to managers like Farnum's. To help those managers keep their theaters attractive and running smoothly, the directory also included two "supply houses" for projector parts (United Theatre Equipment and Michigan Motion Picture Supply, both in the New Film Building); but many other local firms advertised in the *Michigan Film Review*: for example, Premier Scenery Studios, General Theatre Display and Advertising, Theatrical Advertising, Sign & Poster, Simpson Cartage Service, and Exhibitors Film Delivery.

Reciprocally, imagine you are an exchange man, that same year, mapping the territory of the city in order to circulate your company's films efficiently and profitably. Your branch office would have an inventory of the area's picture theaters and a record of past rentals—but those apparently no longer survive. That inventory probably paralleled the listings in the Detroit City Directories, which totaled 125–130 theaters by late 1917.[2] Of those, fewer than ten advertised on a regular basis in the Sunday *Free Press*, and even fewer in the Sunday *News-Tribune*.

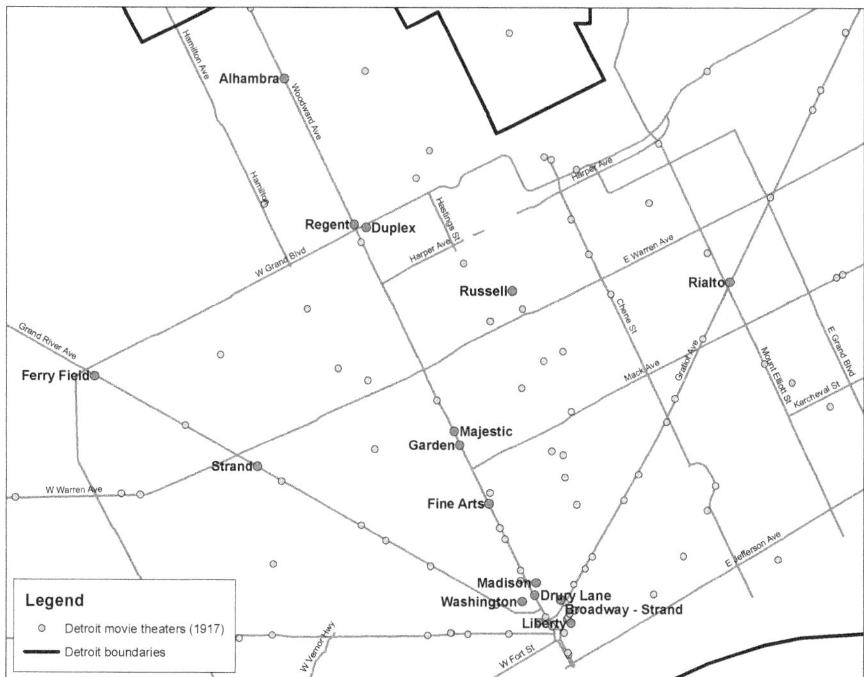

Fig. 1.2. 1917 Detroit map of major theaters.

But five major theaters would have been the prime venues for first-run book-ings. Nearly all were owned by one of three entrepreneurs, were located either in the downtown center just below Grand Circus Park or to the north along Woodward Avenue, and had seating capacities of 1,000 or more: John Kunsky's Washington (1,862 seats) and Madison (1,965 seats);[3] Phil Gleichman's Broadway Strand (1,488 seats); and C. H. Miles's vaudeville houses, the Majestic (1,760 seats) and Regent (2,150–3,600 seats), in the New Center and North Woodward areas, respectively.[4]

The next tier of theaters included Kunsky's downtown Liberty (720 seats), Garden (950 seats), and Alhambra (1,475 seats),[5] plus the smaller Drury Lane (600 seats), Fine Arts (582 seats), and Forest (592 seats) also ranged north along Woodward; Kunsky's Strand (1,384 seats) on Grand River, the Ferry Field (1,325 seats) on West Grand Boulevard, and the Stratford (1,025 seats) on Dix, to the northwest and west, respectively; and the Rialto (1,334 seats) on Gratiot, the Duplex (1,250 seats) on East Grand Boulevard, and the Del-The (1,076 seats) on Mack, to the east.

Among the third group of theaters, the Garden and the Forest (reportedly a "social center" for a Jewish community)[6] alone seemed close to ethnic neigh-borhoods, and the only others with 900 to 1,000 seats were the Farnum and the

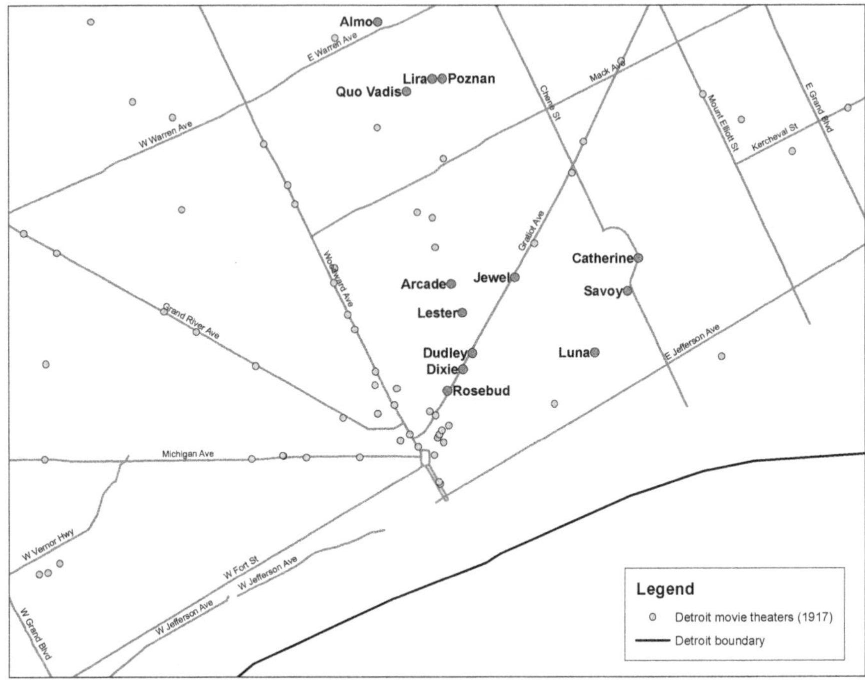

Fig. 1.3. 1917 Detroit map of neighborhood theaters.

Russell, both of which opened in or near Hamtramck in 1917[7]—but neither of which initially advertised in newspapers.

Exchange managers likely gave very low priority to the smaller ethnic neighborhood theaters, but these theaters do become visible when one compares city directories, maps of neighborhood locations, and later studies and directories.[8] In Lower Poletown, for instance, the Arcade, Catherine, Jewel, Luna, Poznan, and Savoy all seated only 330 to 490 people each.[9] In the nearby Italian community, both the Lira and the Quo Vadis seated fewer than 400 people each.[10] In Upper Poletown, from Lake Shore Junction into Hamtramck, again most theaters had between 300 and 400 seats each: the Clay, Dreamland, Fredro, Home, Pastime, Perrien, Poland, and Rozmaitosci.[11] That was the norm until the Iris (880 seats) opened in 1916, followed by the Farnum and the Russell. In or near the west side Polish neighborhood, the Eagle, Olympic, and Victoria had between 334 and 385 seats each; only the Crystal was larger, with nearly 600 seats. In the Hungarian community of Del Ray, the Crescent and the Del Ray also seated fewer than 400 apiece, and another theater, the Arcadia, had closed in 1916. One theater located in the black community, the Pekin, had closed in 1915,[12] but three others were the Dixie, Rosebud, and Dudley (all with fewer than 400 seats)—and the last of these

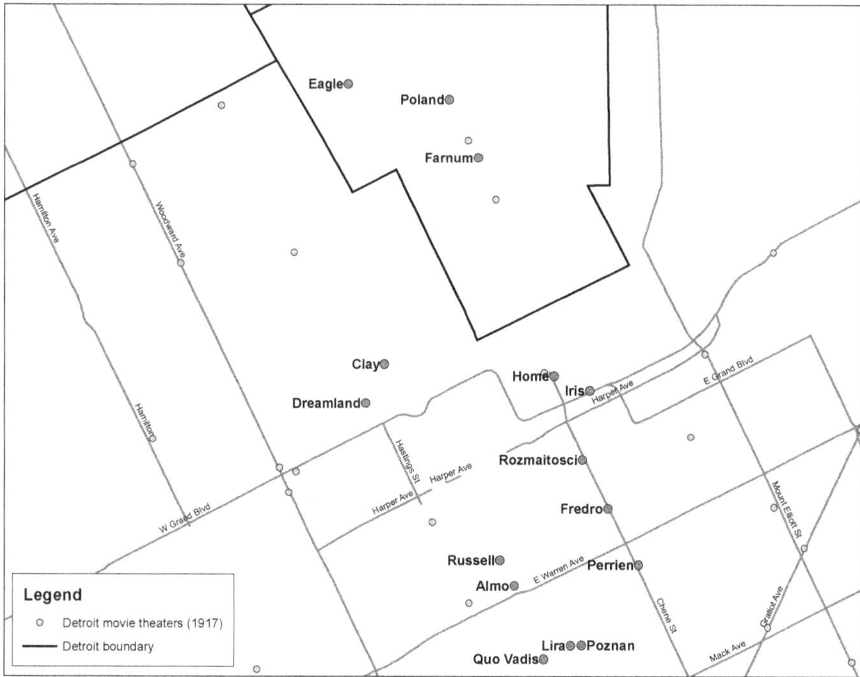

Fig. 1.4. 1917 Detroit map of neighborhood theaters.

closed in 1921.[13] Many of these ethnic neighborhood theaters will become important to the discussion later in this chapter and in chapter 2, when they began
advertising in local newspapers, as well as in chapter 3, because they were listed
as venues for local newsreels.

This chapter aims to track the circulation of films, largely feature films, serials,
and short comedies (chap. 3 will take up nonfiction films), describing and analyzing
the interrelations of distribution and exhibition over space and time between 1916
and 1925.[14] Rather than treat distribution and exhibition as two separate branches
of the movie industry, the following pages explore their nexus as a complex site of
circulation, especially attentive to the inclusion and exclusion of different ethnic
communities, and sometimes situated within larger cultural, social, and/or economic contexts. The specifics of that circulation come from Detroit's four main
newspapers, the *Michigan Film Review*, Kunsky's *Weekly Film News* (more on that
as a source in chap. 2), the trade press, and other local resources. Perhaps most
significantly, this cultural history of the movies in a unique metropolis during
a decade of exceptional growth and transformation, economically and socially,
seeks to address pertinent questions about the sources, methods, and evidence
that scholars use in writing about silent American cinema history.

Detroit's Movie Market to the End of the Great War: I

First, what can be gleaned from the *Free Press* and *News-Tribune* in the year or so prior to late 1918? Unlike some other newspapers, neither carried many promotional ads placed by major motion picture companies. Paramount had included the *News-Tribune* as a venue for the second of its weekly national campaigns in 1915–1916,[15] and that campaign closed in May with a characteristically long vertical ad for a pseudo contest prodding moviegoers to sign ballots to support the company's "decent" features as a counter to "sensational and suggestive pictures."[16] That month, shortly after leaving the Motion Picture Board of Trade,[17] Metro opened its own campaign in the same paper with a similarly designed ad promoting its stars and urging moviegoers to pick up its "Pictures Magazine" at their local theater.[18] The Metro campaign ran through the fall and winter, with one ad that claimed "its Name . . . guarantees you a fine evening's entertainment," another that heralded its "great stars in great plays made by great directors," and a third that seemed to apologize for not making "all the motion pictures" but boasted that at least it did make "the good ones."[19] The only other companies to advertise were Mutual and Pathé, which placed typically large ads promoting their new serials throughout 1917. For Mutual, there was one—*The Railroad Raiders*, starring Helen Holmes—whose first episode could be seen in a dozen Detroit theaters, including the Pastime and the Rosebud.[20] For Pathé, there were at least four: *Patria*, produced by Hearst's International Film Service, with Mrs. Vernon Castle; *The Fatal Ring*, with Pearl White; *The 7 Pearls*, with Mollie King; and *The Hidden Hand*, with Doris Kenyon.[21] All other companies in the industry seemed content to let theater managers sell their brands, stars, and special photoplays, in their newspaper ads, their lobbies, or their slides for upcoming stars or films.

In May 1916, a *News-Tribune* column summed up how a typical moviegoer chose his entertainment: He "generally looks first to see who is starred at a theater. If the star of the day is a favorite . . . he next learns in what play he or she is appearing. If it is a play he cares to see, he pays the price of admission."[22] Whether or not one accepts this generalization (and the moviegoer's gender), it does prompt a question: Can one track the circulation of particularly popular films and favorite stars in 1916–1917, even if sources are limited and nearly all theaters referenced are downtown or in the north, west, and east areas of the city that were largely white, middle class, or skilled working class? The answer is yes, to some extent, because a few specific films and/or stars seemed especially popular at those theaters, although one can only conjecture about the films' circulation through the city's one hundred other venues and their reception by audiences.

Half a dozen films and stars make prominent appearances in late 1916, which suggests that rental exchange bookings were hardly ironclad and could change quickly over time. One of the more interesting films is Metro's *Romeo and Juliet*, starring Francis X. Bushman and Beverly Bayne, which the company promoted with a full page of five production stills in the *News-Tribune* in late September 1916.[23] After opening at the Regent in late October and running for another week "by special request," the film showed up at the Fine Arts in mid-November and at the Stratford in mid-December.[24] By contrast, Fox's *Romeo and Juliet*, starring Theda Bara, competed with the Metro film for only one week at the Broadway Strand; and Metro celebrated its version with a late December ad urging fans to ask their neighborhood theaters to book it.[25] Artcraft's first feature, *Less Than the Dust*, starring Mary Pickford,[26] also is relatively easy to track: It opened at the Majestic for a two-week run in mid-November, transferred immediately to the Liberty, and had two- and one-day runs at the Alhambra, Strand, and Stratford in December.[27] Selznick Picture's *War Brides*, starring Alla Nazimova, also premiered at the Broadway Strand in mid-November, reappeared at the Liberty a week later, featured at the Del-The's "Grand Opening" on December 24, moved to the Rialto and Alhambra for two-day runs in early January, and finally screened at the Nettie B (525 seats) in mid-January.[28] Premiering as well at the Broadway Strand in late December was *The Foolish Virgin*, starring Clara Kimball Young, which ran for two weeks before appearing in late January for two days at the Strand, Alhambra, and Rialto, as well as one Sunday at the Garden.[29]

During the first half of 1917, five different rental exchanges contracted with Kunsky for exclusive, extended runs of their big features at the Washington. The first was Selig's *The Crisis*, adapted from the American novelist Winston Churchill's Civil War novel, which screened for three weeks in November and December 1916.[30] Not until mid-June 1917 did it reappear at the Strand for a two-day run.[31] The second big feature was Fox's *A Daughter of the Gods*, starring Annette Kellerman, which ran for a record six weeks in December 1916 and January 1917.[32] At the same time, both the Alhambra and the Strand exploited Kellerman's appeal with one-day screenings of her earlier *Neptune's Daughter*.[33] Coming next to the Washington was Universal's *20,000 Leagues Under the Sea*, shown for four weeks in February; followed by Triangle Film's *Civilization* for three weeks in March.[34] Finally there was Rex Beach's *The Barrier*, which also ran for three weeks, in April; it, too, returned for only one day at the Garden in early September.[35] Another strategy marked Paramount-Artcraft's distribution of films with its most popular stars, Pickford and Fairbanks.[36] It arranged for *A Poor Little Rich Girl* to open at the Madison, Kunsky's new palace cinema, in March.[37] The following month, it contracted for two-week screenings of Fairbanks's *In Again–Out Again* at the Washington; shortly thereafter, also for two weeks, came Pickford's *A Romance of the Redwoods*.[38] In late June, it was the turn of *Wild and Woolly*, followed immediately by Pickford's patriotic special, *The Little American*.[39] In the midst of these paired films, *Enlighten Thy Daughter*, an unusual "state rights" feature "endorsed by press and clergy," occupied the Washington for two weeks in late April.[40] As a very different spectacle attraction, D. W. Griffith's *Intolerance* enjoyed a special screening at the Detroit Opera House from early May to early June and then returned to the Washington for one week in mid-November.[41] Finally, a unique ad for *The Deemster*, adapted from a Hall Caine novel and also distributed as a long-delayed, state rights film, offers a rare glimpse of its circulation through eighteen neighborhood theaters—including the Crystal, Iris, and Quo Vadis—for one- and two-day runs in early December.[42]

The popularity of certain films and stars also allowed some companies to address the demand for return engagements through the rest of 1917. Besides Chaplin comedies, which circulated constantly to theaters large and small, Vitagraph reissues of several short films starring Kimball Young also screened as an extra attraction, for instance, at the Alhambra.[43] Moreover, the star's own feature, *The Dark Silence*, returned "by popular demand" to the Garden in early July, along with Fairbanks's *In Again–Out Again* several days later.[44] After the United States entered the Great War in April, it is little wonder that Pickford's *The Little American* reappeared "by popular demand," at the Alhambra on a Saturday in early October and at the Strand on Monday in mid-November.[45]

During the Great War, of course, few European films could be imported into the United States. Just as the country intervened in the war, however, its close alliance with France led the Brady-International Service to purchase a series of five French feature films starring famous actresses and distributed by World Pictures.[46] The first was *Mothers of France*, with Sarah Bernhardt, which the Broadway Strand screened for a week in mid-April 1917, after which it reappeared as a Monday "special feature" at the Alhambra in mid-June.[47] On Saturday that same week in June, the Strand featured *Atonement*, with Régina Badet, the alleged "vampire of France"; a month later, again on Saturday, Badet returned to the Strand in *The Golden Lotus*.[48] At the very end of June, also on Saturday, the Strand promoted Suzanne Grandais [*sic*] as "the 'Mary Pickford' of France" in *Her Naked Soul*.[49] The last film in the series, *When True Love Dawns*, with Grandais, finally appeared at the Alhambra on Monday in mid-November.[50] Kunsky's second-run theaters could have shown these French features as summer program "fillers," yet three of them were featured prominently on Saturdays. And this suggests that their real function, in Detroit and elsewhere, was propagandistic (and explicitly in the case of *Mothers of France*), perhaps especially for women on the home front. By contrast, Harry Raver, a New York entrepreneur, was able to import no more than two Italian films starring Maciste, the famous "giant of *Cabiria*."[51] *The Marvelous Maciste* apparently did not make it to Detroit,[52] but the Orpheum featured *The Warrior* on its vaudeville program in mid-March 1918, and the Regent did likewise in early April.[53] Both theaters highlighted the film's wartime story set in the snowy Italian Alps, a story allegedly based on Maciste's "actual experiences . . . when he was captured by Austrians on the wrong side of the border" and his heroic feats in escaping a detention camp.[54]

Detroit's Movie Market to the End of the Great War: II

For a unique perspective on the circulation of films, especially in 1918, the weekly *Michigan Film Review* proves invaluable. First of all, what can one draw from the commercial advertisements that supported this rare trade journal from late 1917 through late 1918? As expected, ads for the branch offices of major film rental exchanges were prominent, from the more recent firms devoted to features—World Film or Box Office Attraction, Triangle, Goldwyn, Metro, Fox, Select—to older companies—General Film, Mutual, Pathé, Universal, George Kleine. But even more ads came from companies located in the city. Some were exchanges: the Madison, which leased feature films booked in Kunsky's first-run theaters to others in the state,[55] and Dawn Masterplay, which, after releasing "new prints" of "sure fire winners," purchased limited state rights to distribute Griffith's *Hearts of the World* (1918).[56] But many came from local exchanges dealing in reissues or older film prints. Strand Features exploited the popularity of current films by booking Helen Gardner's six-reel *Cleopatra* (1912), and two-reel versions of William S. Hart features, as well as older Chaplin and Arbuckle comedies.[57] Standard Film Service boasted a big list of older short-reel comedies and cartoons and also subcontracted with companies such as Madison to truck their films around the city.[58] Even Triangle and Kleine got into the reissue business with, respectively, Fairbanks and Hart features and one-reel *Broncho Billy* westerns, with Kleine alleging that it was "swamped with contracts" from theaters "aching" for those westerns—but, tellingly, neither the cowgirl nor Indian pictures that were quite popular in the early 1910s.[59] All these ads suggest that regional distribution involved a crowded field of local rental exchanges competing to exploit the ever-increasing number of film titles on the market, both features and shorts. Moreover, as a corollary, it raises the question of how much the overall industry depended on the continuing circulation of popular older films and reissues, usually but not exclusively to second- and third-run houses.[60]

Intriguingly, Paramount-Artcraft did not advertise in the *Review* until late 1918.[61] By contrast, after setting up "a publicity-efficiency department" in every one of its exchanges, the company had developed a prominent presence in the newspapers.[62] In summer 1918, it launched a third national campaign of weekly advertising, and that campaign targeted readers of the *Detroit News* from early July through mid-October.[63] Every ad occupied half a page in the Sunday paper's "Photoplays" section, and the ads consistently exhibited a box-within-a-box design. Framing the central box, which promoted Paramount-Artcraft films, was a series of smaller ads for the weekly or daily programs of more than a dozen different picture theaters contracted to screen one or more of the company's features. Most of the centered ads privileged a single star—William S. Hart, Mary Pickford, Elsie Ferguson, Douglas Fairbanks, Marguerite Clark, Charles Ray, and Wallace Reid—but one heralded the director Cecil B. DeMille, and

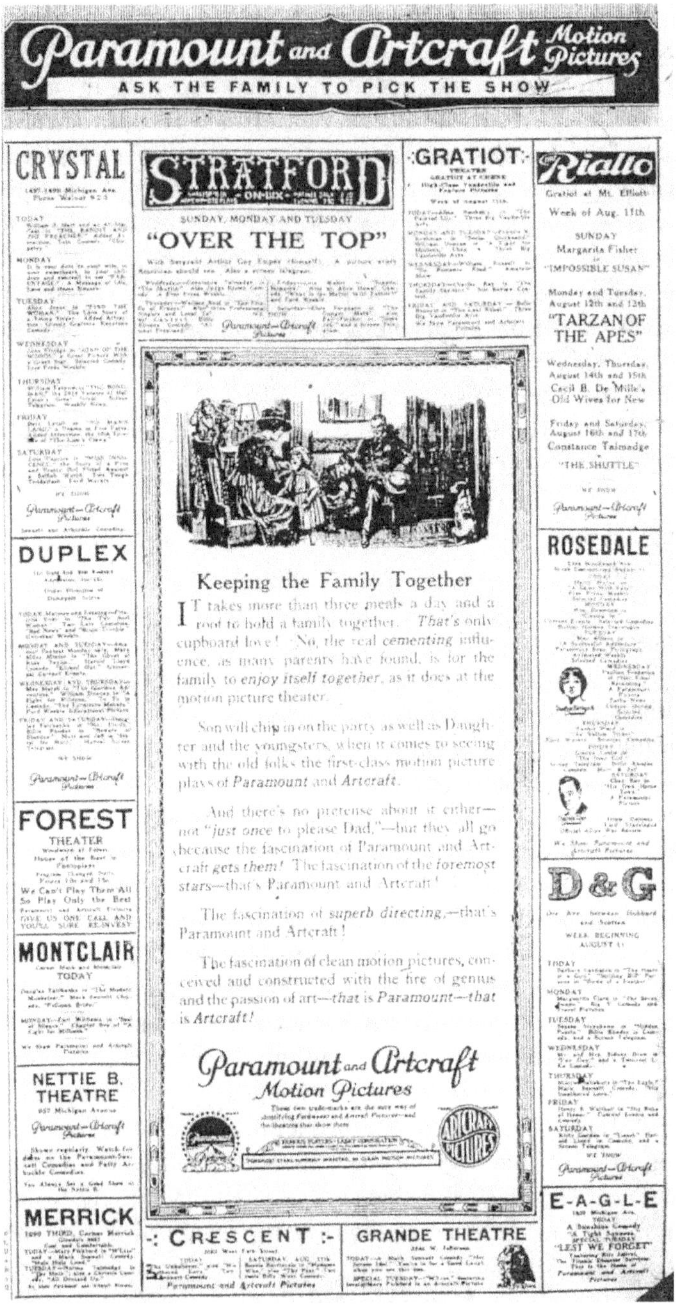

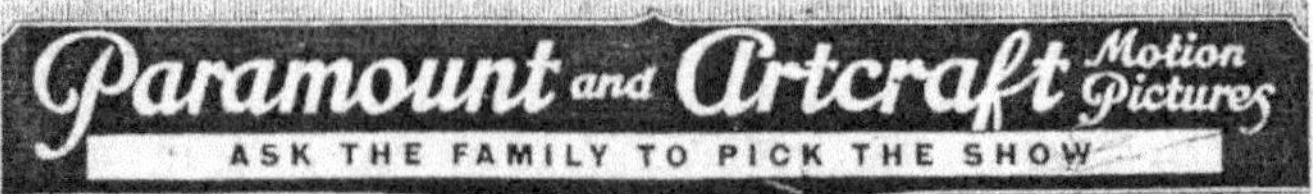

Fig. 1.5. Paramount-Artcraft ad, *Detroit Sunday News* (August 11, 1918): 11.

another concocted a silly doggerel for Mack Sennett comedies. While two ads simply displayed the Paramount and Artcraft trademarks, three others depicted the company's desired audience of a distinctly well-off family or couple: urging "Dad" to join a mother and two kids one evening (their chauffeur waits outside), encouraging older couples to feel young again, and claiming that the company's films are "keeping the family together." In the text of a fourth ad, "we" leave the house library for seats in a theater playing a Paramount-Artcraft feature, to "live a life in two hours." What nearly all four ads do is bind together families, "clean, worth-while" films, favorite stars, and an enjoyable theater experience through the Paramount-Artcraft brand. Only one other company advertised, but in the *Free Press*, in early 1918. This was "World Pictures Brady-Made," which simply listed its four current features that could be seen at twenty-four "representative Detroit theaters."[64] Unlike the Paramount-Artcraft ads, World Pictures' two ads included two Polish neighborhood theaters rather than just one.

Although the *Michigan Film Review*'s weekly directory listed two dozen or more "Detroit Film Exchanges," there was no directory for a host of companies advertising products and services essential to distribution and exhibition in the region. Many of these, as expected, sold or rented theater products and services to exhibitors—from projector parts[65] and screens, such as L. J. Gardiner's much-praised Velvet Gold Fibre Screen manufactured in the city,[66] to stage set plans,[67] posters and frames,[68] and printing options for theater programs of various shapes, sizes, and styles.[69] Two rival companies, Simpson Cartage Service and Exhibitors Film Delivery, trucked film cans from the downtown train depot to exchanges and theaters and back again.[70] A specialist in building theaters, Frank Farrington, used an ad to promote its construction of a dozen major Detroit picture theaters and nearly a hundred others in North America.[71] Perhaps the most surprising was the Metropolitan Film Company, known for "making titles, slides, and special films for theaters."[72] In March 1918, together with the *Detroit Free Press*, the company began to produce and distribute a weekly newsreel of local current events (see chap. 3).[73] Within months, the *Detroit Free Press Film Edition* was playing on at least fifty Detroit and southeast Michigan theater programs.[74] With this newsreel, Metropolitan Film may have seen an opportunity to expand its business to theaters other than those that could either afford to rent national newsreels or, like several in the Kunsky chain, compile their own.[75]

Detroit-area theaters had little incentive to advertise, but the *Review* did grant them occasional attention. The state's Exhibitors Association meetings received front-page coverage—as did John Kunsky himself in a few articles and notices, especially once he became the state's representative to First National Exhibitors Circuit.[76] Remarkably little attention was given to the largest theaters (either downtown or north along Woodward), all of which programmed a single feature film for a full week, allegedly the most for any city in the country.[77] By contrast, the trade weekly twice singled out the extent of smaller theater bookings along Woodward: eleven showed Paramount-Artcraft features, and eight offered daily program changes, with features supplied by World Film (likely second- or third-run bookings).[78] Not all of this attention was positive. The *Review* admitted there was criminal activity in the local industry, which included embezzlement charges against the Fine Arts manager and the Adams treasurer.[79] It also criticized exhibitors' practice of making "cut-outs on features and comedies," excising material they considered padded or unfit for their audiences.[80] Most threatening to the *Review*, however, was unionization. It branded as "agitators" those who were trying to unionize the "poster men, examiners, inspectors, and shipping clerks" employed by the exchanges and belittled their arguments.[81] Yet, despite this opposition, the exchange workers (some of them women), backed by the operators' and musicians' unions, succeeded, which meant more "trouble."[82] All this was evidence that the trade weekly was more supportive of the film exchanges than any other sector of the industry in a largely nonunion city.

The impact of the Great War, unsurprisingly, also preoccupied the *Review*. A crucial issue was the admission tax, imposed by the US government in early November 1917, that required exhibitors to pay 15¢ per reel of film per day to help finance the country's involvement in the war. The tax was so controversial that nearly one hundred exhibitors in the Detroit area initially refused to accept it.[83] This prompted a big campaign for compliance, which led to a two-page ad signed by a dozen of the city's major exchanges and a front-page article in which Kunsky and his partner, George W. Trendle, explained why they favored the war tax.[84] While the opposition held firm for weeks,[85] the *Review* printed a list of the downtown and other large theaters that were in compliance, as well as another list of neighborhood theaters, including the Free Poland and Quo Vadis, in the Polish and Italian communities.[86] Twenty-five of Kunsky's employees were among the men who enlisted in the war effort,[87] and at one point in the summer of 1918 the state's draft officials issued a "Work or Fight" order that would have forced projectionists to either become soldiers or work in a war factory.[88] Although they quickly were excluded from the order, some operators had already enlisted, and Kunsky made plans to train women in case of a shortage.[89] The *Review* strongly urged exhibitors to participate in the third Liberty Loan drive; besides the ten prints of ten different trailers in constant circulation, the Ford Motor Company contributed even more prints of its film *Liberty Bonds—How and Why They Are Made*.[90] And the Alhambra won praise for a special night of performances, including the city's "Liberty band of 100 pieces," that raised $15,000, credited to the nearby Northern High School students.[91]

The US involvement in the Great War also may have played an important role in Detroit's reinstitution of local film censorship, which, after apparently lapsing for several years, now was endorsed by the *Review* and the State Federation of

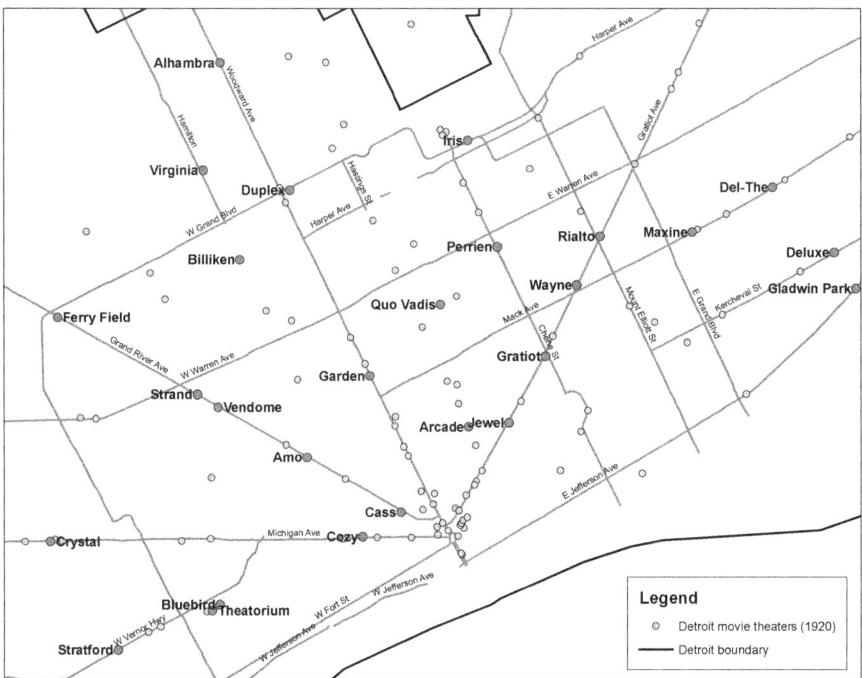

Fig. 1.6. 1920 Detroit map of selected theaters.

Women's Clubs.[92] In early April 1918, the Detroit Police Commission assigned Royal A. Baker the arduous task of serving as the city's chief censor.[93] Baker was a unique figure whose aspirations as a scenario writer made for a relatively cozy relationship with the movie industry.[94] Usually quite lenient in his censoring role, especially in contrast to Chicago's censors, he once criticized those condemning the industry for "being all wet when they say the motion pictures influence persons to commit crimes."[95] Acknowledging that good exchanges had nothing to fear from Baker, the *Review* summarized each monthly censorship report. In April, "twenty-two pictures were suppressed entirely and 115 cut-outs were made in other films," although none were named.[96] In May, the report was more extensive, encompassing everything from censored posters, gaming booths, side shows, and wrestling matches to "stolen property recovered, and parts eliminated" from motion pictures, plays, circuses, and carnivals.[97] In June, five motion pictures were listed as "condemned."[98] Intriguingly, the one title singled out was *War Brides* (apparently a re-release), which had enjoyed such popularity in late 1916; now that American troops were in Europe and protests had erupted in Pennsylvania and Missouri, the film was judged to "advocate peace under any circumstances" and thus "seriously hamper the successful prosecution of the war."[99] Still, three years later, *Exhibitors Herald* could report that "Detroit exchanges and exhibitors are not afraid of unfair censorship while Royal A. Baker is on the job."[100]

In July 1918, the *Review* did print a "complete list" of Detroit movie theaters, with names, addresses, and (some estimated) seating capacities.[101] One might question its completeness (the Farnum is missing), but the list did seem to attribute to all theaters the same level of importance. In fact, one downtown theater manager endorsed this leveling: "The small theatres are the educators for the big theatres—they get people started to the movies and then these people want to go to the bigger theatres."[102] The number of theaters, according to city directories and other scant sources, continued to expand. The most important was the Adams (1,770 seats), which Kunsky first opened as a legitimate theater at Grand Circus Park, then converted to a picture palace in April 1918.[103] Yet other "bigger theaters" appeared as well: the Lincoln Square (1,850 seats), the Lyric (1,000 seats), and Kunsky's De Luxe (1,466 seats)—the first two, respectively, on the city's western and northern edge; the latter in the "elite Indian Village" area near Belle Isle Park.[104] Another followed the Farnum and the Russell in what an ad described as "foreign neighborhoods"[105]: the New Home (1,000 seats), which replaced the Home, in Hamtramck.[106] There, too, in a patriotic move that anticipated Polish independence in the war's aftermath, the Poland changed its name to Free Poland. Together with newspaper ads, the *Review*'s list provides especially valuable data for mapping the precise location of the city's theaters and their concentration in certain areas and districts by 1918. What is particularly striking is that 25 percent to 30 percent of the total were located in or near Polish, Italian, Jewish, and Hungarian neighborhoods, most of them overflowing with recent immigrants.

Finally, what films—according to both the *Michigan Film Review* and the newspapers—were either especially popular or seemed to have a big impact in Detroit in 1918? Two films garnered special attention: Fox's *Cleopatra* (starring Theda Bara) and the Kleine-Edison "patriotic war picture," *The Unbeliever*.[107] Promoted as the "real sensation of the year," *Cleopatra* premiered at the downtown Washington in February, where 52,122 people saw it during the first week of a three-week run; in July, the Washington rebooked a reduced eight-reel version for another week, a print that apparently then featured one month later at the Miles (another downtown vaudeville theater) and the Strand, as well as three months later at the west side Maxine (774 seats).[108] Adapted from a novelette first serialized in *Ladies' Home Journal* and reprinted several times as a book (the latest in 1918),[109] *The Unbeliever* played to equally large crowds at the Majestic, where it ran for five weeks in March and April (allegedly, the longest run in the country).[110] The first week's screenings included a troop of Marines marching across the stage before a backdrop of a ship bound for France and a Detroit girl, Marjorie Kaye, singing "Throw Me a Kiss from Over the Sea."[111] By June, the *Review* claimed it was doing record business throughout the state, second only to *The Birth of*

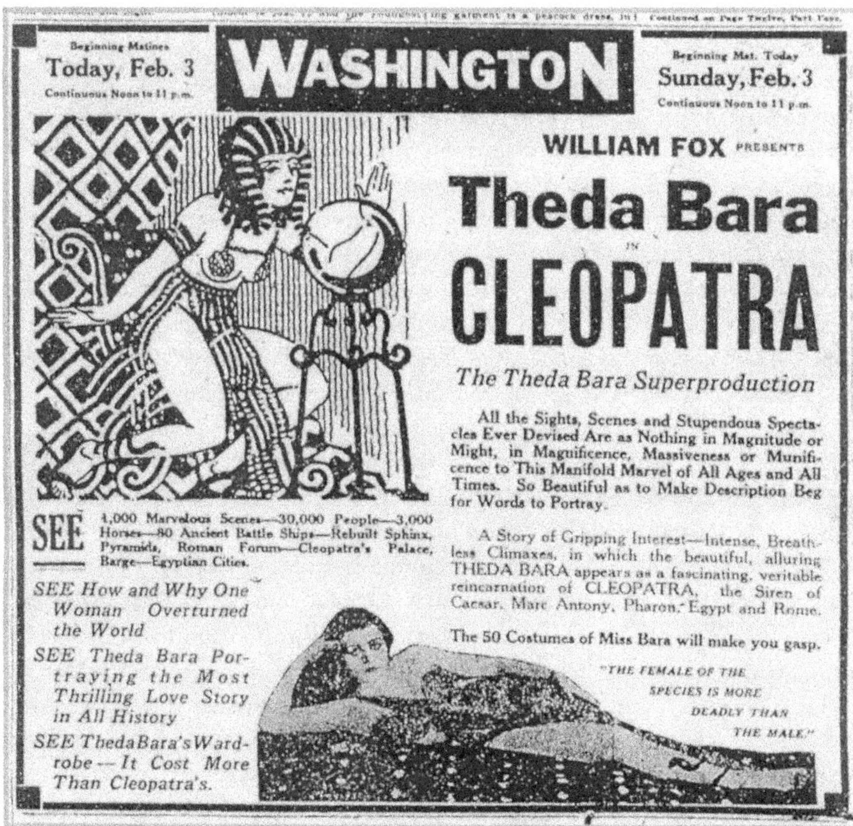

Fig. 1.7. Washington Theater ad, *Detroit Sunday News* (February 3, 1918): 10.

a Nation.[112] A patriotic "war documentary," *My Four Years in Germany*, based on a book by the former US ambassador James W. Gerard, also opened at the Washington in late April, one year after the nation entered the Great War.[113] After the film played for five weeks in Detroit, the Madison Film Exchange booked it throughout the state, with ad testimonials from pastors, military officers, and the Federation of Women's Clubs.[114] It's no surprise that Charlie Chaplin's *A Dog's Life* broke a record at the Madison Theatre and D. W. Griffith's *Hearts of the World* had an exclusive run of three months at the Detroit Opera House.[115]

So, what seemed to draw Detroit movie audiences in 1918? War pictures and stars: notably Theda Bara, whose *Salome* later played for two weeks at the Adams; Chaplin; and Douglas Fairbanks, whom the Alhambra honored with an "All Fairbanks Week."[116] In fact, the popularity of Fairbanks, Hart, and Pickford led Paramount-Artcraft to order six prints each of their films for first-run screenings in Detroit-area theaters.[117]

Patterns and Changes in Detroit's Movie Market to 1922

The end of the Great War nearly coincided with the "Spanish flu" epidemic that devastated Europe and spread westward through North America, largely transmitted by returning soldiers. Beginning in October 1918, state boards of health decided to close movie theaters, along with many other entertainment venues whose business depended on drawing large crowds.[118] According to *Photoplay Magazine*, "ten thousand picture theatres—80% of the total in the United States and Canada—closed for a period varying from one week to two months."[119] Film production largely halted, and the major distributors jointly agreed not to release any new films between October 15 and November 9.[120] Initially, the Detroit area seemed to escape the brunt of the epidemic, but that soon changed, and the governor ordered "every Michigan theatre, public gathering, dance hall, skating rink, pool room, etc." closed "for an indefinite period."[121] The epidemic's effect on Detroit's moviegoing is clear from the absence of advertisements and pages or columns devoted to the movies in the city's newspapers. While the *Free Press* simply reinstated its Sunday pages of columns and ads on November 10, the *News* took note of the movies' return with a syndicated column on what actors had been doing during their month-long "vacation" and with columnist Harold Hefferman expressing his relief that, after seventeen days without movies, "Detroit is cheerful again."[122] Accentuating that cheer, city theaters reopened just in time for the *Detroit Free Press Film Edition* to screen its footage of "Detroit's 'War-End' Celebration."[123]

Lacking extant issues of the *Michigan Film Review* makes it a challenge to track the patterns and changes of film circulation in the Detroit area after the war. Sources now are restricted to city directories and scattered references in the newspapers.[124] That said, according to the directories, in 1918–1919 several major companies opened rental exchange offices (Box Office, Famous Players, Fine Art, First National, and United Artists, all located in the Mack Building), joining the established firms of Goldwyn, Metro, Pathé, Select, Universal, and Vitagraph.[125] Others such as Fox, General Film, George Kleine, Mutual, and Triangle closed or no longer were listed; nor was Paramount-Artcraft, but that was because Famous Players-Lasky now distributed its features through its own regional exchange office. While some local exchanges that once rented reissues, second- or third-run features, or older films also disappeared (Dawn Masterplay, Four Square, and Jewell), others remained (Standard Film, State Film, and Strand Features), and still others popped up (Capitol Film, Exhibitors Booking, Film Clearing House, and Lefkey & Zapp) but did not last long.[126] In 1920–1921, World Film closed its office; Warner Bros. opened a branch; and nearly a dozen small local rental exchanges appeared, yet few survived in the midst of the economic depression. Survivors included Detroit Film, Equity Film, Favorite Film, Kempson

Pictures, and Merit Film. Distribution in Detroit, as in most large cities by the early 1920s, was dominated by the industry's consolidation into half a dozen or more major companies—what Kia Afra calls "a limited oligarchy"[127]—at least two of which, Paramount and First National, now either contracted with or owned outright thousands of theaters.[128] City directories, however, suggest that distribution may have been just lucrative enough for some local companies to sustain a more or less thriving secondhand business on the margins.

Newspaper ads offer more detailed information on the circulation of films, at least from the major companies. During the first half of 1919, exhibitors continued to promote movie stars, titles of adaptations (novels or plays), and even a few filmmakers (D.W. Griffith, Thomas Ince, Maurice Tourneur) to attract moviegoers, but the Paramount, Artcraft, and Famous Players-Lasky trademarks, however small in size, did appear sometimes in ads for films—from *The Hope Chest*, with Dorothy Gish, and *Branding Broadway*, with William S. Hart, to Cecil B. DeMille's *For Better, For Worse*, with Gloria Swanson.[129] Beginning in the second half of 1919, companies began to change their tactics. In early September, Fox gained some financial interest in one of Kunsky's downtown theaters, which became the William Fox Washington; and Fox's name soon branded its frequent westerns starring Tom Mix.[130] In November, several ads included the label "a Universal Picture," one of which added this line: "Carl Laemmle offers Dorothy Phillips [in] *The Right to Happiness*."[131] In early 1920, the Madison started promoting one film after another—from *In Old Kentucky*, with Anita Stewart, and *Pollyanna*, with Mary Pickford, to *The Woman Gives*, with Norma Talmadge—as "a First National attraction."[132] At the same time, the label "Selznick Pictures" also was being stamped on films such as *The Woman Game*, starring Elaine Hammerstein.[133]

As the top-ranked distributor, Paramount launched its second national campaign with a full-page ad in the *Free Press*, designating early September 1919 as "National Paramount Artcraft Week."[134] This ad blocked out the programs for six of the best venues, twenty-nine others in Detroit (but only the Catherine and Crescent in ethnic neighborhoods), and nine "out-of-town theatres." Among the graphics in the first ad was a large crowd of people and two automobiles before a palace theater showing Paramount-Artcraft films; atop the second was a drawing in which a well-dressed couple looked out over a crowded theater audience to a screen displaying the Paramount logo. Later large ads in the *News* claimed that the company produced "exactly the kind of motion pictures that you would make if you were master of the world" and urged moviegoers to look for lobby posters, billboards, newspaper ads, and theater programs in order to plan their viewing of the company's "first-rate pictures."[135] Surprisingly, in late 1919 Samuel Goldwyn mounted a national ad campaign to make his company a viable competitor—promoting *Jinx* with Mabel Normand, *Jublio* with Will Rogers, and

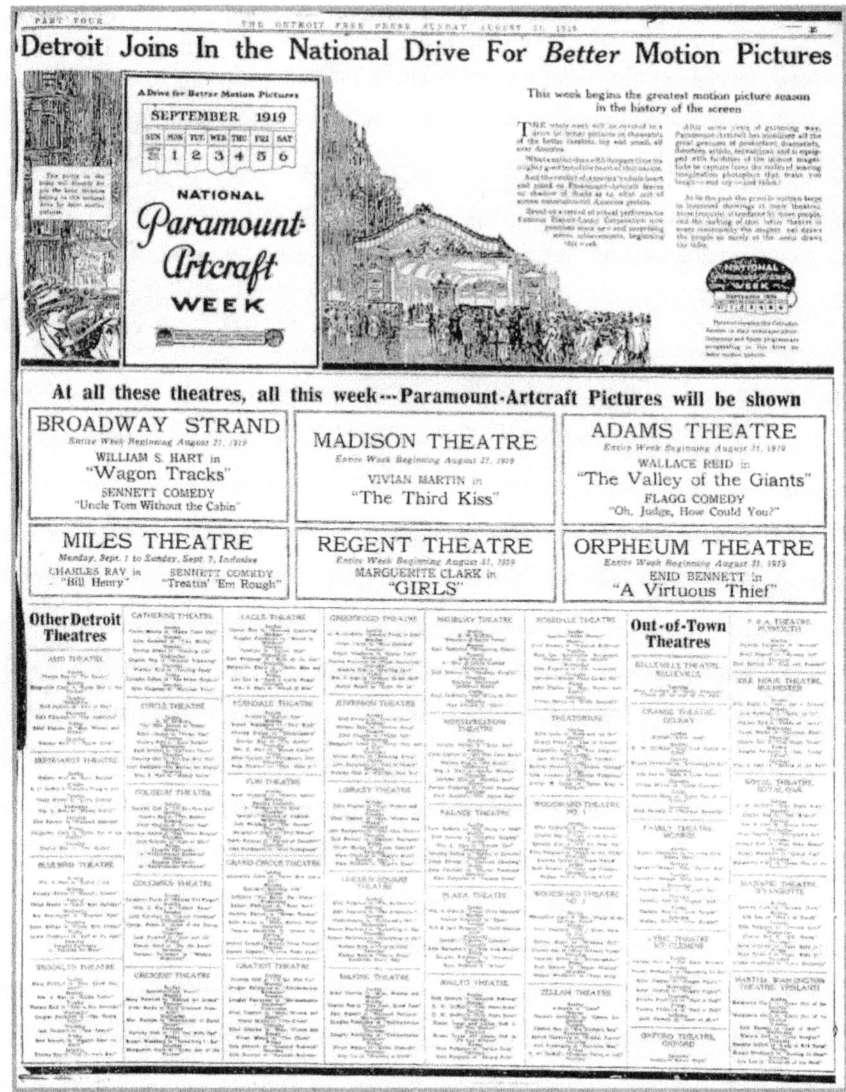

Fig. 1.8. Paramount-Artcraft ad, *Detroit Sunday Free Press* (August 31, 1919): 4.16.

Toby's Box with Tom Moore.[136] The same day that Paramount announced its "third annual drive for motion pictures" in early September 1920,[137] Goldwyn's campaign culminated in an ad promising that movie fans would find "the first fifteen" of sixty pictures set for release during the 1920–1921 season only "in the best theatres."[138] In January 1921, however, Paramount upped the ante with a full-page ad addressing readers directly: "what 1921 and Paramount Pictures have in store

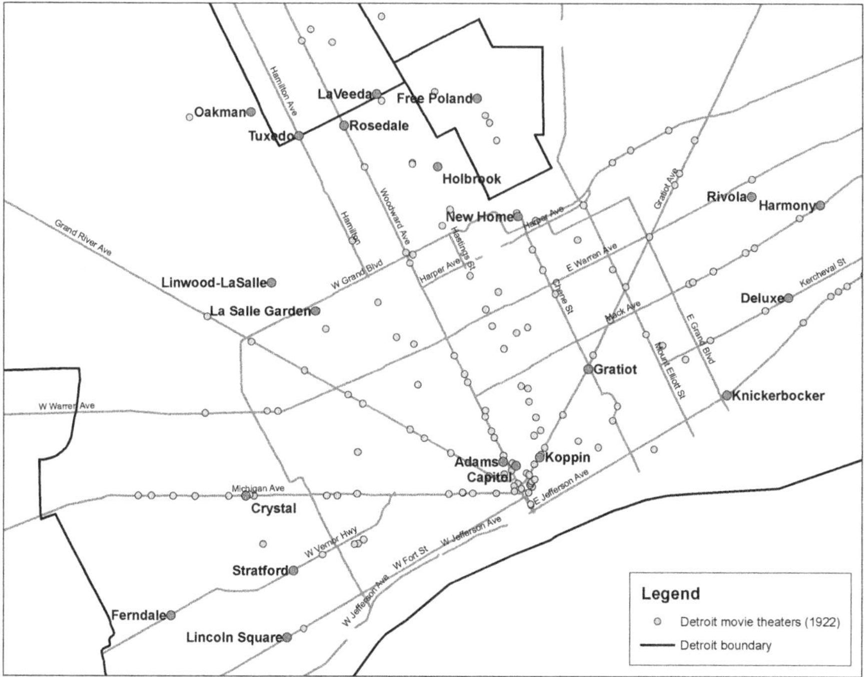

Fig. 1.9. 1922 Detroit map of selected theaters.

for you." The ad included a long column of current and coming films and stars, an equally long list of theaters playing those films in the city and elsewhere in the state (a dozen were ethnic neighborhood theaters), and a graphic of well-dressed moviegoers (of all ages) in a huge line leading to a "Paramount Pictures" theater.[139] The Broadway Strand also designed a contest (for prize tickets) that asked readers to "count the number of times the word 'Paramount'" could be found in a full page of ten ads that surrounded its own.[140] In early September, as expected, the company welcomed moviegoers to the "4th Annual Paramount Week" in a large ad listing three tiers of theaters: first, the Broadway Strand, Madison, and Adams; second, twenty-three more theaters (the Iris and Crystal were still prominent); and last, nearly fifty others in the city and "out-of-town."[141]

The landscape of commercial exhibition venues also began to shift in 1920–1921 under the dual pressures of the economic depression and persistent population expansion. Small downtown theaters such as the Princess and the Royale closed by 1922. So did a larger theater located on the east side, the Duplex (1,250 seats), in 1921;[142] and so did the Pulaski (formerly the LaBelle) in Del Ray. Other small theaters, particularly in ethnic neighborhoods, underwent a name change that seemed to either erase their origins or elevate their status, as if through a process of "Americanization": the Lester became the People's in 1918; the Lira, the Lockwood in 1919; the Amuse U, the Lancaster in 1921; the Rozmaitosci, the Premier in 1922. The Free Poland reverted to simply the Poland in 1921. More significant was the 1920 opening of the Koppin (1,500 seats) in Black Bottom's entertainment district. The Koppin would soon become the top "musical institution in black Detroit";[143] in 1921 it was already an important enough venue to be named in the Paramount ad.[144] Most striking, however, was the construction of large cinemas in areas near the city limits and in the suburbs, as more and more people (largely white) sought out spacious lots away from the crowded city center and swelling ethnic neighborhoods. A new "Dexter-Linwood" commercial area defined by Linwood, Oakman, Woodrow Wilson, and Tuxedo, just west of Highland Park, saw the building of three such theaters between 1919 and 1921: the Oakman (1,213 seats), the Linwood-LaSalle (1,400 seats), and the Tuxedo (1,800 seats).[145] Erected farther south, but still near the Boston-Edison district, was the La Salle Garden (1,990 seats). Others arose in the suburbs: the Ferndale (995 seats) on the eastern edge of Dearborn in the west, the Washington (1,128 seats) in Royal Oak, the Rivoli (1,010 seats) in Warren, and the Harmony (1,322 seats) in Grosse Pointe. Exceptions, whether in location or size, were few; they included the Holbrook (764 seats) in Lake Shore Junction in 1920; the La Veeda (528 seats) on the southeastern edge of Highland Park in 1922;[146] and Kunsky's picture palace, the Capitol (3,367 seats), which that same year joined the Madison and Adams encircling the new city center around Grand Circus Park.[147]

Coincident with the armistice, both the *News* and the *Free Press* suddenly began running weekly ads for loosely defined neighborhood theaters—those that the *News* argued "sustain the motion picture industry."[148] Paramount-Artcraft's national campaign had established a precedent for the *News*. In early July, the company designed a kind of picture frame for the initial ad (and those that followed), composed of smaller ads for seventeen theaters, perhaps to show how widely its films circulated in the city. A few theaters were prestigious and/or large: the Stratford, Duplex, and Rosedale (965 seats) to the north on Woodward; the Gratiot (1,025 seats), Plaza (760 seats), and Rialto on the east side; and the Lincoln Square and Rex (865 seats) on the west side.[149] The rest were smaller, and two—the Crystal and the Eagle—were close to the west side Polish neighborhood.[150] After the Paramount campaign ended, seven of those theaters began placing ads in the Sunday edition of the *News* in mid-November,[151] and three weeks later the paper introduced a daily vertical strip of tiny ads for twenty-one neighborhood theaters, arranged alphabetically, and addressed familiarly to readers: "Photoplays at Your Favorite Theater Today."[152] All but three of those listed had never advertised in the paper; while half a dozen had far-from-small seating capacities, only three—the Crystal, Iris, and Jewel—served one each of the Polish communities. By January 1919, this column was running full length down the edge of a Saturday

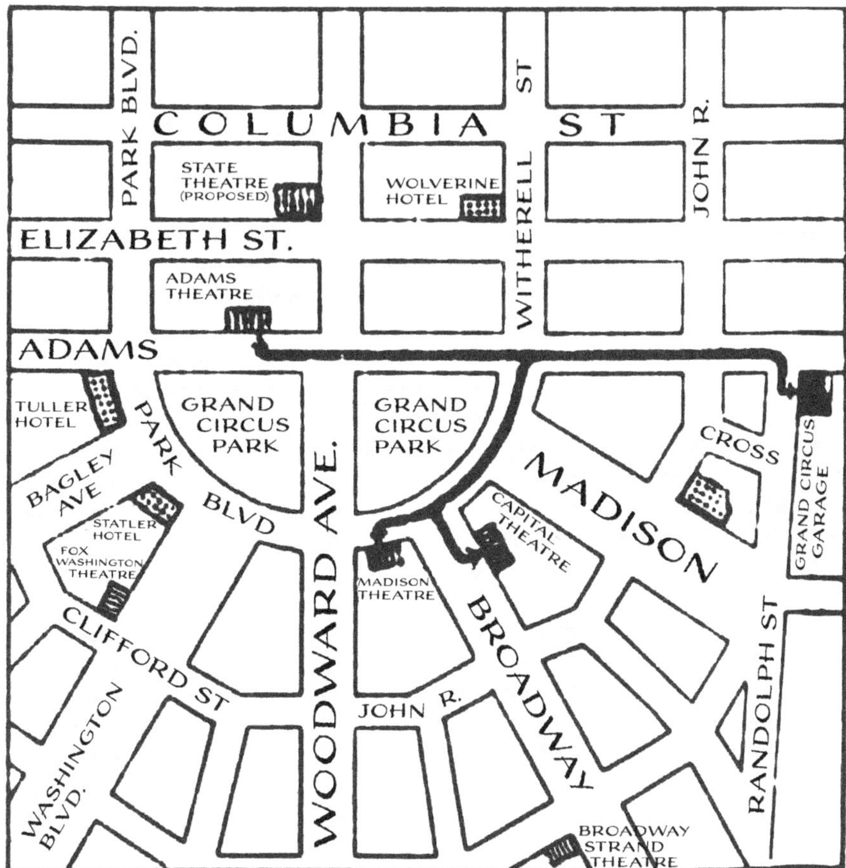

Fig. 1.10. 1923 map of Grand Circus Park, with major theaters and hotels.

page, comprising ads for thirty-five theaters.[153] Most were large theaters scattered across the city; only the enlarged Catherine, with the Crystal and Iris, served the Polish communities, and none were located in the Italian community or Black Bottom. At year's end, this column was listing featured attractions at forty-two theaters.[154] Only half a dozen were neighborhood theaters seating fewer than 500 people; among the rest were several new entries: the Knickerbocker (923 seats) near the Belle Isle Bridge on the east side; the Ferndale on the far west side; and the Drury Lane, Fine Arts, and Norwood (505 seats)—all located conveniently along Woodward from north of Grand Circus Park to midtown.[155] Another half dozen served ethnic neighborhoods: the Crescent in Del Ray, the Arcade and Catherine in "Lower Poletown," and the Iris and Oakland (358 seats) near Hamtramck.

In mid-November 1918, the *Free Press* began printing its own weekly column of ads, headed "What's Doing in Neighborhood Filmland."[156] Despite the *News*'s earlier moves, the *Free Press* boldly claimed that its ads were an "innovation" sponsored by theaters for the benefit of their "movie fans."[157] Moreover, only four theaters sponsored ads of their daily program features: the Maxine on the far east side, the Vendome (891 seats) on the far west side, the north side Duplex, and the Iris. A week later, five more theaters contributed ads: the Rialto, on the east side; the Del-The (1,076 seats) and Gladwin Park (894 seats), near Belle Isle Park; the Crystal; and the Virginia (530 seats), near the Boston-Edison neighborhood.[158] Within the next month or two, a few of these theaters stopped advertising, but three others replaced them: the Strand; the Billikin (350 seats), just west of the north side Duplex; and the Gratiot on the east side.[159] All but three of these theaters had large seating capacities; among these "better theaters" (according to the *Free Press*) were the Iris and Crystal, which catered to Polish communities. Reduced to five theaters by March 1919, this block of ads disappeared altogether for four months after early May, then gradually resumed in September.[160] In mid-October 1919, the *Free Press* finally followed the *News* (and the *Journal*) with its own daily vertical column of tiny ads, headed "Today's Show at Your Neighborhood Theatre."[161] The thirty-two theaters listing their featured attraction ranged from prestigious venues—the Alhambra, Del-The, De Luxe, Ferry Field, Garden, Rialto, Stratford, and Strand—to many that were not carried in the *News*—the Amo (384 seats), Beechwood (399 seats), Blue Bird (344 seats), Cass (250 seats), Cozy (389 seats), Theatorium (384 seats), and Wayne (330 seats). Several besides the Iris and the Crystal were located in or near either Polish or Italian neighborhoods, but all were small: the Arcade, Jewel, Perrien, and Quo Vadis. However, the number soon again declined until, by January 1920, the column included no more than twenty venues, and only the Iris, Crystal, and Arcade remained of those located in ethnic areas.[162]

The most popular films and stars in Detroit during 1919 were hardly unusual, and their spatial and temporal dispersal is slightly easier to track. In February, *Mickey*, with "mischievous Mabel Normand," opened for a week at the Majestic, moved north to the Regent, transferred to the Ferry Field and the Del-The in March, returned downtown to the Washington in April and the Ferry Field in June, then turned up later at the Detroit Opera House, Alhambra, and Crystal ("by special request").[163] In May, *Daddy-Long-Legs*, with Pickford, played for one week at the Adams, where "45,575 people saw it," then shifted to the Washington for another week.[164] In June, it featured at the Miles, Ferry Field, and Arcade (in Lower Poletown); in July, at the Liberty and De Luxe; and six months later, at the far east side Arthur (337 seats).[165] In September, *His Majesty, the American*, with Fairbanks, held the screen at the Majestic for two weeks and played another week at the Regent and Orpheum (another Miles vaudeville house); in October, moviegoers could find it across the city, from the Liberty and the Fine Arts to the De Luxe.[166] In November, DeMille's *Male and Female*, with Swanson and Thomas Meighan, premiered at the Broadway Strand for a three-week run; months later, it showed up at other large theaters; and it was the main attraction at the Linwood-LaSalle's grand opening in late April.[167] Based on its 1919 ad, many of these Paramount films also likely played at the Catherine (in Lower Poletown) and the Crescent (in Del Ray), although neither advertised in Detroit papers at the time. Finally, Griffith's *Broken Blossoms*, with Richard Barthelmess and Lillian Gish, featured prominently from early December through January, opening at the Adams and circulating among many theaters already listed, as well as the Frontenac (834 seats) just east of Hamtramck.[168]

Other films either exceeded expectations or created controversy. Metro's *The Brat* demonstrated the drawing power of "the exotic and artful Nazimova"[169] by playing simultaneously at the Majestic, Orpheum, and Regent in October, shifting to others like the Crystal (but apparently not the Iris) in early November, then circulating through much of the city for another three months.[170] Also in October, George Loane Tucker's *The Miracle Man*, with Betty Compson, had a surprising four-week run of six daily shows at the Broadway Strand and returned to the theater in late December; from January through March 1920, it also appeared at the Liberty, Ferry Field (twice), Iris, Strand, Oakman, Alhambra, Lincoln Square, Duplex, Rosedale, and Frontenac.[171] Perhaps most intriguing was Public Health Films's *Fit to Win*, produced by the War Department Commission on Training Camp Activities, whose commercial showings, although approved by the American Social Hygiene Association, the industry contested for months in 1919.[172] Despite the Michigan Commissioner of Health's letter of disapproval sent to exhibitors in early 1919, the Washington arranged exclusive screenings of *Fit to Win* for three weeks in January and booked it for a two-week return run in late March.[173] Perhaps to appease any objections from citizens, the Washington adopted the strategy of admitting "Men Only" to the first engagement and "Ladies Only" to the second. In conjunction with that second screening, the *Free Press* printed an article on efforts by local social welfare organizations to endorse the film.[174] Only in late 1919 did the industry agree to let the Better Photoplay League decide if such "so-called health films" were fit for commercial screening.[175]

The economic depression of 1920–1921 may have slowed investment in new theaters and forced others to close, but it did not necessarily lessen the attraction of the movies. As named directors, Griffith, DeMille, and Chaplin often guaranteed the success of their films. In January 1920, the D. W. Griffith Service reissued a part of *Intolerance* as *The Fall of Babylon* for a roadshow tour with its own special orchestra.[176] This touring production played for three weeks at the city's Orchestra Hall (3,000 seats) in May and June,[177] transferred to the Shubert Detroit (former Opera House) for a fourth week, and later appeared in "popular price" shows.[178] Griffith's new film, *Way Down East*, with Gish and Barthelmess, premiered at the Shubert Detroit in early May 1921; returned (at popular prices) to the Fox Washington for a four-week run in late October; played at other theaters, including the Crystal and Iris in early 1922; and even showed up six months later at the Linwood-LaSalle.[179] DeMille's Paramount films, with Swanson, consistently went over big. In April 1920, *Why Change Your Wife?* played for four weeks at the Broadway Strand and moved on that fall to the Liberty, Alhambra, and probably other Paramount venues.[180] In early September, the company also stocked nine different "neighborhood theaters" with a full week of other Paramount features.[181] In mid-October, DeMille's *Something to Think About* had a three-week run at the Broadway Strand and later carried on at large theaters, although apparently not in ethnic neighborhoods.[182] The Broadway Strand even sponsored a contest (for prize tickets) asking readers to make up the film's title, as often as possible, from letters in nine other businesses' ads that framed its own.[183] Moviegoers could hardly get enough of Chaplin, as his earlier films kept shoring up one theater program after another.[184] When his first feature, *The Kid*, finally arrived in late January 1921, it played two weeks at the Madison and reappeared one month later at the Liberty, Regent, and Orpheum; from February through March, it dominated the programs of at least a dozen theaters, including the Crystal and Iris, and was still screening in November at the far east side Your Theater (774 seats).[185]

Major stars other than Chaplin obviously could guarantee huge audiences as well. Mary Pickford once again took on a tomboy disguise in *Little Lord Fauntleroy*, which held the screen for two weeks at the Adams in late November 1921, before reappearing at other theaters, including the Crystal in early 1922, and then anchoring a summer program at the Alhambra.[186] According to ads for Hudson's department store, Pickford's costume sparked a fashion trend in dresses and blouses trimmed with "Sally collars . . . Lord Fauntleroy style."[187] Douglas Fairbanks exploited his athleticism in historical super productions, beginning with *The Mark of Zorro*, which premiered at the Fox Washington in early December; shifted to the Orpheum at the end of the month; and featured, over the next three months, at many large theaters, including the Iris.[188] Nearly a year later, *The Three Musketeers* opened at the Adams for a four-week run, before circulating, from December to August, through theaters such as the De Luxe, where it shared a week with *Way Down East*.[189] In April and May 1921, director Rex Ingram's *The Four Horsemen of the Apocalypse* opened a special four-week run of two daily shows at the Garrick,[190] a legitimate theater. When the film returned to the Adams (at popular prices) for a three-week run in January 1922, Rudolph Valentino was promoted as its star; for the next five months it featured at theaters that included the Iris and even the Park (676 seats), located just north of Hamtramck and east of Ford's Crystal Palace.[191] In November 1921, Valentino's next hit, *The Sheik*, opened a two-week run at the Broadway Strand; then, during the first four months of 1922, it shadowed *Four Horsemen*

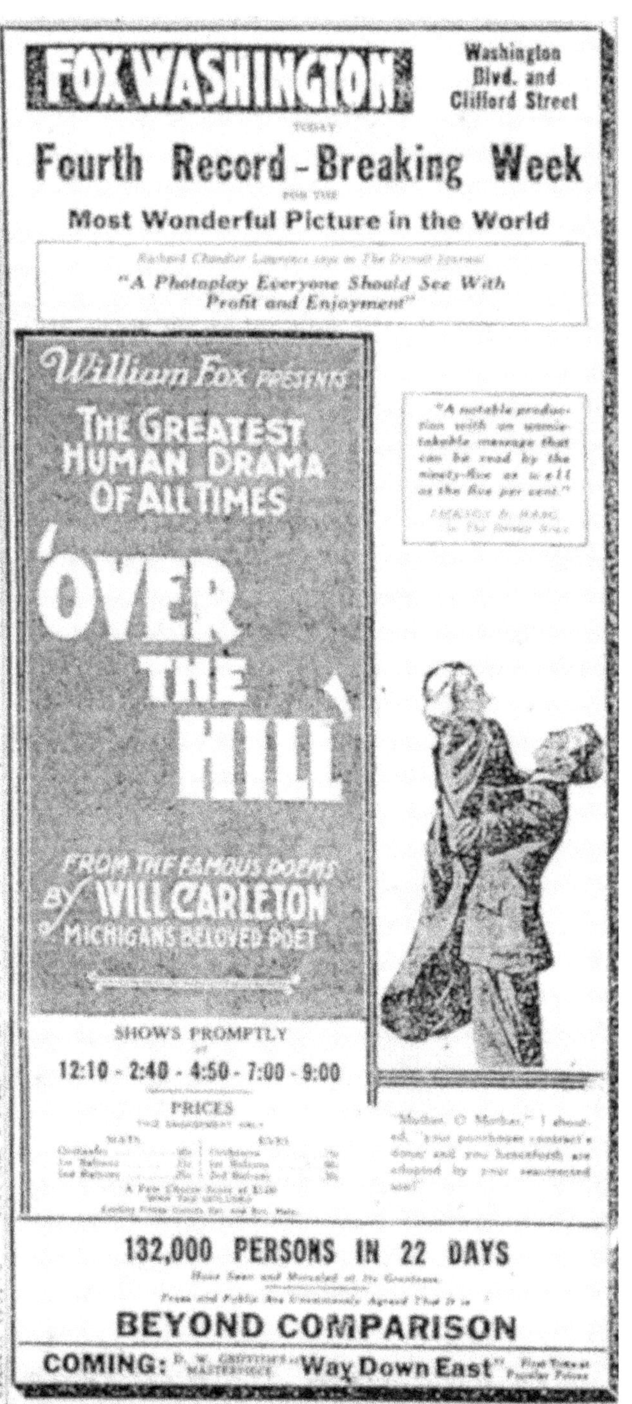

Fig. 1.11. Fox Washington Theater ad, *Detroit Sunday Free Press* (September 25, 1921): 5.9.

in screenings at a dozen theaters, before returning downtown for a week at the Orpheum.[192]

At least two rather different films received special attention in Detroit. One was Paramount's *Humoresque*, based on a Fannie Hurst story published in Hearst's *Cosmopolitan* magazine and directed by Frank Borzage, which premiered at the Broadway Strand in early September 1920, promoted as "the cinema's epic of mother love."[193] Not only did the Broadway Strand sponsor a contest asking readers to put together as many titles of the film as possible from letters in the seven ads surrounding its own,[194] but also it took the unusual step of printing the program for its six daily performances (see chap. 2).[195] Near the end of the film's "record breaking" four-week run, the theater also compiled glowing testimonials from more than a dozen state and city officials and businessmen.[196] From October to December, moviegoers could find *Humoresque* at theaters from the Liberty and the Alhambra to the Iris.[197] Perhaps the most intriguing of these films was Fox's *Over the Hill*, which premiered at the Fox Washington in early September 1921 and ran through October for a record seven weeks.[198] Another "story of mother love," the film was drawn from two "farm ballads" by Will Carleton, "Michigan's beloved poet," which partly explains why "181,000 Detroiters" allegedly had seen it by early October.[199] In late November, a highly unusual ad announced that, in "response to the popular demand," *Over the Hill* would return for the exceptional period of a full week at "24 neighborhood motion picture theatres" in the city and suburbs, from the Drury Lane, Duplex, and Stratford to the Crystal, New Home, La Veeda, Arcade, and Crescent in several different ethnic communities.[200]

In 1921, nearly three years after the armistice, a few foreign film imports began to break into the American market. German films led the way, and one of the first, *Deception*,[201] distributed by Paramount, found exhibitors ready to book it in Detroit. Directed by Ernst Lubitsch, this historical superproduction about Henry VIII and Anne Boleyn played for two weeks at the Broadway Strand in May, reappearing in several large theaters between June and September as well as the Park in March 1922.[202] The *Free Press* highlighted its stars, Emil Jannings and Henny Porten, and also described its set design as a "masterpiece of decorative art."[203] In late August, the Broadway Strand premiered a second German film, *The Golem*, stressing its origin in "the mystic Jewish folk lore of medieval Europe."[204] After screening at the Alhambra and Rialto, it also was booked for a limited engagement at the Iris in early December.[205] Several Italian historical spectacle films soon followed the German imports. In early June 1921, Goldwyn announced its acquisition of *Theodora*, marking "the re-entry of Italian productions into the United States after eight years."[206] Five months later, the film premiered at the Shubert Detroit in twice-daily shows, and Goldwyn advertised the Italian government's sponsorship of this adaptation of a famous Sardou play.[207]

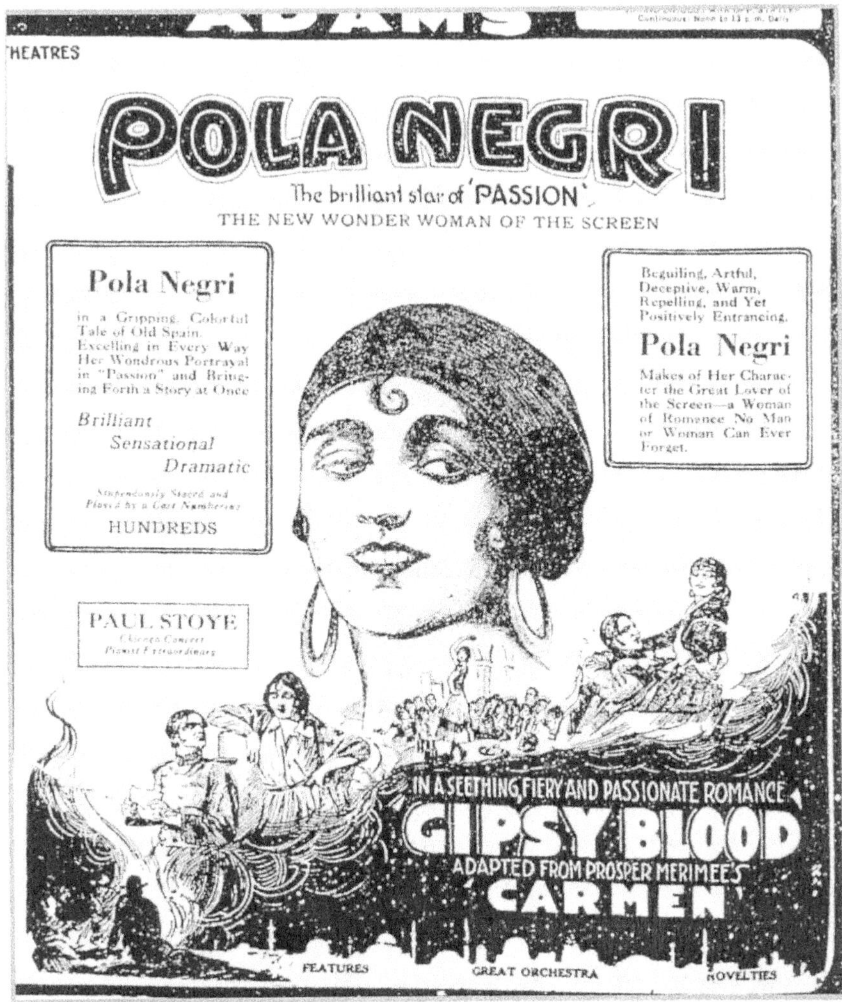

Fig. 1.12. Adams Theater ad, *Detroit Sunday Free Press* (May 22, 1921): 5.10.

In late January 1922, the Adams presented *Theodora* at "popular prices," calling Cleopatra "a mere novice" compared to the Italian film's empress; two months later, the film also had limited engagements at the La Salle Garden and the Tuxedo, but played for a full week at the Farnum and then a weekend at the Park for the Polish community of Hamtramck.[208] At the same time, the re-release print of the famous pre-war film *Quo Vadis?* featured one weekend at both the Crystal and the Iris, and just before the latter theater's Easter week screening of *The Four Horsemen of the Apocalypse*.[209] One has to ask, however, why another German film, *The Cabinet of Doctor Caligari*, seems not to have come to Detroit, especially since it was featured prominently, even in some small towns, elsewhere in the country.[210]

Perhaps the most relevant of these foreign imports, however, were the Lubitsch-directed films of the Polish star Pola Negri.[211] Several syndicated notices preceded First National's premiere of *Passion* at the Adams in February 1921, where "it played to the greatest Sunday crowds in Detroit theatrical history" and, as a result, was held over for a second week.[212] During that extended run, another syndicated article highlighted Negri's "curious combination of the soulful and capricious," "simultaneously intense and fancifully fantastic," most evident in her "remarkably large and expressive eyes."[213] Another article later claimed that, along with *Way Down East* and *The Mark of Zorro*, *Passion* was the box office smash of the season.[214] Although Negri's film circulated through half a dozen major theaters from March to May, it was booked unusually early at the Iris and the Crystal, which served Polish neighborhoods.[215] Exploiting *Passion*'s success, *Gypsy Blood*, Lubitsch's version of *Carmen*,[216] also screened at the Adams in late May, appeared at the Garden and at other theaters that summer, and still could be seen at the Park the following April.[217] Apparently Negri was so popular in Detroit that First National opened *One Arabian Night*, her third Lubitsch-directed film, at the Adams in late September, for its "first showing anywhere in the United States."[218] From October through December, this "oriental" spectacle also had a wide circulation that encompassed many theaters beyond those in the Polish neighborhoods.[219]

By 1921–1922, what seems distinctive about the circulation of films in and around Detroit? Given its prominent advertising campaign, Paramount—more than did any other distributor—appeared bent on securing the city and its environs as one of its principal markets to exploit. At least three Hollywood distributors had arrangements with major downtown theaters to premiere their weekly releases: Paramount, with the Broadway Strand, First National, with the Adams and Madison; and Fox, through a financial stake in the Washington. These arrangements (without the confirmation of contracts) may have given the appearance of a stable exhibition market, but they were far from exclusive and they allowed for flexibility in booking.[220] For second- and third-run screenings, distribution seemed even more fluid and up for grabs, especially in theaters that changed their film programs multiple times a week or even daily. Theater construction continued to boom, despite a short-lived economic depression, but much of that came in the more prosperous outer areas of the city, such as the new commercial district west and south of Highland Park, and in the suburbs to the east, west, and north. Very few new theaters appeared in ethnic neighborhoods, and only the Iris and the Crystal, serving Polish communities, could afford to advertise regularly in newspapers. The more popular films and stars for Detroit moviegoers probably were much the same as elsewhere. Those included titles attributed to Griffith, DeMille, and Chaplin, and stars such as Pickford, Fairbanks, Normand, Swanson, and the newcomer Valentino. But the city's unusually large Polish population may well have enhanced the appeal of the "exotic" European star, Pola Negri.[221] And that appeal likely led First National to make Detroit the privileged site to launch Negri's third German film, *One Arabian Night*.

Securing and Stabilizing Detroit's Movie Market to 1925

Marking off this chapter into a third period of approximately three years may seem arbitrary, especially given the previous section's breakpoint at the end of the Great War. Yet this periodization may have some merit. Although problems like housing conditions obviously remained, the Detroit area evidenced a relatively steady economic recovery from the 1920–1921 depression. At the same time, Hamtramck and Highland Park chose, or were pressured, to incorporate into separate mid-sized cities rather than to become part of the larger booming metropolis. Significantly for this study, new sources of historical information devoted to movie culture appeared in several newspapers. As the circulation of the *Detroit Times* rose substantially after being bought by Hearst, the paper greatly expanded its coverage of the movies. Hamtramck and Highland Park published their own weekly newspapers, which carried ads from quite different neighborhood theaters. Ending this section in early or mid-1925 also coincides with the disappearance of theater ads in those two newspapers, the *Hamtramck News* and *Highland Parke*r, perhaps signaling that each was losing influence compared to that of the three remaining major Detroit papers. Finally, this endpoint comes well before the October 1925 opening of Kunsky's State theater, his fourth picture palace encircling Grand Circus Park, which certified the district as the entertainment center of downtown Detroit.

As film distributors, the major Hollywood companies had solidified their position in Detroit's movie market. According to city directories, while Box Office and half a dozen small firms closed down, others took their place, with Selznick the most important among a similar number of new small firms. However, at least seven Hollywood companies—Paramount, First National, Fox, Universal, Goldwyn, Metro, and Louis B. Mayer—regularly stamped their brand or trademark, as a guarantee of satisfaction, on first-run theater ads for most of their feature films. For example, see the premieres of First National's *Smilin' Through*, starring Norma Talmadge, at the Adams in April 1922; Paramount's *Blood and Sand*, with Valentino, at the Adams in early September; and Goldwyn's *The Christian*, at the Broadway Strand in March 1923.[222] Fox may have had an exclusive arrangement with the Washington, but contracts with other first-run theaters seemed far less exclusive. Paramount and First National were not the only companies to premiere films at the Adams; Universal's *Foolish Wives* opened there in

April 1922; Mayer's *Hearts Aflame*, in January 1923; and Metro's *Scaramouche*, in April 1924.[223] A film's second-run circulation also could follow one of several different paths. *Blood and Sand* left Kunsky's Adams to feature at the Regent and the Miles; *Smilin' Through* transferred only to the Miles from Gleichman's Broadway Strand and then immediately turned up at Kunsky's Alhambra; and *The Christian* bypassed the Regent and the Miles to headline the La Salle Garden and then the Tuxedo, both large theaters well outside the downtown center.[224] Although a film might circulate initially through a certain range of theaters (based on limited newspaper ads), it need not appear at all of them, nor did its trajectory always follow a consistent path. Do all these ads then suggest that at least an implicit arrangement (if not outright collusion) among the three principal theater entrepreneurs determined which theater premiered which Hollywood feature during a particular week—and that, beyond those premiere engagements, Detroit's movie market was relatively open or at least far from closed? Getting answers rather than making guesses could depend on finding business records that at this time are still missing.

Paramount's annual newspaper ad campaigns, however, offer a different, if rather narrow, perspective on film circulation in Detroit. A large ad in late July 1922 urged readers directly to "ask your theatre manager to book" the company's pictures.[225] It listed the titles of an imposing number of forty-one films (and the names of their stars) to be released in the next six months; some of the ads included the name of a director and a scenarist.[226] Another large ad one month later promoted the banners and posters in theater lobbies hailing moviegoers, but most prominently it listed, in block columns, the theaters where Paramount films were being shown that week.[227] Kunsky's Adams, Capitol, and Madison now handled premieres; the Alhambra, Columbia, Deluxe, Ferry Field, Lincoln Square, and Rialto offered second-run screenings; and fifty-one other theaters in the city, along with thirteen in the suburbs, followed with third-run screenings. Among the latter were the Crystal, Farnum, Highland Park, Holbrook, Iris, La Veeda, Park, Perrien, and Premier serving Polish or Jewish communities; the Quo Vadis in the Italian ghetto; and the Crescent in Del Ray. One year later, Paramount designed a different ad that amassed its "artists," at least ten of them directors, into parallel blocks of forty-six small drawings of their faces.[228] While the Madison and the Adams still premiered the company's films (promoting only the titles and stars), second-run screenings shifted to the Regent, Miles, Orpheum, Palace, and Columbia. Third-run theaters were classified into the West Side, East Side, Hamtramck, and Suburban. Polish and Jewish neighborhood theaters were most numerous in and around Hamtramck—the Caniff, Free Poland, Holbrook, Iris, La Veeda, Park, Perrien, Premier—along with the Catherine in Lower Poletown. A similar ad, without the "artists," appeared in late August 1924.[229] Now, the Capitol, along with the Adams and the Madison, again premiered the company's

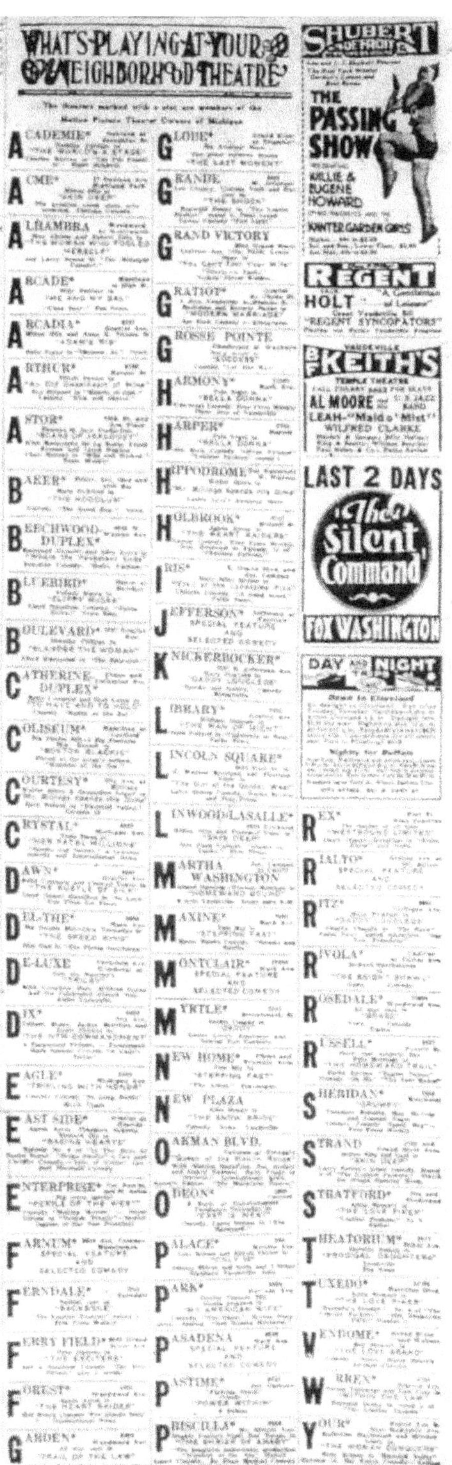

Fig. 1.13. "Neighborhood Theaters" column, *Detroit Times* (September 6, 1923): 18.

films; but the theaters offering second-run screenings had realigned to include the Regent, Miles, and Columbia and diverse others like the Alhambra, Eagle, Ferry Field, Strand, Theatorium, and Victoria.[230] Among the eleven theaters showing third-run films, only the Holbrook, Martha Washington, and Quo Vadis served ethnic neighborhoods.[231] That Detroit was "a National Demonstration Center for Paramount Pictures"—as claimed in an October 1923 ad—supported the company's dominance in the city's movie market.[232]

The commercial venues for film exhibition grew even more stable, even "sedimented," during this period. At least ten theaters closed, nearly all of which had small seating capacities. They included the Our in 1922, the Cass and Columbus in 1923, the East End and Elizabeth in 1925, and the Favorite (the former Dixie) near Black Bottom. In the downtown district, as he centered his enterprises in and around Grand Circus Park, Kunsky shuttered the Princess and Royale in 1922 as well as the Empire in 1925, and sold the Liberty, which closed in 1926. The only large theater to close outside the old downtown hub was the Aladdin (former Gladwin Park) to the east of Belle Isle Park. Interestingly, four theaters changed their names, two of them in different ethnic neighborhoods: in 1922, the Pulaski (formerly the LaBelle) in Del Ray; in 1923, the Enterprise (former Luna) in Lower Poletown; and in 1924, the Royal (former Ludwig) and the Wolverine (former Nettie B) on the west side. Surprisingly few new theaters opened. In 1923, the Astor (732 seats) joined others near the upscale Boston-Edison community; and in 1924, the Republic (400 seats) appeared adjacent to Gleichman's Broadway Strand, which underwent a major renovation that summer.[233] At the same time, the Cinderella (1,897 seats) arose far out on East Jefferson, perhaps to draw more moviegoers from nearby Grosse Pointe. That year the Martha Washington (1,000 seats) also opened, as a vaudeville and movie house, on Joseph Campau Avenue in the northern part of Hamtramck, far from the Dodge Brothers factory on the city's southern edge.

In early January 1923, as a boon to Detroit's movie fans, the *Times* expanded its daily column of theater listings to include more than seventy venues, or half of the total operating in the city.[234] At least twenty-five theaters had never posted newspaper ads before. These columns are invaluable to the cinema historian, because they greatly increase the available data one can use to track the circulation of films. Nearly all of these theaters ranged widely across the city yet were located in largely white neighborhoods, either white collar or skilled working class; none were near the Italian community or Black Bottom.[235] Some had relatively small seating capacities: not only the Odeon (390 seats) and Priscilla (474 seats), both east of Lower Poletown, but also the Jefferson (376 seats) on the far east side. Almost as many, however, were unexpectedly large: the Hippodrome (750 seats), Myrtle (753 seats), and Vendome (891 seats) on the near west side; the Courtesy (816 seats), Harmony (1,322 seats), and Rex (865 seats) on the

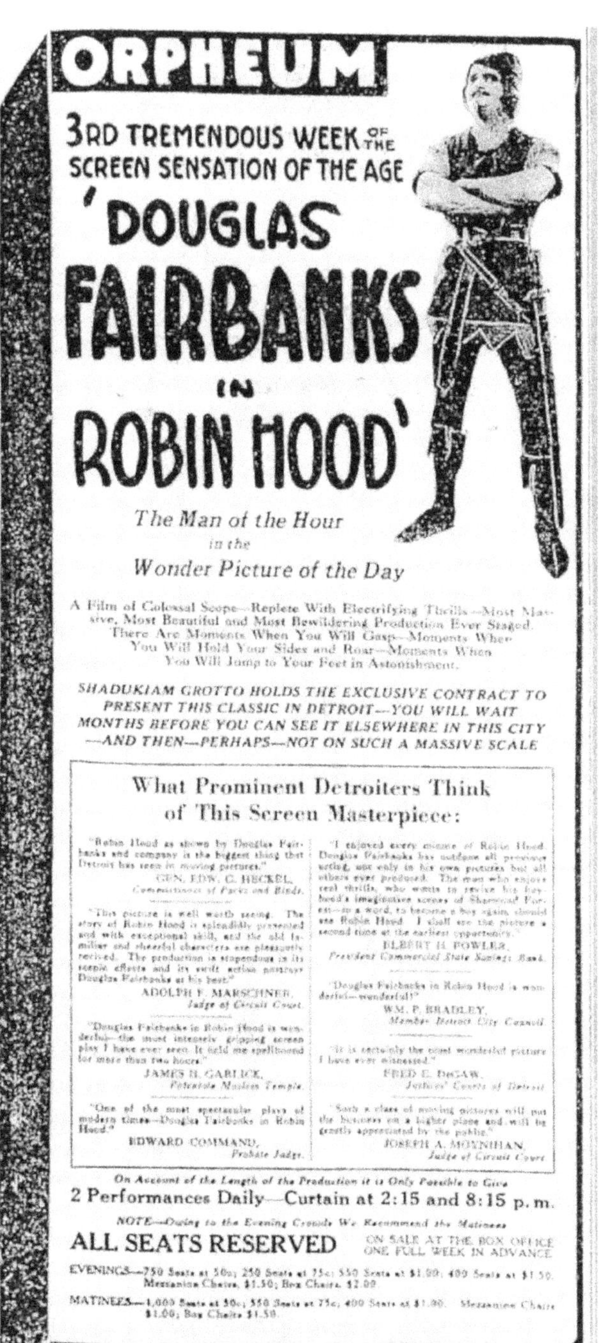

Fig. 1.14. Orpheum Theater ad, *Detroit Sunday Free Press* (November 19, 1922): 5.9.

far west side; the Dawn (894 seats), well east of Hamtramck; the Knickerbocker in the east near Belle Isle; and the Rivola (1,010 seats) in the northeastern suburb of Warren. Only one small theater in Hamtramck, the Pastime (400 seats), joined the nine others in ethnic neighborhoods already posting daily ads.[236] Furthermore, the *Times*'s columns, along with the ads in the *Hamtramck News* and *Highland Parker*, offer a wealth of data for a much fuller analysis of specific theater programs and program changes during these three years (see discussion in chap. 2).

For now, this newspaper advertising offers a means to determine which films and stars seemed especially popular and to track their circulation in the city. At least three films, following the precedent of *The Four Horsemen of the Apocalypse*, received special premieres. In early November 1922, United Artists's *Robin Hood*, directed by Allan Dwan and starring Fairbanks, opened at Miles's downtown Orpheum for what became six weeks of two shows daily.[237] Apparently the Masonic Order of Detroit handled the film's booking; how unusual (or not) this practice of sponsorship was at the time remains to be discovered.[238] After returning to the Adams for two weeks of six shows daily in early March 1923, *Robin Hood* still was playing in early June for four and five days, respectively, at the New Home and Farnum in Hamtramck.[239] In early September 1924, DeMille's *The Ten Commandments* premiered at the New Detroit, a legitimate theater, for a five-week run; several weeks later, the same theater hosted Fairbanks's equally spectacular *The Thief of Bagdad*, which ran there for four weeks and, in early February 1925, returned to the Adams for two weeks, at "popular prices," before circulating through other venues.[240]

Big features with established stars, however, also enjoyed extended initial runs, most of them at the Adams, confirming Kunsky as Detroit's leading movie man.[241] After opening there in mid-March 1922, Griffith's *Orphans of the Storm* (with the Gish sisters) played through mid-April, returned to the Fox Washington in early October, and still could be found at the Rosedale in June 1923.[242] In late December 1922, United Artists's new version of *Tess of the Storm Country*, starring Pickford, featured at the Broadway Strand for three weeks of six shows daily, abetted by five thousand Christmas cards mailed to patrons[243]; the following April the film had three-day runs at the New Home and the Farnum.[244] In late May 1923, Goldwyn's *Enemies of Women*, with Lionel Barrymore, played another three weeks at the Adams and eventually came to the New Home for three days in mid-December.[245] In late March 1924, Metro's *The White Sister*, with Henry King directing Lillian Gish, opened at the Adams for a four-week run and headed a weekend program at the Alhambra in late June.[246] Earlier that month, First National's *Secrets*, with Borzage directing Norma Talmadge, played the Adams for three weeks and eventually featured at the Farnum for three days in mid-October.[247] Finally, after premiering at the New Detroit Opera

House in October 1923, Paramount's epic western, *The Covered Wagon* (directed by James Cruze), ran for four weeks the following summer, again at the Adams, and still served as a special week-long feature at the Martha Washington in late October 1924.[248]

Nearly a dozen films with relatively new stars, however, were equally popular, if not more so; and many also opened at the Adams. In early September 1922, Paramount's *Blood and Sand*, with Valentino, directed by Fred Niblo, premiered there for a three-week run and, in mid-June 1923, was still screening at the Your;[249] in August 1924, Paramount's *Monsieur Beaucaire*, with Valentino, directed by Sidney Olcott, had a similar run at the Adams and, in November, featured for three days at the Martha Washington.[250] In late February 1924, Universal's *The Hunchback of Notre Dame*, starring Lon Chaney, also opened at the Adams for a run of four weeks, allegedly breaking box office records; in mid-August, it featured for four days at the Farnum.[251] In late August 1922, a full-page syndicated article carried in the *Times* announced Paramount's coming release of *When Knighthood Was in Flower*, a Cosmopolitan production starring Marion Davies;[252] after arriving in early November, it held the Adams's screen for four weeks—with Victor Herbert initially conducting his special score—returned "by popular demand" to the Madison in mid-February 1923, and still played the Rosedale in late June.[253] Beginning in late December 1924, another Davies vehicle, Metro-Goldwyn's *Janice Meredith*, ran for three weeks and still featured at the Martha Washington for three days in mid-March 1925.[254] Perhaps the most prominent star, however, was Harold Lloyd, with no less than seven comic features produced by Hal Roach and released by Pathé in a period of two and a half years. Four films—*A Sailor-Made Man*, *Grandma's Boy*, *Dr. Jack*, and *Why Worry?*—had three-week runs at the Madison, the Fox Washington, and the Miles, respectively; the others—*Safety Last!*, *Girl Shy*, and *Hot Water*—opened at the Adams and ran for a full month each. While *Safety Last!* circulated for at least three months, from early April 1923 to early July (appearing simultaneously at the Del-The, Ferndale, and Stratford),[255] *Dr. Jack*, after opening at the Washington in early January 1923, was still screening eight months later at the Iris.[256]

The popularity of at least three sensational films stood out for other reasons. Universal's "super jewel" *Foolish Wives*, directed by and starring Erich Von Stroheim (as a German military officer), opened at the Adams for a three-week run in late April 1922. The initial ad called the film "an Arabian nights tale . . . a shimmering, dizzily-told story of the world's perfumed garden of amours"—with a warning to patrons that it "is of interest only to the adult"; the third week's ad depicted four scantily clad women caught in a spider's web.[257] What especially distinguished the film's promotion, however, were ads in late August that told moviegoers to "see it at your neighborhood theater," listing the forty-six theaters that were showing the film on which days over a two-week period.[258] *Exhibitors*

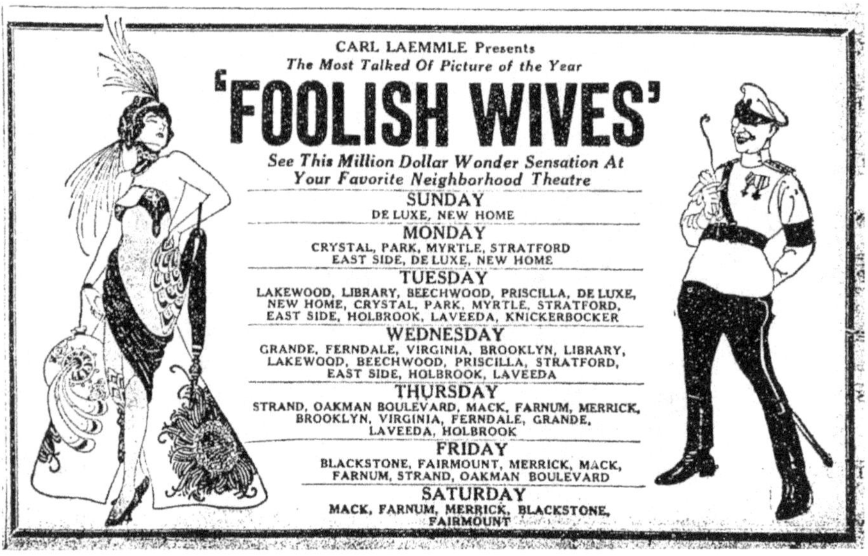

Fig. 1.15. *Foolish Wives* ad, *Detroit Sunday Free Press* (August 20, 1922): 5.9.

Herald picked up Universal's "day-and-date policy of exhibiting big attractions under cumulative or mass exploitation" and printed quotes from most of those theaters: the Stratford, Holbrook, Farnum, New Home, and Park all broke house records.[259] Despite threats from the Motion Picture Producers and Distributors of America (MPPDA) and its chair Will Hays,[260] the "hygienic picture" *Some Wild Oats* played for four months in Detroit, first at the Shubert Detroit and then at the Orpheum, with support from the city's health department, the county medical society, and others.[261] The two theaters adopted the same strategy that had been used three years earlier for *Fit to Win*: They preempted audience objections by scheduling daily "adult" screenings, with Thursday nights for "women only" and Tuesday shows for "men only." Goldwyn's *Name the Man!*, directed by Victor Seastrom and starring Conrad Nagel and Mae Busch, was an unexpected hit, opening at the Broadway Strand in late January 1924 for a three-week run, and in early May still playing for three days at the Farnum.[262] The Broadway Strand deployed several promotional stunts—for example, a telegram allegedly from Seastrom directed at Swedish immigrants, free taxi service at night, and free parking spaces near the theater—but the most intriguing was special stickers plastered around town that capitalized on the controversial mayor's race by admonishing would-be voters to "Name the Man"—an allusion not to the film's accused woman but to Klan supporters of Charles Bowles.[263]

A particularly notable phenomenon during this period was the return screening of certain earlier-released films. In late April 1922, the Madison first

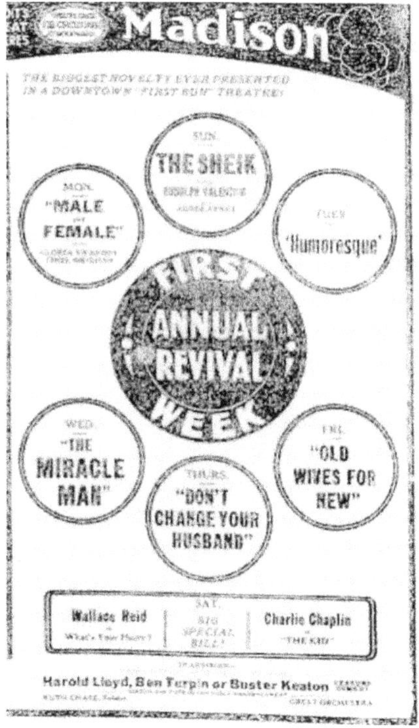

Fig. 1.16. Madison Theater ad, *Detroit Sunday Free Press* (April 30, 1922): 5.6.

promoted this as a "novelty event," a "revival week" in which each day featured a different film from the past three years.[264] Sunday: *The Sheik*; Monday: *Male and Female*; Tuesday: *Humoresque*; Wednesday: *The Miracle Man*; Thursday: *Don't Change Your Husband*; Friday: *Old Wives for New*; and Saturday: *What's Your Hurry?* and *The Kid*. That DeMille directed three of these films seemed to raise his status above all other filmmakers at the time. That year, Griffith's *The Mother and the Law* and Chaplin's *Shoulder Arms* also returned (the latter as a "popular revival" at the Madison), and Pickford's *Daddy-Long-Legs* also had a "revival" at the Fox Washington in August.[265] Only in 1924–1925, however, did a sizable number of older films reappear. Among them were two titles from the Madison's "revival week" two years earlier, *The Miracle Man* and *The Sheik*,[266] but the others encompassed a variety of genres and stars. Some came from as far back as the war period: *The Cossack Whip* (1917), starring Viola Dana; *'Blue Blazes' Rawden* (1918), with Hart; and a war film, *Over the Top* (1918).[267] Others had been released shortly after the war: *Mickey* (1918), starring Normand; *Blind Husbands* (1919), with von Stroheim; and *Over the Hill* (1921) adapted from a Michigan poet's work.[268] Appearing one November weekend in Hamtramck, *The Mark of Zorro* (1921), likely served to promote the next-day release of Fairbanks's *The Thief of Bagdad*.[269] Perhaps most intriguing was another re-release of Griffith's *The Birth of a Nation* that United Artists began distributing to "cheaper theaters" across the country in 1922.[270] The film had a week-long run at the Fox Washington in April 1923, and six months later played for three days at the New Home.[271] Before it appeared for one week at the Farnum, however, Hamtramck's mayor and police commissioner seized the film, "following the filing of a protest by a [NAACP?] committee of negroes."[272] This action seemed to reveal the Polish neighborhood's concern with the growing influence of the Ku Klux Klan.

Finally, a few imported films continued to turn up in scattered Detroit theaters. The most important was Paramount's *The Loves of Pharaoh*, directed by Lubitsch and starring Jannings. In early March 1922, Hugo Riesenfeld had opened the film at New York's Criterion, preceded by "a simple, dignified and graceful Egyptian dance."[273] In late August, the film began a two-week run at the Adams, after which it had a respectable circulation, ranging from the Alhambra in October to the Farnum in February 1923.[274] Two years later, the Martha Washington hosted another Jannings vehicle, *Peter the Great*, for a single Sunday screening.[275] In mid-August 1922, the Iris played a French import, *The Sheik's Wife*, starring Marcel Vibert and Emmy Lynn, for three days, probably in an attempt to capitalize on Valentino's *The Sheik*.[276] The most surprising of these imports, however, was *In the Clutches of the Ochrane*, which had a rare screening at the Farnum in early September 1922.[277] Starring Halina Bruzowna and subtitled in English, this Polish film was set during "the rule of the Russian secret service" before the fall of the Czarist government. This screening suggests how eager moviegoers in the Hamtramck area must have been to see such rare Polish films.

Given the popularity of her German films with Lubitsch, Pola Negri signed contracts to star in a series of American films. In Detroit she was such an attraction that, over two months in late 1922, the *Free Press* published the purported story of her life that stressed her image as an exotic "vampire" figure.[278] After a less than promising beginning in *The Last Payment* (1922),[279] her first really successful film was Goldwyn's *Mad Love*, which broke records at New York's Capitol theater in early 1923.[280] That film followed *Robin Hood* at the Adams, where it played for two weeks in March, and ended its run at the Iris in May and the Farnum in June.[281] Paramount then released five films, directed by experienced filmmakers George Fitzmaurice and Herbert Brenon, that also circulated very well in the city and, as expected, especially in Polish neighborhoods.[282] Fitzmaurice's *Bella Donna* opened at the Adams in early May for a two-week run and was still screening at the Iris and Farnum, respectively, in July and September. A new adaptation of *The Cheat*, directed by Fitzmaurice, also played for two weeks at the Adams in September and then for overlapping days at the Iris and Martha Washington in

November. Brenon's *The Spanish Dancer* received unusual publicity when Paramount chose it to introduce Detroit as its "National Demonstration Center."[283] The film premiered at the Madison for a two-week booking in October, quickly moved to the same Hamtramck theaters at the end of one week and the beginning of the next in late November, and still could be seen at the Cinderella in February 1924. From a one-week run at the Adams in January 1924, Brenon's *Shadows of Paris* went on to the Martha Washington and the Iris, respectively, in March and April, before reaching the Alhambra and the Cinderella in late April.[284] Until Paramount "tamed" her erotic charge in later films,[285] Negri was a major star in the Detroit area, partly due to the large number of her Polish movie fans.

And So . . .

What does this chapter reveal—however restricted to the invested perspectives of rental exchanges and exhibitors—about the circulation of movies and movie stars in a relatively unique metropolis during this period? The rare surviving annual volume of the *Michigan Film Review* suggests that the major film exchanges largely controlled that circulation and, to some extent, controlled how film prints moved from first-run through second- and third-run theaters. Yet exhibitors did have some options of their own within the policies and practices those exchanges put in place. One of those options, which may have been crucial to the industry overall, was to rent prints of the older films and re-issues in which the crowded field of smaller, local exchanges specialized. Moreover, the *Review* offers a detailed map of the network or infrastructure of local businesses required to support the movies as an expanding form of entertainment for an increasing mass of moviegoers. It also shows that both exchanges and exhibitors had to confront a range of problems and issues raised by US intervention in the war.

Unlike the *Review*, after the war the newspapers suggest that, if Paramount clearly was the dominant company distributing films—from the largest first-run theaters to the smallest neighborhood theaters—exhibitors and their patrons within the city and beyond could track a multitude of film titles and movie stars in circulation at any one time. With access to the daily columns of neighborhood theaters, particularly in the *News* and the *Times*, movie fans could readily find out where and when they might see a specific film and/or encounter a favorite star. Along with city directories, the newspapers also make clear that the construction of new picture theaters, large and small, boomed before and after the economic recession of late 1919–early 1921, yet, strikingly, after the recession few of those were located in ethnic neighborhoods. Finally, Detroit movie fans, like moviegoers elsewhere, flocked to the films of Pickford, Fairbanks, Chaplin, Talmadge, Swanson, Meighan, Normand, Lloyd, Valentino, and others, but they especially favored one film and one star with close ties to either the state or specific locales in the city. The film was *Over the Hill*, a "story of mother love" adapted from two much-admired "farm ballads" by "Michigan's beloved poet" Will Carleton. The star was Pola Negri, whose German films directed by Lubitsch were so popular, but whose Polish origins made her a favorite of Detroit's huge Polish immigrant population. While the film looked back with nostalgia at the rural dreamscape of an earlier era, stories about the star embodied a heady present and an immigrant dream for the future. If one view honored a mother at the center of family life, the other heralded the new modern woman, her promises matched by perils.

Notes

1. "Detroit Film Exchanges," *MFR* (December 18, 1917): 13.

2. *Detroit City Directory* (R. L. Polk & Co, 1917), n.p. Between 1915 and 1917, 20 smaller theaters closed while 15 (most of them larger) opened. The police department, however, licensed 117 moving picture theaters, which brought in $2,891.70, or almost exactly the same as came from 30 "theatres"—"Licenses," *Fifty-Third Annual Report of the Detroit Police Department* (Detroit: Detroit Police Department, 1918), 63–64.

3. Kunsky had the Madison constructed as part of a five-story office building; later in 1917, he moved all of his theatrical business offices to the top two floors—"Kunsky, Cinema Magnate, Moves Business Offices, *DFP* (July 4, 1917): 2. I thank Ben Strassfeld for this information.

4. In the 1920s, General Motors promoted the New Center area as a second business district in the city—June Manning Thomas, *Redevelopment and Race: Planning a Finer City in Postwar Detroit* (Detroit: Wayne State University Press, 2013), 66. North Woodward was near the wealthy Boston-Edison community.

5. The Garden also was located in the New Center area; the Alhambra, also in North Woodward.

6. "Girl Stars Predominate Program at Forest," *DJC* (March 30, 1917): 17.

7. "Farnum Theatre Opens," *MFR* (December 11, 1917): 9.

8. The relevant maps for comparative purposes come from Olivier Zunz, *The Changing Face of Inequeality: Urbanization, Industrial Development and Immigration in Detroit, 1880–1920* (Chicago: University of Chicago Press, 1982), 343–347.

9. Accurate seating capacity figures are difficult to determine because later sources (Galbraith and Morrison) do not always agree with listings given out at the time. Depending on the source, the Arcade may have had 650 seats; later as a duplex, the Catherine may have had 716 seats.

10. The next-door location of the Lira and Poznan theaters on East Canfield suggests how blurred the boundaries of the Italian and Lower Poletown neighborhoods were. The Quo Vadis was only one block east of the Lira and Poznan.

11. The Fredro had been an early theater that staged Polish dramas; the Perrien was named for Perrien Park, an "early social and recreational center"—Frank Serafino, *West of Warsaw* (Hamtramck, MI: Avenue Publishing, 1983), 9, 10.

12. A black-owned theater, Mott's Pekin Temple, operated in Chicago's South Side from 1904 to 1917—see Mary Carbine, "'The Finest Outside the Loop': Motion Picture Exhibition in Chicago's 'Black Metropolis,' 1905–1928," *Camera Obscura* 23 (May 1990): 9–41.

13. Originally named the Vaudette, the Dudley apparently was the only theater managed (and perhaps owned) by a black man, Edward B. Dudley—Singh Henry Jines, "Vaudette Theatre, Detroit, Mich.," *Indianapolis Freeman* (June 10, 1916): 5. See also Lars Bjorn and

Jim Gallert, *Before Motown: A History of Jazz in Detroit, 1920–60* (Ann Arbor: University of Michigan Press, 2001), 6.

14. "The term *distribution* is used more commonly within the audiovisual industries to describe the dissemination of films or musical recordings, but circulation goes beyond the practical activity of delivery to capture the cultural resonances of media artifacts and their movement."—Alexandra Bourtros and Will Straw, "Introduction," *Circulation and the City: Essays on Urban Culture* (Montreal: McGill-Queen's University Press, 2010), 6.

15. For an analysis of these two Paramount campaigns, see Richard Abel, *Menus for Movieland: Newspapers and the Emergence of American Film Culture* (Oakland: University of California Press, 2015), 50–53, 54–57.

16. Paramount ad, *DNT* (May 14, 1916): Magazine, 2. Cf. a more generic Paramount ad, *DFP* (February 17, 1916): 6. The attack on "sensational films" also was consistent with Paramount's support for the Hughes bill in Congress, which would have mandated federal censorship—see Kia Afra, *The Hollywood Trust: Trade Associations and the Rise of the Studio System* (Lanham, MD: Rowman & Littlefield, 2016), 40–44.

17. Founded in September 1915, the Motion Picture Board of Trade sought to reconcile the GFC/MPPC and Independents in a producer–distributor alliance that soon collapsed after Metro's desertion—see Afra, *The Hollywood Trust*, 34–36, 47.

18. Metro ad, *DNT* (May 21, 1916): Plays and Players, 6.

19. Metro ads, *DNT* (September 3, 1916): Photoplays, 9, (October 15, 1916): Photoplays, 8, and (March 18, 1917): 4.3. Metro's publicity director was Arthur James—Arthur James, "How Shall I Advertise Pictures," *MPW* (July 20, 1918): 326.

20. Mutual ads, *DNT* (April 1, 1917): n.p., and (April 8, 1917): Photoplays, 6.

21. Pathé ads, *DNT* (March 4, 1917): n.p.; *DFP* (August 5, 1917): C2, (September 16, 1917): 4.10, (September 23, 1917): 4.10, and (September 30, 1917): 4.10; and *DSN* (December 30, 1917): Photoplay, 4. Although sold as a patriotic film during the war, *Patria* made its villains Mexican and Japanese rather than German, given Hearst's pro-German sympathies, which led the US government to insist on cuts and changes before its release—David Nasaw, *The Chief: The Life of William Randolph Hearst* (Boston: Houghton Mifflin, 2000), 257, 261–263; Louis Pizzitola, *Hearst Over Hollywood: Power, Passion, and Propaganda* (New York: Columbia University Press, 2002), 155–161.

22. Edward Stone, "Motion Picture Comment," *DNT* (May 7, 1916): Photoplays, 3.

23. Rotogravure Supplement, *DSFP* (September 24, 1916): n.p.

24. Regent ads, *DNT* (October 22, 1916): n.p., and (October 29, 1916): n.p.; Fine Arts ad, *DNT* (November 19, 1916): n.p.; and Stratford ad, *DNT* (December 17, 1916): n.p.

25. Broadway Strand ad, *DNT* (October 22, 1916): n.p.; and Metro ad, *DNT* (December 3, 1916): 3.

26. For more information on Artcraft's founding in July 1916, as a distributor for Famous Players-Lasky, in parallel with Paramount, see Afra, *The Hollywood Trust*, 67.

27. Majestic ads, *DSFP* (November 5, 1916): The Screen, 4, and (November 12, 1916): 4; Liberty ad, *DSFP* (November 26, 1916): The Screen, 4; Alhambra and Strand ads, *WFN* (December 10, 1916): 13, 15; and Stratford ad, *DNT* (December 24, 1916): Photoplays, 7. The Stratford played the film on Christmas and the day after.

28. Broadway Strand ad, *DSFP* (November 19, 1916): The Screen, 4; Liberty ad, *DSFP* (November 26, 1916): The Screen, 3; Del-The ad, *DSFP* (December 24, 1916): The Screen, 3; Rialto ad, *DSFP* (December 31, 1916): The Screen, 3; Alhambra ad, *WFN* (December 31, 1916): 13; and Nettie B ad, *DN* (January 20, 1917): 9.

29. Broadway Strand ads, *DNT* (December 24, 1916): n.p., and (December 31, 1916): n.p.; Alhambra and Strand programs, *WFN* (January 21, 1917): 13, 15; Garden program, *WFN* (January 28, 1917): 9; and Rialto ad, *DNT* (January 21, 197): n.p.

30. Washington programs, *WFN* (November 26, 1916): 5, and (December 3, 1916): 5; Washington ad, *DNT* (December 10, 1916): 3.

31. Strand program, *WFN* (June 10, 1917): 15.

32. Washington programs, *WFN* (December 31, 1918): 7, and (January 28, 1917): 5.

33. Alhambra and Strand programs, *WFN* (January 7, 1917): 13, 15.

34. Washington programs, *WFN* (February 4, 1917): 5, (February 25, 1917): 5, and (March 4, 1917): 5.

35. Washington programs, *WFN* (March 25, 1917): 7, and (April 8, 1917): 7.

36. Famous Players-Lasky had gained control of Paramount in December 1916, which gave it unusual distribution access through that company as well as through Artcraft—see Afra, *The Hollywood Trust*, 68–69.

37. "The New Madison Theater Is Open," *WFN* (March 11, 1917): 3, 12. The Madison booked a variety of features but never for more than one-week runs.

38. Washington programs, *WFN* (April 29, 1917): 7, and (May 13, 1917): 7.

39. Washington programs, *WFN* (June 24, 1917): 7, and (July 8, 1917): 7.

40. Washington ad, *DNT* (April 15, 1917): 7; Washington program, *WFN* (April 22, 1917): 7. See also the Enlightenment Photoplay ad, *MPW* (February 24, 1917): 1132–1133. The "state rights" region of Michigan also included Ohio and Kentucky—see the US map printed in *MPN* (July 7, 1917): 83.

41. Detroit Opera House ads, *DSFP* (May 7, 1917): 8, and (June 4, 1917): 6; and Washington ad, *DSFP* (November 11, 1917): 4.10.

42. *The Deemster* ad, *DFP* (December 2, 1917): 4.11. See also the Arrow Film ad, *MPW* (February 10, 1917): 809; "Screen Examinations," *MPN* (February 24, 1917): 1250; and Arrow Film ad, *MPW* (April 28, 1917): 536.

43. The films were *Betty in the Lions' Den* and *Dr. LaFleur's Theory*—see the Alhambra programs, *WFN* (August 19, 1917): 13, and (October 28, 1917): 13.

44. Garden program, *WFN* (July 1, 1917): 11.

45. Alhambra program, *WFN* (September 30, 1917): 13; Strand program, *WFN* (November 18, 1917): 15.

46. World Pictures ad, *MPW* (April 7, 1917): 20; and "Lew Fields to Screen 'The Corner Grocery,'" *MPN* (July 14, 1917): 251.

47. Broadway Strand ad, *DNT* (April 15, 1917): 7; and Alhambra program, *WFN* (June 10, 1917): 13.

48. Strand programs, *WFN* (June 10, 1917): 15, and (July 8, 1917): 15. See also "Ready-Made Ad-Talks," *MPN* (July 7, 1917): 74. Badet had been a ballerina and an actress at the Opéra Comique de Paris before beginning to work in French films in 1910—M. Magdalena Brotons Capó, "Bailes, bailarinas y demi-mondaines en el primer cine," in *Presences and Representations of Women in the Early Years of Cinema, 1895–1920*, ed. Angel Quintana and Jordi Pons (Girona, Spain: Fundacio Museu de Cinema, 2018), 216–217.

49. Strand program, *WFN* (June 24, 1917): 15. Grandais was a very popular star in Gaumont comedies and dramas and had founded her own short-lived production company not long before World War I broke out in 1914.

50. Alhambra program, *WFN* (November 18, 1917): 13.

51. Jacqueline Reich, *The Maciste Films of Italian Silent Cinema* (Bloomington: Indiana University Press, 2015), 132. Reich offers an excellent analysis of the production and distribution of Maciste's films, his stardom, and his Italian national identity.

52. For the extent of *The Marvelous Maciste*'s distribution in the United States, see Reich, *The Maciste Films*, 122–130.

53. Orpheum ad, *DSFP* (March 17, 1918): 4.9; and Regent ad, *DSFP* (March 31, 1918): 4.8.

54. "Orpheum," *DSFP* (March 17, 1918): 4.9; and "Regent," *DSFP* (March 31, 1918): 4.17.

55. Madison Film Exchange ad, *MFR* (November 6 1917): 5.

56. Dawn Masterplay ads, *MFR* (February 26, 1918): 7–10, and (June 4, 1918): 1. See also the four-page insert ad in *MFR* (June 18, 1918).

57. Strand Features ads, *MFR* (February 26, 1918): 14, and (November 1, 1918): 6. For the distribution of older Hart features, see also the Victor Film ad, *MFR* (March 12, 1918): 15. Extolling Theda Bara's *Cleopatra*, in its third sensational week in Detroit, Fox Film warned exhibitors not to be misled by the revival of the "cheap version" of Gardner's earlier film—Fox Film ad, *MFR* (February 19, 1918): 6–7.

58. Standard Film Service ad, *MFR* (November 13, 1917): 7; and "Standard Revolutionizes Film Distribution," *MFR* (October 1, 1918): 11.

59. A. J. Reed note, *MFR* (February 12, 1918): 6; and "Big Business on 'Broncho Billy'," *MFR* (March 5, 1918): 10. For an analysis of cowgirl and Indian pictures in the early 1910s, see Abel, *Americanizing the Movies and "Movie-Mad" Audiences, 1910–1914* (Berkeley: University of California Press, 2006), 61–82, 105–123.

60. "What About Reissues?," *MFR* (February 19, 1918): 1.

61. Paramount-Artcraft Pictures ad, *MFR* (October 1, 1918): 16. One reason for the company's lack of advertising may have been the *Review*'s opposition to federal censorship. For its decision to begin advertising, one reason may have been the founding of a competitor, First National, several months earlier, and Kunsky would soon become one of the latter's regional officers.

62. "Paramount Launches New Policy," *M* (August 12, 1916): 387. The Detroit publicity manager was D. Lee Dennison.

63. Paramount-Artcraft ads, *DSN* (July 7, 1918): Photoplays, 3, (July 14, 1918): Photoplays, 3, (July 21, 1918): Photoplays, 3, (July 28, 1918): Photoplays, 3, (August 4, 1918): Photoplays, 3, (August 11, 1918): Photoplays, 11, (August 18, 1918): Photoplays, 11, (August 25, 1918): Feature, 11, (September 1, 1918): Feature, 11, (September 8, 1916): Feature, 12, (September 15, 1918): Feature, 11, (September 22, 1918): Feature, 3, (September 29, 1918): Feature, 11, (October 6, 1918): Feature, 11, and (October 13, 1918): Feature, 10.

64. World Pictures ads, *DSFP* (January 6, 1918): 4.8, and (January 20, 1918): 4.8.

65. United Theatre Equipment and Michigan Motion Picture Supply ads, *MFR* (November 13, 1918): 11, 15.

66. L. J. Gardiner ads, *MFR* (March 26, 1918): 2–3, and (April 9, 1918): 15; "Detroit Now Has Largest Screen Factory in World," *MFR* (April 9, 1918): 2. Gardiner would later supervise management of Kunsky's "residential theaters."

67. Premier Scenery Studios ad, *MFR* (January 1, 1918): 8.

68. General Theatre Display and Advertising ad, *MFR* (October 15, 1918): 7.

69. Fred T. Grenell ad, *MFR* (November 6, 1917): 13; Theatrical Advertising ad, *MFR* (November 20, 1917): 8; Songram Distributing ad, *MFR* (April 9, 1918): 15; "New Program Idea Going Big," *MFR* (April 9, 1918): 2; Theatre Sign & Poster ad, *MFR* (June 4, 1918): 15; and "Fred Grenell Expands," *MFR* (June 4, 1918): 15.

70. Simpson Cartage ad, *MFR* (November 13, 1917): 15; Exhibitors Film Delivery ads, *MFR* (April 16, 1918): 15, and (October 1, 1918): 7.

71. Frank Farrington ad, *MFR* (May 7, 1918): 8.

72. Metropolitan ad, *MFR* (May 21, 1918): 14.

73. "Metropolitan Co. to Produce News Weekly," *MFR* (February 26, 1918): 4; "Metropolitan Now Making News Weekly," *MFR* (March 12, 1918): 2; and Metropolitan ad, *MFR* (March 12, 1918): 7.

74. Metropolitan ad, *MFR* (May 21, 1918): 14.

75. See, for instance, the Madison, Washington, and Liberty program listings in John Kunsky's house organ, *WFN* (November 18, 1917): 3, 5, 7.

76. See, for instance, "Preparing for Meeting, November 27," *MFR* (November 13, 1917): 1; "Kunsky and Trendle Favor Film Tax—Explain Why," *MFR* (November 27, 1917): 1; "Michigan Exhibitors Fraternize in Detroit," *MFR* (December 4, 1917): 1; and "Kunsky Buys More Pictures," *MFR* (December 18, 1917): 11. Interestingly, in October 1922, differences among Detroit exhibitors were evident in that neither Kunsky or his theater managers nor any Miles theater managers attended the Third Annual Convention of the state's Motion Picture Theatre Owners, for which Phil Gleichman served as vice president—"Michigan League Sets Fast Pace in Subscribing $11,000," *EH* (October 28, 1922): 53, 70, 97.

77. "Nine Detroit Theatres Use Pictures Full Week," *MFR* (March 26, 1918): 2. The downtown Liberty shifted to two program changes per week—"New Policy for Liberty Theatre," *MFR* (February 19, 1918): 1.

78. "Some Business," *MFR* (November 6, 1917): 10; and "Eight Woodward Avenue Theatres Show World," *MFR* (March 26, 1918): 4.

79. "Emmett Sorge Caught in New York," *MFR* (December 4, 1917): 4; and "Theatre Treasurer Skips with $4,000," *MFR* (February 5, 1918): 7.

80. "Relative to Making Cut-Outs," *MFR* (March 5, 1918): 1.

81. "Attempt to Unionize Help in Film Exchanges Meets Strong Opposition," *MFR* (July 16, 1918): 1. This front-page article praised the exchanges' working conditions and refused to believe that any manager would insult "girls" on his staff. See also "Organization Stopped," *FD* (July 22, 1918): 5.

82. In 1918, the trade weekly reluctantly reported that the operators' and musicians' unions had won wage increases—"Detroit Operators Demand Increased Wages," *MFR* (August 6, 1918): 15; and "Musicians Asking $7 Increase," *MFR* (August 20, 1918): 1. See also "Film Help Unionize and Get Charter—Look Out for Trouble," *MFR* (August 27, 1918): 2.

83. "The Film Tax," *MFR* (November 13, 1917): 1.

84. "The Truth About the War Tax!," *MFR* (November 13, 1917): 4–5; and "Kunsky and Trendle Favor Film Tax—Explain Why," *MFR* (November 27, 1917): 1.

85. "Detroit Exhibitors Still Pat on Film Tax," *MFR* (November 27, 1917): 1.

86. "Detroit Exhibitors Paying Film Tax," *MFR* (December 18, 1917): 1; and "Others Paying the Film Tax," *MFR* (December 25, 1917): 1.

87. "Kunsky Loses 25 Employees," *MFR* (January 15, 1918): 2.

88. "Shortage of Motion Picture Operators Looms Greater," *MFR* (June 25, 1918): 1.

89. "Operators Not to Be Taken," *MFR* (July 9, 1918: 1.

90. "How Michigan Exhibitors Can Help the Third Liberty Loan," *MFR* (April 9, 1918): 1.

91. "Alhambra Has Big Patriotic Night," *MFR* (April 23, 1918): 4.

92. "Beware of Censorship," *MFR* (March 5, 1918): 2. At the national level, the Anti-Defamation League of B'nai B'rith persuaded Famous Players-Lasky to cut objectionable scenes in *She Loved Him Plenty* and Griffith to correct the crucifixion scene in *Intolerance*—"Co-Operation Against Offensive 'Jewish Comedy' Pledged to Detroit Committee by Famous Players-Lasky Corporation," *DJC* (September 20, 1918): 1; and Milton Alexander, "The B'nai Brith and the Anti-Defamation Movement," *DJC* (February 14, 1919): 5.

93. "Detroit to Have Police Censorship Again," *MFR* (April 2, 1918): 1. His only assistant was Lester Potter.

94. For more information on Baker as Detroit's chief censor, see Ben Strassfeld, "Indecent Detroit: Regulating Race, Sex, and Adult Enterprises, 1950–1975" (PhD diss., University of Michigan, 2017), 59–61.

95. "Miles of Film Cut by Censors," *DFP* (March 27, 1921): 5.1.

96. "Detroit Film Censors Report for April," *MFR* (May 7, 1918): 1.

97. "Detroit Censorship Bureau Report for May," *MFR* (June 11, 1918): 3.

98. "Censorship Bureau, Detroit," *MFR* (July 16, 1918): 8.

99. "War Brides' Film Banned in Detroit," *MFR* (June 11, 1918): 1; and "National Issue When Pennsylvania Calls 3 Films Unpatriotic," *MPN* (May 5, 1917): 2809. In Baltimore, however, a Ford's Theater screening gave "a percentage of the receipts . . . to Allied Charities"—"How Pictures Are Booking," *MPN* (April 7, 1917): 2485.

100. Harry E. Nichols, "With the Detroit Filmmen," *EH* (June 12, 1920): 75.

101. "Complete List of Detroit Picture Theatres," *MFR* (July 30, 1918): 11.

102. "Manager McGee Says," *MFR* (November 27, 1917): 4.

103. "Announcing the Adams Theatre," *WFN* (July 29, 1917): 3, 12; and Adams ad, *DSFP* (April 7, 1918): 4.9.

104. "Lyric, Cadillac, Opens," *MFR* (February 5, 1918): 1; "New Theatre Is Near Completion," *MFR* (April 9, 1918): 8; "Jack Mowatt to Manage Lincoln Square Theatre," *MFR* (April 2, 1918): 10; and Andrew Craig Morrison, *Opera House, Nickel Show, and Palace* (Dearborn, MI: Greenfield Village, 1974), n.p.

105. Fred T. Grenell ad, *MFR* (November 6, 1917): 13.

106. "New Home to Open Easter," *MFR* (January 1, 1918): 9.

107. Despite its box office success, *The Unbeliever* could not save either Edison or Kleine from closing down feature film production—Joel Frykholm, *George Kleine and American Film: The Movie Business and Film Culture in the Silent Era* (London: Palgrave, 2015), 102–195.

108. "'Cleopatra' Does Enormous at Washington," *MFR* (February 5, 1918): 1; "'Cleopatra' The Real Sensation of the Year," *MFR* (February 12, 1918): 1; Arthur B. Benson ad, *MFR* (February 19, 1918): 6–7; and "'Cleopatra' Rebooked into Washington," *MFR* (July 23, 1918): 2. See also the Washington ads, *DSFP* (February 3, 1918): B7, and (August 4, 1918): C7; the Miles ad, *DSN* (September 8, 1918): Feature, 10; the Strand ad, *DSN* (September 22, 1918): Feature, 3; and the Maxine ad, *DSFP* (November 17, 1918): C7.

109. Leslie Midkiff DeBauche, *Reel Patriotism: The Movies and World War I* (Madison: University of Wisconsin Press, 1997), 137. The story has a rich young man enlist in the Marines and, as a result of the war, overcome his prejudices against religion, Germans, and the working class.

110. "'The Unbeliever' at the Majestic Theatre," *MFR* (March 12, 1918): 1; "'The Unbeliever' Has All Detroit Talking," *MFR* (March 19, 1918): 6; Kleine ad, *MFR* (March 19, 1918): 8–9; Kleine ad, *MFR* (March 26, 1918): 4; Majestic ad, *DFP* (March 31, 1918): C9; "'The Unbeliever' Still Holds Record," *MFR* (June 18, 1918): 8; and Kleine ad, *MPN* (June 8, 1918): 3370–3371.

111. DeBauche, *Reel Patriotism*, 128–129. The manager of the Majestic explained his strategy for drawing such crowds in Jacob Smith, "How McGee Put On 'The Unbeliever,'" *MPW* (March 30, 1918): 1804. For other successful exhibition strategies, see "2 Big Stage Spectacles Employed in Presenting 'The Unbeliever' in Indianapolis," *MPN* (May 18, 1918): 2969; and "Good Advertising and Clever Staging Puts Over 'Unbeliever' for a Record Week," *MPN* (June 1, 1918): 3269.

112. By June, "Keline had fifty prints of *The Unbeliever* in circulation"—Frykholm, *George Kleine and American Cinema*, 105. Preceding both *Cleopatra* and *The Unbelievers*, a version of *The Birth of a Nation* reappeared at the Washington for two weeks in January and then toured the state for at least a month—"Washington Books 'Birth of a Nation,'" *MFR* (January 15, 1918): 6; "The Birth of a Nation," *MFR* (January 29, 1918): 4; and "The Birth of a Nation," *MFR* (February 5, 1918): 2.

113. "'My Four Years in Germany' Opens at Washington Theatre," *MFR* (April 23, 1918): 2.

114. "'My Four Years in Germany' in Its Second Week," *MFR* (April 30, 1918): 14; "Will Stay a Fifth Week," *MFR* (May 14, 1918): 2; and Madison Film ad, *MFR* (June 11, 1918): 4–5. See also the Washington ad for *My Four Years in Germany—DSFP* (May 5, 1918): C11.

115. "Chaplin Breaks Madison House Record by $3,000," *MFR* (May 7, 1918): 1; and "'Hearts of the World' Holds Detroit Record," *MFR* (September 10, 1918): 6. The Detroit Opera House theater was called The Campus. See also "'Hearts of the World' Doing Immense Business at Residential Detroit Theatres," *MFR* (October 8, 1918): 8; and "13 Weeks Record Detroit 'Run,'" *DSFP* (November 5, 1922): Cosmopolitan, 5.

116. "'Salome' Second Week at Adams," *MFR* (September 24, 1918): 1; and "'All Fairbanks Week' at Alhambra," *MFR* (May 21, 1918): 7.

117. "Paramount Takes More Prints," *MFR* (November 6, 1917): 10. Paramount also ordered seven prints of its serial *Who Is Number One?* for first-run circulation in southeast Michigan—"A Booster for Paramount Serial," *MFR* (November 6, 1917): 12.

118. "Many Michigan Theatres Closed on Account of Epidemic," *MFR* (October 15, 1918): 1. For a good overview of trade press reporting on the epidemic's impact, see Richard Koszarski, "Flu Season: Moving Picture World Reports on Pandemic Influenza, 1918–1919," *Film History* 17, no. 4 (2005): 466–485. For a more specific analysis focused on Detroit, see Ben Strassfeld, "Infectious Media: Debating the Role of Movie Theaters in Detroit During the Spanish Influenza of 1918," *Historical Journal of Film, Radio, and Television* (March 2017): 1–19.

119. Alfred A. Cohn, "The Spanish Invasion," *PM* (January 1919): 76.

120. "All Releases Will Be Held Back for Four Weeks," *MFR* (October 15 1918): 1.

121. "Every Michigan Theatre Indefinitely Closed by Governor Sleeper," *MFR* (October 22, 1918): 1. Unfortunately, no other issue of the *Review* seems to survive beyond this date.

122. Harold Hefferman, "Films Regain Old Footing," and "Filmists Vary Layoff Hours," *DSN* (November 10, 1918): Feature, 9.

123. *Detroit Free Press Film Edition* ad, *DSFP* (November 10, 1918): C8.

124. The information in this paragraph is based on the *Detroit City Directories* of 1919–1920, 1920–1921, and 1922–1923.

125. For further information on the initial years of these corporate organizations, see Kia Afra, *The Hollywood Trust* (Lanham, MD: Rowan & Littlefield, 2016), and Richard Koszarski, *An Evening's Entertainment* (New York: Charles Scribner, 1990).

126. Harry Garson Productions, which first appeared in 1916–1917, tried to break into distribution with several features starring Blanche Sweet, but apparently could not sustain the costs of first-run rights.

127. Afra, *The Hollywood Trust*, 122.

128. Afra, *The Hollywood Trust*, 123, 130.

129. Madison and Broadway Strand ads, *DSN* (January 5, 1919): Photoplay, 9–10; and Madison ad, *DSFP* (May 11, 1919): 4.15. Warners made a rare appearance in promotions of "former Ambassador James W. Gerard's 'Beware,'" in a large Broadway Strand ad, *DSFP* (June 1, 1919): 4.14.

130. Washington ad, *DN* (September 6, 1919): 11; and William Fox Washington ads, *DSN* (September 14, 1919): Photoplay, 14, and *DSFP* (September 14, 1919): 4.12, (December 14, 1919): 4.24, and (February 1, 1920): 4.12.

131. William Fox Washington and Grand Circus ads, *DSFP* (November 2, 1919): 4.20.

132. Madison and Adams ads, *DSFP* (January 18, 1920): 4.12, (January 25, 1920): 4.12, and (April 18, 1920): 4.15.

133. Adams ad, *DSFP* (March 28, 1920): B17.

134. Paramount-Artcraft ad, *DSFP* (August 31, 1919): 4.15.

135. Paramount-Artcraft ads, *DSN* (June 12, 1919): Feature, 17, and (October 12, 1919): Feature, 17.

136. Goldwyn Motion Pictures ads, *DFP* (December 8, 1919): 8; *DSFP* (January 4, 1920): 4.14, and (February 15, 1920): C12.

137. Paramount ad, *DJ* (September 5, 1920): 8.

138. Goldwyn Pictures ad, *DSFP* (September 5, 1920): D4; and Paramount Week ad, *DSFP* (September 5, 1920): D5.

139. Paramount ad, *DSFP* (January 9, 1921): C14. Those theaters included the Clay, Dreamland, Farnum, Holbrook, Perrien, and Russell in and around Hamtramck; the Acme and Highland Park (600 seats) in Highland Park; the Jewel in Lower Poletown; the Quo Vadis in the Italian neighborhood; and the Crescent in Del Ray.

140. Broadway Strand ad, *DSFP* (January 9, 1921): C15.

141. Paramount ad, *DSFP* (September 4, 1921): 4.5. The third tier now included the Farnum and Perrien in Hamtramck, the Rosebud and Luna in Lower Poletown; the Quo Vadis in the Italian neighborhood; the Koppin in Black Bottom, and the Crescent in Del Ray.

142. City directories, the *Michigan Film Review* directory, and other sources all list this Duplex (1,250 seats) on East Grand, south and east of Hamtramck.

143. Lars Bjorn, *Before Motown: A History of Jazz in Detroit, 1920–1960* (Ann Arbor: University of Michigan Press, 2001), 3, 7, 11. Bessie Smith gave an especially memorable performance at the Koppin in 1921. Paul Shirley recalls being attracted, in the early 1920s, to the female dancers of the Blackbirds and Brown Skinned Models—see "Paul B. Shirley," in Elaine Latzman Moon, *Untold Tales, Unsung Heroes: An Oral History of Detroit's African American Community, 1918–1967* (Detroit: Wayne State University Press, 1994), 48–49.

144. The Koppin's proprieter was Henry Koppin of the Geo. F. Koppin Amusement Company, which also owned the Comique, La Salle, Rosebud, and Woodward 1 & 2. The Koppin's manager was Edward B. Dudley, after his own theater closed in 1921. "Theater Chains: Michigan," *Wid's Daily Yearbook* (1921): 237.

145. See, for instance, the Oakman's "grand opening" ads, *DSFP* (December 28, 1919): C14; and *DSN* (December 28, 1919): Photoplay, 8; and the Tuxedo's grand opening ads, *DN* (October 22, 1921): 6; and *DSFP* (October 23, 1921): 5.12. The Tuxedo offered variety programs of vaudeville and pictures, changed twice a week. The Zemon-Wettzmann Company opened the Linwood-LaSalle, with a supposed seating of 1,600—Harry E. Nichols, "With the Detroit Filmmen," *EH* (June 12, 1920): 75.

146. The La Veeda was named after a popular Castillian Fox-Trot, "strange and seductive, thrilling and wonderful"—Jerome H. Remick ad, *DSFP* (June 27, 1920): 3.14.

147. Capitol ad, *DSFP* (January 8, 1922): 5.11, and *DFP* (January 12, 1922): 10.

148. Jackson D. Haag, "First Run Films and Neighborhood Cinemas," *DN* (September 19, 1920): 19.

149. Paramount-Artcraft ad, *DNT* (September 1, 1918): 11. This north side Duplex, at Woodward and E. Grand, is missing from the published books on the city's theaters as well as the list in the *Michigan Film Review*; consequently, its seating capacity is unknown.

150. An ad for the Catherine in "Lower Poletown" also appeared just this once.

151. See the Crystal, Duplex, Eagle, Grande, Gratiot, Montclair, and Rialto ads, *DSN* (November 10, 1918): 10–11.

152. "Photoplays at Your Favorite Theater Today," *DN* (November 30, 1918): 12. The *Journal* introduced a daily vertical strip of nineteen theaters slightly later—"Go to the Movies Today at Your Favorite Theater," *DJ* (December 22, 1919): n.p. At its peak, this strip included thirty-one theaters—"Go to the Movies Today," *DJ* (March 6, 1920): 9.

153. "Photoplays at Your Favorite Theater Today," *DSN* (January 18, 1919): Photoplay, n.p.

154. "Photoplays at Your Favorite Theater Today," *DSN* (December 7, 1919): Photoplay, 5.

155. The Knickerbocker, not far from the Gladwin Park/Aladdin, was located in an entertainment district that included three dance halls: Jefferson Beach, the Pier, and the Palais de Dance—Björn, *Before Motown*, 5, 16–17.

156. "What's Doing in Neighborhood Filmland," *DSFP* (November 17, 1918): C7.

157. The *Free Press*'s claim also was puzzling because newspapers in Chicago, for instance, had been printing twice-weekly or even daily block ads for scores of neighborhood theaters going back at least to 1914—Abel, *Menus for Movieland*, 90, 94.

158. "What's Doing in Neighborhood Filmland," *DSFP* (November 24, 1919): C7.

159. Se, for instance, "Filmland," *DSFP* (December 15, 1918): B13, and (December 22, 1918): B11. The Billiken, however, closed in 1924.

160. See, for instance, "Filmland," *DSFP* (March 9, 1919): C14; and the Ferry Field, Rialto, Strand, and De Luxe ads, *DSFP* (September 14, 1919): C12.

161. "Today's Show at Your Neighborhood Theatre," *DSFP* (October 19, 1919): C21.

162. "Today's Attractions at Your Neighborhood Theatres," *DFP* (January 9, 1920): 8. For a few months that summer, the Jewel replaced the Arcade as the "representative" of "Lower Poletown"—"Today's Attractions at Your Neighborhood Theatre," *DSN* (May 30, 1920): 3.10; "Today's Attractions at Your Neighborhood Theatre," *DFP* (June 27, 1920): 3.15; and "Today's Best Motion Picture Program," *DFP* (September 26, 1920): 3.15.

163. Majestic ads, *DN* (February 8, 1919): 11 and *DSN* (February 9, 1919): Photoplay, 6; Regent ad, *DSN* (February 16, 1919): Photoplay, 6; Ferry Field ad, *DSN* (March 2, 1919): Photoplay, 14; Del-The ad, *DN* (March 22, 1919): 13; Washington ad, *DSFP* (April 6, 1919): 4.11; Ferry Field ad, *DSFP* (June 22, 1919): 4.12; Detroit Opera House ad, *DN* (September 6, 1919): 11; Crystal ad, *DFP* (October 15, 1919): 14; and Alhambra ad, *DN* (October 18, 1919):15.

164. Adams ad, *DSN* (May 11, 1919): Photoplay, 17; and Washington ad, *DSN* (May 18, 1919): Photoplay, 5.

165. Miles ad, *DSN* (June 1, 1919): Feature, 18; Ferry Field ad, *DSN* (June 8, 1919): Photoplay, 15; Arcade ad, *DN* (June 21, 1919): 14; Liberty ad, *DFP* (July 3, 1919): 11; De Luxe ad, *DSFP* (July 27, 1919): 4.10; and Arthur ad, *DSFP* (January 4, 1920): Photoplay, 13.

166. Majestic ads, *DSN* (August 31, 1919): Photoplay, 16, and (September 7, 1919): Photoplay, 12; Orpheum and Regent ads, *DSN* (September 21, 1919): Photoplay, 12; De Luxe ad, *DFP* (October 8, 1919): 5; Liberty ad, *DSN* (October 12, 1919): Photoplay, 15; and Fine Arts ad, *DN* (October 18, 1919): 15.

167. Broadway Strand ads, *DSN* (November 30, 1919): Photoplay, 16, (December 7, 1919): Photoplay, 5, and (December 14, 1919): Photoplay, 11; Liberty ad, *DFP* (March 3, 1920): 10; Garden ad, *DFP* (October 5, 1920): 12; Gratiot ad, *DFP* (April 13, 1920): 4; and Linwood-LaSalle ad, *DSFP* (April 25, 1920): 3.18. *Male and Female* was the first DeMille film to gross more than $1,000,000 (at a cost of less than $170,000)—David Pierce, "Success with a Dollar Sign," in Paolo Cherchi Usai and Lorenzo Codelli, eds., *L'Eredità DeMille* (Pordenone, Italy: Le Giornate del Cinema Muto, 1991), 316.

168. Adams ad, *DN* (December 6, 1919): 11; Ferry Field ad, *DSFP* (January 4, 1920): 4.15; Lakewood ad, *DSFP* (January 11, 1920): 4.12; Del-The ad, *DFP* (January 15, 1920): 9; Liberty, Frontenac, and Arcade ads, *DSFP* (January 18, 1920): 4.14; and Alhambra ad, *DSFP* (January 25, 1920): 4.11.

169. Although praising Nazimova, trade press reviews were not kind to the film—for example, "The Brat," *PM* (December 1919): 73. Herbert Blache directed the film from a scenario by June Mathias; supposedly "Nazimova herself" and Charles Bryant first wrote an adaptation

from a Maude Fulton play produced by Oliver Morosco—Metro ad, *MPN* (August 23, 1919): 1646.

170. Miles Theaters ad, *DSN* (October 19, 1919): Photoplay, 12; De Luxe and Ferry Field ads, *DSN* (November 2, 1919): Photoplay, 11; Liberty ad, *DSN* (November 9, 1919): Photoplay, 17; Crystal ad, *DFP* (November 10, 1919): 8; Strand ad, *DSN* (November 23, 1919): Photoplay, 17; Gratiot ad, *DFP* (December 4, 1919): 6; Stratford ad, *DN* (December 27, 1919): 12; Baker ad, *DFP* (January 10, 1920): 14; Alhambra ad, *DFP* (January 22, 1920): 4; and Arcade ad, *DSFP* (February 8, 1920): Photoplay, 11.

171. Broadway Strand ads, *DSN* (October 5, 1919): Photoplay, 19, (October 12, 1919): Photoplay, 18, (October 19, 1919): Photoplay, 15, (October 26, 1919): Photoplay, 17, and (December 21, 1919): Photoplay, 11; Liberty ad, *DSFP* (January 4, 1920): 14; Ferry Field ads, *DSFP* (January 11, 1920): 4.13, and (February 1, 1920): 4.12; Iris ad, *DFP* (January 21, 1920): 8; Strand ad, *DSFP* (January 25, 1920): 4.12; Oakman ad, *DFP* (January 30, 1920): 10; Alhambra ad, *DFP* (February 3, 1920): 8; Lincoln Square ad, *DSFP* (February 8, 1920): Photoplay, 11; Duplex and Rosedale ads, *DSFP* (February 15, 1920): Photoplay, 22; and Frontenac ad, *DSFP* (March 14, 1920): B17.

172. Public Health Film ads, *EH* and *M* (April 12, 1918): 13, and (April 19, 1918): 14; "Association Goes After 'Fit to Win,'" *MPW* (May 24, 1918): 1141; "'Fit to Win' Gets into Court," *MPW* (May 24, 1918): 1153; and "Misguided Propagandists," *EH* and *M* (May 31, 1918): 25. Raymond McKee, who had starred in *The Unbeliever*, played the main character of Billy Hale in *Fit to Win*—see the advertisement reproduced in DeBauche, *Reel Patriotism*, 131.

173. Washington ads, *DSN* (January 12, 1919): Photoplay, 11, (January 19, 1919): Photoplay, 11, (March 23, 1919): Feature 7.

174. "Social Welfare Campaign Endorses 'Fit to Win' Film," *DSFP* (March 30, 1919): 4.12.

175. "Better Film Fight Won!" *PM* (November 1919): 92, 110–111.

176. D. W. Griffith Service ad, *MPW* (January 24, 1920): 530; and "Griffith Releases 'Fall of Babylon,'" *MPW* (January 24, 1920): 616.

177. The trade press noted the Orchestra Hall performances that included the dancer "Madja and her Nautch girls"—"Orchestra Hall 'Goes Over,'" *EH* (June 26, 1920): 73.

178. Orchestra Hall ads, *DSFP* (May 23, 1920): 3.18, and (June 6, 1920): 3.16; Shubert Detroit ads, *DSFP* (June 13, 1920): 3.14, and (August 29, 1920): 3.16; La Salle Garden ad, *DSFP* (December 19, 1920): 5.14; and Liberty ad, *DSFP* (January 2, 1921): 4.24. All ads now promoted Constance Talmadge as the film's star.

179. Shubert Detroit ad, *DSFP* (May 8, 1921): 5.5; Washington ad, *DSPF* (October 23, 1921): 5.12; Liberty ad, *DSFP* (January 1, 1922): 5.8; Alhambra and Garden ads, *DFP* (January 23, 1922): 4; Crystal and Iris ads, *DSFP* (January 29, 1922): 5.11; Maxime ad, *DSFP* (February 19, 1922): 5.10; and Linwood-LaSalle ad, *DT* (September 19, 1922): n.p.

180. Broadway Strand ads, *DSFP* (April 4, 1920): 3.17, and (April 25, 1920): 3.17; and Liberty ad, *DSFP* (August 29, 1920): 3.15. The Broadway Strand ads use publicity cuts other than those reproduced in *EH* (April 10, 1920): 52.

181. "Special Programs" ad, *DJ* (September 5, 1920): 7. The theaters were the Ferry Field, Library, Gratiot, Rosedale, Lincoln Square, Iris, Acme, Rialto, and Duplex.

182. Broadway Strand ad, *DSFP* (October 17, 1920): 3.16; Ferry Field ad, *DSFP* (December 5, 1920): 5.12; Rialto ad, *DFP* (December 23, 1920): 5; Alhambra and De Luxe ads, *DFP* (January 3, 1921): 7; and Maxime ad, *DFP* (February 18, 1921): 4. *Something to Think About* was the second DeMille film to gross more than $1,000,000—Pierce, 316.

183. Broadway Strand ad, *DSFP* (October 24, 1920): 5.8. The businesses ranged from shirts and corsets to candy and cigars, and the ad took a full page in the "Automotive" section.

184. See, for instance, the *Charlie Chaplin Review* in the Washington ad, *DSFP* (May 30, 1920): 3.9.

185. Madison ad, *DSFP* (January 30, 1921): 5.11; Regent, Orpheum, Liberty, Alhambra, Ferry Field, Garden, and Strand ads, *DSFP* (February 27, 1921): 5.13–14; Miles, Crystal, Del-The, and Iris ads, *DSFP* (March 6, 1921): 5.11; and Your ad, *DSFP* (November 6, 1921): 5.11.

186. Adams ads, *DSFP* (November 27, 1921): 5.11, and (December 4, 1921): 4.11; La Salle Garden ad, *DSFP* (January 1, 1922): 5.9; Liberty ad, *DSFP* (January 29, 1922): 5.10; De Luxe and Crystal ads, *DSFP* (February 12, 1922): 5.13; and Alhambra ad, *DT* (August 6, 1922): Feature, 4.

187. See, for instance, the Hudson's ads, *DFP* (February 18, 1922): 7, and (April 22, 1922): 7.

188. Washington ad, *DSFP* (December 5, 1920): 5.13; Garden ad, *DSFP* (January 16, 1921): 5.12; Iris ad, *DFP* (February 4, 1921): 7; Your ad, *DSFP* (February 13, 1921): 5.13; and Frontenac ad, *DFP* (March 8, 1921): 6.

189. Adams ads, *DSFP* (October 16, 1921): 5.11, and (November 6, 1921): 5.11; Liberty and De Luxe ads, *DSFP* (December 25, 1921): 5.9; Crystal ad, *DSFP* (January 15, 1922): 5.10; Tuxedo ad, *DSFP* (January 29, 1922): 5.11; Maxime ad, *DSFP* (February 5, 1922): 5.10; and Alhambra ad, *DT* (August 19, 1922): 5.

190. Garrick ads, *DSFP* (April 17, 1921): 5.9, (May 1, 1921): 5.5, and (May 8, 1921): 5.5.

191. Adams ads, *DSFP* (January 1, 1922): 5.9, and (January 15, 1922): 5.11; Alhambra and Garden ads, *DSFP* (March 19, 1922): 5.11; Strand and De Luxe ads, *DFP* (March 24, 1922): 14; Rialto ad, *DFP* (March 31, 1922): 10; Iris ad, *HN* (April 14, 1922): n.p., and Park ad, *HN* (May 19, 1922): n.p.

192. Broadway Strand ad, *DSFP* (November 27, 1921): 5.11; Liberty ad, *DFP* (January 23, 1922): 4; Linwood-LaSalle ad, *DFP* (January 30, 1922): 4; Strand and De Luxe ads, *DFP* (February 2, 1922): 10; Crystal ad, *DFP* (March 6, 1922): 8; New Bernhardt ad, *HN* (March 10, 1922): n.p.; Lakewood ad, *DFP* (March 14, 1922): 12; Tuxedo ad, *DSFP* (March 26, 1922): 5.10; Park ad, *HN* (March 31, 1922): n.p.; and Orpheum ad, *DSFP* (April 2, 1922): 5.12.

193. Broadway Strand ad, *DSFP* (September 5, 1920): 5.3. The Adams also put on an unusually widespread and varied publicity campaign for *What's Your Hurry?*, with Wallace Reid—"How They Do It in Detroit," *MPN* (November 27, 1920): 4173.

194. Broadway Strand ad, *DSFP* (September 5, 1920): 5.9. See also "'Humoresque' Shows at Broadway Strand Week of September 5," *DJC* (September 3, 1920): 5.

195. Broadway Strand ads, *DFP* (September 7, 1920): 22.

196. Broadway Strand ads, *DSFP* (September 19, 1920): 3.17, and (September 26, 1920): 3.16.

197. Liberty ad, *DSFP* (October 31, 1920): 4.13; De Luxe ad, *DSFP* (November 21, 1920): 4.14; Iris ad, *DSFP* (November 28, 1920): 4.12; and Alhambra ad, *DSFP* (December 5, 1920): 5.12.

198. Washington ads, *DSFP* (September 4, 1921): 5.6, and (October 16, 1921): 5.10.

199. Washington ads, *DSFP* (September 11, 1921): 5.6, (September 18, 1921): 5.9, and (October 9, 1921): 5.10. See also the Fox ad, *MPW* (November 3, 1921): 26; and William Fox's "Statement," *MPW* (November 26, 1921): 364. The film also took in extremely high box office grosses in New York, Chicago, Boston, and San Francisco—Fox Film ad, *MPW* (November 26, 1921): 365.

200. *Over the Hill* composite ad, *DSFP* (November 20, 1921): 5.10.

201. As *Anna Boleyn*, this film premiered in Weimar, Germany, in March 1920.

202. Broadway Strand ads, *DSFP* (May 8, 1921): 5.8, (May 15, 1921): 5.9, and (May 22, 1921): 5.11; La Salle Garden ad, *DSFP* (June 5, 1921): 5.8; Liberty ad, *DSFP* (June 19, 1921): 5.7; Duplex ad, *DSFP* (September 4, 1921): 5. 3; and Park ad, *HN* (March 10, 1922): n.p.

203. "Europe's Great Actors in Leading Roles in Stupendous Historic Film," *DSFP* (May 8, 1921): 5.7; and "Screen Architecture Brings Back Picturesque Days of 16th Century," *DSFP* (May 15, 1921): 5.7.

204. Broadway Strand ad, *DSFP* (August 28, 1921): 5.7. Ads did not mention the film's star, Paul Wegener. The Detroit chapter of the Intercollegiate Zionist Association held a discussion of *The Golem* shortly after its initial screening—"I.Z.A. to Discuss Work of Congress," *DJC* (September 9, 1921): 6.

205. Rialto ad, *DFP* (November 21, 1921): 9; Alhambra ad, *DFP* (November 25, 1921): 5; and Iris ad, *DFP* (December 7, 1921): 5.

206. "'Theodora' Marks Return of Italian Films to the United States," *DSFP* (June 5, 1921): 5.9.

207. Shubert Michigan ad, *DSFP* (November 6, 1921): 5.8. The actress playing Theodora was Rita Jolivet, who earlier had survived the sinking of the Lusitania.

208. Adams ad, *DFP* (January 23, 1922): 4; La Salle Garden ad, *DFP* (March 20, 1922): 8; Tuxedo ad, *DSFP* (April 2, 1922): 5.10; Farnum ad, *HN* (March 17, 1922): n.p., and Park ad, *HN* (April 21, 1922): n.p.

209. Iris ad, *HN* (April 7, 1922): n.p.; and Crystal ad, *DSFP* (April 9, 1922): 5.11.

210. See, for instance, the Majestic ad, *[Reno] Nevada State Journal* (August 20, 1921): 4; St. Regis ad, *Trenton [New Jersey] Times* (August 31, 1921): 11; Hippodrome ad, *Fort Wayne Sunday News-Sentinel* (October 2, 1921): 37; "6th St. Theatre," *Coshocton [Ohio] Tribune* (October 24, 1921): 6; and Strand ad, *Iowa City Press-Citizen* (November 18, 1921): 5.

211. For an astute analysis of Pola Negri's star figure in the United States, see Diane Negra, "Immigrant Stardom in Imperial America: Pola Negri and the Problem of Typology," in Jennifer Bean and Diane Negra, eds., *A Feminist Reader in Early Cinema* (Durham, NC: Duke University Press, 2002), 374–403.

212. "Screen Chat," *DSFP* (October 24, 1920): 4.15; "Pola Negri Takes Blasé New York by Storm," *DSFP* (January 30, 1921): 5.9; Adams ad, *DSFP* (February 13, 1921): 5.15; Adams ad, *DFP* (February 14, 1921): 8; and Adams ad, *DSFP* (February 20, 1921): 5.10. As *Madame Dubarry*, this film had premiered in Berlin in September 1919.

213. "Pola Negri's Type Is a Curious Combination," *DSFP* (February 20, 1921): 5.9.

214. Karl R. Kitchen, "Some Film Hits That 'Gross' Millions," *DSFP* (April 3, 1921): 5.7. The Capitol Theatre in New York City "filled every one of the 5,000 seats at every one of the five shows a day for two weeks, or a total of 350,000 persons—First National ad, *MPW* (January 1, 1921): 28.

215. Iris and Strand ads, *DSFP* (March 27, 1921): 5.9; Crystal and Garden ads, *DFP* (April 11, 1921): 7; and Alhambra ad, *DSFP* (May 1, 1921): 5.9.

216. *Carmen* had premiered in Berlin in December 1918.

217. Adams ad, *DSFP* (May 22, 1921): 5.10; De Luxe ad, *DSFP* (June 26, 1921): 5.7; Garden ad, *DSFP* (July 10, 1921): 5.7; and Park ad, *HN* (April 14, 1922): n.p. See also the trade press quotes in "You'll Need a Larger House," *MPW* (June 4, 1921): 481. Perhaps this Negri film prompted the import of "an elaborate French production," *Gypsy Passion*, which played for a week at the Washington in April 1922—Washington ad, *DSFP* (April 9, 1922): 5.11.

218. Adams ad, *DSFP* (September 25, 1921): 5.8. As *Sumurun*, this film had premiered in Berlin in September 1920. See also the selection of production photos for *One Arabian Night* in *ETR* (September 10, 1921): 1023. Beginning in late November, Fox's *Queen of Sheba* exploited the popularity of Lubitsch's film with a three-week run at the Washington, and the following spring Fox announced a "Sheba Week," during which the film featured at twenty-seven theaters, including seven in ethnic neighborhoods—Washington ads, *DSFP* (November 20, 1921): 5.11, and (December 4, 1921): 5.10; and the Fox ad, *DSFP* (April 16, 1922): 5.9.

219. Iris ad, *DSFP* (October 30, 1921): 5.11; Garden and Linwood-LaSalle ads, *DSFP* (November 6, 1921): 5.11; and Alhambra ad, *DSFP* (November 27, 1921): 5.10.

220. There was one man, Tom Ealand, "who book[ed] the only first-run open spots in Detroit"—Harry E. Nichols, "With the Detroit Filmmen," *EH* (June 12, 1920): 75.

221. Negri's background also appealed to Jewish communities—"Famous Jewish Movie Picture Actress Coming to America," *DJC* (November 16, 1921): 8.

222. Adams ads, *DSFP* (April 16, 1922): 5.10, and (September 3, 1922): 5.8; and Broadway Strand ad, *DSFP* (March 11, 1923): 3.14.

223. Adams ad, *DSFP* (April 30, 1922): 5.7, (January 7, 1923): 3.11, and (April 20, 1924): Feature, 8.

224. Regent ad, *DSFP* (December 3, 1922): 3.11; Miles ads, *DSFP* (December 31, 1922): n.p. and (May 28, 1922): 5.11; Alhambra ad, *DSFP* (June 11, 1922): 5.11; La Salle Garden ad, *DSFP* (April 22, 1923): 3.9; and Tuxedo ad, *DSFP* (April 29, 1923): 3.11.

225. Paramount ad, *DT* (July 29, 1922): 7. A slightly earlier ad marking the company's "10th Anniversary" also included the Koppin in the Black Ghetto—Paramount ad, *DSFP* (March 12, 1922): 517.

226. Among the directors were Cecil B. DeMille, Fred Niblo, James Cruze, Frank Borzage, George Fritzmaurice, and Alfred Green. Nine women counted among the scenarists: June Mathis, Jeanie Macpherson, Beulah Marie Dix, Ouida Bergere, Clara Beranger, Julia Crawford Ivers, Olga Prinszlau, Josephine Lovett, and Lorna Moon.

227. Paramount ad, *DSFP* (September 3, 1922): 5.11.

228. Paramount ads, *DSFP* (September 2, 1923): Feature, 12, and *DSN* (September 2, 1923): Metropolitan, 8.

229. Paramount ad, *DSFP* (August 31, 1924): Feature, 10.

230. Allan Dwan, the sole filmmaker, was the director of *Manhandled*.

231. More than sixty theaters in cities and towns outside Detroit many have compensated for the reduced number of third-run theaters in the city.

232. Paramount ad, *DSFP* (October 14, 1923): Feature, 18. See also "Detroit Named as 'Key' City for First Showing of Paramount Films," *DSFP* (October 14, 1923): Feature, 7.

233. Broadway Strand ad, *DSN* (July 27, 1924): Metropolitan, 4. The renovations included matching interior and exterior colors, new lighting effects, a rebuilt stage, and a reequipped projection booth.

234. "What's Playing at Your Neighborhood Theatre," *DT* (January 7, 1923): 3.4.

235. This generalization about theater locations in relation to demographics is based on Maps 13.2 and 13.3 in Zunz, *The Changing Face of Inequality*, 344–347.

236. The Pastime and White Star offered Merry Christmas and Happy New Year greetings to moviegoers in the *HN* (December 26, 1924): n.p.

237. Orpheum ads, *DSFP* (November 5, 1922): 5.9, and (December 10, 1922): 5. 11. In Chicago, all kinds of window displays and other tie-ins promoted the film's run at the Grand Opera House; whether similar tie-ins were staged in Detroit is unclear—"Big Drive Precedes Fairbanks Premiere," *ETR* (November 4, 1922): 1471.

238. "Detroit Masons Lease House for Showing of 'Robin Hood,'" *MPW* (November 11, 1922): 147.

239. Adams ads, *DSFP* (March 4, 1923): 3.12, and (March 11, 1923): 3.15; New Home and Farnum ads, *HN* (June 1, 1922): n.p.

240. New Detroit ads, *DSFP* (September 7, 1924): Feature, 6, (October 5, 1924): Feature, 11, (October 26, 1924): Feature, 9, and (November 16, 1924): Feature, 9; and Adams ad, *DSFP* (February 1, 1925): n.p.

241. Other established stars with initial runs of two weeks or less included Swanson's *Her Gilded Cage* at the Madison and Charles Ray's *A Tailor-Made Man* at the Broadway Strand, both

in early September 1922. In addition, Tom Mix westerns appeared every two months or so for one-week runs at the Fox Washington.

242. Adams ads, *DSFP* (March 12, 1922): 5.15, and (April 2, 1922): 5.13; Washington ad, *DSFP* (October 1, 1922): 5/9; and Rosedale ad, *DT* (June 25, 1923): 8.

243. Broadway Strand ads, *DSFP* (December 24, 1922): Feature, 6, and (January 7, 1923): 3.10. "Big Exploitation Campaign in Middle West for 'Tess of the Storm Country,'" *MPW* (January 6, 1923): 71. In early May 1924, another Pickford film, *Dorothy Vernon of Handon Hall*, did premiere at the New Detroit, but it stayed for only two weeks.

244. New Home and Farnum ads, *HN* (April 13, 1923): 5, and (April 27, 1923): 5.

245. *Enemies of Women* was adapted from another Vicente Blasco Ibanez novel and directed by Alan Crosland. Adams ad, *DSFP* (May 27, 1923): Feature, 11; and New Home ad, *HN* (December 7, 1923): 8.

246. Adams ads, *DSFP* (March 23, 1924): Feature, 9, and (April 13, 1924): Feature, 8; Alhambra ad, *DSFP* (June 29, 1924): Feature, 8. Despite this lengthy run, trade press articles and ads excluded Detroit from their assessment of *The White Sister*—"Saunders, Back from Trip, Discusses 'White Sister,'" *MPW* (January 19, 1924): 192; and Metro ad, *MPW* (February 23, 1924): 604–605.

247. Adams ads, *DSFP* (June 1, 1924): Feature, 8, and (June 15, 1924): Feature, 8; and Farnum ad, *HN* (October 10, 1924): n.p. Although information on Detroit businesses is unclear, *Secrets* offered exhibitors a wealth of promotional tie-ins from window displays of clothes and shoes, flower arrangements, and cosmetics to "driving bally," old high-wheeled bicycles, and old-fashioned photographs—"When You have 'Secrets'—TELL THE TOWN," *FD* (September 27, 1924): 37; "After You Book the Picture," *FD* (September 27, 1924): 39–40; and "Breaking the Records With 'Secrets,'" *FD* (September 27, 1924): 41.

248. New Detroit Opera House ad, *DSFP* (October 28, 1923): 5.9; Adams ads, *DSFP* (July 20, 1924): Feature, 10, and (August 10, 1924): Feature, 10; and Martha Washington ad, *HN* (October 17, 1924): n.p. *The Covered Wagon, Janice Meredith, Dorothy Vernon of Haddon Hall*, and *The Sea Hawk* were among eight 1924 films based on novels published by Grosset & Dunlap—Grosset & Dunlap ad, *ETR* (August 16, 1924): inside front cover.

249. Adams ads, *DSFP* (September 3, 1922): 5.8, and (September 17, 1922): 5. 9; and Your ad, *DT* (June 13, 1923): 17. A variety of promotional tie-ins accompanied *Blood and Sand*—"Featuring the Frame" and "'Blood and Sand' Gets Campaign," *ETR* (September 16, 1922): 1065, 1069; and "Lively Displays," *ETR* (September 30, 1922): 1185. *Blood and Sand* was adapted from yet another Vicente Blasco Ibanez novel.

250. Adams ads, *DSFP* (August 17, 1924): Feature, 7, and (August 31, 1924): Feature, 8; Martha Washington ad, *HN* (November 21, 1924): n.p.

251. Adams ads, *DSFP* (February 24, 1924): 5.12, and (March 16, 1924): Feature, 7; and Farnum ad, *HN* (August 15, 1924): n.p. See the Universal ad that lists the daily box office figures for the first two weeks—*FD* (March 12, 1924): 6. Universal also advertised the film in the *Saturday Evening Post*—Universal ad, *MPW* (August 16, 1924): 506.

252. Nasaw, *The Chief*, 323–325.

253. "When Knighthood Was in Flower," *DSFP* (August 27, 1922): 4; Adams ad, *DSFP* (November 5, 1922): 5.8; Madison ad, *DSFP* (February 18, 1923): 3.12; and Rosedale ad, *DT* (June 30, 1923): 5. See also Victor Herbert, "Writing Music for 'When Knighthood Was in Flower,'" *EH* (August 26, 1923): 76. Undercrank Productions recently released a Blu-Ray/DVD print of the film, preserved by the US Library of Congress.

254. Adams ads, *DSFP* (December 28, 1924): Feature, 6, and (January 11, 1925): Feature, 6; and Martha Washington ad, *HN* (March 13, 1925): n.p. Although it is unclear whether

Metro-Goldwyn did the same for Detroit, the company promoted the film in Cleveland with a public library display and large photos of Davies in major department stores—"'Janice Meredith' Gets Public Library's Aid," *ETR* (January 7, 1925): 43.

255. Adams ads, *DSFP* (April 1, 1923): 3.11, and (April 15, 1923): 3.11; and Del-The, Ferndale, and Stratford ads, *DT* (July 5, 1923): 12.

256. Washington ads, *DSFP* (January 7, 1923): 3.10, and (January 21, 1923): 3.12; and Iris ad, *HN* (August 17, 1923): 1. Again, it is unclear how many of Pathé's promotional novelties, teasers, and stunts for *Dr. Jack*, for instance, circulated in Detroit—"Pathé Issues Attractive Novelties for 'Dr. Jack,'" *ETR* (December 2, 1922): 32; "'Dr. Jack' Teasers a Denver Campaign," *MPW* (February 3, 1923): 468; and "Unique Gags Devised for 'Dr. Jack,'" *ETR* (February 24, 1924): 665.

257. Adams ads, *DSFP* (April 30, 1922): 5.7, and (May 14, 1922): 5.15.

258. *Foolish Wives* ads, *DSFP* (August 20, 1922): 5.9, and (August 27, 1922): 5.8. The same ads appeared on the same days in the *Detroit Sunday Times*. The film initially returned to the Broadway Strand for a one-week run in late July—Broadway Strand ad, *DSFP* (July 23, 1922): 5.13.

259. Harry E. Nichols, "Day-and-Date Runs for Big Features Detroit Success," *EH* (September 23, 1922): 40.

260. "Disregards Hays Plea," *EH* (July 22, 1922): 29. In Portland, Oregon, the mayor and city council overturned the local censorship board's ban of the film—"Portland's Mayor Overturns Censors," *V* (April 28, 1922): 46.

261. Shubert Detroit ads, *DSFP* (July 2, 1922): 5.9, and (July 9, 1922): 5.9; and Orpheum ad, *DSFP* (October 15, 1922): 5.10. A year later, the Washington screened *Twilight Sleep*, "the much discussed film on child birth," once each afternoon, for "ladies" only—Washington ad, *DSFP* (June 10, 1923): Feature, 11.

262. Broadway Strand ads, *DSFP* (January 27, 1924): 5.8, and (February 10, 1924): 5.12; and Farnum ad, *HN* (May 2, 1924): n.p. June Mathis adapted the scenario from a Sir Hall Caine novel of the same title. Goldwyn ballyhooed the box office success of *Name the Man!* with a two-page trade press ad full of theater posters, including those of the Broadway Strand in Detroit—Goldwyn ad, *ETR* (March 8, 1924): 2–3.

263. "Interested Swedes in English Picture," *MPW* (March 8, 1924): 133.

264. Madison ad, *DSFP* (April 30, 1922): 5.6.

265. Farnum ad, *HN* (March 31, 1922): n.p.; Madison ad, *DT* (June 10, 1922): 4; and Washington ad, *DSFP* (August 5, 1922): 5.10.

266. Martha Washington ads, *HN* (June 27, 1924): n.p., and (July 18, 1924): n.p.

267. Iris ads *HN* (January 18, 1924): 8, and (April 4, 1924): n.p.; and Shubert Detroit ad, *DSFP* (August 3, 1924): Feature, 12. *The Cossack Whip* may have owed its initial success, and revival, to a climactic scene in which the star's character whips a hypocritical minister—Frykholm, *George Kleine and American Cinema*, 85.

268. New Home ad, *HN* (January 11, 1924): 8; Broadway Strand ad, *DSFP* (June 8, 1924): Feature, 7; and Washington ad, *DSFP* (February 22, 1925): Feature, 9.

269. Martha Washington ad, *HN* (October 26, 1924): n.p.

270. Melvyn Stokes, *D. W. Griffith's The Birth of a Nation: A History of "The Most Controversial Motion Picture of All Time"* (New York: Oxford University Press, 2007), 241.

271. Washington ad, *DSFP* (April 29, 1923): 3.11; and New Home ad, *HN* (October 5, 1923): 5.

272. Farnum ad, *HN* (October 12, 1923): 8. Stokes, 241; "Hamtramck Bans Film, 'The Birth of a Nation,'" *DFP* (October 16, 1923): 6; and "Mayor Stops Showing of Griffith Film Here," *HN* (October 19, 1923): 1. NAACP protests already had led to bans of *The Birth of a Nation* in other states, such as Ohio and West Virginia.

273. "'Loves of Pharaoh' a Fine Property," *MPW* (March 4, 1922): 40. A later "special bulletin to Southern Enterprises managers" suggested that theaters enhance their shows with "mild incense burning within the theatre, foyer or lobby"—*MPW* (September 23, 1922): 285.

274. Adams ad, *DSFP* (August 20, 1922): 5.8, and (August 27, 1922): 5.7; Alhambra ad, *DSFP* (October 15, 1922): 5.11; and Farnum ad, *HN* (February 16, 1923): n.p.

275. Martha Washington ad, *HN* (October 3, 1924): n.p. After Dimitri Buchowetski directed Pola Negri in *Men*, he was identified, perhaps wrongly, as the "Polish director who made 'Peter the Great.'" Paramount ad, *FD* (January 20, 1924): 22.

276. Iris ad, *HN* (August 11, 1922): n.p. Vitagraph distributed this "French special production"—"'Sheik's Wife' Wins Praise of N.Y. Papers," *ETR* (March 18, 1922): 1102.

277. Farnum ad and "Picture Shows Poland Under Russian Rule," *HN* (September 1, 1922): n.p. How this film was booked at the Farnum is unclear; there is no reference to it in the trade press. Around the same time, the Jewish National Fund Committee screened *The New Jewish Palestine*, promoting pioneer settlers, at McCallister Hall (near Central High School, on Cass and Warren) —"Jewish Homeland Shown in Movies," *DJC* (June 2, 1922): 1; "Social and Personal," *DJC* (June 9, 1922): 8; and "Interesting Films Portray Palestine," *DJC* (June 16, 1922): 1.

278. "Pola Negri," *DFP* (October 12, 1922): 14; "Pola Negri's Romance," *DSFP* (October 15, 1922): Magazine, 9; and "Pola Negri's Career—Her Own Story," *DSFP* (October 29, 1922): Magazine, 3.

279. Miles ad, *DFP* (January 23, 1923): 4; and Roy E. Marcotte, "The Reel Players," *DFP* (January 25, 1922): 12.

280. Goldwyn ad, *FD* (March 6, 1923): 3; and Goldwyn ad, *ETR* (March 17, 1923): 11.

281. Adams ads, *DSFP* (March 18, 1923): 3.11, and (March 25, 1923): 3.11; Iris ad, *HN* (May 11, 1923): n.p.; and Farnum ad, *HN* (June 22, 1923): n.p.

282. Paramount ads, *ETR* (March 31, 1923): 1; *MPW* (March 31, 1923): 483, and (October 20, 1923): 1821; and *EH* (March 1, 1924): 13.

283. See the special advertisement for Pola Negri and *The Spanish Dancer* within the Paramount ad, *DSFP* (October 14, 1923): Feature, 18.

284. Martha Washington ad, *HN* (March 28, 1924): n.p.; and Iris ad, *HN* (April 4, 1924): n.p.

285. See Negra, "Immigrant Stardom in Imperial America," 395–400.

ENTR'ACTE 2

Detroit Area Picture Theaters

THE FOLLOWING THEATER NAMES, ADDRESSES, AND SEATING CAPACITIES (where available) are drawn from Detroit city directories, a 1918 *Michigan Film Review* directory, extant copies of the *Weekly Film News* (1916–1919), newspaper stories and ads, and two 1970s books of theater profiles. Addresses are complicated by the fact that the city changed street numbers in 1922, so theater address numbers prior to that date appear in brackets. Seating capacities sometimes varied according to different sources.

Acme, 17 W. Davison Ave., Highland Park (closed in 1925)
Adams, 44 [20] W. Adams, 1,770 seats (opened in 1917)
Aladdin, 9636 E. Jefferson Ave., 894 seats (formerly Gladwin Park, closed in 1924)
Alhambra, 9426 [2124] Woodward Ave., 1475 seats
Almo, 5136 [1138] Russell St., 378 seats
Amo, 3121 [473] Grand River, 384 seats
Amuse-U, 10533 [3201] W. Jefferson Ave., 1,200 seats [renamed the Lancaster in 1921]
Arcade, 2416 [406] Hastings St., 460 seats
Arcadia, 9159–9167 [2195] Gratiot Ave., 522 seats
Arthur, 8730 Harper, 337 seats (opened in 1921)
Astor, 8652 12th St., 732 seats (opened in 1923)
Baker, 3420 [562] Bagley Ave., 384 seats?
Bandbox, 2647 [343] Grand River Ave., 282 seats (formerly Duchess until 1918)
Beechwood, 5010 W. Warren Ave., 399 seats (made into duplex in 1919)
Bell, 4216 [396 Dix Ave.] W. Vernor Hwy., 344 seats (closed in 1921)
Bernhardt, 1495 Chene St., 382 seats
Bijou, 62 Monroe St., 314 seats
Billikin, 1054 [288] Holden St., 350 seats (closed in 1924)
Blackstone, 2647 Michigan Ave., 288 seats (formerly Jewell)
Blue Bird, 3205 [501] Bagley Ave., 344 seats (formerly Beecher until 1916)
Boulevard, 7237 [1573] Gratiot Ave., 400 seats
Broadway Strand, 1333–1337 [35–41] Broadway, 1,488 seats
Brooklyn, 1302 [372] Michigan Ave., 300 seats
Capitol, 1526 Broadway, 3,367 seats (opened in 1922)

Cass, 1933 [117] Grand River Ave., 250 seats (closed in 1923)

Castle, 3412 [584] Hastings St., 1,000 seats

Catherine, 1540 [300] Chene St., 398 seats

Chopin, Michigan Ave. and Chopin, 400 seats (opened in 1922)

Cinderella, 13305–09 E. Jefferson Ave., 1,897 seats

Circle, 2814 [502] Hastings St., 658 seats (turned into Yiddish vaudeville theater in 1921)

Clay, 1150 [354–66] Clay Ave., 390 seats

Coliseum, 331 Greenwood, 562 seats

Colonial, 2615 [421] Woodward Ave., 1,566 seats (opened in 1917)

Columbia, 50 [18] Monroe St., 1,000 seats

Columbus, 1042 [326] Watson Ave., 282 seats (closed in 1923)

Comique, 1249–51 [13–15] Broadway, 587 seats

Courtesy, 6041 [767–73 Dix Ave.] W. Vernor Hwy., 816 seats

Cozy, 1042 [314] Michigan Ave., 389 seats

Crescent, 7736 [2050] W. Fort, 371 seats

Crystal, 4645 [1497] Michigan Ave., 589 seats (opened in 1916)

D & G, 4035 [341 Dix Ave.] W. Vernor Hwy., 384 seats (Ila until 1917, closed in 1921)

Davison, 1708 [194] E. Davison Ave., 329 seats (opened in 1918)

Dawn, 8342 Gratiot Ave., 894 seats (opened in 1916)

Del Ray, 8022 [2238] W. Jefferson Ave., 398 seats

Del-The, 8935 Mack Ave., 1,076 seats (opened in 1916)

De Luxe, 9355 Kercheval Ave., 1,466 seats (opened in 1918)

Dix, 4418 W. Vernor Hwy., 400 seats

Dixie, 574 [454] Gratiot Ave. (renamed Favorite and closed in 1924)

Doric, 5455 [1269] Grand River Ave., 398 seats (formerly Northwestern until 1922)

Dreamland, 7510–16 [230] Oakland Ave., 393 seats

Drury Lane, 1534 [256] Woodward, 600 seats?

Dudley, 674–76 [244] Gratiot Ave., 399 seats (formerly Vaudette until late 1916)

Duplex, 3076 E. Grand Blvd, 1,250 seats in two auditoria (closed in 1922)

Duplex, Grand near Woodward[1]

Eagle, 6345 [1827] Michigan Ave., 344 seats (closed in 1926)

East End, 11510 [2548.5] E. Jefferson Ave., 365 seats (closed in 1925)

East Side, 2717 [795] Gratiot Ave., 650 seats

Elizabeth, 2986 [742] Franklin St., 294 seats (closed in 1925)

Empire, 1251 [189–91] Woodward Ave., 530 seats (closed in 1923)

Empress, 540 [106] Woodward Ave., 300 seats

Englewood, 11562 [1040] Oakland, 398 seats (formerly Villa until 1917, closed in 1923)

Enterprise, 713 [161] St. Aubin St., 480 seats (formerly Luna until 1924)

Family, 1 Cadillac Square, 926 seats

Farnum, 9048 Jos. Campau Ave., Hamtramck, 900 seats, (opened in 1917)

Ferndale, 7815 W. Vernon Hwy., 995 seats (opened in 1919)

Ferry Field, 6541 W. Grand Blvd., 1,325 seats (opened in 1916)

Ferry Park, 7331 [1701] Grand River Ave.

Fine Arts, 2954 [526] Woodward Ave., 582 seats

Forest, 4635 [875–877] Woodward Ave., 592 seats

Fox Washington, 1505–13 [89] Washington Blvd., 1,862 seats (simply the Washington until 1919)

Fredro, 5317 [1093–97] Chene St., 400 seats

Frontenac, 7206 [1396] Harper, 834 seats?

Fun, 1052 [318] Michigan Ave., 339 seats

Garden, 3929 [727–29] Woodward Ave., 950 seats

Globe, 3520 [568–70] Grand River Ave., 853 seats

Grand Circus, 2115 [301] Woodward Ave., 560 seats

Grande, 8024 [2240] W. Jefferson Ave., 976 seats (enlarged to 1,837 seats circa 1921)

Gratiot, 2306 [722–24] Gratiot Ave., 1,025 seats

Greenwood, 5401–5403 Hamilton Ave., 360 seats

Hancock, 4758 Hastings Ave., 600 seats (opened in 1922)

Harmonia, 3848 [750] Russell St. (closed in 1917)

Harmony, 11205 Mack Ave., 1,322 seats (opened in 1921)

Highland Park, 13843 [2965] Woodward Ave., 600 seats

Hippodrome, 3646 [1128] W. Warren St., 750 seats

Holbrook, 8747 Russell St., 764 seats (opened in 1920)

Home, 6420 [1450] Chene St., 299 seats

Imperial, 7030 Michigan Ave., 378 seats (opened in 1920)

Iris, 2314 E. Grand Ave., 880 seats (opened in 1916)

Jefferson, 11008 [2422–24] E. Jefferson Ave., 376 seats

Jewel, 1450 [448] Gratiot Ave., 490 seats

Knickerbocker, 1427 E. Jefferson Ave., 923 seats

Koppin, 528–30 Gratiot Ave., 1,500 seats (opened in 1920)

Kramer, 5741 Michigan Ave., 1,732 seats (opened in 1920)

Lakewood, 14243–49 [3231] E. Jefferson Ave., 1,240 seats

La Salle, 1042 [200] Randolph, 298 seats

La Salle Garden, 6515 14th St., 1,990 seats (opened in 1920)

La Veeda, 11759 Oakland St., Highland Park, 528 seats (opened in 1922)

Liberty, 1020 Farmer St./149 Bates, 720 seats (closed 1926)

Library, 8525 [1981] Gratiot Ave., 367 seats

Lincoln, 4647 [1433] Michigan Ave., 276 seats (formerly Columbia, closed in 1919)

Lincoln Square, 6034 W. Fort St., 1,850 seats (opened in 1918)

Linwood-LaSalle, 8229 Linwood Ave., 1,400 seats (opened in 1920)

Lockwood, 1527 [421] E. Canfield Ave. (formerly Canfield, then Lira until 1919)

Ludowry, 1459 Michigan, 394 seats

Luna, 161 St. Aubin St., 330 seats

Lyric, 421 [121] Michigan Ave., 320 seats

Mack Ave., 7731–35 [995] Mack Ave., 425 seats

Madison, 22 Witherell, 1,965 seats (opened in 1917)

Majestic, 4136 [760] Woodward, 1,760 seats

Martha Washington, 10315 Jos. Campau Ave., Hamtramck, 1,000 seats (opened in 1924)

Maxine, 7641 [969] Mack Ave., 774 seats

Medbury, 5848 [1268] Hastings St., 372 seats

Merrick, 5138 [1090] 3rd Ave., 598 seats

Metropolitan, 1659 W. Fort, 380 seats (closed in 1918)

Michigan, 231 Michigan Ave. (formerly Cadillac)

Miles, 192 Griswold, 1,679 seats

Monarch, 5507 [1543] Michigan Ave. (closed in 1917)

Monroe, 204 [54] Monroe St., 313 seats

Montclair, 10739 [1751] Mack Ave., 465 seats

Mt. Elliott, 6041 [1573] Mt. Elliott Ave., 342 seats

Myrtle, 3515 [665] 17th St., 384 seats (enlarged to 750 seats in 1926)

National, 118 [40–44] Monroe St., 758 seats

New Home, 6421 [1451] Chene St., 1,000 seats

Norwood, 6533 [1507–09] Woodward Ave., 505 seats

Oakland, 9008 [636] Oakland Ave., 358 seats

Oakman, 12728-40 Woodrow Wilson St., 1,213 seats (opened in 1919)

Odeon, 1791–1811 [443–37] Concord St., 390 seats

Olympic, 4820 [1490] Michigan Ave., 336 seats

Orpheum, 27 Lafayette Boulevard, 1,873 seats

Our, 8767 [721–23] Kercheval, 395 seats (closed in 1922)

Palace #1, 130–132 [48] Monroe, 1,369 seats

Palace #2, 6010 [1354] 14th St., 397 seats

Park, 2628 E. Davison Ave., 676 seats (opened in 1922)

Pasadena, 9232 [1420] Mack Ave., 386 seats

Pastime, 8615 Jos. Campau Ave., Hamtramck, 400 seats

People's, 2238 [372] Hastings, 298 seats [formerly Lester until 1918]

Perrien, 4738–48 [930] Chene St., 350 seats

Petite, 4151 [771] Grand River Ave.

Plaza, 11641 [2601] E. Jefferson Ave., 760 seats

Poland, 9643 Jos. Campau Ave., Hamtramck (renamed Free Poland, 1918–1921)

Poznan, 423 E. Canfield, 340 seats

Premier, 5741 [1229] Chene St., 352 seats (formerly Rozmaitosci until 1922)

Princess, 520–22 [98] Woodward Ave., 360 seats (closed in 1922)

Priscilla, 2946 [710] Mt. Elliott Ave., 474 seats (formerly Louis until 1923)

Pulaski, 8576 [2432] W. Jefferson Ave. (formerly La Belle until 1923)

Quo Vadis, 13557–59 [361] E. Canfield Ave., 385 seats

Regent, 7314 [1554] Woodward Ave., 2,150–3,600 seats (opened in 1916)

Republic, 1212 Broadway, 400 seats (opened in 1924)

Rex, 5651 [1457] W. Fort St., 865 seats

Rialto, 6345–47 Gratiot Ave., 1,334 seats (formerly the Pearl)

Rivola, 4703 Cadillac Ave., 1,010 seats (opened in 1922)

Rivoli, 8225 [1131] Mack Ave., 382 seats (formerly Wigwam until 1919, closed in 1923)

Ritz, 6661 [1943] Michigan Ave., 632 seats (formerly Neumann Brothers until 1922)

Roosevelt, 7028–30 Michigan Ave., 378 seats (opened in 1921)

Rosebud, 429 [117–19] Gratiot Ave., 398 seats

Rosedale, 11520 [2394] Woodward Ave., 965 seats

Royal, 100–102 [34] Monroe St., 330 seats (closed in 1922)

Royal, 4711 Michigan Ave. (formerly Ludlow, opened in 1924)

Russell, 5335 [1145] Russell St., 1,406 seats (opened in 1917)

Savoy, 1507–11 [289] Chene St., 470 seats

Sheridan, 7414 [342] Kercheval Ave., 375 seats

Star, 2836 [852] Michigan Ave., 353 seats (closed in 1922)

Strand, 4730 [968] Grand River Ave., 1,384 seats

Stratford, 4651 W. Vernor Hwy./547 Dix, 1,025 seats

Theatorium, 3323–27 [531 Baker] Bagley Ave., 384 seats

Tuxedo, 11738 Hamilton St., 1,800 seats (opened in 1921)

Universal, 831 [236] Michigan Ave., 307 seats

Vendome, 4481 [885–87] Grand River Ave., 891 seats

Victor, 77 Victor Ave., Highland Park (opened in 1916)

Victory, 3455-57 [1009] Michigan Ave., 385 seats (formerly Victoria until 1921)

Virginia, 8237 [1227] Hamilton Blvd., 530 seats

Warfield, 5126 [1030] Hastings St., 376 seats

Warren, 3818 [1180] W. Warren Ave., 550 seats

Washington, 422 S. Washington Blvd, Royal Oak, 1,128 seats (opened in 1922)

Wayne, 3323 [977] Gratiot Ave., 330 seats

White Star, 9229 Jos. Campau Ave., Hamtramck, 360 seats

Willis, 4190 [780] Hastings St., 399 seats

Wolverine, 3301–07 [957] Michigan Ave., 504 seats (formerly Nettie B until 1924)

Woodward #1, 1016 [148] Woodward Ave., 268 seats

Woodward #2, 2511 [395] Woodward Ave., 330 seats (opened in 1918)

Your, 3748 [1070] E. Forest Ave., 774 seats

Zellah, 5467 [481] Moran Ave., 385 seats

Note

1. This north side Duplex, at Woodward and E. Grand, is missing from the published books on the city's theaters as well as the list in the Michigan Film Review; consequently, its seating capacity is unknown.

ENTR'ACTE 3

John H. Kunsky and George W. Trendle

JOHN H. KUNSKY (1875–1952) WAS A FIRST-GENERATION POLISH American; his father had emigrated from the Polish territories in 1868.[1] At the turn of the century, Kunsky was a superintendent in the Caille Brothers factory, which made slot machines, candy machines, and gambling devices—before he and Arthur Caille opened the Casino, Detroit's first nickelodeon, in March 1906.[2] The two men formed Casino Amusement Enterprises, and by 1907 they managed as many as nine storefront theaters in and around Monroe Street.[3]

By early 1910, George W. Trendle (1891–1972), a young lawyer and bookkeeper whose major client was Casino Amusement, had joined the two partners. Three years later Kunsky bought out Caille's interest in the Casino's growing circuit of theaters.[4] That circuit began with the Royale (the renovated Casino) in 1908; this was followed by the downtown Columbia, a vaudeville theater designed by architect C. Howard Crane, which opened in October 1911—with 1,000 seats, a small orchestra, and a pipe organ.[5] Other large theaters, also designed by Crane, came soon after: the Garden (900 seats) in December 1912, the Liberty (720 seats) in September 1913, the Washington (1,860 seats) in August 1914,[6] the Alhambra (1,475 seats) in 1915, and the Strand (1,380 seats) in September 1915.[7] The Liberty (the former Central Presbyterian Church at Farmer and Bates) was around the corner from the Royale; the Washington (at Washington and Clifford) was located a block or two south of Grand Circus Park; the Garden could be found farther north on Woodward near midtown; the Strand (at Grand Avenue and 14th Street) and the Alhambra (at Woodward and Kenilworth) were built, respectively, north-west of downtown and south of Highland Park to the north, the latter serving the Boston-Edison community, one of the city's wealthiest white residential areas.[8] Because of Trendle's astute handling of the financial side of the business,[9] Kunsky made him general manager of the theater circuit[10] and put him in charge of planning and financing the slightly later Madison (variously cited as having 1,800, 2,300, or 3,100 seats)[11] and Adams (1,770 or 2,000 seats), which would become the first picture palaces constructed on the north side of Grand Circus Park—the new "heart of the business and hotel district," and soon to be dubbed "Kunsky Circle."[12]

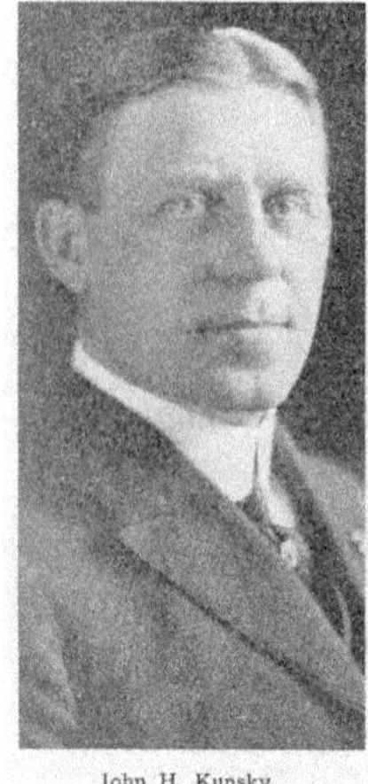

John H. Kunsky.

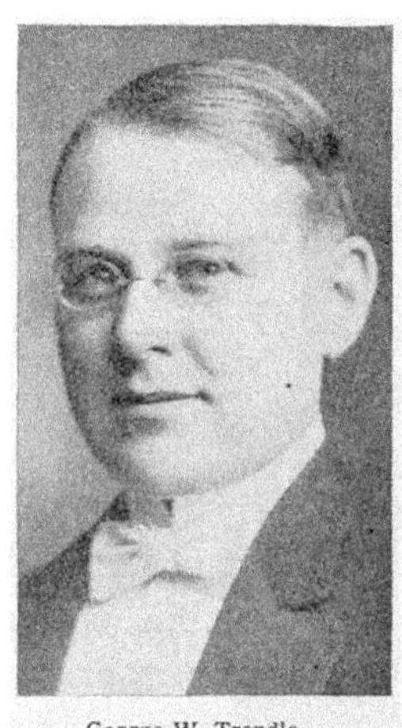

George W. Trendle.

Fig. EA3.1. John H. Kunsky, *Moving Picture World* (March 6, 1915): 1434.

Fig. EA3.2. George W. Trendle, *Moving Picture World* (March 6, 1915): 1434.

By 1917, according to the *Detroit Free Press*, Kunsky's theatrical enterprises had grown to include "the Madison Film Exchange, the Casino Feature Film Company, the Madison Realty Company, Metro Film Exchange, and the *Weekly Film News*."[13] As the public spokesman for these enterprises, Trendle was invited to talk about censorship to the Detroit Federation of Women's Clubs in early 1917 and was elected president of the Detroit Theater Managers' Association in early 1919.[14] That year, Kunsky himself became a leader of the new First National Exhibitors Circuit.[15]

Ten years later, Kunsky and Trendle sold their cinema chain to the Paramount Pictures Publix Division,[16] and together then entered the radio business. After Kunsky changed his surname to King in 1936,[17] the King-Trendle Broadcasting Corporation eventually controlled ten radio stations in Michigan; they were all sold to ABC in 1946.[18] Trendle also became well known as a producer of such popular radio shows as *The Lone Ranger* and *The Green Hornet*.

Notes

1. *DFP* (April 20, 1868): 1.

2. Mary Bickel, *Geo. W. Trendle* (New York: Exposition Press, 1971), 30, 33; Andrew Craig Morrison, *Opera House, Nickel Show, and Palace* (Dearborn, MI: Greenfield Village & Henry Ford Museum, 1974), n.p. See also "Kunsky Is Millionaire Owner of Theatre String," *MPN* (February 1916): 600.

3. Sydney Ware, "The Casino Amusement Co.," *Billboard* (November 23, 1907): 20. In June 1908, Kunsky and Caille put on two shows at their Lafayette Theater for the *Detroit Free Press's*

four thousand newsboys—"Free Press to Give 'Newsies' Treat to Lafayette Theater," *Detroit Free Press* (June 9, 1908): 6.

4. "New Amusement Company Formed," *DFP* (March 13, 1910): 5; "Council Order Seems Ominous," *DFP* (September 30, 1910): 3; "Kunsky to Run Film Shows Alone," *DFP* (February 9, 1913): 8; and Bickel, *Geo. W. Trendle*, 35.

5. Michael Hauser and Marianne Weldon, *Detroit's Downtown Movie Palaces* (Chicago: Arcadia, 2006), 7, 14; and Morrison, *Opera House, Nickel Show, and Palace*, n.p.

6. In the summer of 1914, Kunsky leased and renovated the Washington, which the previous summer had opened, and proved unsuccessful, as a legitimate theater—"Detroit," *V* (August 9, 1914): 20.

7. For further information on these and other new picture theaters, see "Dozen Theatres Are Being Erected in Detroit," *MPN* (October 1914): 78; and "Strand Theater, Detroit, Mich.," *MPW* (December 11, 1915): 2001. See also the photograph and brief profiles of the Kunsky theater managers in "A Coterie of Theatre Managers," *MPW* (January 23, 1915): 530.

8. The area around the Alhambra was almost exclusively white; the area around the Garden was largely residential with a mixed population of white-collar, skilled, and unskilled workers (likely Polish to the east); the area around the Strand was residential, with a white population of white-collar and skilled workers, and commercial, with nearby factories such as American Malting Works, Williams Pickle Factory, and Northway Motor Company—Olivier Zunz, *The Changing Face of Inequality: Urbanization, Industrial Development, and Immigrants in Detroit, 1880–1920* (Chicago: University of Chicago Press, 1982): maps 12.3, 12.6, 13.2, and 13.3. Kunsky's staff described all three as "neighborhood theaters"—"The Neighborhood Theater," *WFN* (January 21, 1917): 8.

9. "Huge New Theater Will Seat 3,600," *DFP* (May 5, 1916): C11.

10. Bickel, *Geo. W. Trendle*, 55, 57.

11. "New Madison Theater, Acme of Motion Picture Palaces," *DFP* (March 9, 1917): 12; and "Million Dollar Detroit House Opens," *MPN* (March 24, 1917): 1897. For a description of the planned exterior and interior, see "Latest Kunsky Theatre in Detroit to Seat 3,100," *MPN* 13, no. 24 (1916): 3790. The Madison had set afternoon and evening performance times of 12:00, 2:00, 4:00, 5:45, 7:30, and 9:15. The Madison allegedly earned a profit of $400,000 in 1919—Bickel, *Geo. W. Trendle*, 61.

12. "Announcing the Adams Theater," *WFN* (July 29, 1917): 3, 12. The Adams initially served as a "high class dramatic theater" with a stock company, but soon turned into a picture palace.

13. "Kunsky, Cinema Magnate, Moves Business Offices," *DFP* (July 4, 1917): 14. Kunsky opposed the term *movies* as undignified—see his quoted letter in W. Stephen Bush, "The Dreadful Word," *MPW* (October 30, 1915): 760.

14. "Movie Man Wants Broad Censorship," *DFP* (January 27, 1917): 6; and "City Theater Men Pick 1919 Officers," *DFP* (January 15, 1919): 6. The Detroit branch allegedly had a "Photoplay club of more than 600 women members who [were] constantly watching motion picture productions about the city."

15. "John H. Kunsky Enterprises Join First National Expansion Plans," *EH* (December 1919): 53. Kunsky may have had a summer home in nearby Walkerville, Ontario, for he hosted a party there for "First National members" in late May 1920—Harry E. Nichols, "With the Detroit Filmmen," *EH* (June 12, 1920): 75.

16. "Detroit Movie Pioneer, John King, Dies at 77," *DFP* (January 3, 1952): 7.

17. "Kunsky Changes Name," *DFP* (June 20, 1936): 7; and "Kunsky Changes Name," *Billboard* (June 27, 1936): 35.

18. "Detroit Movie Pioneer Dies," op. cit.

2

MOVIES, LIVE ACTS, AND THE THEATRICAL EXPERIENCE

Programming Practices in the Motor City

Mr. Rothaphel believes that the artistic presentation [of the exhibitor] is the most important element; Mr. Goldfish, that the picture itself is the thing.

Genevieve Harris, *Chicago Post* (December 7, 1918)

Attendance at the presentation of a motion picture today is not merely the witnessing of the picture itself, but of hearing superb renditions of music, enjoying the wonderful beauty of interpretative dancing, and the marvelous lighting effects which convert the scenes on the film into a wonderland of delight.

Los Angeles Evening Express (December 10, 1919)

WHAT WOULD DETROIT MOVIEGOERS EXPECT TO FIND IN their picture theaters between late 1916 and early 1925? This chapter addresses that question by looking more closely at the program practices in a range of theaters. Although features were especially prominent on most programs, theaters essentially mounted variety shows in which "the successful exhibitor [became] as much a 'producer' of pictures as a manufacturer," especially in the "arrangement of the program."[1] My aim, therefore, is to take up questions that, first of all, moviegoers might have asked about the variety shows in which short films and live acts could be attractions as alluring as features. What specifically would they want to know about the weekly or daily programs of any one of several theaters? Would they be mainly interested in movie stars and their feature films, as too often has been assumed, or would they be just as drawn to certain kinds of shorts and/or live acts? Whether they were relatively new moviegoers or devoted fans in the process of setting routines for attending certain theaters, on certain days and at certain times, what were the starting times for programs and what would seat tickets cost? What if they wished to plan their moviegoing in advance rather than drop in whenever time and money allowed—as some would have done during the nickelodeon era? Such questions about Detroit's movie culture obviously are of keen interest to cinema historians as well. Here, then, I seek a better understanding of the variety shows that typified picture palaces as well as neighborhood theaters, large and small. Moreover, within any one of those theaters—a "paradoxical place," writes Gabriele Pedullà, in which "many different and often opposed functions are brought together in a single space"[2]—how did what was put on change from one week or month to another and especially over the course of these years? Finally, do the advertisements and surviving programs suggest something about who theater managers imagined made up their audiences, at one time or another, and what in particular may have appealed to those audiences?

As in chapter 1, newspaper ads certainly are an important source to consult in addressing these questions. Initially those were limited to a handful of the largest theaters, from Kunsky's Washington, Liberty, and Madison to the Broadway Strand, Majestic, and Regent. Their number gradually rose through 1917–1918 and then began to increase dramatically around the end of the Great War, so that by 1922, nearly half of the city's theaters were advertising in brief daily entries within a standardized column in one of two Detroit papers. Moreover, during the 1920s, weekly theater ads appeared in surviving neighborhood newspapers in Hamtramck, Highland Park, and elsewhere. Between 1916 and 1919, however, the "house organ" of the Kunsky theater chain, the *Weekly Film News*, becomes an especially rich source. Much as the *Michigan Film Review* proved invaluable in chapter 1, here, too, are surviving copies of the *Weekly Film News*, for they include more or less full programs for the downtown Washington, Madison, Adams, and Liberty as well as for the neighborhood theaters, the Alhambra, Garden, and Strand—and occasionally for the older and smaller downtown Empress and Royale. Augmenting these rare sources after 1918 are scattered copies of house organs from the Broadway Strand, Fox Washington, and Lincoln Square, a few copies of Kunsky's even later *Photoplay Weekly*, and at least two newspaper ads reproducing weekly program sheets for the Majestic and the Broadway Strand.

Programming Practices During the Great War

As a context for delving into Kunsky's *Weekly Film News*, some background is useful. In the early 1910s, moviegoers attending a picture theater in many cities and towns could pick up what the industry dubbed "house organs"—from daily single sheets to weekly program booklets. Generally, theater managers or their press agents compiled these from "the clip sheets sent out by the various film companies," along with purchased "cuts to illustrate the [film] stories, often giving them a local spin."[3] In early May 1913, in his *Moving Picture World* column, Epes

Winthrop Sargent began to take note of such localized publicity formats.[4] Within a year, he was giving practical advice about "the right way and the wrong way to make up a house organ" in order to attract and retain customers, whether or not a manager advertised in a local newspaper.[5] By early 1915, his examples ranged from metropolitan palace cinemas to ordinary picture theaters in small towns. While suggesting some design changes in the weekly four-page booklet put out by the flagship Stanley theater in Philadelphia,[6] he had nothing but praise for the weekly eight-page *Garden Chat* that Miss Reda S. Rauch was editing for the Garden Theater in Des Moines, wishing only that she could expand it to include more ads as well as more of her "brightly written" matter.[7] Five theaters in Dallas had a great idea, he thought, in jointly getting out "8,000 copies weekly" of a single publication, but he found its pages too haphazardly arranged.[8] Sargent's advice was clearly respected, for he kept receiving requests to assess publications like the weekly *Spotlight* "designed to cater only to those movie patrons who attend Galesburg [Illinois] theaters."[9] And he provided evidence of Paramount's successful publicity strategies by hailing several exhibitors who created house organs either by inserting their own program pages inside each week's *Paramount Magazine* or by simply binding the company's "heralds" into a "luxurious" thirty-six-page weekly booklet enclosed within the theater's own cover.[10]

In the fall of 1915, *Motion Picture News* mounted an even more extensive campaign to promote house organs through its unsigned "Live Wire Exhibitors" column. Rarely did the *News* follow the *World* in making an example of "ineffective publicity."[11] Instead, in October the *News* launched a weekly "House Organ Series" that offered exhibitors models of "effective theatre advertising," beginning with the four-page *Duluth Photoplay News* from the Rex and Lyric theaters.[12] Some of these models came from big cities: the Calhoun theater's high-quality cover illustrations in Minneapolis; several pages from the *Belmar Film Forecast* for the Rowland and Clark theaters in Pittsburgh; or the deluxe *Saxe Weekly* for the Saxe chain of six theaters in Milwaukee.[13] Yet just as many represented what enterprising exhibitors could do in small cities or towns: the Majestic's four-page weekly *Movie Fan* in Grand Junction (Colorado), with a circulation of two thousand; the Heyburn's four-page weekly booklet in Evanston (Illinois); or the thirty-two-page *Movieland*, "published fortnightly by E. H. Hulsey for his chain of five Texas theaters, located in Dallas, Galveston, Houston, and Waco."[14] Several house organs came in distinctive formats: the Family theater in Batavia (New York) published a folder of eight pages, with each page devoted to a different day of the week; the Sheridan in Brooklyn and the La Salle in South Bend (Indiana) distributed four-page weekly folders small enough to slip into a vest pocket.[15] Perhaps the most unusual were those put out by three California theaters (the Franklin in Oakland, the Sequoia in Sacramento, and the Liberty in San Jose) and the Swanson Circuit of theaters in Salt Lake City, all of which took the popular "shape of newspapers," and which the *News* admired for their "excellent make-up and . . . attractiveness."[16]

House organs were notoriously ephemeral, usually tossed in the trash, as Sargent noted, once they had served their initial use.[17] Hardly any survive, unlike legitimate theater and vaudeville house programs, which theatergoers sometimes collected in scrapbooks and which subsequently found their way into a library or an archive. Even if they do survive, house organs can be difficult to locate.[18] The *Weekly Film News* is one of the very few extant—with more than fifty issues, dating from May 1916 to April 1919, in the possession of a Detroit private collector.[19] Edited first by Howard O. Pierce and then Harry R. Guest,[20] the *Weekly Film News* was given free to patrons of Kunsky's Detroit theaters. The first issue appeared on January 10, 1915,[21] but the date of the last remains unknown. Initially this 8"×10" house organ had light gray covers, ran sixteen pages, and included not only half a dozen full-page theater schedules but also stories of stars, half-tone photos, gossip items, synopses of featured films, an editorial column, and dozens of local ads. Sometime in early 1916, the *Weekly Film News* expanded to twenty pages, with the front and back covers now printed in color (like *Photoplay* and *Motion Picture Magazine*), adding several new columns and snapshot film reviews. During these first two years, fifty thousand copies of each issue allegedly were in circulation.[22] In late January 1917, the *Weekly Film News* returned to its original format of sixteen pages, with light gray covers, and a reduced circulation of thirty-five thousand copies.[23] By late June 1918, if not earlier, it was cut further to eight pages, now absent ads, and with each page—other than the covers—devoted to a different one of Kunsky's six main theaters.[24] By 1919, those few issues still extant ran only four pages and focused exclusively on the flagship picture palaces: the Washington, Madison, and Adams.

The period of September 1916 through May 1917 offers an initial baseline for analyzing the programming practices of Detroit's picture theaters. Here the *Weekly Film News*, supplemented by newspaper ads, serves as a primary source. Three of Kunsky's downtown theaters—the Washington, Liberty, and Madison—presented programs that ran unchanged for a full week. In early September, the Washington featured Fannie Ward in Paramount's *Each Pearl a Tear* (accompanied by "musical selections" by the theater's "augmented orchestra"), along with a tenor soloist; Burton Holmes's *Climbing the Austrian Alps*; and a "first-run comedy."[25] The theater offered six afternoon and evening shows daily, starting "promptly" at 12:10, 2:05, 4:00, 5:45, 7:30, and 9:20; tickets ranged from 10¢ for an afternoon balcony seat, to 15¢ or 25¢ for an evening seat on the main floor. When the Madison opened in early March 1917, it featured Mary Pickford in *A Poor Little Rich Girl*, a *Pathé-Hearst Weekly*, Pathé's color travel film of Barcelona, a lyric soprano, "Detroit's favorite tenor," and its orchestra and organist.[26]

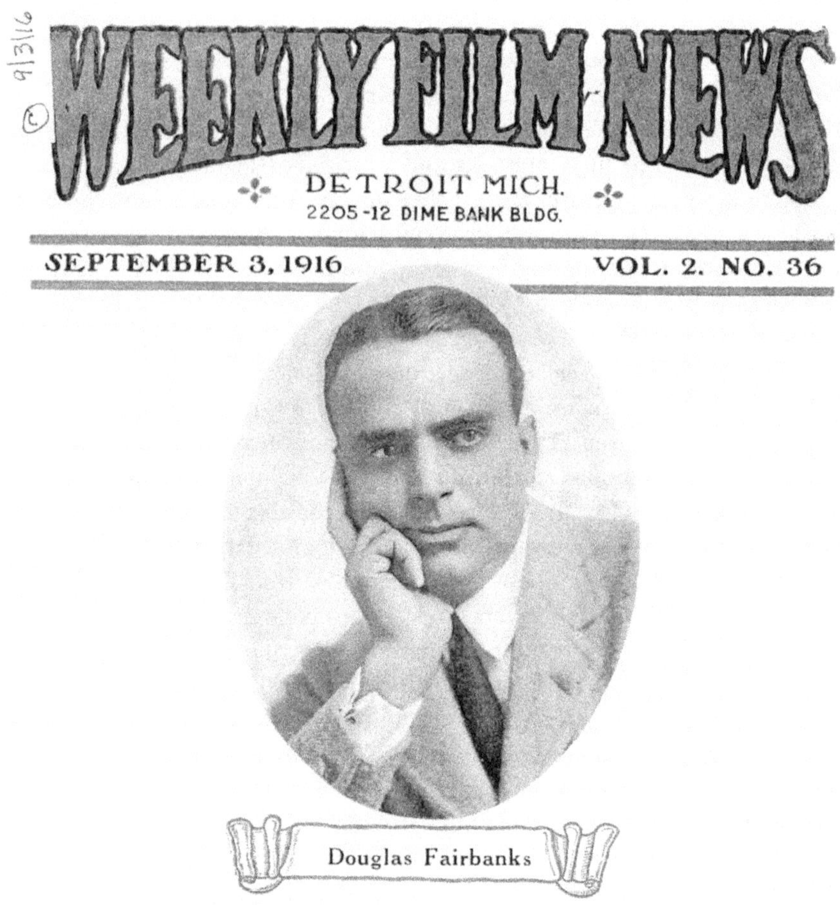

Fig. 2.1. *Weekly Film News* (September 3, 1916): front cover.

This theater also offered six afternoon and evening shows daily, at 12:00, 2:00, 4:00, 5:45, 7:30, and 9:15; tickets ranged from 15¢ for matinees to 75¢ for main floor loges in the evening. In September 1916, the Broadway Strand presented a similar program, featuring Theda Bara in *Her Double Life*, a male singer, a *Mutt and Jeff* comedy, and a "topical review."[27] For its six daily shows, tickets cost from 10¢ for matinees to 25¢ for evenings. Weeks later the Majestic featured Frank Keenan in

The Thoroughbred, a Keystone comedy, a *Mutt and Jeff* comedy, *The B. of C. Americanization Campaign*, and songs by Henry Santrey.[28] There were three afternoon and evening shows daily at 2:00, 7:00, and 9:00, and tickets ranged from 10¢ for matinees to 25¢ for evenings. A week later, the Regent featured Mabel Taliaferro in *God's Half Acre*, a Drew comedy, the "Regent Weekly and Regent Travelogue," a cartoon comedy, and a "20-piece orchestra."[29] This North Woodward theater also presented three afternoon and evening shows daily at 2:00, 7:00, and 9:00; balcony tickets cost 10¢, and box seats were 35¢.

As evidence of what appealed to their audiences, all of these theaters, with few exceptions,[30] not only offered programs with a variety of films and live acts but also prominently promoted a movie star's name, followed by the title of the star's feature film. That was also the case with Kunsky's large neighborhood theaters, which generally changed their programs daily. On Thursday in mid-September 1916, the Alhambra featured Sessue Hayakawa in *The Honorable Friend*, a Max Figman comedy, and a *Hearst International Weekly*.[31] Daily matinees were at 2:30, and evening shows at 7:00 and 8:45; tickets cost from 10¢ to 25¢ (for boxes). Two weeks earlier on Thursday, the Strand featured Lillian Gish in *An Innocent Magdalene*, a Keystone comedy, and a "Strand Topical Review."[32] Its daily schedule and ticket prices were the same as the Alhambra's. The same week on Wednesday, the Garden featured Mme Petrova in Metro's *Playing with Fire* and Roscoe Arbuckle's *The Other Man*.[33] It, too, offered three shows daily, but all seats cost only 10¢. This ticket price suggested that the Garden likely drew some of its audience from Polish and Italian neighborhoods on the near east side. A few theaters with newspaper ads also changed their programs daily: The Stratford offered just one matinee and evening show[34]; the Fine Arts presented continuous programs from 2:30 to 11:00 (tickets ranged from 10¢ to 25¢)[35]; the Ferry Field advertised "travelogues, comedies, and other films," and a soprano soloist, all along with the feature on its daily matinee and two evening shows (seats cost from 10¢ to 15¢)[36]; and the Rialto listed a topical review, comedy, travelogue, and xylophone soloist with the feature for its one matinee and two evening shows (seats also cost from 10¢ to 15¢).[37] At least one other theater with ads changed its programs twice a week. The Duplex advertised only its stars and features for matinee and evening shows in its two auditoriums, with tickets costing from 10¢ to 25¢ (for boxes).[38]

Yet stars and films hardly were the only attractions drawing audiences—or those assumed to be of a higher class. The Washington promoted its amenities: the "ladies' retiring room," the "gentlemen's smoking room," the foyer room where parcels could be checked free, and a lobby telephone.[39] The Madison's amenities were no less accommodating, with an office next to the ticket booth where one could consult the manager.[40] In one ad, the Regent singled out its own "handsomely appointed lounges" and "cosy corners" that gave the second floor a distinctive sense of "hominess."[41] Another ad stressed the Regent's wide aisles and

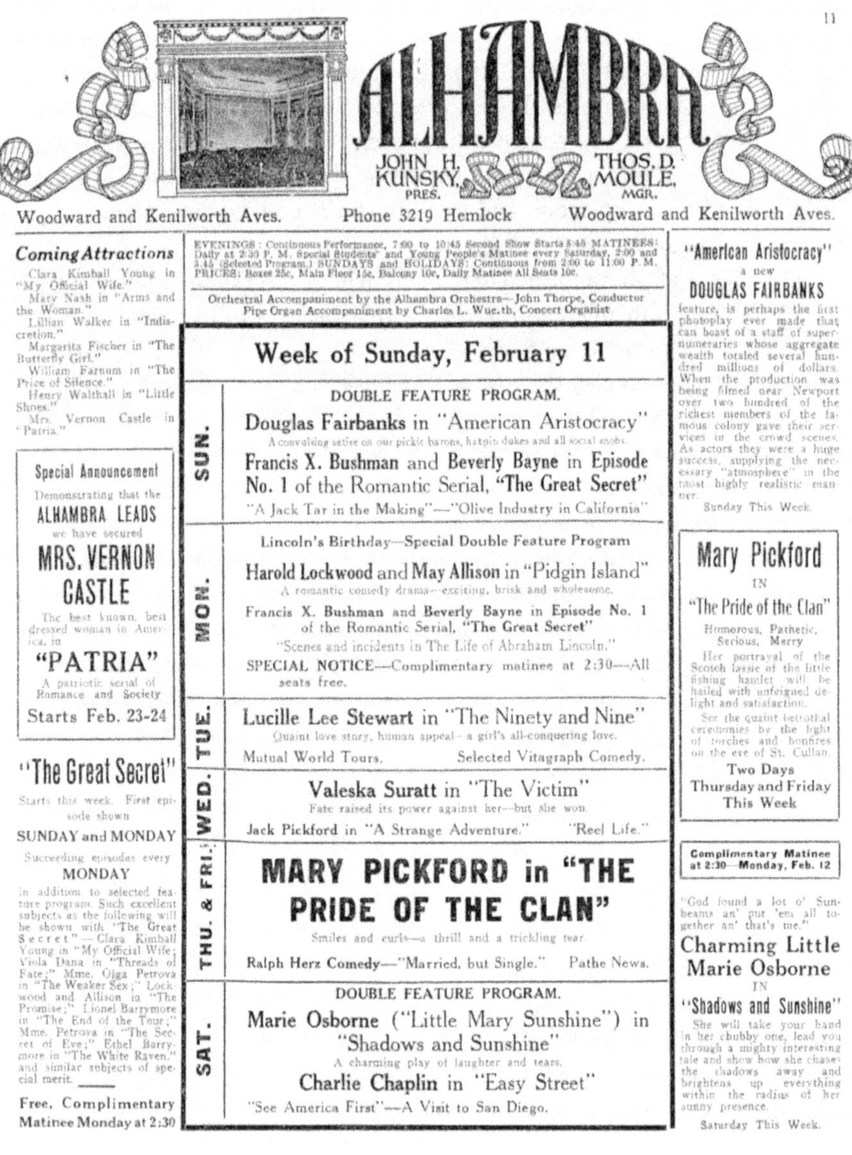

Fig. 2.2. Alhambra Theater programs, *Weekly Film News* (February 11, 1917): 11.

roomy seats "set at a restful angle."[42] A third praised the allegedly unique "acoustic properties" that enhanced the "volume, mellowness of tone, [and] delicate shading of the music," which made its theater experience "so restful and enjoyable."[43] In late November 1916, the Washington also called attention to its orchestra's "special musical selections" accompanying screenings of *The Crisis*.[44] That same week, the Garden headlined the appearance of Tom Lahey, the "popular band singer," whose song sheet music was available at the Jerome Remick store in the city.[45] The following week, the Garden's chief attraction was Milton Wallace, "the popular New York baritone," whose songs Jerome Remick also published.[46] Two other Kunsky theaters offered another amenity: children's matinees. The Alhambra featured *Pinocchio* one Saturday in early December; the Strand, *Alice in Wonderland* a week later, urging parents to "send the children to the matinee or bring them in the evening."[47] By contrast, several older downtown theaters booked occasional "adults only" films: in November, backed by a Michigan Child Welfare League testimonial, the Drury Lane ran *It May Be Your Daughter* for two full weeks; in December, the New Bijou showed *The Unborn* for a week, calling it a "sensational . . . birth control picture."[48]

During the first half of 1917, several program changes stand out, especially in Kunsky's theaters. As mentioned in chapter 1, the Washington became the venue for multiple-week runs of four "big pictures": Fox's *A Daughter of the Gods*, starring Annette Kellerman; Universal's *20,000 Leagues Under the Sea*; Thomas Ince's *Civilization*; and Rex Beach's *The Barrier*.[49] For each of these features, the theater scheduled only two daily screenings, at 2:15 and 8:15, and raised ticket prices from as low as 25¢ to as high as $1.00 and to $1.50 for the Kellerman spectacular. Each program also listed no other accompanying short film or live act. By contrast, at the same time the Regent adopted a twice-weekly change of feature films, beginning in early January with *The Traveling Salesman* (starring Frank McIntyre) Sunday through Wednesday, and *The Evil Eye* (starring Blanche Sweet), Thursday through Saturday.[50] Several other Kunsky theaters began to offer two-day runs of special films. At the Strand, these included *The Foolish Virgin* (featuring Clara Kimball Young), *The Pride of the Clan* (starring Mary Pickford), *Civilization*, and the first serial episode of *Patria* (with Mrs. Vernon Castle)—all on Monday and Tuesday.[51] At the Alhambra, *Civilization* screened on Tuesday and Wednesday; *Snow White* (starring Marguerite Clark) on Wednesday and Thursday; *Pride of the Clan* on Thursday and Friday; and a local film, *Behind the Scenes in a Big Detroit Hotel*, on Sunday and Monday in early January.[52] At least one other theater adopted a program of two-day runs: in early January, the Rialto screened *The Rise of Susan* (starring Kimball Young) on Monday and Tuesday.[53] The Garden also favored programs dubbed "double bills," often offered on Mondays or Tuesdays, and at least once paired Fairbanks and Hart features.[54] In either case, do these extended or "fattened" programs suggest that some theater managers were making an extra effort to attract audiences during what could have been the slowest days of the week?

Music obviously continued to constitute an important feature of the theater experience in certain venues. The Washington spotlighted the original musical scores, along with the composer or arranger, which its "augmented orchestra" performed during the screenings of all four of its "big pictures." Toward the end of *The Barrier*, the orchestra played one character's farewell "Song of the North," and its sheet music was "on sale in the lobby."[55] The Regent took another tack, supposedly quoting a patron: "I make it a point to go to the Regent at least once a week to listen to the magnificent pipe organ. It is the best I have ever heard."[56] When the Madison opened, the *Weekly Film News* described the visual spectacle of the "heavy green velour curtain," bearing a painting of James Madison's home," which rose to reveal a "work of art" stage setting" for the "gay crowd" of "prominent Detroiters."[57] Besides its own orchestra, the Madison also continually heralded its soloists: a lyric soprano and especially a tenor, Harold Jarvis, who sang at only two or three matinees a week.[58] Particularly intriguing were the special inducements that the Washington deployed to lure audiences to *A Daughter of the Gods*. In early January, "every lady attending matinee performances" would receive "a beautiful souvenir art calendar for 1917, showing Annette Kellerman in a Classic Pose."[59] A week later, the *Weekly Film News* offered a vivid account of how "one of the most exciting moments" in the film was produced: the destruction of "a great Moorish city . . . wiped out by fire while terror-stricken thousands flee through its gates and leap off its walls."[60] Perhaps the most outlandish come-on, in a *Detroit News-Tribune* ad, compared Kellerman's measurements to those, allegedly, of Cleopatra and Venus.[61]

As some of these programs suggest, with the exception of the Liberty and Garden, Kunsky theaters seemed intent on attracting and retaining high-class customers. This is explicit in a Washington ad, noting that called-for carriages could pick up spectators at the end of matinee and evening shows, as well as in a short note on one Alhambra program: "Keep your copy of the Film News on the library table for ready reference."[62] Yet one specific strategy established by early 1917 was aimed at all classes of movie fans. This was the regular promotion of the stars and feature films that would appear at a Kunsky theater the following week. The Washington was a strong advocate of such promos, often printing a long description of the coming film that encircled and dominated the current week's program listing. In early May, the description of *A Romance of the Redwoods* (with Pickford) also included a reference to "the direction of the famous Cecil B. DeMille" and "the two authors, Cecil B. DeMille and Jeannie Macpherson."[63] Yet, with less fanfare, the Liberty, Strand, Alhambra, and Garden all adopted this strategy as well. In late January, the next week's listings included Anita Stewart in *The Glory of Yolanda* at the Liberty and Viola Dana in *The Cossack Whip* at the Garden.[64] In early February, the promoted films were *The Pride of the Clan* at the Alhambra and both that film and the first serial episode of *The Great Secret* (with Francis X. Bushman and Beverly Bayne) at the Strand.[65] These "coming attraction" promotions at Kunsky theaters likely were a boon to movie fans. As was the "schedule of photoplay serials," starting in April 1917, that listed where other kinds of fans could see specific episodes of three or four serials each week at the Garden, Strand, or Alhambra. Both strategies allowed moviegoers to make plans well in advance, deciding which stars, features, or serials they were especially interested in; where; and more precisely, when. In short, such promotions began to establish a kind of efficiency system at the local level of consuming entertainment.

Surviving issues of the *Weekly Film News* continue to serve as the primary source for Kunsky theaters through 1917; from then until the end of the Great War, however, program information for the increasing number of Detroit theaters has to come from newspaper ads. From the summer of 1917 on, the Washington, Madison, and Liberty programs seem more or less standardized. The latter two theaters headlined a feature and a star each week, accompanied by other attractions, and they consistently promoted the next week's feature and star. Among those other attractions, the Madison began screening new "editions" of *The Battle of the Somme* in July, while the Liberty each week promoted a serial—from *The Neglected Wife* (with Ruth Roland) to *The Seven Pearls* (with Mollie King).[66] The Washington offered the films of popular stars around holidays: *Wild and Wooly* and *The Little American* each for two-week runs before and after July 4; and DeMille's *Joan the Woman* (starring Geraldine Farrar) for two weeks before Christmas.[67] Among the theater's other attractions, starting that summer, were the "entertainers" Emmons and Colvin and a continuing series of "pictured" O. Henry short stories.[68] In their daily changed programs, the Alhambra, Strand, and Garden all highlighted their stars in large boldface type far more than they did their films, and they promoted at least one star and feature (or comedy) coming the following week. In mid-September, among the extra attractions for the Alhambra's fall season were a *Ford Weekly* (Monday and Tuesday), a serial episode of *The Fatal Ring* (with Pearl White), a Burton Holmes Travelogue, an O. Henry "featurette," several new comedies, the *Universal Weekly* (Wednesday) and the *Pathé Weekly* (Friday), as well as an "augmented orchestra."[69] At the same time, the listed extra attractions at the Garden were fewer; as another sign that the Garden's audience was different, however, they included episodes from three different serials: *The Gray Ghost*, with Priscilla Dean and Eddie Polo (Wednesday); *The Mystery of the Double Cross*, with Mollie King (Thursday); and *The Fighting Trail*, with William Duncan (Saturday).[70]

Unlike in Chicago, very few movie stars made personal appearances in Detroit. During the 1916 Christmas holidays, Kimball Young introduced each screening of *The Foolish Virgin* during its first week at the Broadway Strand.[71] During the Thanksgiving holidays a year later, Myrtle Stedman appeared all week at the Madison, to "sing several songs and . . . also give a short talk on 'Romance and Humor in the Motion Picture Studio.'"[72] Stedman's singing is further evidence of music's importance as an attraction in the city's largest picture theaters. The Majestic not only touted its orchestra and trio of singers but also paired musical numbers with specific films. In late April 1918, Italian Street Singers synced up with screenings of George Beban's *One More American*; two weeks later, a Song

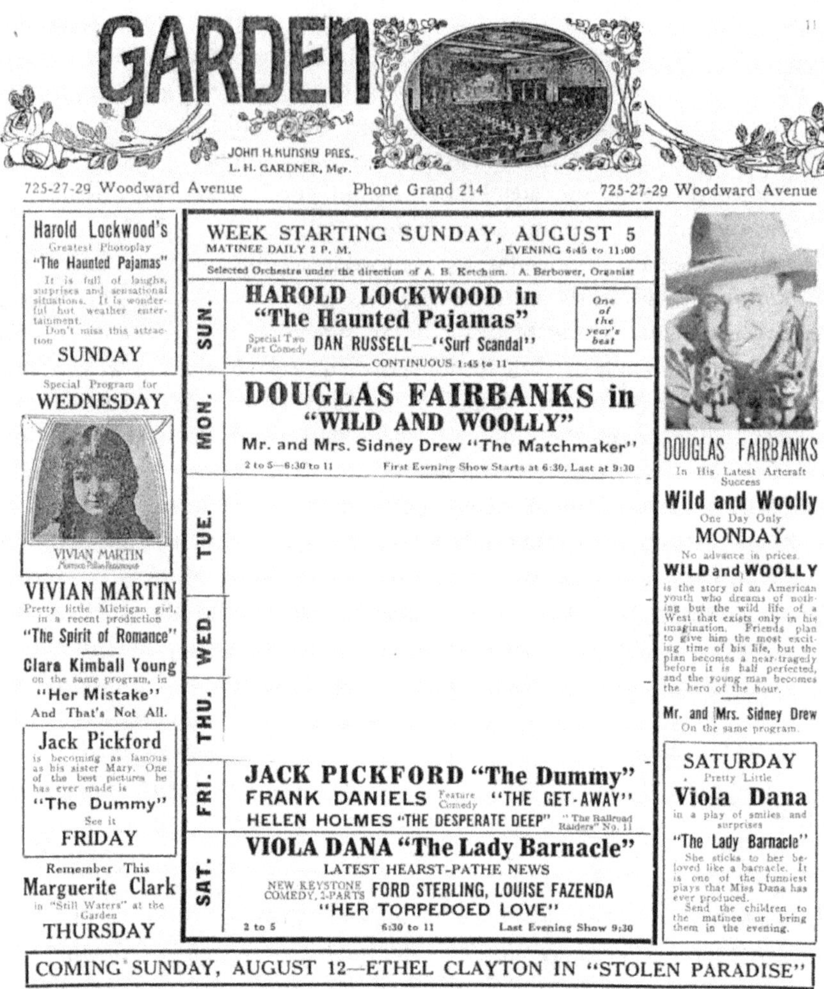

Fig. 2.3. Garden Theater programs, *Weekly Film News* (August 5, 1917): 11.

Revue of Southern Melodies complemented *A Pair of Sixes*, with Taylor Holmes.[73] In October, Ye Old Time Songsters accompanied the picturesque film of Midwest farm life, *A Hoosier Romance*, starring Colleen Moore.[74] The Broadway Strand sometimes promoted its musical numbers as much as its feature films: all week in early June 1918, Eddie McGrath sang Jerome Remick's "latest ballad," "When We Meet in the Sweet Bye and Bye"; in September, a "chorus of 60 girls" performed "a new edition of the Animated Song Sheet."[75] Even the Washington, in August, underscored its "captivating musical accompaniment" for the return engagement of *Cleopatra*, but also the theater could not resist claiming that "Theda Bara's fifty costumes can be carried in a cigar box. They will make You Gasp."[76] When the Regent reopened in early September, after resuming vaudeville programs throughout the summer, its half-page ad offered the well-to-do residential areas of North Woodward a daily "variety program" of three performances, with ticket prices of 20¢ to 55¢. Yet the principal attraction of those programs was J. Ward Hutton, the director of "the largest orchestra west of New York"; organist Wayne Brilliant; and baritone soloist Henry Santrey.[77]

Finally, in the summer of 1918, a select number of neighborhood theaters began to advertise in the newspapers.[78] In its daily changed programs, the Crystal sometimes paired a feature with a comedy or a singer; one Saturday in early July it advertised a feature, a Sennett comedy, and a *Ford Weekly.*[79] More than a dozen theaters accompanied the Paramount ad campaign from July through October. Most listed only that day's feature film, perhaps along with a comedy—for example, *Denny from Ireland*, with Shorty Hamilton, at the Catherine.[80] Others featured each day's main attraction(s), and a couple theaters included their performance times and ticket prices. The Crystal offered continuous programs from 2:00 p.m. to 11:00 p.m. and accompanied its features and stars with a comedy and a travelogue "every day" and different serial episodes on Wednesday, Thursday, and Friday.[81] The Rosedale presented daily matinees and two evening performances of a feature film, along with a comedy and other attractions. The Stratford screened double bills on Monday and Tuesday and added a serial episode on Friday; the Rialto offered feature films in two-day runs. With varied one- and two-day programs each week, the Gratiot was the only theater to advertise "three big vaudeville acts" on some nights, sponsor a "song review contest" on Thursday, and make Friday a "patriotic night"—and ticket prices were never more than 10¢. Over the course of the summer and fall, other theaters joined Paramount's ad campaign, and at least two were unusually specific. Ticket prices for matinee and two evening performances at the Lincoln Square ranged from 10¢ to 30¢ (for loges).[82] Although it also screened features in two-day runs, the theater seemed especially proud of its "select concert orchestra" and "mammoth pipe organ." The Duplex offered the fullest descriptions for its two-day programs, with tickets costing 10¢ to 15¢. In early August, on Wednesday and Thursday, the lengthy program included Pauline Frederick in Paramount's *Madame Jealousy*, Sennett's *Ladies First*, a serial episode of *A Fight for Millions*, a *Ford Weekly*, and "W. J. Dickey in popular songs."[83]

During this initial three-year period, Detroit theaters do not offer a clear-cut answer to Goldfish and Rothaphel's argument about what most attracts moviegoers. On the one hand, stars and their feature films usually stand out either in surviving Kunsky theater programs or in newspaper ads—even for neighborhood theaters. Yet sometimes other program attractions, such as serial episodes, comedies, newsreels, and travel films, gain nearly equal attention. On the other hand, many large theaters boast of their orchestras and pipe organs, whether accompanying the films or playing overtures and closing numbers; along with some neighborhood theaters, they also promote soloists performing current as well as "classic" popular songs. Moreover, a few large theaters highlight their interior spaces as comfortable, convenient environments, especially for well-to-do patrons. Although it is risky to generalize, the *News* ads, in particular, suggest that moviegoers may have frequented neighborhood theaters largely in the evenings and on weekends, except when they could spend an afternoon at one of the premier theaters.

Movies, Music, Dances, and Scenic Settings: Programming Practices to 1922

Following the end of the Great War, short films continued to bolster the variety shows of the major first-run theaters. One staple was nonfiction—newsreels, travelogues or scenics, as well as other "educational" films (see chap. 3). An even more prominent genre was the comic series, which theaters seemed unable to do without. Older Chaplin comedies, of course, circulated widely and often, but what about new releases? Here, Sennett comedies proved a reliable draw, for the Broadway Strand made them an unusually frequent attraction on its weekly programs. In April 1919, the theater boldly promoted "Mack Sennett's Big 3" (Chester Conklin, Ben Turpin, Charles Lynn) in *The Foolish Age*; within two years Turpin had become the star Sennett player, from *She Sighed by the Seaside* in June to *Love and Doughnuts* in November.[84] *Mutt and Jeff* comedies were less publicized by the Broadway Strand through the first half of 1919, but when Fox took over the Washington in September, the series became one of that theater's regular program items.[85] Harold Lloyd comedies occasionally were advertised that year, but they became a major attraction only in 1920: first at the Fox Washington, beginning in February with *Capt. Kidd's Kids*, and then the following year at the Madison, from *Number, Please?* in January to *Never Weaken* in November.[86] Also in 1920, Larry Semon comedies played second fiddle to features on an irregular basis at the nearby Adams.[87] Finally, in January 1921, the Madison announced the first of half a dozen films by Buster Keaton, the "new comedy star of the screen," after which such titles as *The Playhouse* and *The Boat* appeared later that year, respectively, at the Madison and Adams.[88]

Along with these comedies, an increasing number of special events and live acts were luring audiences. Films dealing directly with the war did not last long into 1919: at the Majestic, a short, *Egyptian Soldiers in France*; and at the Detroit Opera House, the Committee on Public Information (CPI) feature *Under Four Flags*, along with *Battle of Vilmy* [sic] *Ridge* (reenacted by "Michigan State

Troops") and the Liberty Band onstage.[89] From late April into June, however, the Majestic adopted a policy that admitted returning soldiers with "wound stripes" free to its shows.[90] This was but one of many local appeals, and most of those, perhaps as expected, targeted women. One week in May, the same theater touted the locally produced *Majestic Baby Show*—"see your baby in the movies."[91] From August through February 1920, the Adams presented a series of seasonal fashion shows onstage, "with live models" from half a dozen of "Detroit's exclusive shops."[92] In early September 1920, the Regent exploited that week's engagement of *Suds* (starring Pickford) to display in its lobby a new "Federal Washer" that it promised to "give away free to some woman patron."[93] In late August 1921, together with the Detroit Shoe Dealers' Association, the Majestic sponsored a contest for "lady" patrons with a "perfect foot."[94] That year the Madison as well as the Adams resumed seasonal fashion shows, with the addition in September of the short, *Shoe Fashion Revue*; in August, the Broadway Strand booked the *Parisian Style Show*, as an "extra added attraction [with] stunning New York models."[95] Later that fall, in conjunction with the feature *Ladies Must Live* (with Betty Compson), the Broadway Strand gave to "every lady attending" that week a free sample of the star's favorite "Day Dream Perfume."[96]

Not surprisingly, stars themselves remained one of the major lures for Detroit moviegoers, and not only in feature films. In early 1919, the Adams included among its short films *Stars As They Are* and *Photoplay Supplement*, both featuring off-camera views of selected stars; that summer, during a showing of *Upstairs and Down*, the Madison gave out autographed photos of the film's star, Olive Thomas.[97] But the striking new "novelty" for theaters was the personal appearances of more and more stars. One of the first, in late May 1919, was George Beban, who accompanied his latest feature at the Majestic, *Hearts of Men*.[98] Others that year were "9 Bathing Beauties from the Sennett Studios," whom the Broadway Strand promoted more than its Sennett feature, *Yankee Doodle in Berlin*.[99] By 1921, personal appearances were becoming more common. When, in February, the Madison played *One Man in a Million*, Beban returned to perform a shortened playlet of his famous *Sign of the Rose*.[100] In early May, Kimball Young came to the Madison for screenings of *Straight from Paris*; in October she returned to make three daily appearances for showings of *What No Man Knows*.[101] In late August, Turpin headlined the Adams's program with "a side-splitting burlesque vaudeville act."[102] Six weeks later, Theda Bara took the Adams stage "three times daily . . . in a novel presentation" that introduced the aptly named *Wife Against Wife*, although she was not its star.[103] In early December, William Desmond appeared at the Regent in conjunction with *Dangerous Toys*, but he also conducted "screen tests on the stage," supposedly to discover whether "some Detroit girl" might bring a "new face" to the movies.[104] Two weeks later at the Madison, Rex Beach, the popular novelist and screen writer, spoke to audiences during the first three days' screenings of his latest feature, *The Iron Trail*.[105]

Yet the most consistent program attractions came in one or more forms of music. Some, of course, featured in the vaudeville programs at the Regent; the Miles; the Orpheum; and, at least from September 1919 to October 1920, the Majestic. The Adams, Madison, Fox Washington, and Broadway Strand all touted their orchestras and pipe organs. Typically, their musical numbers opened and closed each program as well as accompanied the headline feature and various shorts. At times, a theater underscored that accompaniment: In early 1919, the Broadway Strand's three-week run of *The Unpardonable Sin*, starring Blanche Sweet, was "aided by a symphony orchestra of forty pieces";[106] as late as December 1921, the Fox Washington played *A Connecticut Yankee in King Arthur's Court* with the "original New York musical score."[107] In early 1919, the Broadway Strand also promoted "Eddie McGrath and his 9 Minstrels" on a par with the feature, *The Mystery Girl*, starring Ethel Clayton.[108] Three months later, the same theater paired another Clayton feature with the "special musical attraction" *Moonlight on the Levee*, performed by "New Orleans Pickaninnies."[109] After that, minstrel shows disappeared from picture theaters, at least in ads; instead, jazz became a special musical attraction, as at the Detroit Opera House in August, along with the return of *Tillie's Punctured Romance*.[110] These undoubtedly were white rather than black jazz musicians (the latter were headline acts at the Koppin): for example, the Royal Jazz Band, "apostles of jazz and pop," which, in February 1920, the Fox Washington oddly paired with *A Tale of Two Cities*.[111] By contrast, in late March 1921, the Broadway Strand introduced Paramount's *The Faith Healer* with an "Easter Fantasy" in which the theater's orchestra performed "Entry of the Gladiators" (with Roman scenery) as well as *The Messiah*'s Hallelujah chorus.[112]

Nearly as important were instrumental soloists of all kinds: cello, piccolo, harp, xylophone, and violin players. The Adams even booked one "premier celloiste," Hélène Réjane, "direct from the great Strand and Rivoli Theatres, New York."[113] But singers were the principal attraction, as either soloists or duos. Emmons and Colvin were fixtures at the Adams from early 1919 well into 1921.[114] At the same time, a consistent favorite with audiences was the baritone Henry Santrey, who initially performed at the Majestic, even promoting a revival of *Mickey* with a song of the same title a week before the feature.[115] In late August, he made a "triumphant return" to sing Irving Berlin tunes at the Detroit Campus, then turned up the following week as an "extra added attraction" at the Ferry Field.[116] A week later he was back at the Detroit Campus, moderating a "popular song contest" in which "15 leading music publishers will provide contestants and audiences will judge winners."[117] In September 1921, the reconstituted duo of Colvin and Audrey took out a special ad for their performance at the Madison of the very topical tune "When Grand Circus Park Was Uptown."[118]

Santrey's promotion of *Mickey* was not an anomaly; in late September 1919 the Broadway Strand had Margaret Postel sing "The Miracle Man" one week before the month-long run of that feature film.[119] A similar tactic involved booking a musical group whose performance could be coordinated with a feature film: in early September 1919, the Broadway Strand paired a cowboy quartet with Hart's *Wagon Tracks*; later the Madison may have booked the same cowboy quartet to accompany another western—*The Sky Pilot*.[120]

The period immediately after the Great War saw major metropolitan picture theaters developing elaborate stage settings and preludes for their programs and even spectacular prologues that introduced special feature films. As Ross Melnick has amply demonstrated, S. L. "Roxy" Rothaphel was a crucial figure in this development, but others shared the honor. Throughout 1918, Sid Grauman had been staging prologues to his features at the Million Dollar Theatre in Los Angeles.[121] In early 1919, also in Los Angeles, "D.W. Griffith staged his own thirty-minute prologue for *The Greatest Thing in Life* . . . at Jay Clune's Auditorium."[122] Rothaphel had long produced "unitary texts" that integrated films and live acts in programs at various theaters in New York City and elsewhere, but he was unsuccessful in turning that into a standardized product through the Rothaphel Unit Programme Company.[123] In early December 1919, he regained national attention with an "original" presentation of *Soldiers of Fortune* at the California Theatre in Los Angeles. The stage show began with "an atmospheric prelude" featuring "Senor and Senora Espinosa in Spanish dances . . . joined by Manuela V. Budrow, 'the Spanish Prima Donna,' together with Her Chorus of Vocalists and Instrumentalists" aided by the theater's concert orchestra.[124] And that's when *Motion Picture News* initiated a weekly column that listed the full theater programs, including preludes, in selected cities—not only in New York but also in Atlanta and Detroit, where theaters adopted these practices, even if gradually.[125]

According to ads, the Adams may have staged the first "special scenic presentation" to frame its screening of Griffith's *Broken Blossoms* in December 1919.[126] Four months later, the Madison presented a "special musical-scenic prologue" for Griffith's *The Idol Dancer*, "with the champion Samoan Hula Dancer Lily Houkelani and her 5 dusky Samoan knights playing those soft sensuous airs of the South Seas."[127] In May, the Adams followed suit with a "scenic-musical prologue" for Beach's *The Silver Horde*, along with "the Alaskan nightingale Una Laska."[128] Also that month, the Orchestra Hall's showing of Griffith's *The Fall of Babylon* included "the international dancing sensation Madja . . . with her Egyptian Nautch girls."[129] In late August, the Madison' featured *The Soul of Rafael* (starring Kimball Young) and "an elaborately staged prelude with the celebrated tenor Caesar Nesi direct from the Capitol Theater New York assisted by the Singing Monks."[130] That fall, the other first-run theaters began to stage such special attractions.[131] In October, the Majestic framed its screening of *Civilian Clothes* (starring Thomas Meighan) and live performances with "a marvel in stage lighting . . . From Dusk to Dawn."[132] That same month, the Broadway Strand mounted an "interpretative introduction" to *The Right to Love* (starring Mae Murray) and then staged "the polka of 1865" as a "scenic prelude" to Cecil B. DeMille's *Something to Think About* (starring Swanson).[133] In December, as a "holiday attraction," the Broadway Strand presented a "musical and scenic prelude" that included a ballet number, "Dance of the Hours," before its screening of William C. DeMille's *Midsummer Madness*.[134] Indeed, dance numbers were such a popular live act at the time that theaters could smartly pair them with features: "La danse grotesque" with *Madame Peacock* (starring Alla Nazimova) at the Madison; a "Pygmalion dance" with *Idols of Clay* (starring Murray) and a "gypsy dance" with *The Passionate Pilgrim*, both at the Broadway Strand; and the "dancing maidens of the Orient" with *Kismet* (starring Otis Skinner) at the Adams.[135]

During the first six months of 1921, the Broadway Strand, Majestic, and Madison continued to produce special preludes and prologues. In late March, the Majestic presented an "impressive stage prologue" for Arbuckle's feature comedy, *Brewster's Millions*.[136] In April, the Broadway Strand opened with the "Scotch Prelude Dancers" before screenings of "the seventh wonder of the film world," an adaptation of James M. Barrie's *Sentimental Tommy* (starring Mabel Taliaferro).[137] Perhaps the most intriguing of these pairings was the Broadway Strand's prelude, staged by Francis A. Mangan, which differed in the extreme from DeMille's *Forbidden Fruit*, starring Agnes Ayres. It staged scenes of the home hearth and grand ballroom entrance from *Cinderella*, with three local actors, and accompanied by "music and incidental numbers taken from Gounod's opera, 'Romeo and Juliet.'"[138] By contrast, in May, the Madison introduced *Bob Hampton of Placer*, which included a reenactment of Custer's last fight, with a "special prologue" that featured "a whole band of Blackfoot warriors and squaws" led by "Chief Sparkling Water."[139] Especially striking later that year was the "Oriental Prelude" that the Broadway Strand paired with Valentino's *The Sheik*. That prelude included an "oriental dance," the "solo dance 'Amitra,'" and "song numbers," arranged and directed by the "ballet master" Theo J. Smith.[140] Sennett's *Love and Doughnuts*, starring the cross-eyed Turpin, probably came as a blessing "comic relief" to this "artistic" prelude and intensely romantic feature. If the ingredients of competing Detroit picture theaters often differed greatly from one venue to another, their audiences could probably feel whipsawed as much as soothed by the wildly varying combinations of preludes, prologues, and features.

The precise order in which a theater organized its films and live acts into a single, recurring weekly program during this period has long eluded cinema historians. Here, certain Detroit sources offer some tantalizing answers. The most important, of course, are surviving issues of the *Weekly Film News*. Beginning in late 1918 (if not earlier), these Kunsky house organs list specific programs of

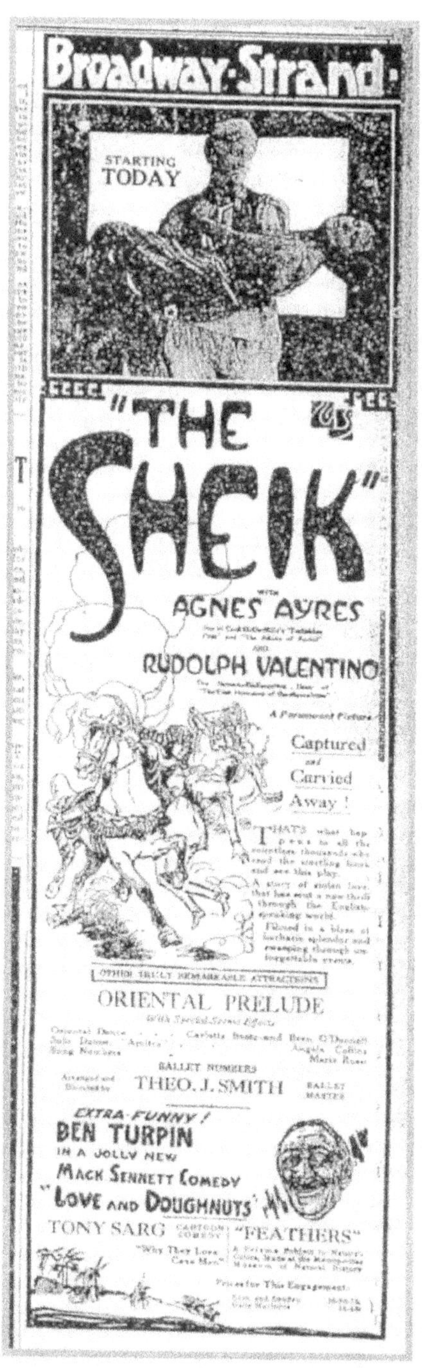

Fig. 2.4. Broadway Strand Theater ad, *Detroit Sunday Free Press* (November 27, 1921): 5.11.

numbered "acts" for the Washington, Madison, and Adams. During the week of December 8, the Washington opened with orchestra and organ musical selections, followed by the *Washington News Pictorial*, a Burton Holmes Travelogue, a tenor solo, *Quicksand* with Dorothy Dalton heading the cast; it closed with a selected comedy.[141] The Madison presented a Tchaikovsky overture, a topical review (drawn from "Pathé, Ford Motor Co. and other sources"), a Robert Bruce scenic, the CPI's "official war review," two soprano solos, *Too Many Millions* with Wallace Reid and others in the cast, a selected comedy, and finally an organ solo. The Adams also opened with an orchestral overture, then a Newman Travelogue, a baritone solo, the *Adams Weekly Review*, Ditmar's Animal Studies, and *A Lady's Name* with Constance Talmadge heading the cast; it closed with a "Katzenjammer Kids" comedy. Three weeks later, the order of the Washington and Madison programs was much the same.[142] The Adams, however, opened with an "inauguration of the grand organ"; slightly rearranged its next five "acts"; and ended with *Arizona*, a feature starring Fairbanks. In late March 1920, the Fox Washington and Madison programs again were little changed.[143] But the Adams now opened with a *Bray Pictograph*, followed by an orchestral overture, the *Adams Weekly Review*, songs by Emmons and Colvin, *Common Clay* with Fannie Ward heading the cast, and Sennett's *The Village Smith*; it closed with an organ solo. And the management asked patrons to assess its new stage setting, "under the title of 'Spring,' a musical and scenic surprise."

The last *Weekly Film News* issues reveal that the Washington, Madison, and Adams programs remained quite standardized. For the week of April 6, 1919, the Washington offered an orchestral and organ overture, a *Washington News Pictorial*, a Burton Holmes Travelogue, contralto Joan Young Saunders, a *Ford Weekly*, *Mickey*, and a selected comedy.[144] For the week of April 20, the Madison presented an orchestral overture from "Madame Butterfly," *Madison Topical Review*, a selected scenic subject, soprano Estelle J. Carey, *Little Women*, a selected comedy, and an organ solo.[145] For the week of April 27, the Adams had a *Bray Pictograph*, Victor Herbert's "The Only Girl" as a special concert number, an *Adams Weekly Review*, a selected scenic, Emmons and Colvin, *Experimental Marriage* (starring Constance Talmadge), James Montgomery Flagg's burlesque "The Last Bottle," and organ solos.[146] All three theaters offered continuous programming from noon to 11:00 p.m., whereas the Madison and Adams noted that the orchestra and organ accompanied the one afternoon and two evening programs; only the organ accompanied the others. The Madison had the highest ticket prices: 30¢ for the balcony, 40¢ for the main floor, 55¢ for balcony loges, and 75¢ for main floor loges. The Adams was the same, except that both the mezzanine and boxes cost 55¢. Less prestigious now, the Fox Washington not only was slightly cheaper but also divided the main floor into two sections: 20¢ for the gallery, 30¢ for the balcony, 55¢ for the last seven rows of the main floor and 30¢ for the rest. Each theater, of course, had lower ticket prices for matinees.

Fig. 2.5. Majestic Theater ad, *Detroit Sunday Free Press* (July 13, 1919): 4.11.

At least four other programs survive and suggest important differences between theaters, as well as over time. In mid-July 1919, the Majestic inserted a full program listing in its large advertisement for the Paramount-Artcraft special *The Woman Thou Gavest Me*. That program opened with a "Hungarian Comedy" overture conducted by Prof. J. Ward Hutton, followed by the *Free Press Film Edition* of current events, singers Miller & Dempsey, the feature, the "latest Sunshine Comedy" *Merry Jailbirds*, and the organist's "Exit March."[147] Shorter than those at the Kunsky theaters, the program also played only three times a day, at 2:30, 7:00, and 9:00 p.m.; and the Majestic promoted the matinee show costing only 10¢. In October 1920, a rare Fox Washington program reveals a program also shorter than before: the "Cavalleria Rusticana" overture, *Washington Animated Review*, a *Mutt and Jeff* cartoon, soloist Eva Tremayne, and "the 1920 cine-melodrama" *While New York Sleeps*. Shown every afternoon was an episode of the "virile, romantic" serial *Bride 13*—suggesting that its audience was less "high-minded" than before. A last page then promoted "the next attraction, Tom Mix in his very latest thriller *The Texan*." About the same time, unusually specific listings marked two Broadway Strand programs. The first introduced the record-breaking four-week run of Paramount's *Humoresque*. The lengthy program opened with "Pomp and Circumstance" as an overture, followed by *Modern Centaurs* (daredevil cavalry men), "My Cavalier" sung to Cavalier Tableaux, the Chester comedy *Four Times Foiled*, an "Interpretative Introduction" in five parts to the feature "Fannie Hurst's immortal play *Humoresque*"; it closed with an organ "potpourri."[148] A month later, the same theater offered a similar program, but with several different "acts." This time an overture of half a dozen pieces preceded *Idle Hours with Screen Stars*, a clown "bally-hooing" [*sic*] the comedy *The Big Show*, an "Introductory Setting" for the feature consisting of two stage scenes, *The Right to Love* (starring Mae Murray), and an organ number.

Both of these Broadway Strand programs are especially noteworthy. The second named half a dozen of its "professional" executive staff: house manager, publicity (Fred T. Grenell, whose printing company earlier had sold programs for theaters), musical director, organists, operators, and chief electrician. Patron conveniences included a ladies' retiring room, gentlemen's smoking and retiring rooms, checking room for ladies, and drinking fountains. A notice recommended specific actions in case of a fire. There were six daily performances: 12:15, 2:00, 3:45, 5:30, 7:10, and 9:00 p.m. The two mid-afternoon and evening "de luxe" shows included "numbers by the Broadway Strand orchestra, vocal and instrumental solos"; the other two had only organ accompaniment. Ticket prices had increased: 30¢ for the second balcony, 50¢ for the first balcony, 75¢ for the lower floor, and $1.15 for loges (reserved for evening shows). Matinee tickets cost nearly 50 percent less. Of most interest on both programs, however, are the specific times listed when each "act" was scheduled to begin. These starting times probably represent

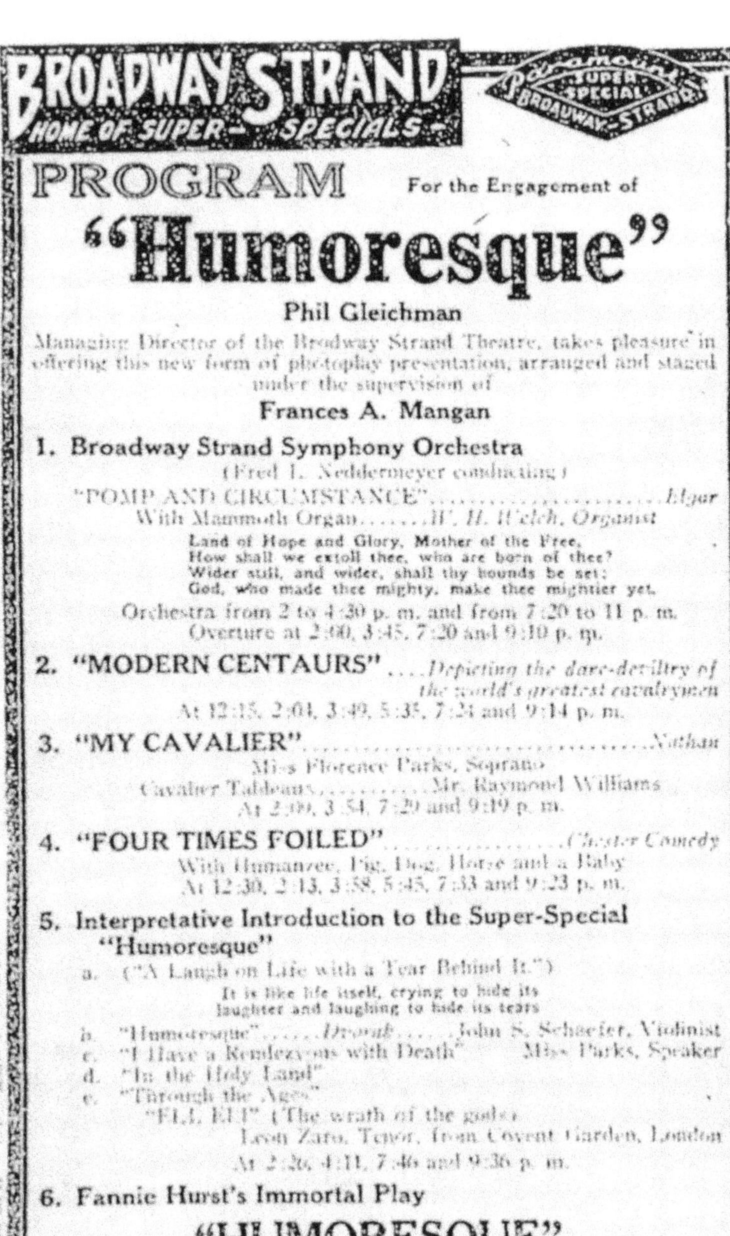

Fig. 2.6. Broadway Strand Theater ad, *Detroit Free Press* (September 7, 1920): 22.

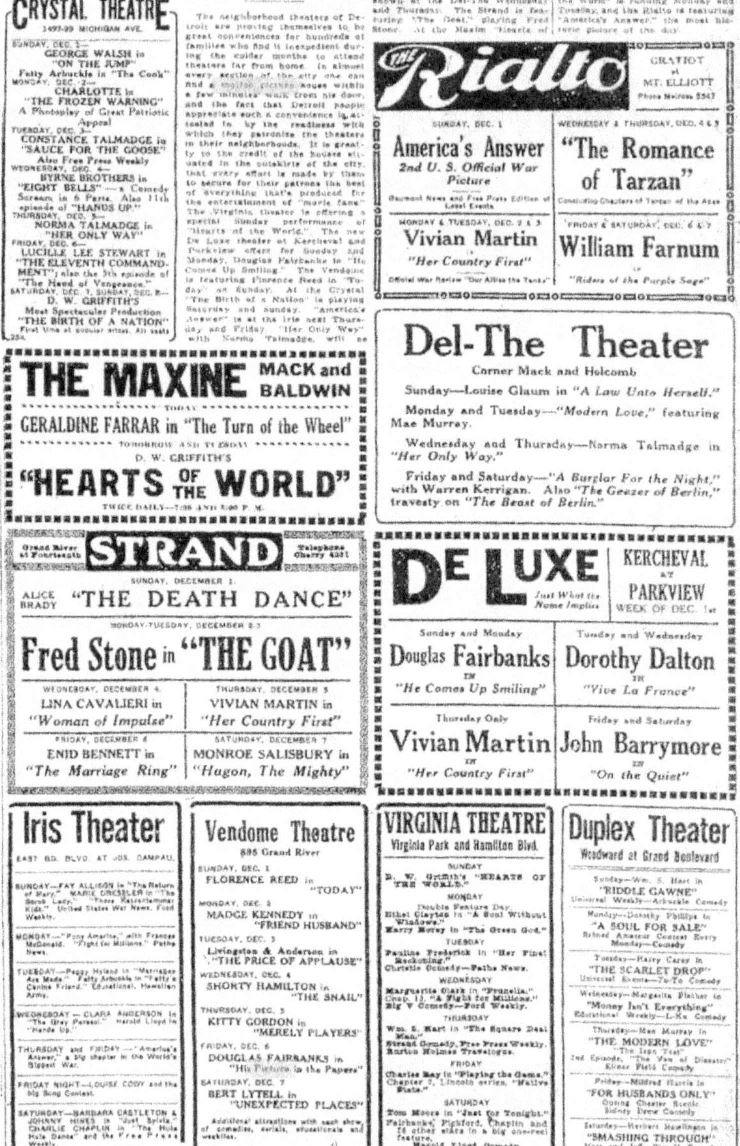

"What's Doing in Neighborhood Filmland"

CRYSTAL THEATRE
1497-99 MICHIGAN AVE.
SUNDAY, DEC. 1—
GEORGE WALSH in "ON THE JUMP"
Fatty Arbuckle in "The Cook"
MONDAY, DEC. 2—
CHARLOTTE in "THE FROZEN WARNING" A Photoplay of Great Patriotic Appeal
TUESDAY, DEC. 3—
CONSTANCE TALMADGE in "SAUCE FOR THE GOOSE" Also Free Press Weekly
WEDNESDAY, DEC. 4—
BYRNE BROTHERS in "EIGHT BELLS" — a Comedy Scream in 6 Parts. Also 11th episode of "HANDS UP"
THURSDAY, DEC. 5—
NORMA TALMADGE in "HER ONLY WAY"
FRIDAY, DEC. 6—
LUCILLE LEE STEWART in "THE ELEVENTH COMMANDMENT"; also the 5th episode of "The Hand of Vengeance."
SATURDAY, DEC. 7, SUNDAY, DEC. 8—
D. W. GRIFFITH'S Most Spectacular Production "THE BIRTH OF A NATION" First time at popular prices. All seats 25c.

The neighborhood theaters of Detroit are proving themselves to be great conveniences for hundreds of families who find it inexpedient during the colder months to attend theatres far from home. In almost every section of the city one can find a motion picture house within a few minutes' walk from his door, and the fact that Detroit people appreciate such a convenience is attested to by the readiness with which they patronize the theaters in their neighborhoods. It is greatly to the credit of the houses situated in the outskirts of the city, that every effort is made by them to secure for their patrons the best of everything that's produced for the entertainment of "movie fans." The Virginia theater is offering a special Sunday performance of "Hearts of the World." The new De Luxe theater at Kercheval and Parkview offers for Sunday and Monday, Douglas Fairbanks in "He Comes Up Smiling." The Vendome is featuring Florence Reed in "Today" on Sunday. At the Crystal "The Birth of a Nation" is playing Saturday and Sunday. "America's Answer" is at the Iris next Thursday and Friday. "Her Only Way" with Norma Talmadge, will be shown at the Del-The Wednesday and Thursday. The Strand is featuring "The Goat," playing Fred Stone. At the Maxim "Hearts of the World" is running Monday and Tuesday; and the Rialto is featuring "America's Answer," the most historic picture of the day.

THE RIALTO
GRATIOT at MT. ELLIOTT
Phone Melrose 2547
SUNDAY, DEC. 1
America's Answer
2nd U. S. Official War Picture
Gaumont News and Free Press Edition of Local Events
MONDAY & TUESDAY, DEC. 2 & 3
Vivian Martin "Her Country First"
Official War Review "Our Allies the Tanks"
WEDNESDAY & THURSDAY, DEC. 4 & 5
"The Romance of Tarzan"
Concluding Chapters of Tarzan of the Apes
FRIDAY & SATURDAY, DEC. 6 & 7
William Farnum "Riders of the Purple Sage"

Del-The Theater
Corner Mack and Holcomb
Sunday—Louise Glaum in "A Law Unto Herself."
Monday and Tuesday—"Modern Love," featuring Mae Murray.
Wednesday and Thursday—Norma Talmadge in "Her Only Way."
Friday and Saturday—"A Burglar For the Night," with Warren Kerrigan. Also "The Geezer of Berlin," travesty on "The Beast of Berlin."

THE MAXINE MACK and BALDWIN
TODAY
GERALDINE FARRAR in "The Turn of the Wheel"
TOMORROW AND TUESDAY
D. W. GRIFFITH'S
"HEARTS OF THE WORLD"
TWICE DAILY—2:00 AND 8:00 P. M.

STRAND
Grand River at Fourteenth   Telephone Cherry 4321
SUNDAY, DECEMBER 1.
ALICE BRADY "THE DEATH DANCE"
MONDAY-TUESDAY, DECEMBER 2-3
Fred Stone in "THE GOAT"
WEDNESDAY, DECEMBER 4. LINA CAVALIERI in "Woman of Impulse"
THURSDAY, DECEMBER 5 VIVIAN MARTIN in "Her Country First"
FRIDAY, DECEMBER 6 ENID BENNETT in "The Marriage Ring"
SATURDAY, DECEMBER 7 MONROE SALISBURY in "Hugon, The Mighty"

DE LUXE Just What the Name Implies   KERCHEVAL AT PARKVIEW   WEEK OF DEC. 1st
Sunday and Monday Douglas Fairbanks IN "He Comes Up Smiling"
Tuesday and Wednesday Dorothy Dalton IN "Vive La France"
Thursday Only Vivian Martin IN "Her Country First"
Friday and Saturday John Barrymore IN "On the Quiet"

Iris Theater
EAST GD. BLVD. AT JOS. CAMPAU.
SUNDAY—FAY ALLISON in "The Return of Mary," MARIE DRESSLER in "The Scrub Lady," "Those Katzenjammer Kids," United States War News, Food Weekly.
MONDAY—"Pony Amarino," with Frances McDonald, "Fight for Millions," Pathe News.
TUESDAY—Peggy Hyland in "Marriages Are Made," Fatty Arbuckle in "Fatty's Canine Friend," Educational, Hawaiian Army.
WEDNESDAY—CLARA ANDERSON in "The Gray Parasol," Harold Lloyd in "Hands Up."
THURSDAY and FRIDAY—"America's Answer," a big chapter in the World's Biggest War.
FRIDAY NIGHT—LOUISE CODY and the big Song Contest.
SATURDAY—BARBARA CASTLETON & JOHNNY HINES in "Just Sylvia," CHARLIE CHAPLIN in "The Hula Hula Dance" and the Free Press Weekly.

Vendome Theatre
895 Grand River
SUNDAY, DEC. 1 FLORENCE REED in "TODAY"
MONDAY, DEC. 2 MADGE KENNEDY in "FRIEND HUSBAND"
TUESDAY, DEC. 3 Livingston & Anderson in "THE PRICE OF APPLAUSE"
WEDNESDAY, DEC. 4 SHORTY HAMILTON in "THE SNAIL"
THURSDAY, DEC. 5 KITTY GORDON in "MERELY PLAYERS"
FRIDAY, DEC. 6 DOUGLAS FAIRBANKS in "His Picture in the Papers"
SATURDAY, DEC. 7 BERT LYTELL in "UNEXPECTED PLACES"
Additional attractions with each show, of comedies, serials, educationals and weeklies.

VIRGINIA THEATRE
Virginia Park and Hamilton Blvd.
SUNDAY D. W. Griffith's "HEARTS OF THE WORLD."
MONDAY Double Feature Day. Ethel Clayton in "A Soul Without Windows." Harry Morey in "The Green God."
TUESDAY Pauline Frederick in "Her Final Reckoning." Christie Comedy—Pathe News.
WEDNESDAY Marguerite Clark in "Prunella." Chap. 11, "A Fight for Millions." Big V Comedy—Ford Weekly.
THURSDAY Wm. S. Hart in "The Square Deal Man." Strand Comedy, Free Press Weekly. Burton Holmes Travelogue.
FRIDAY Charles Ray in "Playing the Game." Chapter 7, Lincoln series, "Wallys Plate."
SATURDAY Tom Moore in "Just for Tonight." Fairbanks, Pickford, Chaplin and 14 other stars in a big one-reel feature. Harold Lloyd Comedy.

Duplex Theater
Woodward at Grand Boulevard
Sunday—Wm. S. Hart in "RIDDLE GAWNE" Universal Weekly—Arbuckle Comedy
Monday—Dorothy Phillips in "A SOUL FOR SALE" Related Amateur Contest Rerry Monday—Comedy
Tuesday—Harry Carey in "THE SCARLET DROP" Universal Events—Toto Comedy
Wednesday—Margarita Fischer in "Money Isn't Everything" Educational Weekly—L-Ko Comedy
Thursday—Mae Murray in "THE MODERN LOVE" "The Iron Test" 2nd Episode, "The Van of Disaster" Kleine Field Comedy
Friday—Mildred Harris in "FOR HUSBANDS ONLY" Outing Chester Scenic Sidney Drew Comedy
Saturday—Herbert Rawlinson in "SMASHING THROUGH" Mutt and Jeff—Big V Comedy

Fig. 2.7. "Neighborhood Filmland" column, *Detroit Sunday Free Press* (December 1, 1918): 4.10.

another phase of efficiency management in the movie industry: they ensured that all those staffing the theater—from musicians to operators, ushers, and ticket sellers—maintained a tight ship for each show. More tellingly, the listings imply that patrons, picking up the programs beforehand at the box office, could decide what might interest them later in the day or week and, consequently, at what point they might even plan to enter and/or exit the theater. Moreover, if they picked up the program in the lobby, they would know what to expect when they did enter the auditorium. In other words, these listings allowed patrons to manage their own moviegoing.

And what would moviegoers expect to find in their neighborhood theaters, which an early "Filmland" column in the *Detroit Sunday Free Press* claimed were "almost as numerous as neighborhood groceries"?[149] If "one can find a motion picture house within a few minute walk from [one's] door," that column added (whether true or not), then the neighborhood theater was the perfect venue to "answer the question of 'what to do of an evening.'"[150] Many of these theaters may have distributed weekly or daily program sheets to their patrons, but a significant number began to advertise in the newspapers, probably as a publicity strategy to either increase or at least maintain their local audiences. The few that posted relatively complete programs, as had those accompanying the earlier Paramount ads, did so for just weeks. Among them were the Iris (on the south edge of Hamtramck) and the smaller Virginia (to the north and just west of Woodward), both of which listed daily variety shows of a feature and two, three, or four short films.[151] The great majority, however, offered minimal information, other than their address. Even the weekly listings of large theaters—from the west side Strand or Maxine to the east side De Luxe or Del-The—named only the star and feature playing on a particular day.[152] As if confirming the "Filmland" column's claim, nearly all ads seemed to assume that readers already would know or at least have heard of a theater's hours of operation and its ticket prices. The North Woodward Duplex was a rare exception: Evening shows began at 7:00 and 9:00; Saturday matinees ran from 2:00 to 5:00; Sunday shows were continuous from 2:00 to 11:00; and regular tickets cost 10¢–15¢ but were 5¢–10¢ for Saturday matinees.[153] Another was the near west side Merrick (598 seats), which had continuous operating hours from 2:00 to 11:00, with ticket prices of 15¢–30¢ for evening and Sunday shows and 10¢–15¢ for Saturday matinees.[154]

Not surprisingly, neighborhood theaters usually advertised a short comedy to accompany the feature on their programs. In mid-November 1918, the Duplex listed at least one comic film each day, sometimes adding a title or a star: on Monday, an Arbuckle comedy; on Saturday, Sunshine's *Roaring Lions on the Midnight Express*.[155] That same week the Iris offered a comic film almost as often: on Tuesday, Billy West in *The Orderly*; on Wednesday, Harold Lloyd in *Bees in His Bonnet*; on Saturday, a Marie Dressler comedy.[156] In mid-December, the Billiken also listed a comic film each day: on Sunday, Arbuckle's *Mabel and Fatty's Wash Day*; on Monday, a Lonesome Luke comedy, with Harold Lloyd; on Wednesday, Billy West's *His Day Out*; on Friday, a Big V comedy; and on Saturday, another Lloyd comedy.[157] If one focuses instead on a single day, a month later one finds that twenty of thirty-five tiny theater ads in the *News* included a comedy: a Harold Lloyd film at the Alhambra, Sennett comedies at the Arcade and Grande, and Arbuckle's *Fatty the Aviator* at the Rex.[158] In October later that year, on one day, twenty-three of thirty-two similar ads in the *Free Press* listed a comedy: Sennett comedies at the Beechwood, Boulevard, and Frontenac; Sunshine comedies at the Blue Bird, Eagle, and Iris; Harold Lloyd films at the Courtesy, Quo Vadis, and Strand; Larry Semon comedies at the Lakewood and Theatorium; and Arbuckle's *A Desert Hero* at the Louis.[159] Finally, nearly a year later, similarly in the *Free Press*, thirteen of twenty theater ads promoted comedies: a Hank Mann comedy at the Crystal, Maxine, and Your; a Sunshine comedy at the Oakman and Strand; a Larry Semon film at the Del-The; and a Sennett comedy at the Rialto.[160] Comedies were such a popular attraction that, no matter their size (from the Strand to the Louis) or their location (from the Oakman to the Quo Vadis), neighborhood theaters had as much incentive as first-run venues to book them, and just as often.

Although serials also frequently appeared in neighborhood theaters, ads listed them apparently more often in some venues than in others. In late November 1918, the Duplex had the first episode of *Wolves of Kultur* on Monday, the last two episodes of *A Fight for Millions* on Wednesday and Thursday, and the first episode of *The Iron Test* on Thursday; the Iris showed episode 12 of *A Fight for Millions* on Monday and episode 8 of *Hands Up* on Wednesday; and the Crystal advertised episode 10 of *Hands Up* on Wednesday and episode 4 of *The Hand of Vengeance* on Friday.[161] In late January 1919, again focusing on a single day, one finds that only six of the thirty-five theater ads in the *News* had a serial on their Saturday program, and two of those theaters were large and relatively upscale: the Lincoln Square with episode 2 of *Lightning Raiders*, and the Stratford with episode 4 of *The Lure of the Circus*.[162] In October that year, eight of the thirty-two theater ads in the Wednesday issue of the *Free Press* included a serial episode. Yet all of those except the Garden were small, and most were in or near Polish and Italian neighborhoods.[163] By September 1920, also in the *Free Press*, only three out of the twenty theater ads even listed a serial, yet two of those were important theaters: the Ferry Field advertised episode 12 of *The Third Eye* on Saturday, while the Rialto showed the same episode the following Monday and Tuesday.[164] It can be difficult to generalize about either the precise frequency of serial screenings or the kinds of venues in which they tended to appear, as ads became more minimal over the two-year span of the economic depression: in late 1919 they seem restricted to small neighborhood houses in or near ethnic neighborhoods, but a year later others were playing in a very few major theaters.

Whether as newsreels, travelogues, or "educationals" of one kind or another, nonfiction films were a slightly more consistent neighborhood theater attraction. In late November 1918, the Duplex had a *Universal Weekly* on Sunday, Tuesday, and Wednesday as well as a scenic on Friday; the Iris showed a *Ford Weekly* on Sunday, a *Pathé Weekly* on Monday and Wednesday, different "educationals" on Tuesday and Thursday, and a *Free Press Weekly* on Friday and Saturday.[165] In late January 1919, focusing on a single day, one finds that seven of the thirty-five theater ads in the *News* listed a nonfiction film on their Saturday program: the *Gaumont Weekly* at the Arcade, the *De Luxe Graphic* at the De Luxe, the *Free Press Weekly* at the Iris and Montclair, an "Official War Review" at the Fine Arts and Rosedale, and *Pathé News* and *Screen Magazine* at the Rialto.[166] In October that year, nine of the thirty-two theater ads in the *Free Press* had one kind of nonfiction film or another on their Wednesday program: a *Free Press Weekly* at the De Luxe, Lakewood, and Maxine; an unnamed newsreel and travel film at the Alhambra; a *Pathé News* at the Rialto; a Bruce Scenic at the Amo, and another scenic at the Blue Bird; a *Screen Magazine* at the Gratiot; and a Pictograph news film at the Quo Vadis.[167] By early September 1920, also in the *Free Press*, only three of twenty-three ads listed a nonfiction film on their Saturday program, but two very different east side theaters played one or two titles every day of the following week: the Library (399 seats) had a *Free Press Weekly* on Sunday and Monday, a travelogue on Tuesday and Wednesday, a *Ford Weekly* on Thursday and Friday, and a *Paramount Magazine* on Saturday; the Rialto (1,334 seats) had a *Free Press Weekly* and *Screen Magazine* on Sunday, a *Pathé News* on Monday and Tuesday, a *Free Press Weekly* and *Pathé Review* on Wednesday and Thursday, and a *Pathé News* and *Holmes Travelogue* on Friday and Saturday.[168] This great discrepancy in the *Free Press* between a small set of daily ads and just a few weekly ads makes it even more difficult to generalize about either the frequency or the venues for nonfiction films (see chap. 3).

Given that most newspaper ads were miniscule and live acts would be an added expense, it is surprising to find a number of theaters promoting them, if only occasionally. A few supplemented their shows with vaudeville: As before, the Gratiot continued to offer three daily acts; in January 1919, the Iris once included the "Orpheus Comedy Four" on Sunday, the "Fan Tan" on weeknights, and "two acts of high-class entertainment" on Saturday; in mid-August even the 384-seat Theatorium listed "vaudeville" in its tiny *News* ad.[169] Much like the first-run theaters, several large houses considered their orchestras and pipe organs worthy attractions: The Ferry Field consistently noted its "symphony orchestra" and "Duplex organ"; the Rialto praised its orchestra and organ's "proper musical

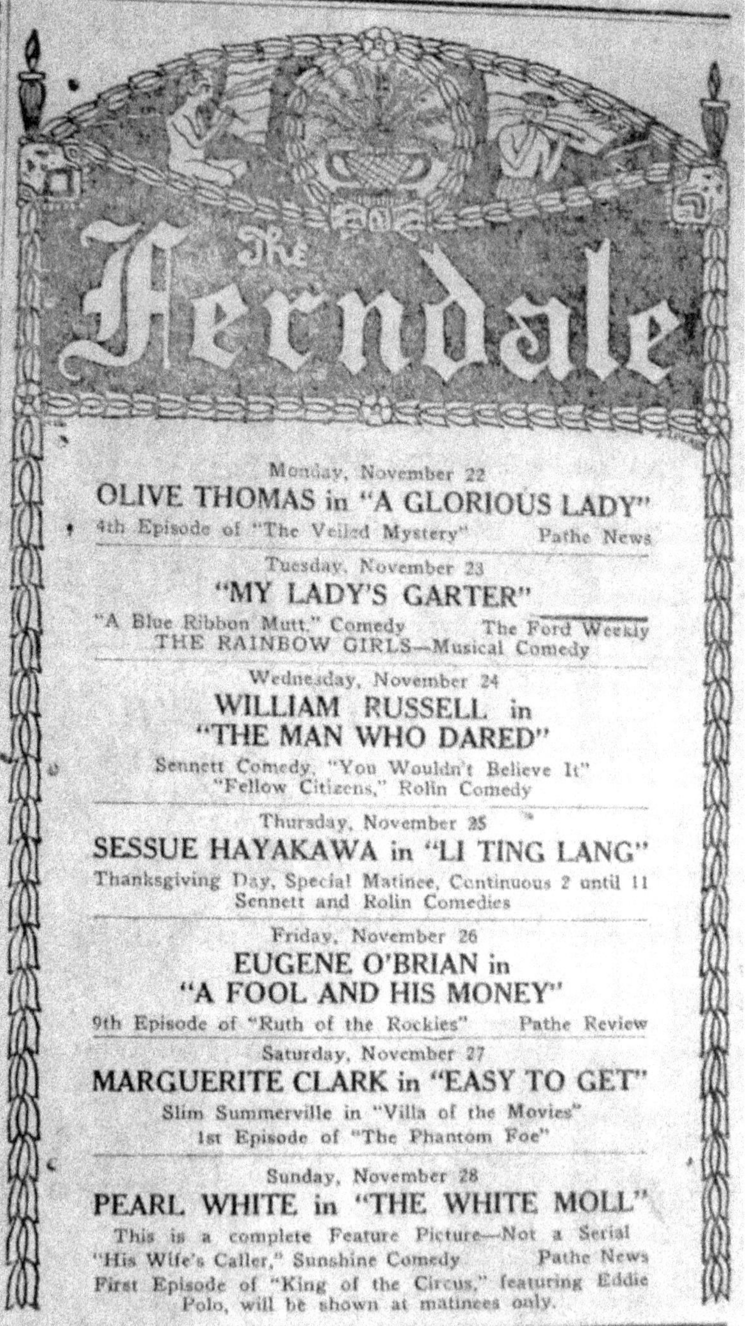

Fig. 2.8. *Ferndale News* (November 18, 1920): n.p.

interpretation"; for its "grand opening" in late December 1919, the Oakman promoted its "special orchestra music"; and for its opening week in September 1920, the Iris "augmented" its orchestra.[170] In consecutive weeks in November 1918, the Iris also featured soloists Sammy Mandell—"Detroit's Youngest Veteran of the Spanish-American War"—and Stella Duinan, then had Louise Cody lead a song contest every Friday at least through mid-January.[171] On a different note, in September 1919, the Ferry Field featured the "extra attraction" of Henry Santrey and his "New York Society Jazz Band" before they embarked on a "state tour." Two years later, the Rialto would offer Christmas weekend performances by an "8-Girl Jazz Band."[172] In late April 1919, Kunsky's De Luxe hosted one of the more unusual live events: following the last screening of *A Midnight Romance* (starring Anita Stewart) Tuesday through Thursday, moviegoers could enjoy dancing in the lobby and foyer until midnight.[173]

In late 1920, two large neighborhood theaters on the far west side placed weekly ads in the *Ferndale News*, with details of their daily programs. In early November, The Ferndale highlighted stars and their features, as expected, but it also named each accompanying short and live act.[174] Comedies played every day except Monday and Friday. A *Pathé News* or *Pathé Review* appeared on Monday, Friday, and Sunday; a *Ford Weekly*, on Monday. Serials were restricted to two days: episode 2 of *The Veiled Mystery* on Monday; episode 7 of *Ruth of the Rockies* on Friday. The Saturday program also included a "two-reel Western drama," and the Tuesday program featured nine "Rainbow Girls" performing a "musical comedy." While the "Rainbow Girls" remained a fixture on Tuesdays through the rest of the year, in late November serials proliferated: episode 4 of *The Veiled Mystery* on Monday, episode 9 of *Ruth of the Rockies* on Friday, episode 1 of *Villa of the Movies* on Saturday, and episode 1 of *King of the Circus* (with Eddie Polo) on the Sunday matinee.[175] With its change of feature films four times a week, the Lincoln Square offered equally full, yet different, programs that same month.[176] Vaudeville was a major attraction almost every day, with "Jim Dell's Song Review" on Monday–Tuesday and "Harold Brow and His Yankee Land Girls" on Sunday. Comedies were a constant, including "Will Rogers and His Funny Sayings" on Monday–Tuesday. The *Gaumont News* appeared on Sunday; *Movie Chats* or *Screen Snapshots* on Monday–Tuesday, and the *Free Press Weekly* on Wednesday–Thursday. There were only two serials: episode 7 of *Bride 13* on Monday–Tuesday and episode 7 of *The Lost City* on Friday–Saturday. This theater also listed its hours of operation: two regular evening shows, at 7:00 and 9:00; a special children's matinee on Saturday at 2:15; and a continuous program on Sunday from 2:00 to 11:00. Seats (unspecified) normally cost "15-30-40¢," with children admitted for 10¢ at the Saturday matinee.

Finally, a rare surviving program for the Lincoln Square's "grand fall opening" in early September 1921 is no less revealing about the theater's variety shows.[177] In what was billed as an "all star Paramount week," vaudeville remained an attraction, with a special Sunday performance of fifteen "clever, classy kids," likely local, putting on "The Juvenile Follies." Comedies appeared each day; newsreels, less often: a *Ford Weekly Deluxe* of "Topics of the Day" on Sunday, and a *Free Press Weekly* on Wednesday–Thursday. Two serials recurred as before: episode 4 of *The Yellow Arm* on Monday–Tuesday, and episode 6 of *Do or Die* (starring Eddie Polo) on Friday–Saturday. This program also gave front-page attention to the theater's orchestra and organ. The Lincoln Square's hours of operation were unchanged, but regular ticket prices were slightly lower, perhaps because of the economic downturn: 10¢ for children, 25¢ for adults, and 35¢ for loge seating. Following the practice of the downtown venues, the theater made a few "suggestions to theatergoers": take note of the exits in case of fire, as well as the ladies' and gent's restrooms off the foyer; "tell the usher where you would like to sit"; and, in a typical disciplinary move, avoid "talking, giggling, reading the titles aloud [which] are annoying to those intent on the picture." The Lincoln Square also followed the established practice of promoting the "feature attractions for next week": Lloyd's *I Do* on Wednesday–Thursday, and *Wet Gold*, "directed by Ralph Ince," on Friday–Saturday.

Assuming that upscale theaters such as the Ferndale and Lincoln Square on the city's western edge, the North Woodward Alhambra and Duplex, and the De Luxe and Del-The on the east side, as well as smaller venues from the Crystal to the Quo Vadis, may be representative, variety shows likely continued to characterize neighborhood theaters nearly everywhere in and around Detroit—and some resembled small-time vaudeville programs from a decade or so earlier, but with movies now the featured acts. Moreover, the more prestigious venues were adopting the programming practices initiated earlier by the Kunsky, Gleichman, and Miles flagship theaters, so that their audiences could enjoy a theatrical experience supposedly similar to those in New York or Los Angeles: "hearing superb renditions of music, enjoying the wonderful beauty of interpretative dancing, and [delighting in] marvelous lighting effects."[178]

Movies and Live Performances, to 1925

From 1922 on, these flagship theaters tended to consolidate and extend the programming practices established after the Great War. The downtown Miles and Orpheum as well as the North Woodward Regent continued to make movies part of their prominently advertised vaudeville acts. The Broadway Strand promoted its musical acts nearly as much as its movies: In February 1922, paired with *The Law and the Woman* (starring Betty Compson) was an "All Girl Jazz Carnival [of] 12 Singers, Dancers, Musicians"; in March, with DeMille's *Fool's Paradise*, it was "Barry & Milton and their 8 Dancing Dolls, a joyous frolic of song dance and music."[179] At the same time, the Madison called attention one week to "8 Native Musicians [in] The Royal Marimba Band" and another week to the "Sutherland Saxo Six."[180] In February, the Adams had the Royal Marimba Band together with the "short-reel feature," *The White Mouse*; the following month, for several days, not only stars Lillian and Dorothy Gish but also director D. W. Griffith appeared onstage to speak about the theater's premiere of *Orphans of the Storm*.[181] Shortly after it opened in January, the Capitol booked George Beban and "his entire company" for yet another stage production of his enduring "Italian" classic, *The Sign of the Rose*.[182] In March, Victor Herbert, "America's Famous Composer and Director," agreed to act as "guest conductor" for the Capitol's daily special noon "symphonic concert"—the feature that week, *Come on Over*, was merely an added attraction.[183] Surprisingly, the midtown Majestic no longer showed movies and was home to the "Woodward Players," a local theater company that was successful enough to put on a repertory of plays there during the next few years.[184]

Detroit now was important enough for Hollywood to make the flagship theaters part of its publicity efforts to arrange personal appearances. Stars of one kind or another showed up more frequently to engage audiences, especially at the new Capitol. In late February 1922, Irene Castle, then starring in *French Heels*, twice daily performed "her exclusive vaudeville dancing act with her own dancing partners and special stage setting."[185] In early May Will Rogers, with "his own inimitable act", was the headliner; the following week Kitty Gordon appeared in a "specially-staged novelty" that featured a "dazzling fortune in gowns."[186] In June, "the greatest of all eccentric comediennes, Eva Tanguey," staged a "big new act"; in July, Betty Blythe, the "statuesque screen star" of *The Queen of Sheba*, was a bigger attraction than Paramount's *The Borderland*.[187] Later celebrities, all headliners, included Fatty Arbuckle, who, after his controversial scandal and court trial, was invited to give a daily "personal talk to patrons"; Bebe Daniels, "nicknamed 'vamp of the screen'"; Nita Naldi, Valentino's co-star in *Blood and Sand*; and George Beban once again, in a stage production of *The Greatest Love of All*.[188] Other Kunsky theaters were not left out. In October 1922, Houdini demonstrated his feats of daring on the Madison stage and executed a straitjacket escape "suspended upside down from the roof of the [nearby] Fife building"; in July 1923, together with her starring role in *Human Wreckage* at the Adams, Mrs. Wallace Reid spoke about the personal "wreckage" of her actor husband's drug addiction and death.[189] In August 1924, Baby Peggy appeared at Madison matinees to "greet . . . the little ones of Detroit."[190] Among the stars welcoming fans at the Broadway Strand during these years, the most famous was Mabel Normand, who, in April 1924, accompanied her new feature, Sennett's *The Extra Girl*, and advised fans to take her own experience as a lesson in what not to do with their lives.[191]

Preludes, prologues, and special scores, in conjunction with big features, continued to be an occasional attraction. In October 1922, the Broadway Strand staged an "attractive prelude [of] singers, dancers, and unusual scenic effects" to introduce a two-week run of *Broadway Rose* (with Murray); in February 1923, Griffith's "own musical director and stage effects" accompanied his *One Exciting Night*; that October, the theater paired a two-week run of *The Common Law* with another "scenic prelude," in which, in a canny parallel to the film's story, Miss Detroit modeled for a singing artist; in November 1924, an elaborately staged "prologue extraordinaire" entitled "Spanish Nights" framed *The Siren of Seville* (starring Priscilla Dean).[192] Not to be outdone, the Adams, in February 1924, added a "special choral accompaniment" to its four-week run of *The Hunchback of Notre Dame* (with Lon Chaney) and, in April, staged a "special prologue" for a two-week run of Ingram's *Scaramouche* (with Ramon Novarro and Alice Terry); later that year, a "grand prologue" performed by a "wonder male chorus" framed the four-week run of Frank Lloyd's *The Sea Hawk* (starring Milton Sills).[193] In November 1922, the Orpheum also produced an "elaborate stage setting" for a six-week run of Fairbanks's *Robin Hood*, accompanied by a "special musical score."[194] Not billed as preludes or prologues, the Capitol produced spectacles reminiscent of earlier stage melodramas that likely were integrated into two film shows: in June 1922, "an actual race between two roaring plunging cars" added an extra dimension to *Reported Missing*; in January 1923, "live horseflesh plunging headlong across the Capitol stage" may have enhanced a climactic scene in Ince's *The Hottentot*.[195] The following October, the Madison topped these spectacles with "an actual plane race" accompanying a scene in *Going Up* (starring Douglas MacLean).[196] In May 1922, even the Iris, the large theater near Hamtramck put on a prologue for *School Days* (with Wesley Barry) performed by Cliff Nichols's "9 Clever Knicker Kiddies [and] headed by Barry's double in person."[197]

In programming the Capitol, Kunsky adopted an entertainment strategy different from that of the Adams, which initially had opened as a legitimate theater, without success. The Capitol, instead, would operate as a venue for highly promoted live performances of music and dance as much as for feature films. During the spring and summer of 1922, Arnold Johnson's "celebrated dance orchestra" appeared no less than three times.[198] In August, Henry Santrey returned with his "world famous symphony orchestra" and headlined one week's program ahead of *The Bonded Woman* (with Compson).[199] In September, accompanying her feature *Slim Shoulders*, came "Irene Castle's own fashion promenade" modeled by six "stunning New York girls" who also demonstrated "the latest Castle ballroom dances."[200] Weeks later, Joe Termint's "Eight Harmony Boys" and then Seymour Simons's "10 Syncopated Serenaders" heralded what would become a "syncopation week" series.[201] In early April 1923, the Capitol staged a "musical oddity" called "Grand Opera vs. Jazz," in which a dozen singers and "10 Statler Syncopaters" (from the nearby hotel) competed with one another.[202] "U of M Week" came next, featuring "Paul Wilson's Wolverines," and the band of twelve students

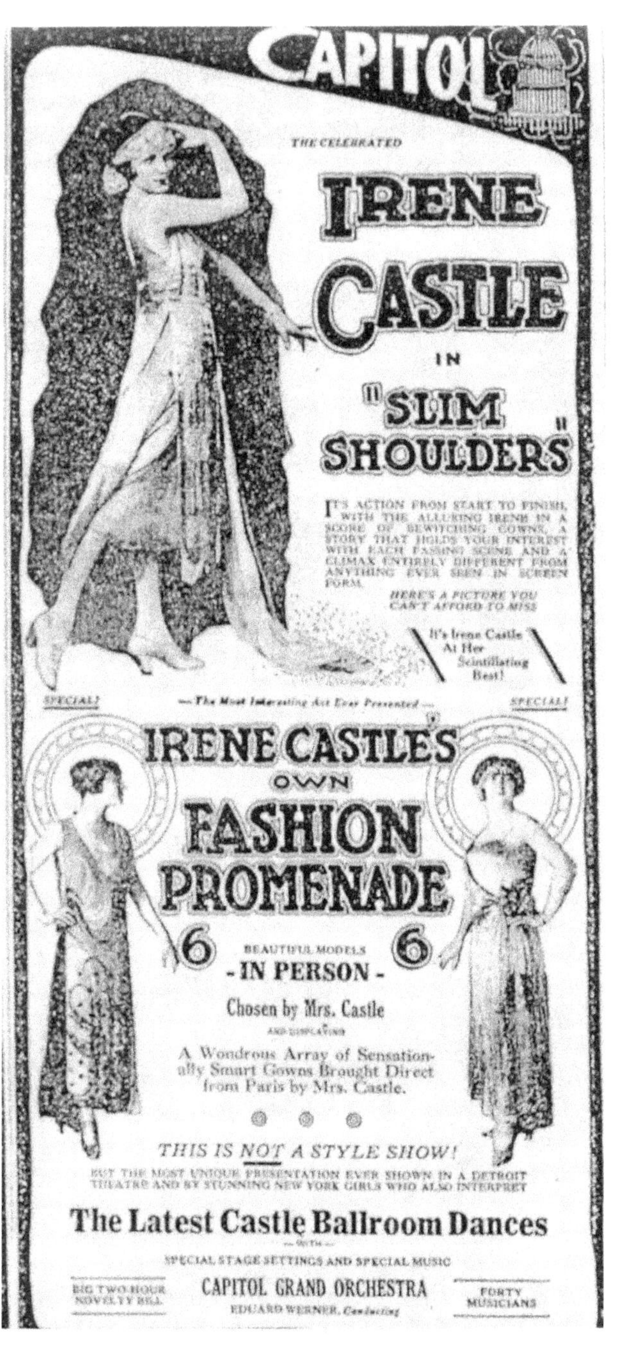

Fig. 2.9. Capitol Theater ad, *Detroit Sunday Free Press* (September 10, 1922): 5.8.

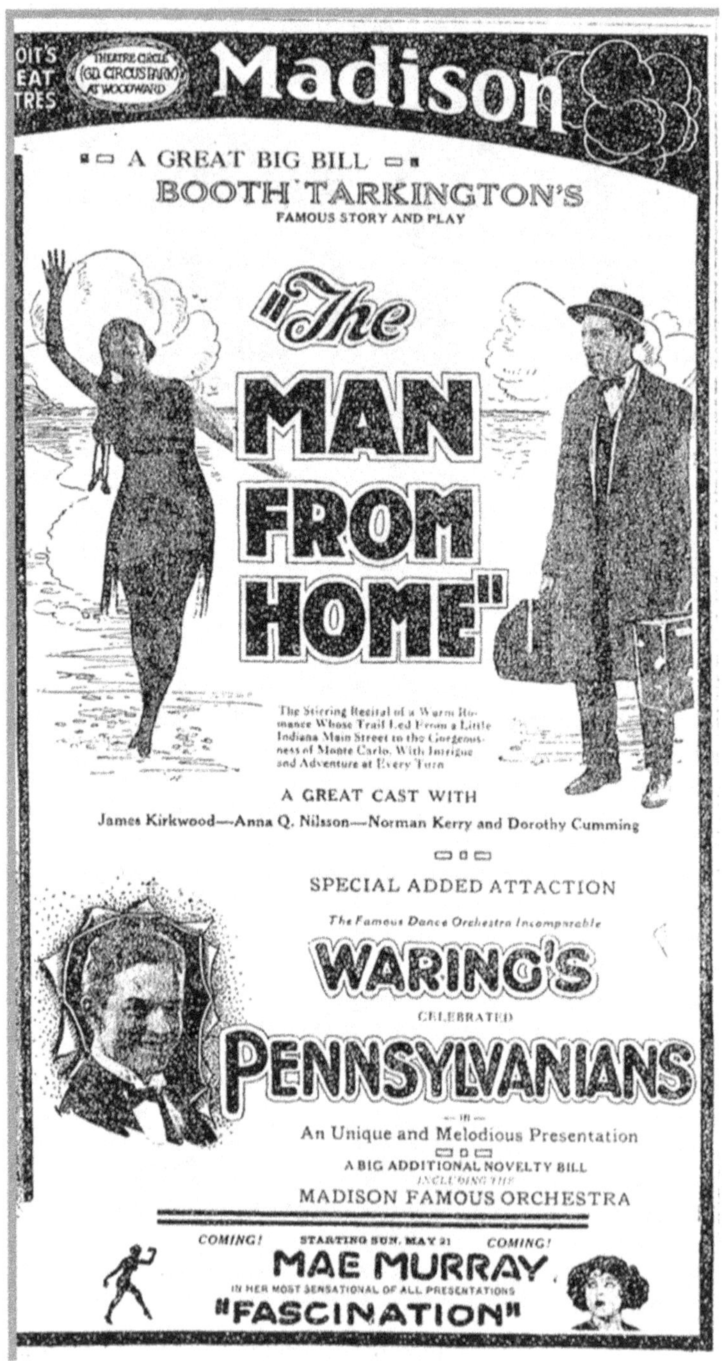

Fig. 2.10. Madison Theater ad, *Detroit Sunday Free Press* (May 14, 1922): 5.15.

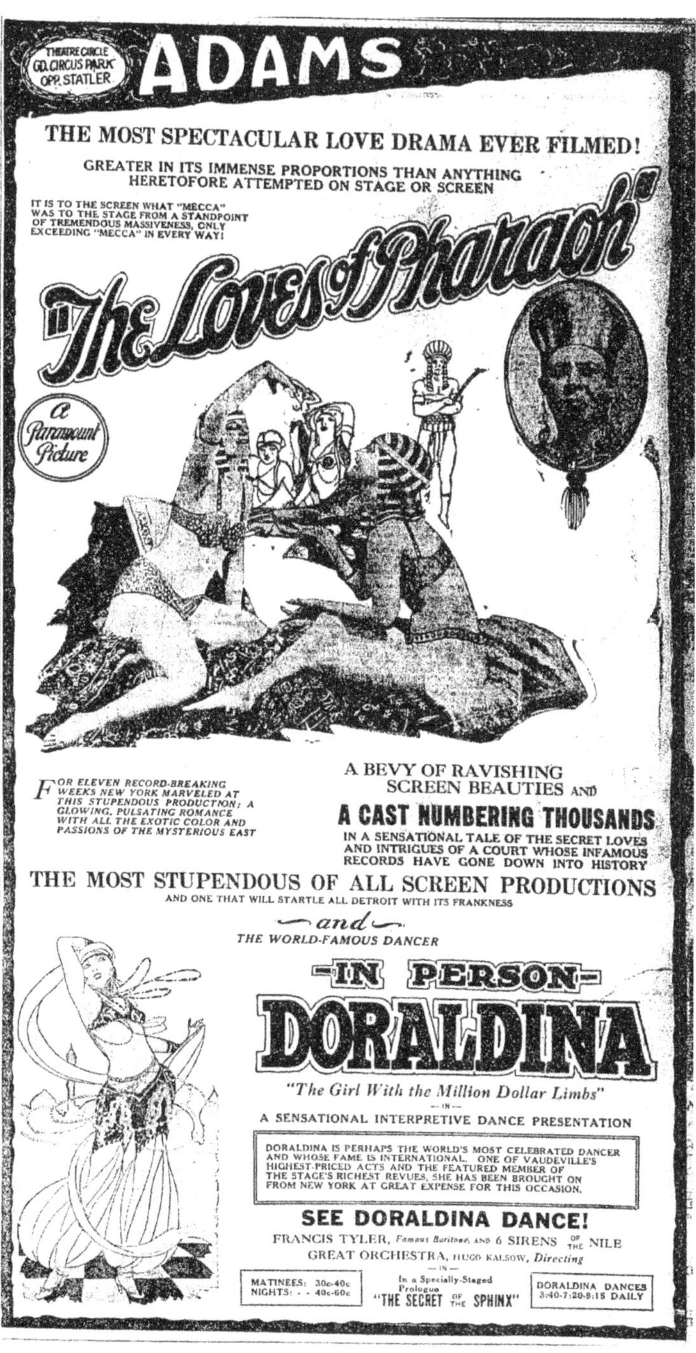

Fig. 2.11. Adams Theater ad, *Detroit Sunday Free Press* (August 20, 1922): 5.9.

returned a year later, followed shortly by Alfred Evans's University Orchestra.[203] In February 1924, the Capitol's "feature act" was Finzel's Arcadia Orchestra, the "creators of OKeh dance records," and its most recent, with fox trots, was on sale close by at Cunningham's Phonograph Shop."[204] In May, Jean Goldkette's orchestra at the city's renowned Graystone ballroom made a special appearance,[205] and for several weeks in September the Capitol promoted one musical group after another: the "6 Brown Bros. 30-piece saxophone band," and a 25-member "choral ensemble" that fronted a stage production titled "A Night in Venice."[206]

A miscellany of live performances featured at the other flagship theaters. One week or another in May and June 1922, audiences could find "Waring's Celebrated Pennsylvanians"—a dance orchestra—at the Madison, the Adams, or even the Capitol.[207] In November, Waring brought his "College Syncopaters" to the Madison for "a half hour of catchy musical delights"; two years later, the Pennsylvanians returned for a month, first to the Capitol and then as the headline act at the Madison.[208] The Adams was especially partial to dance performances: in June 1922, Vera Sabine, "one of vaudeville's biggest dancing acts," accompanied Sennett's *The Crossroads of New York*; in August, Doraldina, "the girl with the million dollar limbs," performed a "sensational interpretive dance" in parallel with *The Loves of Pharaoh*.[209] The Broadway Strand set itself somewhat apart with its focus on musical acts supported by its own orchestra. In early August 1922, the extra attraction was "6 Queens of Syncopation"—that is, "nifty girls in jazz numbers"; in April 1923, the Soli Brothers Marimba Band; in January 1924, Lester, Burns & Cook, a local trio, belting out "your favorite song"; in August, Mlle Melda Allporte, Canada's prima donna"; and one month later, "Irene Berry and her 5 musical muses" performing "hits from songland."[210] At one time or another, nearly every theater tried to attract men by showing off beautiful women: in July 1922, the Capitol constructed a "huge tank of water" for "Lotte Meyer and Her Bathing Beauties" and held a "bathing beauty contest," aptly paired with *Beauty's Worth* (starring Marion Davies); a month later the Broadway Strand headlined "12 sweet lovely luscious darlings" as 'Models of the Surf'"; in April 1923, the Fox Washington staged a "sport and summer style show [with] Martin's Famous Living Models."[211] Perhaps the most unexpected of these live shows took place at the Broadway Strand in November 1922: Frank & Seder's "$25000 Fur Exposition" created a contrasting commercial interpretive frame, lost to us now, for audiences watching the survival tactics employed in *Nanook of the North*.[212]

The live performances that characterized neighborhood theaters could resemble those of the Adams, as did the Strand's promotion, in August 1922, of a "unique dancing act."[213] Yet more often they were very different, if those in Hamtramck are relatively representative. All included vaudeville acts at least once a week, and, from its opening in 1923, the Martha Washington featured four acts all week.[214] Occasionally the Iris brought in musicians like the "Frisco Novelty

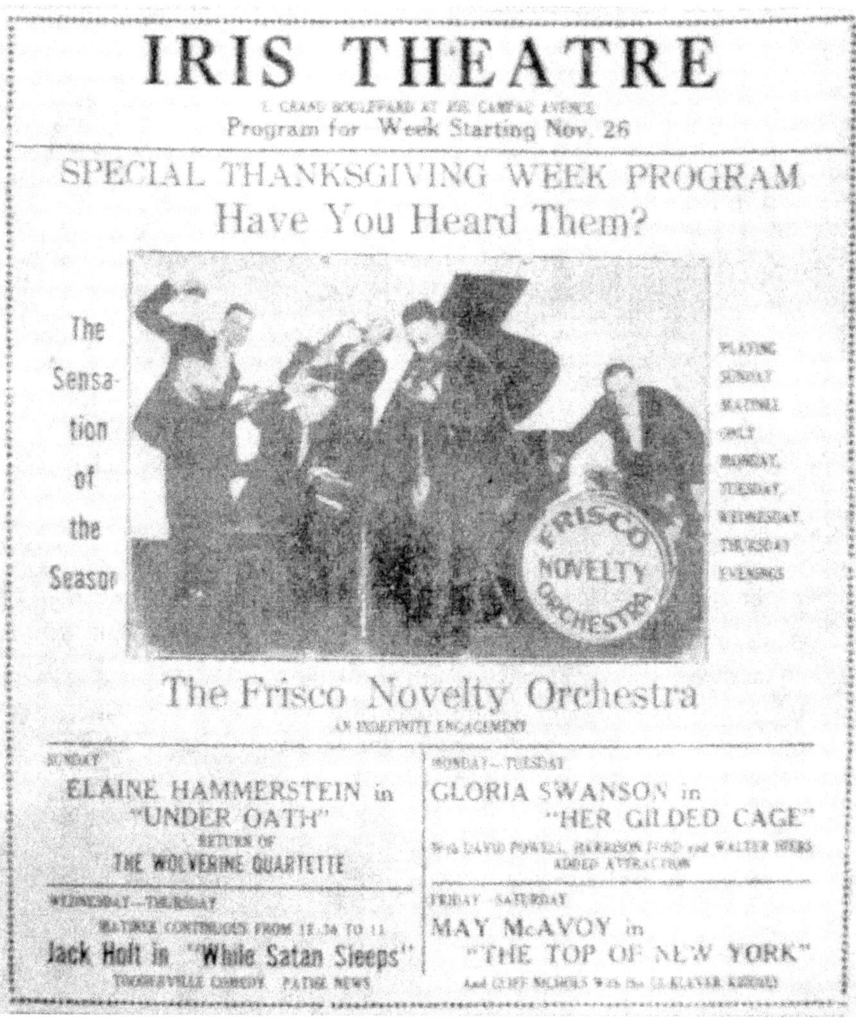

Fig. 2.12. Iris Theater ad, *Hamtramck News* (November 24, 1922): n.p.

Orchestra" or the Wolverine Quartet ("the sensation of Detroit," after performing at the Capitol), and also held song reviews and amateur music contests.[215] But two kinds of local performances stood out, one of which involved young performers. "Bunke's 15 Peppy Youngsters" sang and perhaps danced at the Farnum and the Park, respectively, in March and September 1922.[216] Cliff Nichol's "Klever Kiddies" (now numbering twelve) played at the Iris on Fridays and Saturdays through November.[217] The latter may have been a downscaled version of the "Juvenile Follies," which, in the summer of 1922, began to move through more prestigious neighborhood theaters, from the Ferry Field and Alhambra to the Del-The and Strand.[218] The other local attraction—what the New Home theater advertised several times as a "Big Girl Show"[219]—was especially prominent. No less than five "girl" groups performed regularly in the Hamtramck area. "Pete McCurdy and his Bon Ton Girls" appeared once a week, on different evenings, at the Farnum and the Park and later at the New Home as well.[220] "Harold Brow's Yankeeland Girls" featured on Sundays at the Park and also later at the New Home.[221] Either the "By Jingo Girls" or "Bessie Bright and Her 'Flappers'" performed at the New Home on Fridays.[222] By early 1924, even the Iris on Fridays featured a "girl act" called the "Pom Revue."[223] However risqué the acts these girl groups actually put on, those names may have led audiences, especially those made up of male factory workers, to expect shows that went beyond "decent" vaudeville and verged on salacious burlesque.

Among the short films on nearly all theater programs, whatever their size and location, comedies continued to play a crucial role in attracting audiences. Major comic series made exclusive appearances at specific flagship theaters.[224] The Fox Washington specialized in Al St. John, Clyde Cook, and Sunshine comedies; the Capitol and Adams, in those of Buster Keaton; the Madison, in Larry Semon comedies; and the Broadway Strand, in Lloyd Hamilton, Sennett, and Mermaid comic series. All of those—along with Ben Turpin, Snub Pollard, and Christie comedies—ended up later on other programs, from prestigious venues such as the Ferry Field, Strand, Alhambra, and Oakman to neighborhood theaters like the Iris, Farnum, New Home, and Bernhardt in and around Hamtramck. Once Harold Lloyd began releasing features in early 1922, his comic shorts could be found every week in at least several theaters, sometimes even at the Broadway Strand. Intriguingly, at least according to newspaper ads, Our Gang, Hall Room Boys, and Monty Banks comedies may have first appeared in neighborhood theaters before being listed on downtown theater programs.

Newspapers ads tell a different story, however, about the programming of nonfiction films, especially newsreels. The Fox Washington was the only flagship theater consistently to list its newsreel, *Fox News*, on its weekly programs, even if as a minor attraction. Others only occasionally called attention to special nonfiction features or eventful news films. In May 1922, the Capitol had Martin Johnson's first jungle feature, *Borneo*; a year later, the Madison followed with Johnson's *African Hunt Pictures*.[225] Whereas both of these were added attractions, the Broadway Strand boldly ballyhooed H. A. Snow's *Hunting Big Game in Africa* as its lone feature, in competition that week with the Madison.[226] By contrast, whatever their size or location, neighborhood theaters were much more prone to promote newsreels and other short nonfiction together with their features.[227] In early September 1922, the Strand had at least one sports, scenic, news, and/or local news film every day of the week. The Oakman presented *Fox News* on Sunday, Hearst's *International News* on Monday, and a Holmes Travelogue

PARK THEATRE
DAVISON AND MAINE STREETS

First-Class PHOTO PLAYS, VAUDEVILLE and MUSICAL COMEDY

Program for Week of April 16

SUNDAY, APRIL 16
HAROLD BROW'S YANKEELAND GIRLS IN MUSICAL COMEDY.

On the Screen: "FROM THE GROUND UP," with TOM MOORE.
"WITH STANLEY IN AFRICA." Chapter 9.   COMEDY

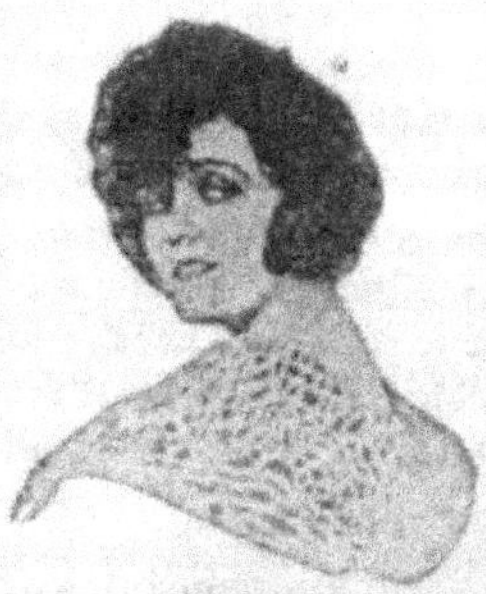

MONDAY, APRIL 17
Special vaudeville, including experts from China and India.

On the screen:

Pola Negri in
"Gypsy Blood"
COMEDY

TUESDAY, APRIL 18
"The Green Comedian"
Goldwyn Feature Comedy.   Fox News

WEDNESDAY, APRIL 19
{All-Star Cast in "Shattered Dreams"
Comedy and Movie Chat.   Also Pete McCurdy and Co. in Musical Comedy

THURSDAY, FRIDAY AND SATURDAY, APRIL 20, 21, 22
STAR CAST IN THE BIG WILLAM FOX PRODUCTION

"Queen of Sheba"

THURSDAY—"ADVENTURES OF TARZAN," No. 5
SATURDAY—"MIRACLES OF THE JUNGLE," No. 12

COMING, SUNDAY, APRIL 23—IRENE CASTLE in "FRENCH HEELS."
COMING SOON—"THEODORA"

Fig. 2.13. Park Theater ad, *Hamtramck News* (April 14, 1922): n.p.

sometimes on Tuesday. The Tuxedo showed the *Detroit News Pictorial* on Sunday through Tuesday and *Pathé News* on Wednesday and Thursday. The Ferry Field often had a travelogue or a review on Sunday and Monday, and a "sport pictorial" on Wednesday and Thursday. The Crystal listed the *Free Press Weekly* on Monday and Hearst's *International News* on Thursday and Friday. Near Hamtramck, the Park showed *Fox News* on Tuesday as well as Friday and Saturday; on the latter days, the Iris had the *Free Press Weekly*. A number of these theaters (the Tuxedo, Strand, and Iris) also offered views of Hollywood such as *Screen Snapshots* on regularly scheduled days at least once a week. Consequently, moviegoers who could attend one of several theaters in their neighborhood may have had a range of choices about not only comedies but also the newsreels and other nonfiction they wished to see, and when.

A similar distinction characterized the programming of serials and series. In their ads, the flagship theaters hardly ever listed a serial episode. The Broadway Strand and Madison played a rare exception, *The Leather Pushers* (a lightly comic boxing series with Reginald Denny), weekly throughout the first half of 1923.[228] Neighborhood theaters, by contrast, often promoted serials almost as frequently as comedies. In the Hamtramck area, fans could enjoy a surfeit of serials, particularly on weekends in the spring of 1922. One week at the Park there was episode 9 of *With Stanley in Africa* on Sunday; episode 12 of *The Secret 4* on Monday; and episode 5 of *Adventures of Tarzan* and episode 12 of *Miracles of the Jungle*, both on Saturday.[229] Two months later, the Iris was showing episodes of *Go-Get-'Em Hutch*, starring Charles Hutchison, on Wednesday and Thursday.[230] That fall the New Home joined the competition with episode 1 of *In the Days of Buffalo Bill* on Sunday and Monday, *The Leather Pushers* on Wednesday and Thursday, and an episode of *Perils of the Yukon* on Friday and Saturday.[231] One week in September, the Crystal (near the west side Polish neighborhood) had episode 7 of *The Timber Queen* on Wednesday and the last episode of *Robinson Crusoe* on Friday; in the following week came episode 1 of *In the Days of Buffalo Bill* on Saturday.[232] The "better" theaters, however, were not above showing serials. That same week in September, the Strand programmed episode 3 of *In the Days of Buffalo Bill* and the Oakman screened episode 12 of *The Perils of the Yukon*.[233] According to ads in the *Highland Parker* (aimed at upscale communities west and south of the city), in one week in early 1924, the Oakman was showing episode 1 of *The Ghost City* on Sunday, episode 13 of *Ruth of the Range* (with Roland) on Friday, and episode 10 of *Beast of Paradise* on Saturday.[234] At the same time, even the nearby Tuxedo scheduled episode 9 of *The Way of a Man* to accompany *The Hummingbird* (with Swanson) on Friday and Saturday.[235]

A relatively random sampling of the *Detroit Times*'s daily columns in mid-January 1923 allows a closer analysis of two pairs of theaters in different neighborhoods. Located within a block of one another on the far east side, the

Dawn (894 seats) and the Library (367 seats) offered programs that seemed to target separate audiences. The Dawn changed features on Sunday, Tuesday, and Thursday, with major releases such as *Broadway Rose* (Mae Murray) and *The Ghost Breaker* (Wallace Reid). Comedies played each day.[236] On Sunday, an Al St. John comedy accompanied the only serial and newsreel—episode 2 of *The Radio King*, and *Free Press Weekly*, respectively. The Library, by contrast, changed features daily and specialized in westerns: *The Lone Hand* (Hoot Gibson) on Sunday, *Good Men and True* (Harry Carey) on Thursday, *Wolves of the Range* (Jack Livingston) on Saturday, and *Wolf Law* (Frank Mayo) on the following Sunday.[237] Each Sunday, it added an episode of *The Timber Queen*, along with the *Free Press Weekly*; also on Thursday came an "educational comedy" and Hearst's *International News*. Serving Lower Poletown, the Catherine and the Luna also seemed to appeal to different audiences. The Catherine changed features daily, with a major release on Sunday—*Smilin' Through* (Norma Talmadge)—but westerns (that is, cowboy films) on Wednesday and Saturday—respectively, *West of Chicago* (Buck Jones) and *Up and Coming* (Tom Mix).[238] That week also featured comedies (Ben Turpin on Sunday), newsreels (Hearst's *International News* on Saturday), and one serial (*In the Days of Buffalo Bill* episode 11 on Thursday). And there were live performances: the local Blackstone Jazz Band on Wednesday and an amateur show on Friday. The Luna's daily change of programs included one major release—*Sauce for the Goose* (Constance Talmadge) also on Sunday—but otherwise minor features and unnamed comedies.[239] Strikingly, there was a serial or a series episode nearly each day: *Cap'n Kidd* (Polo) on Sunday, *The Leather Pushers* on Wednesday, *The Radio King* on Thursday, *Speed* on Friday, and *Man of the North* on Saturday. In either of these neighborhoods, differing by class and ethnicity, fans could find lots of westerns, but only in one could they enjoy just as many serials.

Finally, two surviving issues of Kunsky's *Photoplay Weekly*, along with selected newspaper ads, allow for close analysis of a representative range of theater programs in mid-December 1924 and mid-January 1925.[240] Much like the earlier *Weekly Film News*, the *Photoplay Weekly* included full programs for the Capitol, Madison, and Adams in a twenty-four-page booklet of information about new films and stars, gossip columns, and many ads.[241] For the weeks of December 14, 1924, and January 11, 1925, each theater highlighted its feature film and star, its "special deluxe musical program," and its coming feature attraction.[242] In December, the Capitol had a personal appearance by J. Warren Kerrigan, and in January, the local "Oriole Terrace Beauty Chorus of 20 Girls . . . gorgeously costumed," staging "A Night of Romany."[243] The Madison featured Karl Karey, "the singing pianist [in] special stage settings," and the return of Finzel's Arcadia Dance Orchestra.[244] The Adams presented its resident soprano, Lucille Burke, in "specially staged song numbers" and introduced the Wronski Quartet performing "Colonial Days," in scenic settings to complement *Janice Meredith* (with

Marion Davies).[245] According to ads in the *Detroit Free Press*, during the same weeks, the downtown Fox Washington was now a venue not only for features but also for "Big Girl Shows" like those in Hamtramck theaters—first "12 Detroit Girls in a Sympho-Dance," then "Frazier's Girl Follies"—as well as serials, such as *Galloping Hoofs*, paired with Mix's *Teeth*.[246] The Broadway Strand, by contrast, held to its practice of promoting musical attractions: the "House of David Singing Band," "Al. Strauss' Michiganders" (from the University of Michigan), and song numbers by the Aborn Comic Opera Company.[247]

In December 1924 and January 1925, neighborhood theaters on the city's far western and northern outskirts as well as in Hamtramck complemented their features with quite different attractions. The Ferry Field highlighted local vaudeville acts such as Si Slocum's Syncopaters in "Village Follies," the "Rose Kress Four," and the "Nine O'Clock Revue"—and a personal appearance once by Emma Carus.[248] Along with its features changed twice a week, the La Salle Garden offered other kinds of local musical acts: the Portia Mansfield Dancers, a "Klown Revue," and Harry Bernard's Orchestra.[249] In the Brightmoor suburb, the Virginia played major features such as *Tess of the D'Urbervilles* (with Sweet) on Sunday and *Dorothy Vernon of Haddon Hall* (with Pickford) on Tuesday–Wednesday. In addition, there were two serials on Friday and Saturday, a two-reel western on Monday, unnamed comedies Sunday through Thursday, and newsreels on Sunday and also Tuesday through Thursday.[250] The nearby Redford, which changed features daily—including *Where the North Begins* (Rin Tin Tin) on Sunday–Monday and *Lily of the Dust* (Negri) on Tuesday—eschewed serials and instead played Pathé and Universal comedies every day of the week as well as Pathé, Universal, and Hearst newsreels nearly as frequently.[251] In Hamtramck, the Martha Washington featured five to ten vaudeville acts all week, including the "20th Century Whirl" (a "great girl show"), on Sunday; the "Juvenile Follies" (accompanying Allan Dwan's *Her Love Story*, with Swanson) on Thursday and Friday; and the "Yankeeland Girls" (paired with *Open All Night*, starring Viola Dana and Adolphe Menjou) on Saturday. To entice "ladies," the theater gave out a "dozen free kewpie dolls" on Wednesday.[252] The Farnum, by contrast, promoted features, unnamed comedies, two serial episodes on the weekend, a news weekly on Monday and Tuesday, and three vaudeville acts during the week. Among the latter were familiar "girl shows" like the "Bon Ton Girls" and "Levinsky's Jazzland Girls."[253] Local musical and dance acts, from the "family-oriented" to the risqué, seemed to thrive as program attractions, depending on the location of a theater and its full evening's entertainment."

And So . . .

The archive sources for this chapter produce different perspectives—all from interested businesses and other groups, of course, and not directly from moviegoers—on the programming practices in Detroit's picture theaters. Surviving copies of the *Weekly Film Review*, along with other scattered house organs, reveal a wealth of data about first-run theaters, especially those in Kunsky's chain, up through and just after the Great War. That data includes the number of daily shows and their scheduled starting times, with few theaters still offering continuous programming, except on Sundays. It also offers the specific order of films and other acts on a scheduled program, allowing customers not only to plan their moviegoing in advance but also perhaps to decide when to enter and leave. And it includes ticket prices pegged to a sliding scale, depending on where seats are located, when one goes to the movies (in the afternoon or evening), whether one is an adult or a child, and if what's playing is a big spectacle film or an "ordinary" feature. According to newspaper ads, even most neighborhood theaters posted starting times for their two or three daily shows, which extended the regularizing of moviegoing nearly everywhere in the city.

What both the *Weekly Film Review* and newspaper ads confirm, however, is that, throughout these years, picture theaters overwhelmingly put on a full "evening's entertainment." Although the feature film and its star(s) often were the main attraction, even first-run programs always offered a few short films (comedies, newsreels or "magazines," travel or nature films, and sometimes serial episodes) and one or more live acts of music or dance. The variety show, consequently, was characteristic of nearly every kind of theater, except when a big spectacle film was the exclusive attraction. In fact, a live act could be promoted as much as a feature film. This was especially the case with a prologue or prelude that required a special stage setting to introduce and complement a feature film; an orchestra or a band (either the theater's own musicians or those on tour); and popular soloists, duos, and trios. Here, first-run theaters could differ markedly from certain neighborhood theaters: if the former hosted well-known touring orchestras of syncopated or jazz performers and dancers, the latter tended to program local talent, especially in the "Big Girl Shows" of theaters in and around Hamtramck. And these ethnic neighborhood theater shows may have offered young women a job opportunity to go along with others like usher, ticket seller, musician, and so on.

The range of programming practices, together with the spatial distribution of theaters in the city, also raises questions about audience demographics that demand further study. If first-run theaters were probably easily accessible for well-to-do patrons, to what degree were they also accessible for working-class people, especially in ethnic communities? More specifically, would Black Bottom residents attend certain downtown theaters like the Liberty and even the Fox Washington but not the major Kunsky palace cinemas?[254] How crucial for ethnic communities was the city's transit system—its routes, its cost, and its scheduled runs on particular days and at particular times of day? Could neighborhood theaters assume that their patrons came from within walking distance, or did some, especially the larger ones outside ethnic communities, rely more on automobile traffic and the major arteries of the transit system? For further hints of audience demographics, depending on the changes in time and place, see the movie puzzle contests sponsored by newspapers, covered in chapter 4.

Notes

1. "How Exhibitor Can Become 'Producer,'" *MPN* (December 28, 1918): 3873. Quoted in Ross Melnick, *American Showman* (New York: Columbia University Press, 2012), 10.

2. Gabriele Padullà, *In Broad Daylight: Movies and the Spectator After the Cinema*, trans. Patricia Gaborik (Brooklyn, NY: Verso, 2012), 28.

3. J. W. Martin, "The House Organ and Its Place in Theatre Advertising," *MPN* (January 22, 1916): 357. Martin was the *News*'s "Milwaukee correspondent."

4. Epes Winthrop Sargent, "Advertising for Exhibitors," *MPW* (May 17, 1913): 696.

5. Epes Winthrop Sargent, "Advertising for Exhibitors," *MPW* (May 16, 1914): 960, and (June 20, 1914): 1679–1680.

6. Epes Winthrop Sargent, "Advertising for Exhibitors," *MPW* (February 6, 1915): 819.

7. Epes Winthrop Sargent, "Advertising for Exhibitors," *MPW* (March 13, 1915): 1600.

8. Epes Winthrop Sargent, "Advertising for Exhibitors," *MPW* (March 6, 1915): 1440.

9. Epes Winthrop Sargent, "Advertising for Exhibitors," *MPW* (March 27, 1915): 1923.

10. Epes Winthrop Sargent, "Advertising for Exhibitors," *MPW* (March 27, 1915): 1923, and (April 24, 1915): 547.

11. "Live Wire Exhibitors," *MPN* (October 23, 1915): 52, and (November 20, 1915): 56. See also "Live Wire Exhibitors," *MPN* (September 18, 1915): 57, and (December 25, 1915): 74.

12. "Live Wire Exhibitors," *MPN* (October 9, 1915): 55.

13. "Live Wire Exhibitors," *MPN* (November 30, 1915): 59, (November 20, 1915): 56, and (February 12, 1916): 829.

14. "Live Wire Exhibitors," *MPN* (November 20, 1915): 56, (November 27, 1915): 59, and (December 11, 1915): 60.

15. "Live Wire Exhibitors," *MPN* (December 18, 1915): 58, (February 26, 1916): 1135, and (March 11, 1916): 1434.

16. "Live Wire Exhibitors," *MPN* (December 11, 1915): 60, and (January 15, 1916): 219.

17. Epes Winthrop Sargent, *Picture Theater Advertising* (New York: Moving Picture World, 1915), 83.

18. Another surviving house organ is "The Picture News," published by the Saenger Amusement Company of Shrevesport, Louisiana, under the general management of E. V. Richards Jr. This was a four-page weekly bulletin that covered eight picture theaters within the Saenger circuit—in Shrevesport, Monroe, Alexandria, and Texarkana (Texas). The E. V. Richards Collection at the Ransom Center (University of Texas-Austin) contains fragments of this house organ from 1916, with three others from early 1914. Thanks to Martin Johnson for telling me of this house organ, to Nathan Koob (a former doctoral student at the University of Michigan) for taking time from his own research to locate these fragments, and to Ginny Agnew for photographing them.

19. For an in-depth analysis of the "Weekly Film News" and a reproduction of one issue, see Richard Abel, "House Organs and the Detroit *Weekly Film News* in the 1910s," *Film History* 27, no. 3 (2015): 137–179. These copies came to my attention through Michael Hauser, publicity manager of the Detroit Opera Company and an active member of the Theatre Historical Society of America. He acquired them in separate purchases at two different auctions. I am deeply

grateful that he allowed me to photocopy his collection and gave his permission to reproduce selected pages from this rare house organ.

20. For information on Pierce, see "Casino Theatres Will Have Publicity Organization of Their Own," *MPN* (December 19, 1914): 60; and "Correspondence: Detroit," *MPW* (December 19, 1914): 1709. For information on Guest, see "Accessory News Section: Michigan," *MPN* (June 10, 1916): 3637; and "Detroit Notes," *MPW* (May 19, 1917): 1167.

21. "Bright New House Organ," *MPW* (January 30, 1915): 704. A request for copies of the initial two issues, both dated, appears in *WFN* (January 21, 1917): 8.

22. "Casino Theatres Will Have Publicity Organization of Their Own," *MPN* (December 19, 1914): 60; "Correspondence: Detroit," *MPW* (December 19, 1914): 1709; and "Michigan News Letter," *MPW* (November 27, 1915): 1695.

23. "Kunsky's Begun a 'Sure-Enough' Film Publication," *MPN* (July 21, 1917): 380.The cover of the September 9, 1917, issue is reproduced in "What Theater Men Are Doing," *M* (October 20, 1917): 835. Charles H. Darrell soon was listed on the magazine's masthead as "advertising manager," while also serving as manager of the Alhambra. See the editorial page of *WFN* (September 9, 1917): 8.

24. This second reduction in pages largely excluded "all commercial advertising" and may have occurred in early 1918, as stated in "Charles H. Darrell New Manager at Adams," *DFP* (December 15, 1918): B11. This cannot be confirmed, however, for Hauser's collection includes no issues between December 9, 1917 and June 23, 1918.

25. Washington program, *WFN* (September 3, 1916): 7.

26. "The New Madison Theater Is Open!," *WFN* (March 11, 1917): 3, 15; and Madison ad, *WFN* (March 18, 1917): 3.

27. Broadway Strand ad, *DNT* (September 10, 1916): 9.

28. "Detroit Theaters Offer Splendid Variety This Week" and Majestic ad, *DSFP* (September 24, 1916): 4.9. "B. of C." refers to the Detroit Board of Commerce.

29. Regent ad, *DNT* (September 17, 1916): 3.

30. One exception was *The Crisis*, whose ten reels the Washington screened, without any other attractions listed, for three weeks—Washington ads, *DNY* (November 26, 1916): 7, and (December 10, 1916): 3.

31. Alhambra program, *WFN* (September 17, 1916): 13.

32. Ibid., 15.

33. Garden program, *WFN* (September 3, 1916): 11.

34. Stratford ad, *DNT* (November 5, 1916): n.p. The ad did not list ticket prices.

35. Fine Arts ad, *DNY* (November 19, 1916): 7.

36. Ferry Field ad, *DNT* (December 3, 1916): n.p.

37. Rialto ad, *DNT* (December 31, 1916): n.p.

38. Duplex ads, *DNT* (September 24, 1916): 6, and (October 1, 1916): 3.

39. Washington program, *WFN* (September 3, 1916): 7.

40. Madison program, *WFN* (March 25, 1917): 5.

41. Regent ad, *DNT* (December 3, 1916): n.p.

42. Regent ad, *DNT* (December 24, 1916): n.p.

43. Regent ad, *DNT* (December 10, 1916): 3.

44. Washington program, *WFN* (November 26, 1916): 5.

45. Garden program, *WFN* (November 26, 1916): 11.

46. Garden program, *WFN* (December 3, 1916): 11.

47. Alhambra program, *WFN* (November 26, 1916): 13; Strand program, *WFN* (December 3, 1916): 15.

48. Drury Lane ads, *DNT* (November 12, 1916): 3, and (November 19, 1916): n.p.; and New Bijou ad, *DNT* (December 10, 1916): 3. The following spring, during National Baby Week, the Drury Lane theater featured *Birth*, "for women exclusively"—Drury Lane ad, *DNT* (April 29, 1917): n.p.

49. See endnote 20 in chapter 1.

50. Regent ad, *DNT* (January 7, 1917): n.p.

51. Strand programs, *WFN* (January 21, 1917): 15, (February 11, 1917): 13, (February 25, 1917): 13, and (April 29, 1917): 15.

52. Alhambra programs, *WFN* (January 28, 1917): 11, (February 11, 1917): 11, (March 4, 1917): 11, and (April 22, 1917): 13.

53. Rialto ad, *DNT* (January 7, 1917): n.p.

54. Garden ads, *WFN* (January 28, 1917): 9, (April 1, 1917): 11, (April 22, 1917): 11, and (July 8, 1917): 11.

55. Washington Program, *WFN* (April 8, 1917): 7.

56. Regent ad, *DNT* (January 7, 1917): n.p.

57. "The New Madison Theater Is Open!," *WFN* (March 11, 1917): 3.

58. Madison programs, *WFN* (March 18, 1917): 3, and (May 6, 1917): 5.

59. Washington program, *WFN* (January 7, 1917): 7.

60. Washington program, *WFN* (January 14, 1917): 7.

61. Washington ad, *DNT* (January 20, 1917): 9. Accompanying the columns of measurements were line drawings of each of the three women.

62. Washington ad, *DSFP* (January 7, 1917): 4.2; and Alhambra program, *WFN* (May 6, 1917): 13.

63. Washington program, *WFN* (May 6, 1917): 7. That week's cover also had a photo of DeMille directing Pickford in a scene.

64. Liberty program and Garden program, *WFN* (January 28, 1917): 7, 9.

65. Alhambra program and Strand program, *WFN* (February 4, 1917): 11, 13.

66. Liberty program, *WFN* (June 3, 1917): 9; and Madison program, *WFN* (July 29, 1917): 5.

67. Washington programs, *WFN* (June 24, 1917): 7, (July 1, 1917): 7, (July 8, 1917): 7, and (July 15, 1917): 7; Washington program, *WFN* (December 9, 1917): 5; and Washington ad, *DN* (December 15, 1917): 11.

68. Washington program, *WFN* (June 3, 1917): 7.

69. Alhambra program, *WFN* (September 16, 1917): 13.

70. Garden programs, *WFN* (September 9, 1917): 11.

71. Broadway Strand ad, *DNT* (December 24, 1916): n.p.

72. Madison programs, *WFN* (November 18, 1917), 3, 12, (and (November 25, 1917): 3.

73. Majestic ads, *DSFP* (April 21, 1918): 4.9, and (May 5, 1918): 4.11.

74. Majestic ad, *DSFP* (October 6, 1918): 4.7.

75. Broadway Strand ads, *DSFP* (June 2, 1918): 4.9, and (September 29, 1918): 4.7. The Animated Song Sheet was "a huge drop with bits of black cloth for the notes" for a Liberty Loan song, "For Your Boy and My Boy," and "out through the notes pop[ped] the heads of the 59 girls who [sang] the chorus." See the photograph that accompanied "59 Girls Appear as 'Notes' in Opening Detroit Loan Drive," *MPN* (October 19, 1918): 2541.

76. Washington ad, *DSFP* (August 4, 1918): 4.7.

77. Regent ad, *DSFP* (September 1, 1918): 4.6.

78. In May 1916, the Rosedale, Vendome, and Gratiot briefly listed their weekly programs in shared block advertisements in the *DNT* (May 7, 1916): Photoplay, 3, and (May 14, 1916): Photoplay, 3.

79. Crystal ads, *DFP* (June 9, 1918): 4.9, and (June 30, 1918): 4.7.

80. Catherine ad, *DSN* (July 7, 1918): Photoplays, 3.

81. Ibid. The following descriptions of the Rosedale, D & G, Stratford, Rialto, and Gratiot also come from ads on this page.

82. Lincoln Square ad, *DSN* (September 8, 1918): Feature, 12.

83. Duplex ad, *DSN* (August 4, 1918): Photoplays, 3.

84. Broadway Strand ads, *DSFP* (April 20, 1919): 4.16, (June 19, 1921): 5.7, and (November 27, 1921): 5.11.

85. Broadway Strand ads, *DSFP* (January 5, 1919): 4.9, and (May 4, 1919): 4.15; Fox Washington ad, *DSFP* (September 14, 1919): 4.12.

86. Fox Washington ads, *DSFP* (February 1, 1920): 4.12, and (August 29, 1920): 3.18; Madison ads, *DSFP* (January 2, 1921): 4.22, and (November 6, 1921): 5.11.

87. Adams ads, *DSFP* (June 27, 1920): 3.15, and (October 24, 1920): 4.14.

88. Madison ads, *DSFP* (January 23, 1921): 5.11, and (October 30, 1921): 5.11; and Adams ad, *DSFP* (December 12, 1921): 5.10.

89. Majestic ad, *DSFP* (January 5, 1919): C9; Detroit Opera House ad, *DSN* (January 12, 1919): Photoplay, 11; and Rosedale ad, *DN* (March 22, 1919): 13.

90. Majestic ads, *DSFP* (April 20, 1919): n.p., and (June 1, 1919): 4.15.

91. Majestic ad, *DSFP* (May 25, 1919): 4.15.

92. Adams ads, *DSFP* (August 3, 1919): 4.10, (October 19, 1919): 4.20, and (February 15, 1920): C12. The first was paired with *Oh Boy!* or "Girls and Ginger"; the third, with Olive Thomas in *The Follies Girls*—which meant the programs also could attract men.

93. Regent ad, *DSFP* (September 5, 1920): 5.2.

94. "A Prize for The Lady with a 'Perfect Foot,'" *DJ* (August 31, 1921): 6. The Detroit Shoe Dealers' Association offered three prizes of coupons for purchasing a pair of shoes.

95. Adams ad, *DSFP* (February 27, 1921): 5.14; Madison ads, *DSFP* (September 11, 1921): 5.7, and (October 23, 1921): 5.13; and Broadway Strand ad, *DSFP* (August 21, 1921): 5.7. That summer, the latter theater also promoted its "iced air system"—Broadway Strand ad, *DSFP* (July 10, 1921): 5.7.

96. Broadway Strand ad, *DSFP* (November 6, 1921): 5.10.

97. Adams ads, *DSFP* (February 2, 1919): 4.13, (March 9, 1919): 4.12, and (April 6, 1919): 4.11; and Madison ad, *DSFP* (August 24, 1919): 4.13. Later, among its shorts, the Broadway Strand included *Screen Snapshots*, another series of off-camera views—see the Broadway Strand ads, *DSFP* (August 21, 1921): 4.7, and (October 16, 1921): 5.10.

98. Majestic ad, *DSFP* (May 25, 1919): 4.15. The Fox Washington that year hosted very different personal appearances: Aurora Mardiganian, "the sole survivor of half a million Christian Armenian Girls," who spoke at "morning matinees for ladies only" before screenings of *Auction of Souls*, a rare film about the Armenian genocide; and Audrey Munson, "the world's most famous artist's model," who presented "a series of artistic posings" in conjunction with screenings of her film, *Purity*—see the Fox Washington ads, *DSFP* (May 25, 1919): 4.11, (June 1, 1919): 4.15, and (November 16, 1919): 4.14. For an excellent introduction to Mardiganian, a teenager with limited English, and Selig's *Auction of Souls*, which did not include the elaborate prologue presented in New York, see Anthony Slide, ed., *Ravished Armenia and the Story of Aurora Mardiganian* (Lanham, MD: Scarecrow Press, 1997), 1–18, 203–206.

99. Broadway Strand ad, *DSFP* (September 5, 1919): Photoplay, 11. *Yankee Doodle in Berlin* starred the female impersonator Bothwell Browne, who also appeared in person.

100. Madison ad, *DSFP* (February 13, 1921): 5.14.

101. Madison ads, *DSFP* (May 1, 1921): 5.8, and (October 16, 1921): 5.11. Also at the Madison, in late August, Douglas MacLean performed "nifty little vaudeville acts" to promote *Passing Thru*; three weeks later, Edna Wallace Hopper "in person" headlined the Madison's program, while

Lew Cody did likewise at the Adams in a character sketch titled "Fleurette"—see the Adams ad, *DSFP* (August 28, 1921): 5.7; and Madison and Adams ads, *DSFP* (September 18, 1921): 5.8.

102. Adams ad, *DSFP* (August 21, 1921): 5.7.

103. Adams ad, *DSFP* (October 9, 1921): 5.10.

104. Regent ad, *DSFP* (December 4, 1921): 5.11.

105. Madison ad, *DSFP* (December 18, 1921): 5.10.

106. Broadway Strand ad, *DSFP* (February 23, 1919): 4.12. The film then moved to the Adams, with the "largest theatre orchestra in Detroit"—Adams ad, *DSFP* (March 16, 1919): 4.12.

107. Fox Washington ad, *DSFP* (December 25, 1921): 5.8.

108. Broadway Strand ad, *DSFP* (January 19, 1919): 4.10.

109. Broadway Strand ad, *DSFP* (April 27, 1919): 4.11.

110. Detroit Opera House ad, *DSFP* (August 10, 1919): 4.10.

111. Fox Washington ad, *DSFP* (February 15, 1920): Photoplay, 21. For more on "black society bands" vs. "white society bands," see Lars Björn, *Before Motown: A History of Jazz in Detroit, 1920–1960* (Ann Arbor: University of Michigan Press, 2001), 17–21.

112. Broadway Strand ad, *DSFP* (March 27, 1921): 5.9.

113. Adams ad, *DSFP* (June 5, 1921): 5.9.

114. Adams ads, *DSFP* (March 9, 1919): 4.12, and (March 20, 1921): 5.13.

115. Majestic ads, *DSFP* (January 5, 1919): 4.9, (February 2, 1919): 4.12, and (May 18, 1919): 4.13.

116. Detroit Campus ad, *DSFP* (August 24 1919): 4.12; Ferry Field ad, *DSFP* (August 31, 1919): 4.17. The first ad sported a large close-up of Santrey.

117. Detroit Campus ad, *DSN* (September 7, 1919): Photoplay, 13.

118. Colvin and Audrey ad, *DSFP* (September 11, 1921): 5.3.

119. Broadway Strand ad, *DSFP* (September 28, 1919): 4.15.

120. Broadway Strand ad, *DSFP* (August 31, 1919): 4.17; Madison ad, *DSFP* (May 8, 1921): 5.9.

121. Melnick, *American Showman*, 181–182.

122. Melnick, *American Showman*, 20.

123. Melnick, *American Showman*, 175–180. In early April 1919, Kunsky announced that either the Madison or Adams would be booking "'The 'Rothapfel Program' a complete motion picture entertainment from overture to final curtain"; but neither the house organ nor newspaper ads indicated that such a booking happened—Madison program, *WFN* (April 6, 1919): n.p. For just a week in June, the Colonial did book one "Rothapfel Unit Programme"—see the Colonial ad, *DSFP* (June 22, 1919): 4.12.

124. California Theatre ad, *Los Angeles Examiner Express* (December 5, 1919): 3.5; and "Wonderful Effects at California," *Los Angeles Examiner Express* (December 10, 1919): 29. Quoted in Melnick, *American Showman*, 182.

125. "With First Run Theatres," *MPN* (November 8, 1919): 3444, and (February 12, 1921): 1303. See also "To the Whole Film Industry Greetings," *MPN* (December 27, 1919): 252. Koszarski reproduces a full page from the *Motion Picture News* column in *An Evening's Entertainment*, 49.

126. Adams ad, *DN* (December 6, 1919): 11.

127. Madison ad, *DSFP* (April 4, 1920): 3.18. In ads for Griffith's *Broken Blossoms* the previous December, neither the Orchestra Hall nor Adams listed a prelude or a prologue.

128. Adams ad, *DSFP* (May 9, 1920): 3.16.

129. Orchestra Hall ads, *DSFP* (May 23, 1920): 3.18, and (May 30, 1920): 3.11.

130. Madison ad, *DSFP* (August 22, 1920): 3.14. Rothaphel began managing stage shows at the Capitol in May that year—Melnick, *American Showman*, 187–188.

131. The Madison also continued to offer scenic preludes such as "The Forest Fire" for its screening of *Nomads of the North*—Madison ad, *DSFP* (October 24, 1920): 4.14.

132. Majestic ad, *DSFP* (October 10, 1920): 3.20.

133. Broadway Strand ads, *DSFP* (October 3, 1920): 3.17, and (October 17, 1920): 3.16.

134. Broadway Strand ads, *DSFP* (December 26, 1920): 4.23.

135. Adams ad, *DSFP* (October 10, 1920): 3.19; Broadway Strand ads, *DSFP* (November 28, 1920): 4.12, and (January 9, 1921): 5.13; and Adams ad, *DSFP* (January 9, 1921): 5.11.

136. Broadway Strand ad, *DSFP* (March 27, 1921): 5.8.

137. Broadway Strand ad, *DSFP* (April 17, 1921): 5.8.

138. Broadway Strand ad, *DSFP* (February 13, 1921): 5.13.

139. Madison ad, *DSFP* (May 15, 1921): 5.8.

140. Broadway Strand ad, *DSFP* (November 27, 1921): 5.11.

141. Madison, Washington, and Adams programs, *WFN* (December 8, 1918): n.p.

142. Madison, Washington, and Adams programs, *WFN* (December 29, 1918): n.p. In a New Year's editorial, Harry R. Guest aligned the Kunsky organization with the new city government, welcoming James Couzens as the new mayor and Dr. James Inches as the newly appointed police commissioner.

143. Madison, Washington, and Adams programs, *WFN* (March 30, 1919): n.p.

144. Washington program, *WFN* (April 6, 1919): n.p.

145. Madison program, *WFN* (April 20, 1919): n.p.

146. Adams program, *WFN* (April 27, 1919): n.p.

147. Majestic ad, *DSFP* (July 13, 1919): 4.11.

148. Broadway Strand ad, *DSFP* (September 7, 1920): 22.

149. "Filmland," *DSFP* (December 22, 1918): 4.11.

150. Ibid.; and "What's Doing in Neighborhood Filmland," *DSFP* (December 1, 1918): 4.10.

151. Iris and Virginia ads, *DSFP* (November 17, 1918): 4.7. Virginia ads lasted only to early December; Iris ads, to late February.

152. "What's Doing in Neighborhood Filmland," *DSFP* (December 1, 1918): 4.10.

153. Duplex ad, *DSFP* (November 17, 1918): 4.7.

154. Merrick ad, *DN* (April 26, 1919): 15. Similarly, the west side Rex priced all of its tickets at 15¢—see the Rex ad, *DN* (March 15, 1919): 14.

155. Duplex ad, *DSFP* (November 17, 1918): 4.7.

156. Ibid.

157. Billiken ad, *DSFP* (December 15, 1918): 4.13. *Fatty the Aviator* probably was an older, re-titled short comedy.

158. "Photoplays at Your Favorite Theater Today," *DN* (January 18, 1919): n.p.

159. "Today's Shows at Your Neighborhood Theatre," *DSFP* (October 19, 1919): C21.

160. "Today's Best Motion Picture Program," *DFP* (September 4, 1920): 4. The following week, the Library Theatre also played Sennett comedies Tuesday through Friday—Library ad, *DSFP* (September 5, 1920): D5.

161. "What's Doing in Neighborhood Filmland," *DSFP* (November 24, 1918): 4.7.

162. "Photoplays at Your Favorite Theater Today," *DN* (January 18, 1919): n.p. Episodes of *Wolves of Kultur* were at the Arcade and Vendome; episode 12 of *The Iron Test* was at the Gratiot; and another episode of *The Lure of the Circus* was at the Globe.

163. "Today's Shows at Your Neighborhood Theatre," *DSFP* (October 27, 1919): 6. The other theaters were the Eagle, Frontenac, Jewel, Louis, Perrien, Theatorium, and Wayne.

164. "Today's Best Motion Picture Program," *DFP* (September 4, 1920): 4; and Rialto ad, *DSFP* (September 5, 1920): D3. The other theater was the Gratiot, which had Pathé's *Pirate Gold* on Sunday, *Hindou Gate* on Monday and Tuesday, and *Man Against Man* on Wednesday and Thursday.

165. "What's Doing in Neighborhood Filmland," *DSFP* (November 24, 1918): 4.7, (December 1, 1918): 4.10, and (December 8, 1918): 4.15.

166. "Photoplays at Your Favorite Theater Today," *DN* (January 18, 1919): n.p.

167. "Today's Shows at Your Neighborhood Theatre," *DFP* (October 27, 1919): 6.

168. Gratiot, Library, and Rialto ads, *DSFP* (September 5, 1920): D5. The Lakewood and Merrick also had a *Pathé Review* on Saturday—see the Lakewood and Merrick ads, "Today's Shows at Your Neighborhood Theatre," *DFP* (October 4, 1920): 4. The Gratiot also had a *Ford Educational Weekly* on Monday and Tuesday, a *Paramount Magazine* on Wednesday and Thursday, and a Burton Holmes Travelogue on Friday and Saturday.

169. Gratiot ad, *DSFP* (December 29, 1918): 4.9; Iris ad, *DSFP* (January 26, 1919): 4.11; and Theotorium ad, *DN* (August 16, 1919): 14.

170. Ferry Field ads, *DSFP* (January 5, 1919): 4.9, and (June 13, 1920): 3.15; Rialto ad, *DSFP* (April 27, 1919): 4.11; Oakman ad, *DSFP* (December 28, 1919): 4.14; and Iris ad, *DSFP* (September 5, 1920): D5.

171. Iris ads, *DSFP* (November 17, 1918): 4.7, (November 24, 1918): 4.7, and (January 19, 1919): 4.11. The Billiken also promoted what it called a "refined amateur show" one Thursday evening—Billiken ad, *DSFP* (December 8, 1918): 4.15.

172. "Today's Best Presentations from Filmland," *DSFP* (December 25, 1921): C9.

173. De Luxe ad, *DSFP* (April 20, 1919): 4.16.

174. The Ferndale ad, *FN* (November 4, 1920): n.p.

175. The Ferndale ad, *FN* (November 18, 1920): n.p.

176. Lincoln Square ad, *FN* (November 4, 1920): n.p.

177. Ben Strassfeld discovered this four-page "Lincoln Square Theatre" program in the Detroit Public Library.

178. "Wonderful Effects in California," *Los Angeles Evening Express* (December 10, 1919): 29—quoted in Melnick, *American Showman*, 10.

179. Broadway Strand ads, *DSFP* (February 19, 1922): 5.11, and (March 5, 1922): 5.10.

180. Madison ads, *DSFP* (January 29, 1922): 5.11, and (February 12, 1922): 5.13.

181. Adams ads, *DSFP* (February 12, 1922): 5.11, and (March 12, 1922): 5.15. *The White Mouse* was produced by Selig-Rork and written by James Oliver Curwood—Selig-Rork ad, *MPN* (April 1, 1922): 1974.

182. "George Beban in Italian Characterization Coming to Capitol," *DSFP* (January 22, 1922): 5.9; and Capitol ad, *DFP* (January 23, 1922): 4.

183. Capitol ad, *DSFP* (March 19, 1922): 5.11.

184. Majestic ads, *DFP* (January 12, 1922): 10, (January 23, 1922): 4, and (January 26, 1922): 15.

185. Capitol ads, *DSFP* (February 26, 1922): 5.11. The following week Irene Castle's dance act shifted to the Adams, where it was a major advertised attraction.

186. Capitol ads, *DSFP* (May 7, 1922): 5.11, and (May 14, 1922): 5.15.

187. Capitol ads, *DSFP* (June 18, 1922): 5.8, and (July 30, 1922): 5.8; "Statuesque Screen Star Comes to City in Person," *DSFP* (July 30, 1922): 5.7.

188. Capitol ads, *DSFP* (August 5, 1923): 5.10, (June 17, 1923): 5.18, (November 18, 1923): 5.6, and (April 20, 1924): 5.9.

189. Madison ads, *DSFP* (October 22, 1922): 5.11, and (December 2, 1923): Metropolitan, 8; and Adams ad, *DSFP* (July 15, 1923): 5.15. See also the Adams ad, *DSFP* (November 25, 1923): Metropolitan, 9.

190. Madison ad, *DSFP* (August 3, 1924): 5.11.

191. "Mabel Normand Points to Pitfalls Awaiting Movie-Struck Girls," and Broadway Strand ad, *DSFP* (April 13, 1924): 8, 9.

192. Broadway Strand ads, *DSFP* (October 8, 1922): 5.10, (October 15, 1922): 5.10, (February 4, 1923): 3.10, (October 21, 1923): 5.7, (October 28 1923): n.p., and (November 2, 1924): 5.7. See also the "singing prelude with electrical effects" that led into an English version of *The Christian*—Broadway Strand ad, DSFP (March 11, 1923): 3.14.

193. Adams ads, *DSFP* (February 24, 1924): 5.12, (April 20, 1924): 5.8, and (September 21, 1924): 5.6. See also the two-week run of *The Storm*, enhanced with "thousands of dollars in scenic and sound effects"—Adams ads, *DSFP* (September 24, 1922): 5.11, and (October 1, 1922): n.p.

194. Orpheum ads, *DSFP* (November 5, 1922): 5.9, and (December 10, 1922): 5.17.

195. Capitol ads, *DSFP* (June 4, 1922): 5.12, and (January 14, 1923): 3.9. See also "Theodore J. Smith Dancers and the Premier Quartet," which staged "An Andalusian Idyll" in conjunction with *The Bright Shawl* (starring Richard Barthelmess and Dorothy Gish)—Capitol ad, *DSFP* (May 27, 1923): 5.11.

196. Madison ad, *DSFP* (September 30, 1923): 5.6.

197. Iris ad, *HN* (May 19, 1922): n.p.

198. Capitol ads, *DSFP* (April 9, 1922): 5.10, (May 21, 1922): 5.10, and (July 2, 1922): 5.9.

199. Capitol ads, *DSFP* (August 6, 1922): 5.10, and August 13, 1922): 5.11.

200. Capitol ad, *DSFP* (September 10, 1922): 5.8.

201. Capitol ads, *DSFP* (September 17, 1922): 5.8, and (October 22, 1922): 5.10. "Syncopation" has long characterized European musical composition, but it came into wide circulation in the 1920s, especially for popular dance music: "All dance music makes use of syncopation and it's often a vital element that helps tie the whole track together"—Rick Snoman, *Dance Music Manual: Tools, Toys, and Techniques*, 2nd ed. (Boston: Focal Press, 2009), 44. See also Henry Thies's "Ritz-on-the-Lake Orchestra" of ten musicians and the big show title "Hicksville Follies," with the "Hollywood Blue Streaks" topping five musical acts—Capitol ads, *DSFP* (May 20, 1923): 3.11, (September 23, 1923): 5.6, and (October 19, 1924): 5.6.

202. Capitol ad, *DSFP* (April 1, 1923): 3,10.

203. Capitol ads, *DSFP* (April 8, 1923): 3.11, (April 13, 1924): 5.8, and (April 27, 1924): 5.6.

204. Capitol ad and Cunningham's ads, *DSFP* (February 3, 1924): 4.15.

205. Capitol ad, *DSFP* (May 11, 1924): 5.9.

206. Capitol ads, *DSFP* (August 31, 1924): 5.8, and (September 14, 1924): 5.8. See also "The Sherwoods and their Singing Band of 10 artists"—Capitol ad, *DSFP* (July 27, 1924): 5.7.

207. Madison ads, *DSFP* (May 14, 1922): 5.15, (May 28, 1922): 5.11, (June 18, 1922): 5.9, and (June 25, 1922): 5.13; Adams ads, *DSFP* (May 21, 1922): 5.17, and (June 4, 1922): 5.13; and Capitol ad, *DSFP* (June 11, 1922): 5.8.

208. Madison ads, *DSFP* (November 12, 1922): 5.11, and (October 19, 1924): 5.8; and Capitol ads, *DSFP* (September 28, 1924): 5.11, (October 5, 1924): 5.8, and (October 12, 1924): 5.8. See also the Detroit Letter Carriers' Band, which was promoted as heavily as was the Pennsylvanians—Madison ad, *DSFP* (August 12, 1923): 5.10.

209. Adams ads, *DSFP* (June 11, 1922): 5.9, and (August 20, 1922): 5.9.

210. Broadway Strand ads, *DSFP* (July 30, 1922): 5.8, (April 8, 1923): 3.12, (January 6, 1924): 5.7, (August 17, 1924): 5.6, and (September 21, 1924): 5.7.

211. Capitol ad, *DSFP* (July 16, 1922): 5.9; Broadway Strand ad, *DSFP* (August 13, 1922): 5.11; Fox Washington ad, *DSFP* (April 22, 1923): 3.8.

212. Broadway Strand ad, *DSFP* (September 17, 1922): 5.9.

213. "Movies at Your Favorite Theaters," *DT* (August 15, 1922): 4.

214. Martha Washington ad, *HN* (September 14, 1923): n.p.

215. Iris ads, *HN* (March 3, 1922): n.p., (November 3, 1922): n.p., (November 24, 1922): n.p., (January 9, 1923): n.p., and (January 11, 1924): n.p.

216. Farnum ad, *HN* (March 3, 1922): n.p.; Park ad, *HN* (September 1, 1922): n.p.

217. Iris ads, *HN* (November 3, 1922): n.p., (November 10, 1922): n.p., (November 17, 1922): n.p., and (November 24, 1922), n.p.

218. Ferry Field ad, *DT* (June 2, 1922).

219. New Home ads, *HN* (September 1, 1922): n.p., (September 15, 1922): n.p., and (September 7, 1923): n.p.

220. Farnum ads, *HN* (March 3, 1922): n.p., (March 10, 1922): n.p., and (March 17, 1922): n.p.; Park ads, *HN* (March 10, 1922): n.p., (March 17, 1922): n.p., and April 7, 1922): n.p.; and New Home ad, *HN* (September 3, 1922): n.p.

221. Park ad, *HN* (March 17, 1922): n.p.; New Home ad, *HN* (May 23, 1923): n.p.

222. New Home ads, *HN* (September 8, 1922): n.p.; and (September 22, 1922): n.p. The "By Jingo Girls" also reappeared at the Farnum one Tuesday—Farnum ad, *HN* (September 15, 1922): n.p.

223. Iris ad, *HN* (January 11, 1924): n.p.

224. Rather than referencing these comedies individually, the following information comes from extensive theater ads in the *Detroit Sunday Free Press, Detroit Times, Hamtramck News,* and *Highland Parker* from 1922 through 1924.

225. Capitol ad, *DSFP* (April 30, 1922): 5.6; Madison ad, *DSFP* (May 6, 1923): 3.10.

226. Broadway Strand ad, *DSFP* (May 6, 1923): 3.10. In August 1923, the Madison printed a small listing for news film of President Harding's funeral; in October, it had the "first Detroit showing [of] *Japanese Quake Pictures*"—Madison ads, *DSFP* (August 12, 1923): 5.10, and (September 30, 1923): 5.6.

227. The following specific information comes from the daily "Movies at Your Favorite Theaters" column in the *Detroit News,* between September 4 and 17, 1922, as well as the Iris and Park ads in the *Hamtramck News,* between September 1 and 15, 1922.

228. Broadway Strand ad, *DSFP* (January 28, 1923): 3.10; and Madison ad, *DSFP* (June 3, 1923): 3.17.

229. Park ad, *HN* (April 14, 1922): n.p. That same week the Farnum had episode 8 of *Miracles of the Jungle* on Friday and Saturday—Farnum ad, *HN* (March 10, 1922): n.p.

230. Iris ads, *HN* (May 12, 1922): n.p., (May 19, 1922): n.p., and (May 19, 1922): n.p.

231. New Home ad, *HN* (September 8, 1922): n.p.

232. Crystal ads, *DT* (September 6, 1922): 10, (September 8, 1922): 20, and (September 16, 1922): 5. The east side Your showed the same episode of *The Timber Queen,* but on Thursday, September 7.

233. Strand and Oakman ads, *DN* (September 16, 1922): 5. Just weeks before, the Strand also included a "unique dancing act" on Wednesday, its "double feature day"—Strand ad, *DN* (August 15, 1922): 4.

234. Oakman ad, *HP* (March 26, 1924): n.p.

235. Tuxedo ad, *HP* (March 19, 1924): n.p.

236. Dawn ads, *DT* (January 7, 1923): 3.4, (January 10, 1923): 11, (January 11, 1923): 19, (January 12, 1923): 21, (January 13, 1923): 5, and (January 14, 1923): 7.4.

237. Library ads, op. cit.

238. Catherine ads, op. cit.

239. Luna ads, op. cit.

240. *The Photoplay Weekly* issues are dated December 14, 1924, and January 11, 1925. Thanks to Ben Strassfeld for discovering these rare programs in the Detroit Historical Society Library.

241. *The Photoplay Weekly* was published by Douglas Printing and edited by Howard O. Pierce, general press representative of the Kunsky Publicity department. The ads targeted

an upscale clientele: clothing stores (furs, gloves, lingerie, shoes), a hotel, a ballroom, and a café—and Belcano Facial, with a testimonial by Mary Pickford.

242. All three theaters also listed their Executive Staff and General Staff. The Capitol and Madison listed a supervising manager, house manager, and music director; the Adams, only its manager and musical director. The Capitol also had a chief technician and stage director, chief electrician, orchestral conductor, two organists, two projectionists, and master scenic artist (shared with the other two theaters); the Madison, an orchestral conductor, stage director, chief electrician, two organists (including Marguerite Werner), and two projectionists; the Adams, a manager and musical director as well as a house manager, assistant house manager, orchestral conductor, stage director, two organists, and two projectionists.

243. Capitol programs, *PW* (December 14, 1924): 11, and (January 11, 1925): 11. The Capitol also showed the *Detroit News Pictorial*.

244. Madison programs, *PW* (December 14, 1924): 12, and (January 11, 1925): 12. The Madison also showed the *Detroit News Pictorial*.

245. Adams programs, *PW* (December 14, 1924): 13, and (January 11, 1925): 13. Among its "short screen subjects," the Adam listed only *Kinograms*.

246. Fox Washington ads, *DSFP* (December 7, 1924): 4.21, (December 14, 1924): 5.7, and (January 11, 1925): 5.7.

247. Broadway Strand ads, *DSFP* (December 7, 1924): 4.21, (December 14, 1924): 5.7, and (January 11, 1925): 5.7.

248. Ferry Field ads, *DSFP* (December 7, 1924): 4.19, (December 14, 1924): 5.5, and (January 11, 1925): 5.7.

249. La Salle Garden ads, *DSFP* (December 7, 1924): 4.19, (December 14, 1924): 5.5, and (January 11, 1925): 5.5.

250. Virginia ad, *BJ* (January 15, 1925): n.p.

251. Redford ad, *BJ* (January 15, 1925): n.p.

252. Martha Washington ad, *HN* (December 12, 1924): n.p.

253. Farnum ads, *HN* (December 12, 1924): n.p., and (January 9, 1925): n.p.

254. Further research could determine whether city laws mandated segregated theater seating or whether certain theaters had their own segregated seating policies.

ENTR'ACTE 4

Detroit-Made Films

NONE OF THE CITY'S MAJOR PLAYERS IN THE movie business seem to have considered going into film production, especially feature film production—probably with good reason. In the summer of 1918, H. N. Nelson Attractions briefly ventured beyond its usual nonfiction production with a film initially titled *Red Harrigan*.[1] Later retitled *The Mysterious Mr. Browning*, it featured a few professionals like Paul Panzer (a lead actor in *The Perils of Pauline*) and "many well-known Detroiters."[2] Contrasting "Grosse Pointe's Palatial Residences" with "tenements of the east side," according to an ad, the film played at the Washington, but for only one week. In early 1921, however, Frank L. Talbot, who allegedly had managed several production studios in New York, Boston, and Buffalo, convinced half a dozen Detroit men to join him in forming the Detroit-Made Film Corporation.[3] They included vice president Edward C. Vernier (from a long-time family in Grosse Pointe), secretary Frank C. Cooke (a newspaperman), and members of the board of directors: Jimmy Hodges (a former Orpheum performer), Edward O. Chase (a contractor and builder), Rilla McLain (proprietor of the Palace Gardens amusement park), and architect Joseph G. Rastier.

The company's initial production, entitled *The First Woman*, was written and directed by Glenn Lyons and starred professionals Mildred Harris and Percy Marmont as well as many local actors.[4] Among the locations for shooting were a doctor's residence in Grosse Pointe, the Ritz café, the Fellowcraft Club, the Masonic Temple, and Labadie's Island. *The First Woman* premiered at the Shubert Detroit to appreciative audiences, but its distribution and exhibition are uncertain.[5]

In March 1922, Talbot's company—now the Detroit Motion Picture Corporation—began building a production studio on Vernier Road, north of Jefferson Avenue, in Grosse Pointe. Supposedly, the studio was to have been completed by November 1922, but there is no information to confirm that.[6] In the meantime, the renamed company announced production of another film that summer. Initially titled *Mary*, its presumed stars were Miriam Cooper, Conway Tearle, and Martha Mansfield.[7] But production actually did not begin until late 1923, with a different director, writer, and cameraman and new players, and the

Fig. EA4.1. Shubert Detroit Theater ad, *Detroit Times* (June 3, 1922): 4.

film still was being edited in February 1924.[8] Despite a lawsuit brought by a local actress who charged that the company had reneged on having her star in the film, in December 1923 Talbot supposedly was negotiating with the writer, James Oliver Curwood, for film rights to one of his stories.[9] A tongue-in-cheek newspaper article reported that Talbot was thinking about giving this second film "a snappier name" like *Naked Souls*, "something with a punch and a whallop."[10] But *Mary* proved a financial disaster that made front-page news. After its brief showing in Detroit, no one could be interested to invest in its distribution and further exhibition.[11]

In September 1924, Talbot resigned as the company's president, and the Detroit Motion Picture Corporation filed for bankruptcy.[12] At the same time, in a double blow, Talbot's wife also filed for divorce.[13]

This ballyhooed boom-and-bust story is a familiar one about people unwisely tempted by the lure of easy money in the early movie business. And it must have played out in other cities, even those more favorably disposed to feature filmmaking than was a northern city like Detroit.

Notes

1. Rex G. White, "It's a Wild Life, Making Movies in Detroit," *DSN* (August 4, 1918): Feature, 7; and "First Detroit Made Feature Is Completed," *DSN* (August 4, 1918): 5.1. A Detroit woman supposedly wrote the scenario, and the principal local actors were Edna Mason and Walter Miller.

2. "Made-in-Detroit Picture Play Is Local Feature," and Washington ad, *DSFP* (December 15, 1918): 4.11, 4.12. See also Harold Hefferman, "Detroit Made Picture on Screen This Week," *DSN* (December 15, 1918): 5.1.

3. "Detroit Company Buys Grosse Pointe Site for Erection of Moving Picture Studio," *DSFP* (March 26, 1922): 5.9.

4. "Home Folks Like Detroit Film Play," *DFP* (June 5, 1922): 9. Several production photos appeared in the "Rotogravure Supplement," *DSFP* (December 11, 1921): 5. The final decree in Chaplin's divorce case with Harris had recently been announced—"Final Chaplin Divorce Decree Handed Down," *DFP* (November 17, 1921): 12.

5. Shubert Detroit ad, *DT* (June 3, 1922): 4.

6. "Detroit Company Will Be Making Motion Pictures in Few Weeks," *DSFP* (October 22, 1922): 5.10; "Rushing Work on Picture Studio Screening to Start November One," *DSFP* (September 17, 1922): 5.8.

7. "Work Starts Monday on Second Photoplay to Be Made in Detroit," *DSFP* (June 4, 1922): 5.13.

8. "Skilled Photographer Is Signed by Detroit's Motion Picture Company," *DSFP* (April 29, 1923): 3.9; "Detroit Motion Picture Company Engages Director and Writers," *DSFP* (July 22, 1923): 5.10; "Sets Erected for First Play by City's New Producing Company," *DSFP* (September 30, 1923): Feature, 6; "Stars in City, Filming Starts at Detroit Studio," *DSFP* (November 4, 1923): 3.1; "Snake Charmer Dance Features Closing Scene of Detroit Film," *DSFP* (December 23, 1923): 4.6; "Detroit Soon to See Home-Made Picture," *DFP* (February 14, 1924): 11.

9. "Holds Her Avoirdupois Worth $40 per Pound," *DFP* (October 19, 1923): 2.1; Roy Marcotte, "The Reel Players," *DFP* (December 7, 1923): 24.

10. "'Mary' May Be Called 'Naked Souls;' Name Is Demure, Is Belief," *DSFP* (February 24, 1924): 1.

11. "Film Company's Debts $131,000," *DFP* (September 13, 1924): 1.

12. Ibid.

13. "Mrs. Talbot May Sue for Divorce, Is Hint," *DFP* (September 27, 1924): 1.

ENTR'ACTE 5

The Metropolitan Film Company

THE METROPOLITAN FILM COMPANY WAS ONE OF TWO local film production firms; the other, H. N. Nelson Attractions, specialized in industrial
and advertising films.[1] Apparently founded in early 1917 by M. S. Bailey and
M. J. Caplan, Metropolitan quickly became well known in the city for "making
titles, slides, and special films for theaters."[2] A year later, the *Detroit Free Press*
worked out a contract with Metropolitan to produce and release a local newsreel,
the *Detroit Free Press Film Edition*, whose first issue appeared on March 17, 1918.
By then, "Cappy" Caplan was the sole manager of the company;[3] according to a
later profile, he was deeply involved in the city's social life as a member of numerous clubs, several sports leagues, and many charities.[4] By 1919, Metropolitan was
successful enough to join seven other companies throughout the country in buying a full-page ad in *Reel and Slide Magazine* and promoting its "efficient local
service assured of short length advertising films."[5] In late 1922, the Metropolitan
bought out the rival Nelson company, acquiring "possession and control of [its]
equipment, laboratory, offices and business,"[6] and that acquisition may have led
to a new contract with the *Detroit News* to continue producing the local newsreel,
now retitled the *Detroit News Pictorial*. Besides the *News*, the company's clients
for industrial films grew to include Cadillac, Chrysler, Buick, Hudson, and others.[7] An early example was the one-reel "film of the Starkweather-Buick driveaway
from the Buick plant at Pontiac," in which customers took personal delivery of
seventy-eight cars in one day.[8] Until the well-known firm of Jam Handy relocated
from Chicago to Detroit in the late 1920s,[9] Caplan's company was the city's most
important producer and distributor of short nonfiction films.

Notes

1. "Moving Pictures of Show Goers," *DFP* (January 1, 1917): 15. Nelson's advertising films
allegedly were shown in fifty theaters—H.N. Nelson ad, *DJC* (June 1, 1917): 25.

2. Advertisements, *DFP* (March 3, 1918): C5, (March 7, 1918): 6, (March 10, 1918): C8, and
(March 14, 1918): 8; and the Metropolitan ad, *MFR* (May 21, 1918): 14.

3. Advertisement, *DFP* (August 11, 1918): C6.

4. "Personalities," *Exhibitors Daily Review* (July 7, 1928): 3.

5. Ad Film Distribution Service, *R&L* (April 1919): 48.

6. Roy E. Marcotte, "The Reel Players," *DFP* (October 31, 1922): 12.

EXTRA!!

AT LAST

YOUR LONG WANTED DESIRE IS TO BE REALIZED

The Metropolitan Company

OF

DETROIT

ARE PRODUCING AND RELEASING FOR

The Detroit Free Press

A

Current Event Weekly

OF HAPPENINGS IN DETROIT AND MICHIGAN

THE FIRST WEEKLY WILL BE RELEASED

Sunday, March 17th

AT THE BEAUTIFUL **WASHINGTON THEATRE** DETROIT, MICH.

The Washington Theatre has contracted for the First Run Service of this Picture for Detroit, and it will also be shown each week in the Strand, Alhambra, Garden, Liberty, Columbia and Empress Theatres of Detroit.

HAVE YOU ARRANGED FOR YOUR BOOKING?

We Have a Very Attractive Proposition to Make You Regarding the Booking of This
CURRENT EVENT WEEKLY

Write Us a Letter, Phone Us, or Better Still, Call and See Us and Give Us Your Open Time So We Can Complete Your Program.

The Metropolitan Company

M. S. (BILL) BAILEY
M. J. CAPLAN

23 Elizabeth Street East
DETROIT, MICH.

MAIN
2864

The Film Building Is Just East of Us

Fig. EA5.1. Metropolitan Film Company ad, *Michigan Film Review* (March 12, 1918): 7.

7. Metropolitan Film ad, *Amateur Movie Making* (July 1927): 43.

8. "Buick Driveaway Recorded in Film," *DSFP* (April 24, 1921): 2.3. Supposedly this film was to be exhibited "in 100 Detroit theaters."

9. Rick Prelinger, "Eccentricity, Education and Evolution of Corporate Speech: Jam Handy and His Organization," in *Films That Work: Industrial Film and the Productivity of Media*, ed. Vinzenz Hediger and Patrick Vonderau (Amsterdam, Neth.: Amsterdam University Press, 2009), 211–220; and Rick Prelinger, "Smoothing the Contours of Didacticism: Jam Handy and His Organization," in *Learning with the Lights Off: Educational Film in the United States*, ed. Evin Orgeron, Marsha Orgeron, and Dan Streible (New York: Oxford University Press, 2012), 338–355.

3

"DETROIT-MADE" NEWSREELS AND OTHER SHORT NONFICTION FILMS

See Detroit from your theater seat

Detroit Free Press (May 19, 1918)

See the *News* on the Screen

Detroit Sunday News (October 21, 1923)

THE PREVIOUS CHAPTER STRONGLY SUGGESTS THAT DETROIT EXHIBITORS assumed many in their audiences expected to see, among the extra attractions in their variety shows, not only comedies and serial episodes but also short nonfiction films. Those produced and/or distributed by the major companies included weekly newsreels, "screen magazines," travelogues and scenics, popular science films, and Hollywood "snapshots" of the stars. Yet the most interesting nonfiction, arguably, was "Detroit-Made," not only produced locally but also often circulated as a local attraction. One set of these, newsreels and "screen magazines" produced by the Ford Motor Company, is relatively well known and has received recent scholarly attention.[1] The other, newsreels produced by the Metropolitan Film Company in conjunction with the two largest city newspapers, has, like most local news films of the period, largely faded from view. This chapter examines these "Detroit-Made" nonfiction films for their choice of subjects, the implication of those choices, and their modes of representation, as well as the range and extent of their exhibition. Such a study requires some background: that is, what was the context created by other kinds of nonfiction programming within which these "local" films circulated?

Nationally distributed newsreels comprised a good part of that context. Although newspaper ads offer little sense of newsreels' presence before 1919, surviving issues of the *Weekly Film News* reveal that several were screened frequently in Kunsky theaters—and very likely in others as well. In fall 1916, both *Pathé*

News and Hearst's *International News* appeared on the Washington, Alhambra, Garden, and Strand programs.[2] The following year, the combined *Hearst-Pathé Weekly* featured at the Madison and Garden, while *Pathé News* screened at the Alhambra and the Strand. After the November 1918 armistice,[3] *Pathé News* became a fixture at many neighborhood theaters: the Crescent, D & G, Drury Lane, Ferndale, Globe, and Lakewood. By fall 1920, it showed nearly every week at the Gladwin Park, Norwood, Oakman, and Virginia, as well as sometimes at the Arcade and the Iris—when a special ad celebrated the *Pathé News*'s "tenth anniversary."[4] Hearst's *International News* gradually turned up in neighborhood theaters as well. During one week in June 1923, those theaters included the Blue-bird, Crystal, Forest, Hippodrome, Knickerbocker, Library, Oakman, and Tux-edo.[5] In late 1917, *Universal Weekly* joined the Pathé newsreel at the Alhambra and the Strand; the following year it made scattered appearances at the Adams and Duplex; thereafter, references were less frequent, but it still appeared, alternat-ing with the *International News*, at a theater like the Farnum through December 1924.[6] *Gaumont Weekly* screened at the Washington in May through July 1918, at the Adams in June through September, and at the Broadway Strand in November. By early 1919, its only listings were at the Arcade, Boulevard, and Fine Arts. In late 1919, *Fox News* began an exclusive run at the Washington, after Fox took control of the theater. Within months, *Fox News* was booked at the Fine Arts, Montclair, and Norwood, as well as the Louis and Park in ethnic neighborhoods. By June 1923 it, too, was screening widely: at the Arcade, Doric, East Side, Farnum, Knick-erbocker, Oakman, Ritz, and Theatorium.[7] Yet first-run theaters other than the Washington labeled newsreels, whenever cited, as their own "topical reviews." These seem to have been compiled from a variety of contracted sources; for example, the Madison revealed, beginning in December 1918, that its newsreel was drawn from *Pathé News*, *Ford Weekly*, and other sources.[8]

Throughout 1918, the Majestic and the Madison also served as prominent venues for the Committee on Public Information (CPI) "official war pictures," which aimed to inform the home front and shore up support for the US troops now deeply engaged in the Great War. In December 1917, *Who Leads Our National Army* showed up at most Kunsky theaters. By January and February 1918, however, the Majestic had *Training Officers in the Army*, *Eyes of the Allies*, and *Uncle Sam's Fighting Forces on Sea*, while the Madison offered *The Making of a Man-O-War Man* and *The Boys of the Naval Training Station*.[9] That summer and fall, the Madi-son included a CPI war picture every couple of weeks, one of which, *The Whisper-ing Wires of War*, likely focused on the women who operated the military phone lines that conveyed orders and queries from US command centers to officers at the front.[10] After the war ended in November 1918, CPI war pictures continued to feature at the Madison for several months, among them *Capture of Jerusalem*, *French Colonial Troops*, *Detroit Troops in Russia*, and *Red Cross, Western Front*.[11]

Meanwhile, the Majestic, along with the Washington, supplemented its programs with "official" war films from France and Italy: *The Italian Battle Front*, Kleine's *Behind the Lines in Italy*, and Pathé's *In Alsace Lorraine*.[12] As neighborhood theaters began to advertise in late 1918, the US government films showed up in venues from the Dawn, Fine Arts, Rialto, and Rosedale to the Crystal and Iris in two different Polish communities as well as the Arena Gardens Auditorium near the North End Jewish community.[13] In fact, one of the last to be named was *The 339th Infantry in Russia* at the Crystal in mid-February 1919.

Perhaps the most intriguing nonfiction shorts came in the "screen magazine" series that, particularly after the war, Detroit theaters promoted as much as, if not more than, they promoted national newsreels. Rather than represent current events, these weekly or biweekly series tended to focus on general interest stories similar to, or even drawn from, popular magazines.[14] The earliest was Paramount's Pictograph, which included an "animated cartoon," produced weekly by the Bray Studios in New York.[15] The *Pictograph* first screened at the Alhambra and Strand in fall 1916 and once at the Regent in late December; weekly issues then showed frequently at the Ferry Field and Strand throughout the second half of 1917. That year Bray Studios contracted to make "war propaganda" for several "government departments," and one story, *Training Women Sharpshooters*, seems to have circulated in Detroit.[16] From late 1918 through much of 1919, the *Pictograph* became a fairly regular feature at the Adams but also filled out programs at the Blue Bird, Duplex, Maxime, and Rialto, and at least once at the Quo Vadis. After Goldwyn took over distribution of the *Bray Pictograph* (promoted now for its "Out of the Inkwell" cartoons) in August 1919,[17] Paramount began producing another series, *Paramount Magazine*,[18] which, throughout 1920, showed occasionally at neighborhood theaters like the Amo, Fine Arts, Library, and Virginia and was a regular feature for months at the Baker and Oakman.[19] A minor competitor to the *Pictograph* initially was Mutual Film Corporation's film magazine, *Reel Life*, which the company promoted as "chock full of stuff for the kiddies."[20] An occasional staple at the Strand, beginning in October 1916, *Reel Life* seems to have disappeared by the end of 1917.[21]

Of the several other "magazine" series, the most prominent was *Screen Magazine*, which Universal was releasing in eight monthly issues by February 1918, apparently replacing *Universal Weekly*.[22] *Screen Magazine* featured at the Broadway Strand for several months in early 1919; appeared several times at the Strand, through late 1919; and was listed at least once through 1920 at the Arthur, Courtesy, Dawn, De Luxe, Ferry Field, and Gratiot. Its most frequent screenings, however, occurred at the Rialto, from early 1919 through the fall of 1921. In February 1920, a *Detroit Free Press* column drew particular attention to an issue devoted to the new fashions created by Mme Wade Grenager, especially the Yum Yum frock modeled by Ellen O'Connor.[23] In 1919, not long after World Pictures began

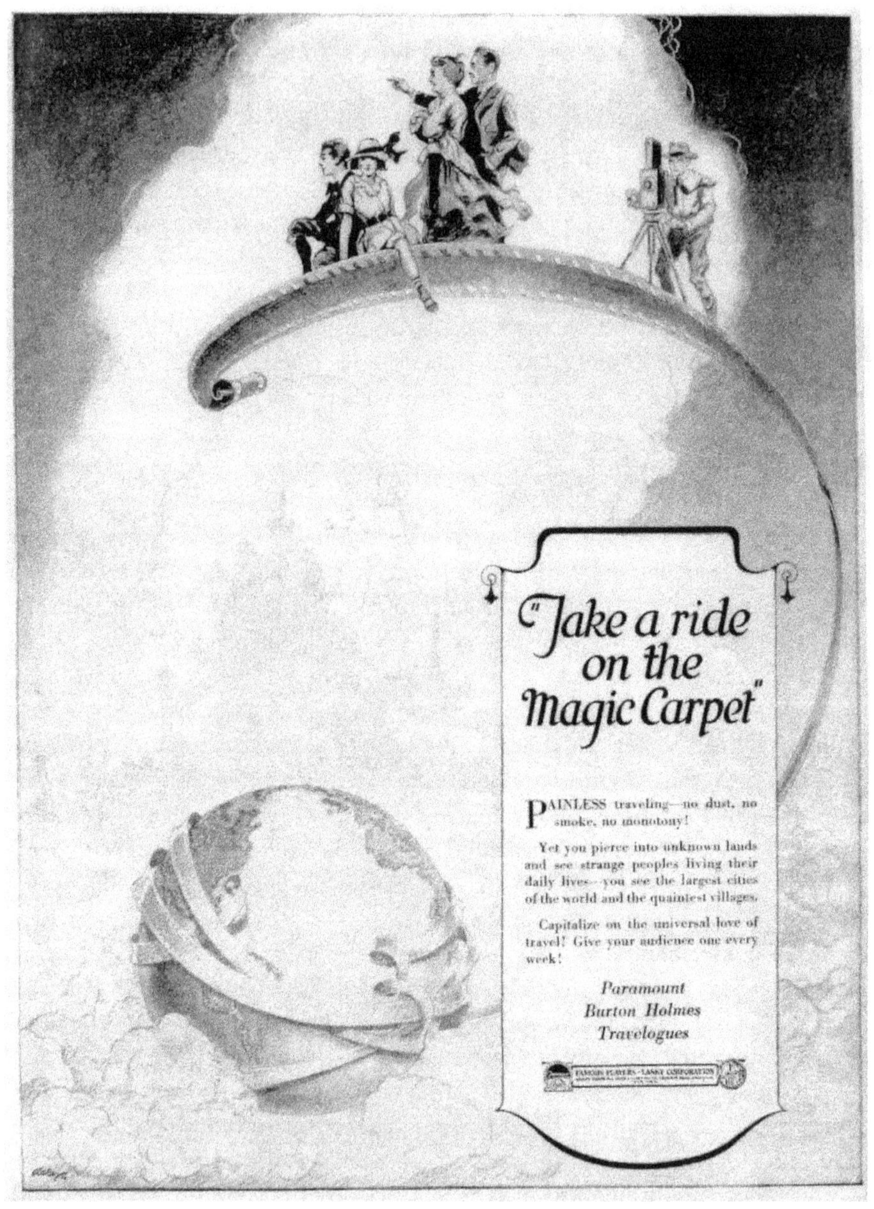

Fig. 3.1. Burton Holmes Travelogue ad, *Motion Picture News* (September 25, 1920): 2334.

distributing *Kinograms*,[24] this magazine series began appearing sporadically at neighborhood theaters such as the De Luxe, Ferry Field, and Norwood. In February 1919, another *Detroit Free Press* column singled out one issue that featured Ring Lardner who, in the persona of "Friend Al," dashed off a quip about finding it "hard for me to move" for the "moving pitcher."[25] By the fall of 1920, *Kinograms* had become a staple at the Drury Lane; nearly three years later, it still was showing at the Dawn, Ferndale, Gratiot, Harmony, Knickerbocker, Linwood-LaSalle, Sheridan, and Stratford.[26] In late 1919, Charles Urban began producing a magazine series, *Movie Chats*, through the Kineto Company.[27] Not until 1922 did weekly issues of *Movie Chats* turn up in Detroit theaters, but they made frequent appearances at the Arthur, Baker, Dawn, Eagle, Greenwood, Iris, Park, Rialto, Vendome, and Warren well into 1923.[28] In 1919, Pathé also added to a large roster of short nonfiction releases its own "screen magazine" series, *Pathé Review*, which gathered together formerly separate subjects—from color travel pictures to "slow motion" films.[29] First listed in late 1919 at the Lakewood, Merrick, and Virginia, by 1923 more than a dozen neighborhood theaters were booking the weekly *Review* as often as the *Pathé News*.[30]

Half a dozen series other than Pathé's displayed the natural wonders of America as well as "exotic" places.[31] Undoubtedly the longest-running travel series was *Burton Holmes Travelogues*, distributed by Paramount. The Washington, Alhambra, and Strand served as the primary venues for the *Travelogues* well into 1919,[32] with specific titles that ranged from *Colorful Ceylon, In Old Ireland*, and *Upper Nile Wonders* to *Through Florida* and *Beautiful Banff*. After the Washington changed hands in late 1919, the *Travelogues*, promoted as a way to "avoid passport tribulations and steamship fees,"[33] could be found now and then for several years in theaters from the Lincoln Square and Oakman to the Koppin.[34] One of the less familiar travel series was *Outing-Chester*. For nearly five months in the last half of 1918, the Adams featured titles such as *A Coorial on the Orinoco, Jungle Joy Riding, Northern Canada*, and *Cuba the Island of Sugar*.[35] For two months prior to November 1919, the Washington screened weekly *Outing-Chester* travelogues, among them *Where They Go Rubbering*; at least through 1920, they occasionally turned up at neighborhood theaters, from the Catherine and Iris to the Knickerbocker.[36] For its part, Mutual offered two travelogue series in parallel with *Reel Life*. From September 1916 to March 1917, issues of *See America First* made frequent appearances at the Alhambra and Strand; from then until August, Mutual's *World Tours*, devoted largely to European cities but also to several in North Africa, took over a similar program slot at the Strand.

Educational Films Corporation, which operated a branch office in the city from 1919 on, distributed three separate nonfiction series.[37] *Ditmar's Animal Pictures* was a special attraction on Majestic and Alhambra programs at various times in 1917–1918.[38] Specific titles ranged from the serious—*The Beaver, Tree Animals*,

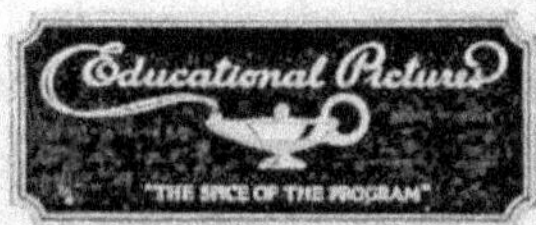

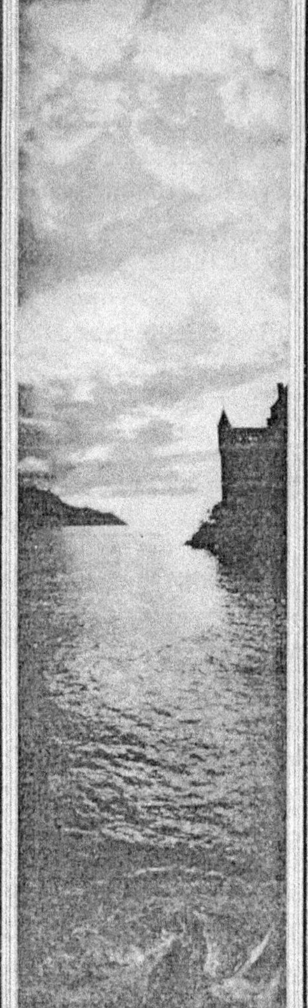

BEAUTY

The scenic pictures made under the direction of Robert C. Bruce are well named the "Scenics Beautiful." They entertain any audience, anywhere—yet they are to the art of motion pictures what the canvases of Rembrandt, Velasquez or Whistler are to the art of painting.

PRE-EMINENCE

For years, Robert C. Bruce pictures have been pre-eminent in the scenic field because they actually tell a story while depicting nature in her most beautiful moods. They entertain, yet they are art.

REGULARITY

Robert C. Bruce is consistent in the quality of his product—produces "Scenics Beautiful" with unparalleled regularity.

Robert C. Bruce's consistency caused the editor of the Exhibitor's Herald to write, "The most remarkable thing about Robert C. Bruce's Scenics, next to their quality, is their regularity of release."

Educational has always released the Robert C. Bruce "Scenics Beautiful."

EDUCATIONAL FILM EXCHANGES, Inc.
E. W. HAMMONS, President

Fig. 3.2. Educational Films Exchange ad, *Motion Picture News* (February 26, 1921): 1596.

and *Foreign Deer*—to the stereotypically comic—*Jungle Vaudeville, Monkey Capers*, and *Orang Apprentice*. The series shifted briefly to the Adams in late 1918 and then had short stays at the Strand and Rialto in early 1919. For several months in late 1918 and early 1919, *Newman's Travels* also screened at the Adams,[39] only to disappear until Newman himself returned in early 1922, along with a photo profile in the *Times*, to lecture on his travel films at the New Detroit.[40] Based on trade press ads, *Bruce Scenics* certainly were much prized for being "to the art of motion pictures what the canvases of Rembrandt, Velasquez, or Whistler are to the art of painting."[41] For much of 1917, *Bruce Scenics* such as *The Heart of Vesuvius, China and the Chinese*, and *Alaskan Wonders* were a constant attraction on the Alhambra's programs. In late 1918, the series featured at the Madison and Ferry Field, with titles like *Acute Spring Fever*. As more and more neighborhood theaters began placing newspaper ads, *Bruce Scenics* became quite visible at the Amo, Arthur, Blue Bird, Ferry Field, and Knickerbocker; in September 1920, the series even returned downtown to the Fox Washington. Throughout this period, cryptic theater ad listings for "scenics" may well have meant the famous "Scenics Beautiful produced by Robert C. Bruce";[42] similarly, those for "travelogues" may have referred to *Burton Holmes Travelogues*.[43]

In case movie fans could not get enough of their adored stars on-screen, in live appearances, or in fan magazines, in early 1919 *Photoplay* introduced a one-reel *Screen Supplement*, promoted as "a gate to the magic land behind the screen."[44] Produced by James Quirk and Julian Johnson, *Photoplay*'s publisher and editor, respectively, the *Screen Supplement* also was distributed by Educational Films.[45] The Adams advertised the series for the first three months, once titling it *The Stars As They Are*. In the second issue, "your favorite picture players—off the screen, at home, and behind the scenes" included Bill Hart, Thomas Ince, Bessie Love, Douglas Fairbanks, Geraldine Farrar, Cleo Ridgely, and Ben Turpin.[46] The *Screen Supplement*'s gateway closed within a year,[47] but Pathé soon took up the idea with a weekly series titled *Screen Snapshots*.[48] In August 1921, the Broadway Strand became an exclusive venue for the series,[49] and the first issue stuffed its one reel with no fewer than eighteen stars "shown . . . in their homes, between times at the studios." Within a year, together with the company's *News* and *Review, Screen Snapshots* was featured at neighborhood theaters from the Ferry Field and the Strand to the Iris. Through the first half of 1923, it continued to appear at theaters like the Arcadia, Garden, Globe, Park, and Rex. Even after CBC Film Sales took over its distribution on "the state right market" in August,[50] *Screen Snapshots* still proved an attraction at the Ferry Field and Tuxedo.[51] Tempting as it may be to think that *Snapshots* especially appealed to movie fans who were unable to see their favorite stars in person during those live appearances at first-run theaters, that does not explain why the series was screening at a "high-class" venue like the Tuxedo in April 1924.

The *Detroit Times*'s "Neighborhood Theater" column, in early June 1923, offers one further perspective on all the recurring newsreels and screen magazines that could attract movie fans in different areas of the city during a single week. The Knickerbocker, near Belle Isle Park, had *International News* on Sunday and Thursday, *Kinograms* on Friday, and *Fox News* on Saturday. The Rialto presented *Pathé Review* on Sunday and *Pathé News* on Monday, Tuesday, and Friday. The Dawn, farther east on Gratiot than the Rialto, showed *Pathé Review* on Tuesday, *Movie Chats* on Wednesday and Thursday, and *Kinograms* on Friday. On the far west side, the Lincoln Square had *Pathé News* on Sunday and *Pathé Review* on Tuesday and Wednesday. The Oakman, just west of Highland Park, screened *Fox News* on Sunday and *International News* on Tuesday and Thursday. While the Iris gave its Polish audiences *Pathé News* on Sunday, the west side Crystal featured *International News* on Thursday and Friday. Yet, during that same week, as later pages will suggest, the local newsreel, the *Detroit Free Press Weekly*, probably appeared on more neighborhood theater programs than any of its national competitors.

"Detroit-Made" Films from the Ford Motor Company

As Entr'Acte 4 demonstrates, the decision to produce "Detroit-Made" feature films hardly turned out to be the business opportunity that Frank Talbot and his investors deluded themselves into expecting. The city did, however, become a relatively important center for producing and distributing short nonfiction films. The most well-known company occupying that center was the Ford Motor Company, which, between 1914 and 1921, released two regular series, the *Ford Animated Weekly* and then the *Ford Educational Weekly*.[52] Both were distributed across the country, sometimes in competition with national newsreels and travel films. Far less known were two firms, H. N. Nelson and Metropolitan Film (the latter bought out the former in late 1922), whose output was nearly as prolific.[53] Of the two, Metropolitan Film was unique in contracting with Detroit's two major newspapers to produce and distribute a local newsreel, the *Detroit Free Press Film Edition* and the *Detroit News Pictorial*. This chapter's analysis of these "Detroit-Made" nonfiction series tracks through three stages:

- First, by focusing on Ford's production and distribution, on the specific films that devoted attention to the Detroit area, and particularly on how both the *Ford Animated Weekly* and *Ford Educational Weekly* circulated in the city's theater programs;
- Second, by drawing on newspaper ads and articles to analyze the subjects represented in the *Free Press Film Edition* and the circulation of its weekly issues in area theaters; and

- Third, by drawing not only on newspaper ads but also on surviving film clips to analyze the choice of subjects included in the *News Pictorial*, how those subjects were framed and organized, and where the weekly issues of this newsreel were exhibited.

Both the *Film Edition* and the *Pictorial* offer a revealing test case for the further study of local newsreels during the silent period and of their possible function (intended or not) for various audiences.[54]

Historical accounts differ about when the Ford Motor Company set up its Motion Picture department in the Highland Park factory, whether in late 1913 or early 1914.[55] The inspiration may have come from Henry Ford himself, after an unnamed company, in mid-1913, convinced him of the value of motion pictures by recording and projecting the process in which "several teams of workers assembled an entire Model T in two and a half minutes."[56] One of the first films the department produced repeated that "time motion study," entitled *How Henry Ford Makes One Thousand Cars a Day*, but its main output became a ten- to fifteen-minute newsreel, the *Ford Animated Weekly*.[57] In order to turn out the newsreel, by fall of 1914 the department itself was operating on an assembly line basis with a technical staff of twenty-four men and six cameramen.[58] Within another year or two, work was divided into thirteen sections: "Administration, Studio and Art Stock, Enlarging Room, Developing Room for 8″×10″ still pictures, Laboratory, Title Making, Print of Films, Perforating, Developing of Films, Drying Room, Assembly Room, Shipping."[59] Ford released the *Weekly* through the company's many automobile dealerships, which screened it in their showrooms and distributed prints for free to both theatrical and nontheatrical venues.[60] Lee Grieveson suggests that the *Weekly* was "widely seen in small towns and rural areas,"[61] but in Detroit the newsreel certainly appeared often at the Alhambra and the Strand until late 1916. Moreover, a random search of newspaper databases reveals that it was shown as the *Ford Detroit Weekly* at least once a week in a range of commercial theaters, including the Alhambra in Canton, Ohio, sponsored by the local Ford dealer.[62] Although promoted and shown in theaters as a newsreel, the *Weekly* clearly served as an advertising film: each issue included at some point a shot of a passing Ford automobile, and the intertitles were printed on a simulated Model T radiator.[63]

Ford discontinued the *Animated Weekly* in late 1916, allegedly because issues had a very short shelf life[64] but probably also because they so overtly advertised the Model T, which lessened their appeal compared to the major national newsreels. Instead, from 1917 through 1921, the Motion Picture department turned to making industrials and travel films released as the *Ford Educational Weekly*.[65] Each issue now focused on a single subject. Examples from 1919 include *The Story of Steel*, a tour of the modern steel mill, as a counter to recent labor strikes; *From*

Special Announcement!

REGARDING

The Ford Weekly

Under a new releasing plan just consummated we will hereafter distribute throughout the State of Michigan the Ford Weekly. We start with the current release, one reel,

No. 115---

"Work or Fight"

Playing all this week at the Majestic Theatre, Detroit

The Ford Weekly is the greatest educational film produced. The Ford Motor Company is spending thousands of dollars in producing the weekly—not for money, not for glory and not for publicity, but because Henry Ford considers the FORD WEEKLY an act for humanity.

IT IS ABSOLUTELY FREE
TO ALL EXHIBITORS

Let us know at once if you want the Ford Weekly—and on what day of each week, so that we can arrange our circuits accordingly. This applies to all exhibitors, whether or not they are now using it.

Sept. 1st We will release Ford Weekly No. 116-- "A Visit to Niagara Falls"

Watch for further announcements of weekly releases.

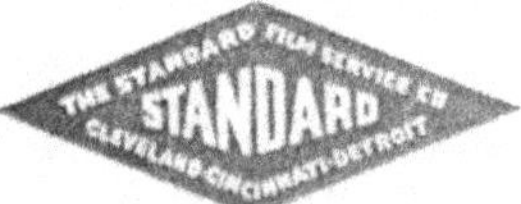

STANDARD FILM SERVICE

Film Building   J. C. FISHMAN, Detroit Manager   Main 6542

Fig. 3.3. *Ford Weekly* ad, *Michigan Film Review* (August 27, 1918): 9.

Mud to Mug, on the process of pottery making; *At the Cross Roads,* a view of correction methods at a federal prison; *The Land of the Ukelele,* a travel tour through Hawaii; *When Black Is Read,* the process of producing a newspaper, perhaps Ford's *Dearborn Independent;* and *Rock of Ages,* a visit to the Stone Mountain quarries near Atlanta.[66] Shortly after the United States entered the war, according to A.B. Jewett, head of the Photographic department, Ford arranged to supply the CPI with "educational films" that, like *The Making of a Man-O-Warsman,* could be shown in Allied countries.[67] Initially, the company itself handled distribution of the *Educational Weekly,* shipping as many as 110 prints of each issue, again for free, to interested theatrical and nontheatrical venues.[68] In late 1918, Ford contracted with Goldwyn to distribute the *Weekly* to theater owners, churches, colleges, and schools; by late 1919, David Lewis claims, circulation had reached a peak of 5,238 theaters.[69] But Ford now began to charge a rental fee for its films, which rose to $1 a week in mid-1920, just as protests broke out over the overt antisemitism spewing from the *Dearborn Independent*[70]—and distribution plummeted to just 1,300 theaters by August.[71] The *Educational Weekly* finally ceased production in December 1921.

Detroit newspaper theater ads, along with the *Weekly Film News,* give a relatively detailed sense of the *Educational Weekly*'s distribution in a metropolis like Detroit. The new *Weekly* continued to feature on Alhambra and Strand programs throughout 1917, and the Ferry Field theater also promoted it frequently from August through December of that year.[72] Many of the films were about travel to cities and events in California and Hawaii in particular, although they covered other cities around the United States as well. Soon these films were joined by industrials such as *How Paper Is Made, Where Cut Glass Comes From, Shoe Industry, Salmon Industry, Making Automobile Wheels,* and *From Tree to Mill.* At the same time, several titles evidenced Ford's contribution to the war effort: *Evolution of Our Flag, Making Steel Plates for Our Merchant Marine,* and *Making Merchant Marine Officers.* In January 1918, the Madison showed a CPI war picture, *Making of a Man-O-War Man,* which might have come from Ford's *The Making of a Man o' Warsman.* From June through August that year, many more theaters included the *Educational Weekly* in their programs: from first-run theaters like the Washington and Majestic to the Rosedale and Virginia as well as the Crystal and Iris. Moreover, the Washington and Majestic sometimes specified their titles. Several were devoted to the war effort: *Canning to Win, Work or Fight* (based on an official state order) and two very different films—first *America at Play* and then *Story of the Ford Eagles*—accompanying the CPI's *America's Answer* at the Majestic.[73] At the same time, the latter film initially played at the Madison as *Ford Eagle Plant.* Yet others were nature films like *Kilauea Volcano;* industrials like *Truth about Liberty Motor;* and nostalgic views of Americana like *Old New England,* which played for several weeks at the Majestic in late 1918.[74]

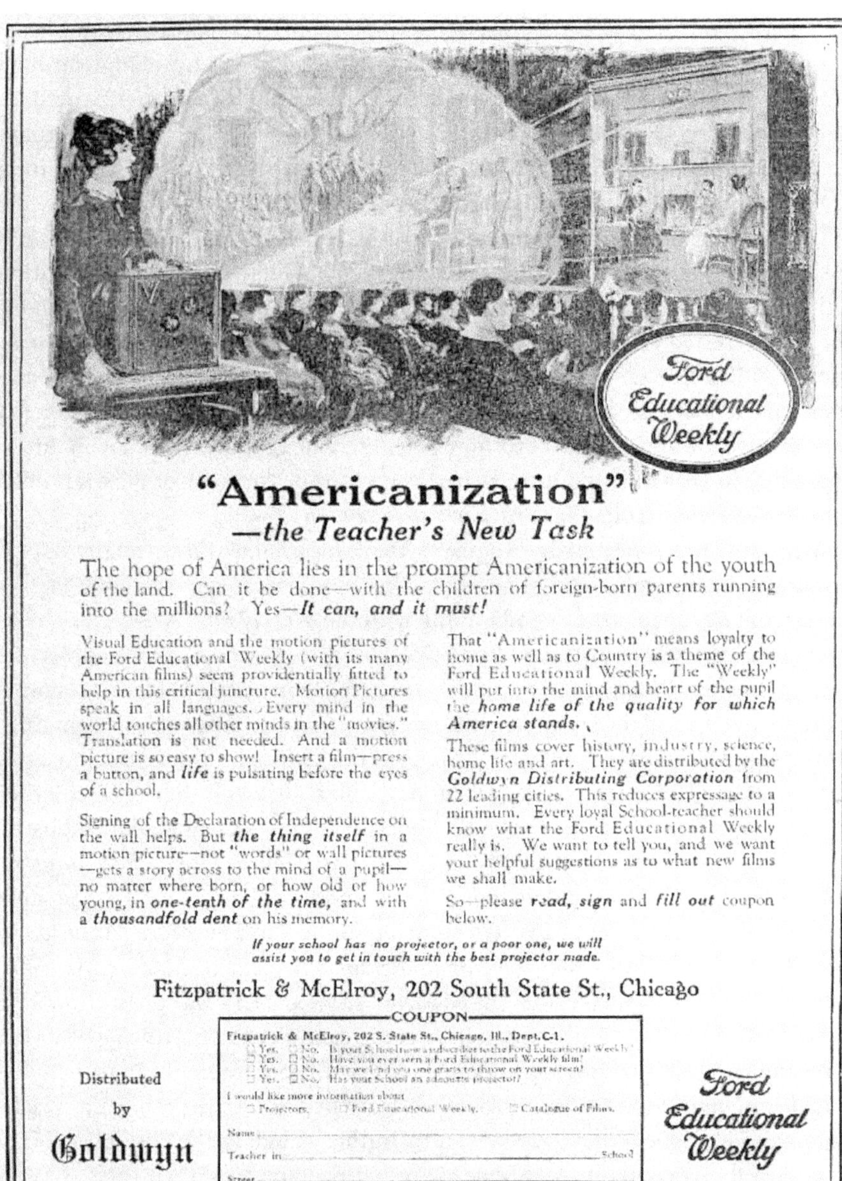

Fig. 3.4. *Ford Educational Weekly* ad, *Moving Picture Age* (February 1920): 7.

For the next two years, the *Weekly* appeared frequently in dozens of neighborhood theaters—as well as the Washington, until the Fox take over in late 1919. Most of those theaters were large and/or in mainly white, middle-class communities or in areas drawing mixed-class audiences: the Alhambra, Boulevard, Blue Bird, Dawn, Ferndale, Fine Arts, Garden, Gladwin, Globe, Grande, Gratiot, Greenwood, Lakewood, Library, Lincoln Square, Linwood-LaSalle, Norwood, Oakman, and Rosedale. Yet the *Educational Weekly* did screen in several ethnic community theaters: the Catherine, Crystal, and Iris. From fall 1920 on, based on neighborhood theater columns in the *Detroit News*, fewer venues advertised these Ford films, although in early September 1921 the Garden took the unusual step of naming a timely *Ford Weekly: Dynamic Detroit*.[75] By the end of 1921, however, only the Garden consistently listed *Ford Weekly* offerings on its programs.[76]

Even before the demise of the *Educational Weekly*, Ford had been urging educators to take advantage of its films for instructional purposes. Ads in *Reel and Slide* and *Moving Picture Age* claimed that the *Weekly* was a "powerful tool for the 'brain factory,'" a typical Ford metaphor for schools, because, in the ballyhoo of boosterism, "it conveys to the American people the message of Industrial Progress, Universal Inspiration and Happiness."[77] Issues of the *Weekly* could "move the World into the Schoolhouse" and continue the work of the Ford English School by supporting "the Teacher's New Task [of] Americanization."[78] In several ads, large drawings depicted specific Ford films—an industrial on ship construction and a historical reenactment of the signing of the Declaration of Independence—being projected to small groups of boys and girls by female teachers. In 1920, well before George Kleine could establish his own "better films" library for nontheatrical distribution,[79] the company introduced the Ford Educational Library as a "practical plan" to supply its films directly to schools, churches, YMCAs, and other nontheatrical venues.[80] While the library gathered fifty-five *Educational Weeklies* into its collection,[81] the Ford Motion Picture Laboratories also produced dozens more, categorized into six subjects: history, regional geography, agriculture, civics and citizenship, industrial geography, and nature studies.[82] Among the specific titles were *Landmarks of the American Revolution*, *Yellowstone Park*, *Farming with a [Ford] Tractor*, *Democracy in Education*, *Iron and Steel*, and *The Honey Bee*. Yet the library, Lewis argues, "never received the widespread support of educational institutions."[83] One reason was that purchasing or renting the films was expensive. In 1922, "the purchase price was set at $50.00 per film and the rental rate was increased from $2.50 per week to $4.25 per week."[84] Despite efforts to make the films available to commercial theaters,[85] Ford stopped promoting the Educational Library in late 1923 and closed it down in 1925.

In 1963, the Ford Motor Company donated its films to the National Archives for preservation and cataloging. Of those, at least two titles from 1920 are easily accessible[86] and invite close analysis. *De-Light: Making an Electric Light Bulb* is an

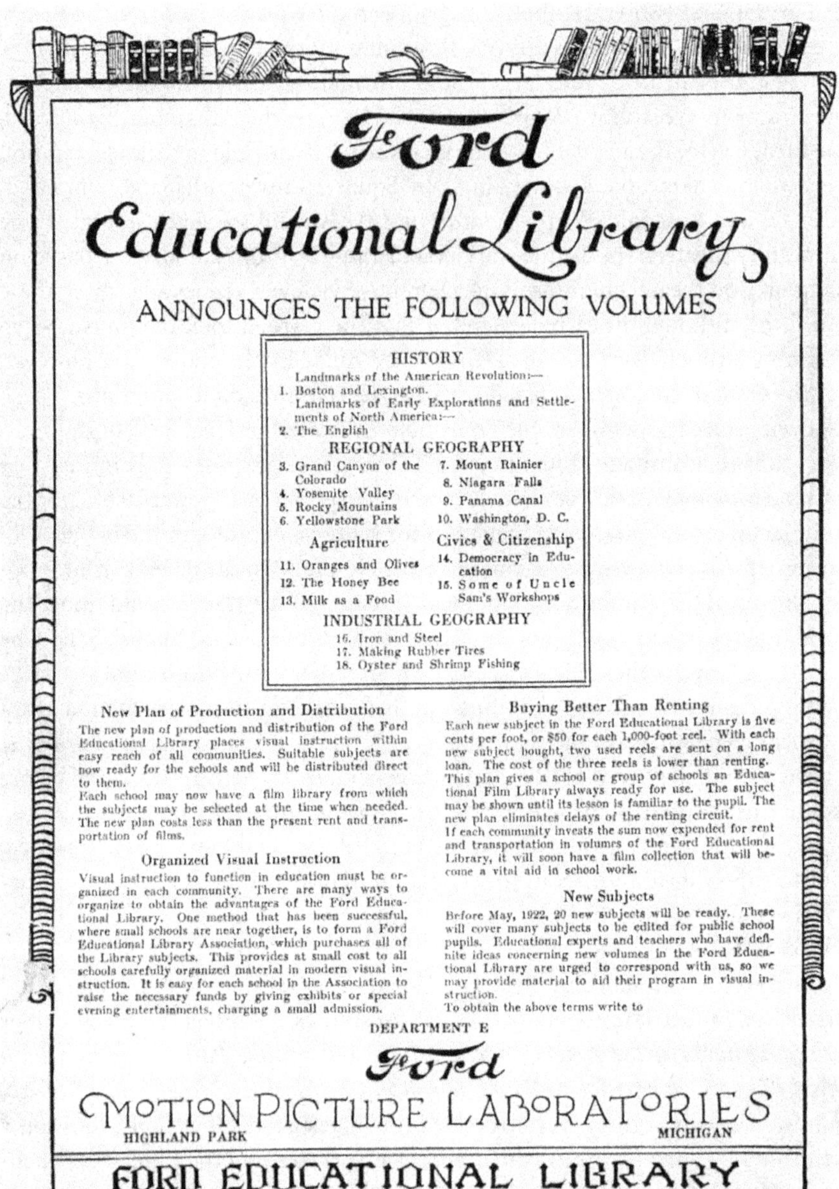

Fig. 3.5. Ford Educational Library ad, *Educational Film Magazine* (February–March 1922): inside front cover.

industrial film (linking Ford and Edison?) that details the processes involved in manufacturing electric light bulbs, from mining tungsten ore to assembling the bulb itself. Twenty-four intertitles describe those processes, illustrated in sepia tinting, at first with single shots and then with an increasing number as each step becomes more intricate, many of them now shown in close shots. The focus consistently falls on the specialized machines engaged in producing the tungsten wiring and glass bulbs and in assembling various components. But workers nearly always are present, sometimes shown only as hands or arms, because most of the processes, Scott Simmon notes, are surprisingly artisanal.[87] Unlike Ford's own assembly-line manufacturing, which required only men, this assembly line relies on a strict gender difference. While men do the initial heavy jobs, women with gloved fingers, small pliers, and tweezers deftly handle the later delicate work on the button rods, wire hooks, and filaments. Framing these processes are a series of woodcut-like drawn images in the intertitles, within which the one constant is a grandmother knitting in the light of a nearby table lamp. But a mirror behind her reveals a smaller image that is different in each intertitle. These smaller images, all but a couple of them involving men, seem to represent an earlier time when work and leisure relied on light from fireplaces, gas lamps, lanterns, and candles. Consequently, they give a sense of historical progress implicitly based on technological advances and assembly-line efficiency. In the end, the electric light bulb allows the grandmother to knit nimbly, well into the night; also, it turns downtown New York City, in the final mirrored long shot at night, into a fairyland "white way" of electric lights, including ad signs for, among others, a Loew's theater.

The second film, *Lights and Shadows in a City of a Million*, seems an anomaly as a *Ford Educational Weekly*. Focused exclusively on Detroit, it looks almost like a local news film.[88] Eighteen intertitles describe, in a rather loose order of black-and-white scenes, some of the health and socioeconomic problems bedeviling the city, and various community efforts to address them. In several early shots, nurses provide medical assistance to the sick, poor, and disabled; and a settlement worker gives a baking lesson to another woman. The "Character Building and Education" section shows boys splashing about in an indoor pool, dozens of seated young men (at least three black men among them) apparently listening to a teacher, and an orphaned girl in bed with a doll and a book. The "Recreation and Settlement Work" section not only includes "foreign mothers" being taught to sew clothes for their children but also invokes the city's housing shortage with a shot down an alley between decrepit wooden buildings. The choice of a specific example, however, singles out Black Bottom by showing two sleepy young black men stumbling out of an old car (not a Ford) supposedly on St. Antoine Street. The final section, "Care of Children," returns to the problem of orphaned children by depicting, first, several children getting out of a new Model T, which has stopped in a middle-class neighborhood, and apparently being shepherded toward a new home offscreen; then, other young children are shown waiting in a Child Welfare Services building; and finally, a blind young man skillfully uses a typewriter to transcribe what he is hearing through the earphones he's wearing. A last shot of a white baby in a crib leads to an intertitle that reveals the film to be an ad promoting the annual campaign for contributions to the Community Fund, an umbrella organization supporting scores of nongovernmental charities.[89] Given that the intertitle has the campaign running for a week, November 15–22, this *Weekly* may have screened at no more than a few upscale North Woodward area theaters, like the Norwood, Oakman, and Rosedale.[90]

This analysis of short nonfiction films produced and distributed by the Ford Motor Company raises several questions for further research. First, the travel and industrial films comprising issues of the *Educational Weekly* must have circulated in competition with others such as *Burton Holmes Travelogues*, *Bruce Scenics*, and Universal Film's industrials. How does the *Educational Weekly*'s choice of subjects compare, then, with those of the competing series of nonfiction films and perhaps also with the subjects in "magazine" series such as Universal's *Screen Magazine*, *Kinograms*, *Movie Chats*, and *Pathé Review*? Did Ford's subjects often, implicitly or explicitly, promote the company as a manufacturer of automobiles and, by extension, specific kinds of tourism—as well as promoting Detroit, at least sometimes, as a booming, civic-minded metropolis? Second, how did Ford's efforts at distributing its films to nontheatrical institutions, particularly to schools, compare with the efforts of other organizations during the early 1920s? Here, those organizations include not only Kleine's film library, started in 1921, but also the YMCA and others such as the Educational Film Corporation, Atlas Educational Film, and state university extension services that advertised in the educational trade journals.[91] Third, what could research in the collection of Ford material at the National Archives further reveal about *Educational Weekly* and the Educational Film Library? Among that material could be correspondence and contracts, documents indicating what stories might have been suggested but not filmed, and outtakes from specific *Weekly* issues.

"Detroit-Made" Local Newsreels from the Metropolitan, I

In the mid-1910s, most local newsreels were produced, distributed, and/or sponsored by regional newspapers—as evidenced in titles that ranged from the *New Orleans Item*'s "Animated Weekly" and the *Minneapolis Tribune*'s "Northwest Weekly"[92] to "Chicago Herald Movies"[93] and the *Chicago Tribune*'s "Animated Weekly."[94] At the same time, major film companies began contracting with large city papers to supply local stories that could be added to their national newsreels, resulting in such titles as the "Indianapolis Star-Universal Animated Weekly"[95]

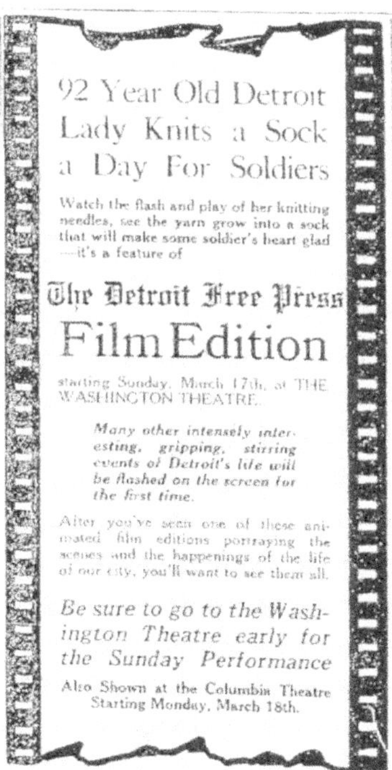

Fig. 3.6. *Detroit Free Press Film Edition*
ad, *Detroit Free Press* (March 14, 1918): 8.

and the biweekly "Selig-Tribune" in Chicago.[96] Given this apparent incorpora-
tion of the local into the national, one might think that newspapers, from the late
1910s on, no longer would be in the business of producing or sponsoring local
newsreels. Not true. In Cleveland, for instance, the *Plain Dealer* announced in
late May 1917 that it was teaming up with the Argus Company, "producers of
educational and industrial films," to make and release a weekly *Motion Picture
Magazine*.[97] In July 1917, the *Detroit Free Press* allegedly approached the *Plain
Dealer*, wanting to know "how to run a motion picture magazine."[98] For whatever
reasons, the Detroit paper did not immediately sign a contract with Metropolitan
Film to produce and release its own *Film Edition* in March 1918. But Metropolitan
probably was a logical choice because it already was experienced in making local
films for theaters."[99] No footage from the *Film Edition* seems to survive, so any
analysis of the *Free Press*'s newsreel has to rely on newspaper advertisements and
frequent daily articles. From those, however, one can gather some sense of each
week's issues and when and where they were shown during the newsreel's five
years of circulation.

The *Free Press* promoted its *Film Edition* to moviegoers with slogans such
as "See Detroit from your theater seat" and "You'll have a bigger, better, more

intimate understanding of Detroit after seeing these films."[99] Newspaper articles usually named "Jim" Lumbard as the newsreel's chief cameraman, but Metropolitan Film must have had others assigned to shoot footage. At some unspecified point Len H. Roos, likely one of the company's cameramen, served for a year as the newsreel's editor.[100] A newspaper article describing the first issue of March 17, 1918, suggests the kinds of stories the *Film Edition* would carry, but not in what order they would appear: stage stars Lillian Russell and DeWolf Hopper visiting the city; a parade and presentation of colors at Camp Custer; Detroit volunteers departing for their barracks in Columbus, Ohio; former police commissioner John E. Whelan's funeral; Red Cross workers making thousands of bandages for the war effort; 92-year-old Mrs. Mary McDonald knitting "a sock a day for the soldiers"; and an editorial cartoon from the pen of G. O. MacConachie, the newspaper's cartoonist.[101] Initially, the *Film Edition* premiered at the Washington on Sunday, moved to the Columbia on Monday, later traveled to the Liberty, Alhambra, Strand, and Garden—all part of Kunsky's dominant chain of theaters—and then transferred to others in the city as well as in Flint, Saginaw, and Monroe.[102] In summer 1918, for unexplained reasons, the newsreel instead began to premiere at Gleichman's downtown Broadway Strand on Sunday, after which it circulated to an increasing number of others in Detroit and southeast Michigan.[103]

During the months before the Armistice in November 1918, the *Film Edition* consistently focused on a certain set of subjects. Stories about local support for American involvement in the Great War appeared nearly every week. In March, Lumbard filmed preparations to train carrier pigeons for war service in France.[104] In early April, he caught several hundred navy recruits marching off to a train bound for Atlanta as well as "a group of women in the snappy uniform for the National League for Women's service" mounting motor trucks for a thousand-mile-journey east with army supplies.[105] A week later, he got an "especially good set of films" of troops from the 551st Michigan regiment handling rapid-firing machine guns.[106] In May, the newsreel paired shots of "1,600 or more Detroit boys marching to stations to entrain for various camps" with others of "a hero of the war, [the] first Detroit man invalided home from France."[107] In June, the stories focused on war material: "aeroplane construction" being investigated by a US Senate committee, "gun mounts being built at a Detroit river shipyard," and a British Britannica tank that "clattered and rumbled" through the streets to be put on display in Cadillac Square.[108] In July, the newsreel acquired official CPI films of Michigan soldiers on the front lines demonstrating their skill in "bayonet, trench, garage, machine gun and heavy artillery practice."[109] In September, by contrast, the newsreel featured women who had replaced men in jobs as "auto mechanics" and as "conductorettes" on the city's streetcars."[110] In October, as the war wound down, Lumbard filmed "Detroit kiddies collecting cast-off garments for unfortunate Belgian children," a successful Liberty Loan rally at Northwestern High School, and a touring troop of Italian Bersaglieri—"the heroes of the Piave . . . who stemmed the tide of the last Austro-German invasion"—marching "jauntily through Detroit streets."[111] And he was there for the "peace celebration" (on November 9), filming "the big crowds that thronged the downtown streets from the minute the city hall bell first rang out the news until nightfall."[112]

Other famous visitors to the city also received special attention. In late March, while Carrie Chapman Catt was "attending the state convention of suffragists," Margaret Youngblood, "Detroit's favorite vaudeville star," was "shown in characteristic poses."[113] A month after Lillian Russell's personal appearance, Marie Dressler arrived and was filmed "'kidding' the huge Liberty Loan crowd in Cadillac Square."[114] In late May, shortly before his death, "Teddy" Roosevelt "spoke before multitudes [and] rode in the big memorial parade."[115] At almost the same time, the "Steel King," Charles M. Schwab, appeared before ten thousand workmen at one of the city's shipbuilding plants.[116] Among the European celebrities on tour were E. D. Swinton, British army general and "inventor of the tank";[117] the duke and duchess of Devonshire and their two daughters who, as British royalty, were visiting the "border city" of Windsor, Ontario;[118] and the famous pianist Ignacy Jan Paderewski and Roman Dmowski, "head of the provisional Polish government in Paris," both of whom were attending a National Polish Congress session in Detroit to plan for Poland's independence after the war.[119]

Newsreel stories celebrating local contributions to the war effort were in keeping with the majority of stories that focused on activities and events that, like Ford's slightly later *Dynamic Detroit*, served to "boost" the city in one way or another—and by extension, the *Free Press* itself. Overall, the stories created an emerging sense of the city's identity, one strongly inflected by class and other interests. Some celebrated the booming manufacturing industries. Prominent were those signaling "Detroit's importance in the building of a merchant marine that will introduce the resources of the Great Lakes to the seven seas."[120] They included scenes of workmen "taking red hot masses of steel and welding them into the huge ribs that form the skeleton of an ocean freighter" and the launching of 3,400-ton cargo ships from Great Lakes Engineering Works in Ecorse.[121] Another story praised "one large meat packing company" for solving its transportation problems, showing "regulation size refrigerator car[s]" being mounted on motor trucks bound for cities in Ohio.[122] In keeping with its "upscale" image, the *Free Press* promoted stories showing how upper-class citizens spent their leisure time. Here they were seen "putting their mounts through fancy paces" at the Cross Country Riding Club and witnessing the Detroit Yacht Club launch of a special motor speedboat, *Miss Detroit III*, which later won "the last heat of the power boat contest."[123] A third story had them experiencing "the moving panorama" of a boat trip through the St. Clair flats, described ostentatiously as the "Venice of

Presenting the World to Detroit's Motion Picture Patrons

IN the war devastated countries of Europe, in Asia, Africa, America, everywhere, there will now be a camera man on the job filming the better news of the hour for Detroit's motion picture patrons. The Detroit Free Press in association with The Metropolitan Company has just contracted for the wonderful Gaumont Weekly which will be released here in conjunction with The Detroit Free Press Film Edition. The Gaumont organization have camera men stationed all over the world—they were one of the first to produce a weekly film of national and international events. With the Free Press Film Edition, folks who attend the better motion picture theaters will have presented to them the news in picture from the world over. You'll not want to miss a single release of this wonderful film.

The Detroit Free Press Film Edition

Produced by The Metropolitan Co., M. J. Caplan, Manager,
IN ASSOCIATION WITH

The Gaumont News and Graphic

Will Be Shown First Today at

The Broadway Strand Theater

41 BROADWAY

The Regent Theater

WOODWARD AND BOULEVARD

Other Free Press Film Edition Releases Today at

Lincoln Square Fort and Military   **Woodward No. 2** 393 Woodward.   **Your** 1070 East Forest.   **Merrick** 1090 Third St.   **Rozmaitosci** 1279 Chene St.

The Free Press Film Edition is shown at these Theaters:

BROADWAY STRAND 35 Broadway.	**REGENT** Woodward and Blvd.
ROSEDALE 2394 Woodward	**DELTHE** 1361 Mack.
FERRY FIELD Grand River and Boulevard.	**LIBERTY** Holly, Mich.
FREE POLAND 2181 Joseph Campau	**BEECHWOOD** 1554 West Warren.
MAXINE Mack and Baldwin.	**AMUSE U** 3281 West Jefferson.
LAKEWOOD 3231 East Jefferson.	**STRATFORD** Dix and Ferdinand.
CATHERINE 300 Chene	**GRANDE** 2240 West Jefferson.
BROOKLYN 875 Michigan.	**CRYSTAL** 1499 Michigan.
JEWEL 448 Gratiot	**LA SALLE** 231 Randolph.
COZY 314 Michigan.	**BAKER** 562 Baker.
ROSEBUD 117 Gratiot.	**ARCADE** 406 Hastings.
DREAMLAND 250 Oakland	**PALACE** 14th and McGraw.
GLADWIN PARK 2034 East Jefferson.	**D & G** 341 Dix.
	EAST SIDE 703 Gratiot

EMPIRE 189 Woodward.	**DUPLEX** Woodward and Blvd.
LUNA 161 St. Aubin.	**MAJESTIC** Jackson, Michigan.
PLAZA 2601 East Jefferson.	**OUR** 721 Kercheval
VIRGINIA 1227 Hamilton.	**LINCOLN SQUARE** Fort and Military.
PERRIEN 935 Chene.	**BILLIKEN** 288 Holden.
WARREN 1180 West Warren.	**NEW HOME** 1433 Chene
COMIQUE 13 Broadway.	**IRIS** Grand Blvd. and Jos. Campau.
ACME Highland Park.	**GRAND CIRCUS** 310 Woodward.
MERRICK 1090 Third.	**EAGLE** 1827 Michigan.
ROYAL Royal Oak.	**WOODWARD No. 2** 393 Woodward.
QUO VADIS Canfield and Russell.	**ROZMAITOSCI** 1279 Chene.
WOODWARD 143 Woodward	**DRURY LANE** 256 Woodward
TILLMAN 957 Michigan.	**YOUR** 1070 East Forest.

See Detroit From Your Theater Chair.

Fig. 3.7. *Detroit Free Press Film Edition* ad, *Detroit Sunday Free Press* (November 17, 1918): 4.3.

America," in words hinting that scenes were tinted and toned.[124] The *Free Press* also featured local women in stereotypical poses—from the "Miss Detroit" contest and a swimming tournament, in which "a bevy of graceful and shapely damsels took part," to a fall fashion show (soon after the influenza epidemic waned) where "lovely girlies . . . trot demurely down a stairway, displaying the nobby, snappy, up-to-the-minute styles in suits, gowns, furs, and hats."[125]

Rarely did the *Film Edition* offer a counterpoint to boosting the city's image, even when it exploited the spectacle of fires at the Monarch Steel Casing Company, at a Gratiot Avenue store during rush hour, and also in fashionable Grosse Pointe.[126] In August, its depiction of the city's garbage-strewn alleys initially could seem surprising, but that week's issue singled out the Public Works Committee's response in a "housecleaning" campaign.[127] Similarly, in early November, the newsreel showed "how influenza spread in the city to epidemic proportions" a month earlier, but again stressed the Board of Health's solution "that so successfully stamped out the plague here."[128] Once the newsreel even took on the city's expensive, inefficient street railway system in something close to satire: it showed Police Commissioner James Couzens (soon to be mayor) "ejected from a D.U.R. car because he refused to pay the six cents fare," which "elicited rounds of applause" from audiences at the Broadway Strand.[129]

The distribution and exhibition of the *Film Edition* during 1918 are quite revealing. Within two months it had become a regular feature at least once a week in nearly forty picture theaters.[130] Aside from the downtown Broadway Strand and Columbia and three outside the city, most of those were located in areas other than the ethnic neighborhoods of recent immigrants. Early in the year, there were few exceptions to this general rule: the Amuse-U and Crescent serving Del Ray's Hungarian community, the Crystal near the west side Polish neighborhood, the Rosebud and Vaudette in Black Bottom, the Iris and Russell on the south edge of Hamtramck, and the Amo near the Crystal Palace in Highland Park. By August, more ethnic neighborhood theaters hosted the newsreel: the Farnum, Free Poland, Iris, New Home, Perrien, Rozmaitosci, and Russell in or near Hamtramck; the Quo Vadis in the Italian community; and the west side Crystal; but only the Crescent in Del Ray and the Rosebud in Black Bottom.[131] And it "premiered" on Sundays at the Rosedale and Rozmaitosci as well as at the Broadway Strand. By the time of the armistice, according to an ad, more than fifty Detroit theaters were screening the *Film Edition*.[132] Besides the ethnic neighborhoods already mentioned, they now included the Arcade, Catherine, Jewel, and Luna in Lower Poletown, the Dreamland near Hamtramck, and the Grande in Del Ray.

Overall, during this initial year, the newsreel must have been a boon to the Metropolitan Film Company, although the company's business records do not survive to confirm that. More pointedly, as the *Film Edition* circulated through so many ethnic neighborhood theaters, its stories seemed to work in sync with the city's Americanization movement campaign. For they repeatedly not only gave recent immigrants a sense of what was so good about living in Detroit but also offered models of behavior and accomplishment to which immigrants could aspire.

As the Great War ended in November 1918, the *Free Press* announced that the *Film Edition* was merging with the "national and international service [of] Gaumont News and Graphic."[133] The announcement added, "The Gaumont service is semi-weekly, the Gaumont News showing the first half of the week and the Gaumont Graphic being presented the latter half of the week." How these two were incorporated into each week's *Film Edition* remains unclear. In any case, during the next two years or more, Gaumont stories made up perhaps half of each week's newsreel issue. Some national news clips continued to focus on the war's aftermath. Several—New York crowds welcoming the American fleet in late December, then Michigan's Eighty-Fifth Army Division in early April—celebrated the return of American soldiers from Europe.[134] Others highlighted the training of aviators, detailed the process by which aerial observation directed artillery fire more precisely, reported "the explosion of 260,000 shells in a Boston munition factory," showed General Jacob S. Coxey proposing another march on Washington with an "army of the unemployed [soldiers]," and honored a Texas Red Cross nurse's funeral.[135] Most news clips conveyed the sense that the country was getting back to "normal." A range of stories represented women, from those "making their debut as voters" in recent primary elections and an aviatrix receiving her license to fly a new "flivver," to "beautiful water nymphs . . . in a bathing suit parade," "society girls in classical dances at Ruth St. Denis's California dance school, Wellesley college girls enjoying physical exercise from "the great out-of-doors to ancient sports," and Annette Kellerman "dedicating a splendid municipal swimming pool at Los Angeles."[136] The *Film Edition*'s attitude toward labor, of course, could not be more different: in December it was "comfort[ed] to see one group of strikers returning to work" at a New Bedford [Massachusetts] cotton mill, alleviating a threat "to the entire textile industry."[137]

The international news clips also continued to present the war's aftermath in a positive light. There were scenes of the signing of the Treaty of Versailles; of the citizens of Rio Janeiro celebrating the treaty in a Peace Jubilee; of "Serbian and Roumanian [*sic*] artists, exiled in France, at work on their artistic creations"; "fine pictures of Lenin [*sic*] and Trotsky addressing their constituents [during] a parade of bolshevist troops"; and, especially apt for the city's Polish communities, scenes of "the patriots of Warsaw celebrating a national fete day in honor of their independence."[138] Several related stories revealed the persistent American bias towards Mexico: a caricature of the "Mexican Navy," whose one ship was sold for junk; and a tongue-in-cheek report on the border town of Mexicali "making active preparations to welcome an influx of thirsty visitors" after Prohibition went into effect.[139] Again, many news clips resumed showing views of "normalcy," especially in France. These included André Citroen, the "Henry Ford of France," posing with his latest model in Paris; the Inter-Allied Games in which "the Allied Armies presented their national sports"; and the resumption of "racing at the famous track at Auteuil."[140] To "captivate the hearts of every woman with the truly feminine love of adornment" (or all those with money to spare), the newsreel produced a show of "chic new hats displayed by a charming actress from the Folies Bergères [and] all the newest creations of the leading French designers."[141]

Well into 1919, the *Film Edition* kept the war's aftermath in the public eye, but from a very local perspective. An especially important way to do that, timed as a kind of Christmas present, was to post a weekly "series of group solider pictures," with twenty in each group.[142] Advertised as a "Welcome Home" series, accompanied by the drawing of a mature soldier embracing his mother, these photos ran through early February 1919: one included a "Detroit marine who received the Croix de Guerre in France."[143] Later stories featured "Red Cross workers preparing huge piles of cast-off clothing of every sort for shipment to the war-torn regions of Europe"; a celebration on Belle Isle for the 339th regiment; another for "the last divisions of Detroit's 'Polar Bears,'" returning from Russia; and General Pershing touring "the city's military establishments" before lunching "at the Dodge ordinance plant."[144] Far more frequent now, however, were local personalities as well as social activities and events. Among those personalities were Mayor-elect Couzens and the new city council at a banquet; the Board of Commerce president, Allan Templeton; and "Detroit theater managers meeting at the Hotel Tuller."[145] That winter, people of all ages "were skating gleefully up and down the lagoons of Belle Isle"; in the spring came displays of Easter flowers, a kite contest at Northwestern High, and "the crowning of the queen of May"; in the summer, "several prominent members of the Detroit Golf Club revel[ed] in their favorite sport," "Lottie Mayer's diving nymphs" engaged in an "eight-mile swimming race," and *Miss Detroit III* again won the gold cup yacht race.[146] In keeping with the newspaper's keen interest in airplanes, the *Film Edition* gave special attention to its cameraman, B. C. Whitman, who captured aerial shots of the city from his "Flying Circus," boosting Detroit's claim to be "the first city in the country to inaugurate aerial passenger transportation."[147]

Surprisingly, the *Film Edition* also highlighted, more often than before, issues and problems in the city, some of which defied solutions. Dangerous industrial fires remained of interest: one at the Wilson Body plant ("a bad one for 1200 workers") and another at the Wadsworth Company (a blaze that "ate its way through the huge factory").[148] In December 1918, former US president Taft tried without success to mediate a "street car labor dispute"; a later strike again created a massive traffic jam; and a Safety First campaign could only offer "how one should and should not alight from a street car."[149] More successful, or at least more lauded, were efforts to serve one-cent noonday lunches at a school in the city's northwestern district, the newspaper's own sponsorship of a "Fresh Air camp" for seventy-five city children, the engineering feat of "moving a four story brick building intact . . . to make way for the large General Motors building," and the charity gifts of "3,000 Christmas packages" for needy children in late 1919.[150] Several stories, however, involved less tractable and more controversial problems. Two focused, with some bias, on ethnic neighborhoods: in one, Sam Giannola led a gang shooting at the county jail, after "many killings" in the Sicilian "settlements"; in the other, the "serious housing shortage" caused by the city's rapid growth gave the more fortunate a glimpse of how others had to resort to "subterfuges . . . in lieu of homes, some humorous, some otherwise."[151] And, despite those "fine pictures of Lenin and Trotsky" shown six months earlier, in January 1919 the newsreel featured the deportation of "35 of the reds caught in this city," as part of "the nation-wide round-up of radicals" during what became known as the "Red Scare."[152]

In late February 1919, the *Film Edition* premiered on Sunday for the first of its full-week runs, not at the Broadway Strand but at the Majestic, through a contract negotiated by its manager, Charles Branham.[153] Branham had been one of four newspapermen who in 1915 founded the *Northwest Weekly* (the regional newsreel in Minneapolis), and the contract entailed some control over *Film Edition* stories because he supposedly had "the staff of Free Press cameramen at his disposal at all times." In June, articles began to give equal attention to its weekly showings at the Temple (a downtown vaudeville house), beginning on Mondays.[154] After the Majestic returned to staging current plays, the *Film Edition* began week-long runs at the Adams starting on Sundays.[155]

The circulation of the *Film Edition* to other theaters changed very slightly in the shift from the Broadway Strand to the Majestic. In early January 1919, an ad noted its Sunday premieres in eight other Detroit theaters—with none in ethnic neighborhoods—as well as in three outside the city. The ad's four columns of theaters showing the newsreel that week, however, included sixty-two in all, nine of which were outside the city. Now twelve were in or near ethnic communities: the Arcade, Catherine, Louis, Luna, and Rosebud (Lower Poletown); the Dreamland, Iris, New Home, and Perrien (Hamtramck); the Acme (Highland Park); the Crystal (west side Polish area); and the Grande (Del Ray). A late March promotional article appended a jumbled list of sixty-two theaters, ten of which were outside the city, with two additional ethnic neighborhood theaters as well: the Park (Hamtramck), and the Lira/Enterprise (Little Italy). For the next year or so, the newsreel's circulation is less easy to track. Fewer than half of the city's theaters advertised in either the *Free Press* or the *News*, and those that did so rarely named their full programs. Moreover, *Free Press* ads listed only the theaters showing issues on Sundays, and their numbers varied from thirteen or fourteen to eighteen or nineteen. While ads often listed the Acme and People's (Lower Poletown), in mid-May 1920 the newsreel's focus on Poland's independence added premieres at two more Polish neighborhood theaters: the Bernhardt (Hamtramck) and the Louis. Even a random search of a full week of neighborhood theater columns in the *News* results in a dearth of data. In early January 1920, no more than eleven theaters listed the *Film Edition* at some point on their programs, with only the Arcade representing an ethnic neighborhood. A year later, the number of theaters remained the same one week, but now the Crystal and the Priscilla (formerly the Louis) replaced the Arcade. By early September 1921, the sixteen theaters naming the *Film Edition* during another week included not one ethnic neighborhood theater.

Throughout this period, the *Film Edition* continued to be distributed in parallel with the *Gaumont Weekly* and the *Graphic*. In January 1921, however, the *Free Press* announced that Gaumont's national and international service had merged with *Kinograms*, and Metropolitan Film would release the consolidated weekly magazine under the *Kinograms* name.[156] The announcement was little more than a publicity piece that assured readers/moviegoers "that cameramen [would be] retained in 40 of the principal centers of the world," including staffs "at various pivotal points." Whether or not the *Film Edition* and *Kinograms* were released together or as separate issues is unclear. In any case, their global reach ended four months later, when the *Free Press* asserted that its newsreel would focus solely on "things that happen in and around Detroit," falsely claiming that this was "a decided innovation for any film 'weekly.'"[157] Later that year, as the Madison took over the Sunday premiere from the Adams, the newspaper kept boasting that its newsreel was unique, the only one of its kind "devoted exclusively to a single city"—which was hardly the case.[158]

Whatever the arrangement was with the Metropolitan Film Company, it allowed the *Free Press* in its ads and puff pieces, from early 1920 to mid-1921, to highlight local "Good Stories," with "punchy, interesting pictures," rather than national and international news.[159] As before, those stories often involved seasonal sports, from winter horse racing, local hockey games, and dance contests to Tigers baseball, a local marathon, summer speedboat races, and the National Women's Tennis Tournament held in the city. They also included social events such as a Masonic barbecue; an Elks Masque Ball; the ceremonial groundbreaking for a new Masonic Temple; and, not to ignore Roman Catholics completely, the Annunciation Church's Silver Jubilee Anniversary of its pastor's ordination.[160] Certain of those now were becoming annual events: the Armistice Day and Memorial Day parades, a May Festival for children, and the Board of Commerce Cruise (with 540 businessmen, relatives, and friends aboard) in June.

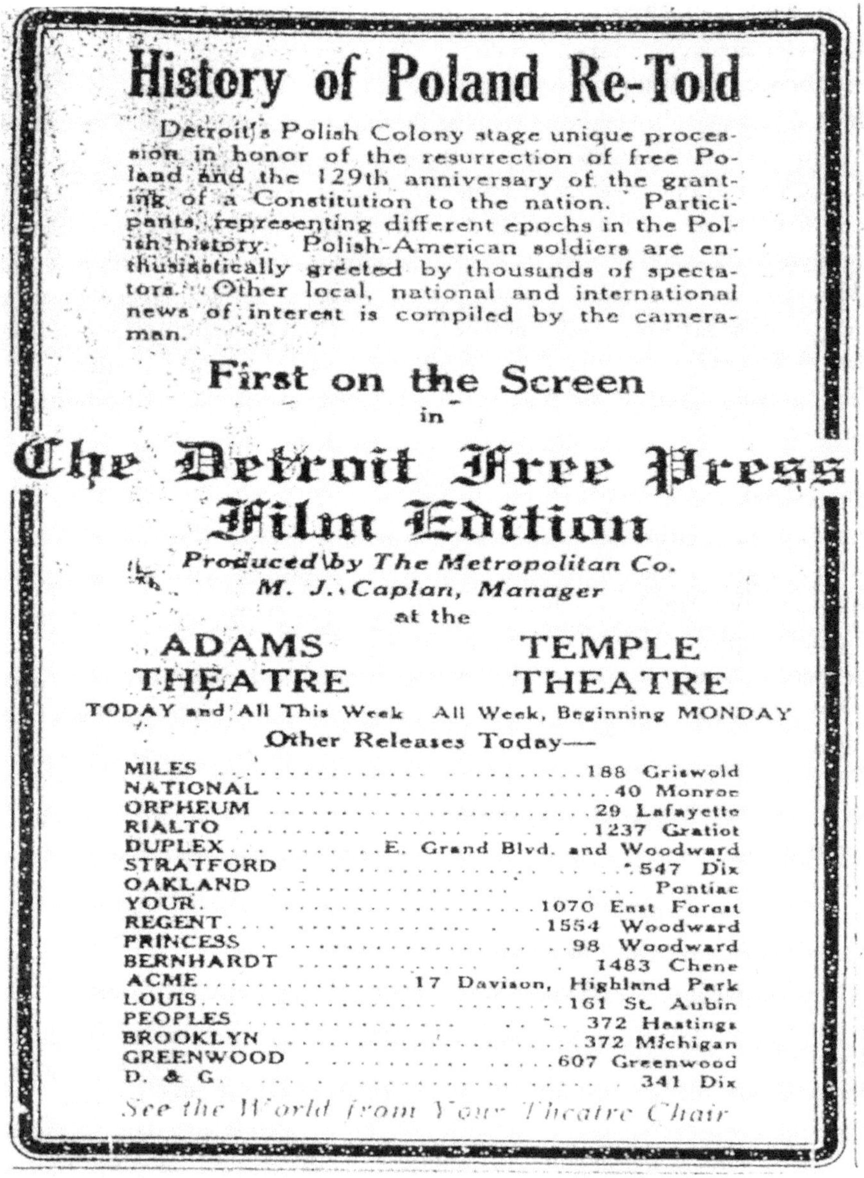

Fig. 3.8. *Detroit Free Press Film Edition* ad, *Detroit Sunday Free Press* (May 16, 1920): 3.18.

While never referring to the recession during this period, the newsreel did continue to show concern for children, from the Old Newsboys' Christmas collection for poor children and the Junior Red Cross Easter baskets for those in hospitals, to school programs such as new physical exercises at Northwestern High, technical departments that trained mechanics, and a cooking class at Algers School that prepared food for the Children's Free Hospital. Among the unusual stories were a "procession in honor of the resurrection of free Poland," in which "Polish Colony" participants represented "different epochs of Polish history"; the investigation of the infamous baseball scandal in Chicago; a "Safety First" parade of wrecked automobiles on Woodward; and Clara Kimball Young's visit to the city, in which she attended a Tigers baseball game.

Once the Metropolitan's contract with Gaumont/*Kinograms* ended, the *Film Edition* went on as before. Its "Good Stories" increasingly conveyed a sense of normalcy, prosperity, and "boosterism." Sports remained a fixture, with the addition of university football games. So, too, did social events like the Rotarian picnic and the Free Press Sunbeam Club meeting, both of which honored local poet "Eddie" Guest.[161] And two events held weeks apart enforced the patriarchal family structure by staging a week of Father and Son Movement "get-togethers" and a Rotarian banquet honoring fathers and daughters. Other events celebrated the city's historical past: there were Danish, Swedish, and French folk dances performed by the Danish Young People's Society; a "Veterans of '61–'98" parade down Woodward; and a pageant involving three thousand school children "picturing in their own way the history of Detroit from the time of Cadillac to the present day." Boosterism was especially strong in a series of industrial subjects that contrasted "making violins by hand" and doing decorative work at the YWCA Arts and Crafts School with building the "largest water filtration plant in the world," constructing a new Belle Isle bridge, and launching the "Greater Detroit" lake steamship. Two stories boasted of manufacturing feats: one company was producing "twelve million pins a day"; another was "devoted exclusively to the manufacture of electric vacuum cleaners [at] one thousand cleaners a day." And the "punchy pictures" for each showed women working at a variety of machines. As had been done in an earlier *Ford Weekly*, in October 1922 the *Film Edition* released a scenic that likely included color: "Mother Nature [was] seen changing her garb of brilliant summer hues for the quieter but harmonious garments of autumn." In late December 1921, the newsreel introduced what would become an annual subject: a summary of the "important events of 1921 [previously] shown on the screen." Not surprisingly, all put Detroit in a good light.

When the Capitol opened in late March 1922, the *Film Edition* premiered there on Sunday, and the following week at the Madison as well. After that, it again became a fixture at the Adams as well as the Shubert Detroit until early June. The late March *Free Press* ad included fifteen other theaters showing the

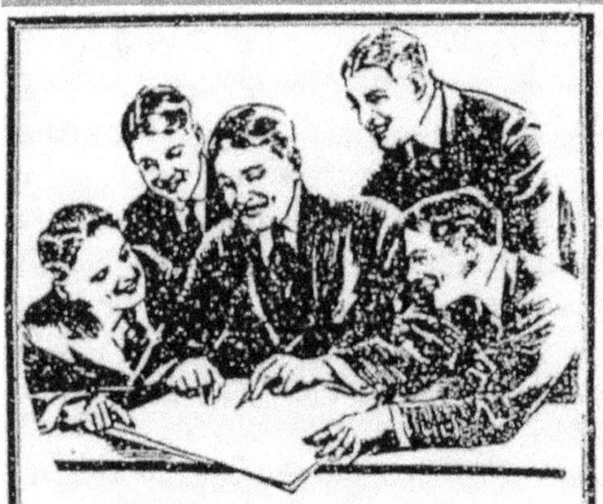

Fig. 3.9. *Detroit Free Press Film Edition* ad, *Detroit Sunday Free Press* (February 19, 1922): 5.9.

newsreel on Sunday; again, none of them screened in ethnic neighborhoods. During the rest of the year, the number of other theaters premiering the newsreel on Sunday decreased to eleven or twelve, depending on the week. Only a few times was an ethnic neighborhood theater among them: the Farnum and Fredro once each, and the Free Poland twice. In early January 1923, fifteen theaters besides the Adams were screening the newsreel's Sunday release, and now that number included the Premier (the former Rozmaitosci). During the remaining months of the *Film Edition*'s existence, the theaters premiering the newsreel on Sunday remained relatively steady but rose to eighteen in early September, including another neighborhood theater, the Enterprise (the former Lira). Once again, the newsreel's circulation throughout the week is difficult to track. Random searches of consecutive neighborhood theater columns for a full week in the *News* and *Times* yield fluctuating results, with very few in ethnic communities. In early January 1922, only ten theaters, including the Crystal, specifically named the *Film Edition* on their programs. In early September 1922, the number rose to thirteen, including the Crystal and Iris. In early January 1923, there were fourteen theaters listing the *Film Edition*, but only the Priscilla was in an ethnic neighborhood. In early September 1923, the number increased to fourteen, with four now in ethnic neighborhoods: the Catherine, Crystal, Iris, and La Veeda. Yet many theater programs simply listed "News" or "Weekly," which could have meant the *Film Edition* as well as one of the national newsreels.

Two of the last *Free Press* ads, however, radically change any conclusion one might be tempted to draw. While the number of theaters showing the *Film Edition* on Sunday remained at eighteen, whether premiering at the Capitol or the Adams, the ads now listed nearly eighty others that screened the newsreel at some time during that week. Some of those had been named previously; but among the many that had not, an unexpectedly high number were in or near ethnic neighborhoods. Most were located in one of the three Polish areas: the Crystal (west side); the Arcade, Catherine, People's, Priscilla, Rosebud, and Savoy (Lower Poletown); and the Clay, Holbrook, Iris, Park, Martha Washington, and White Star (Hamtramck). Two were not far from Ford's Crystal Palace: the Highland Park and the La Veeda. Two others were near Del Ray: the Crescent and the Grande. Only one now was in Little Italy: the Quo Vadis. Lastly, there was the Koppin in Black Bottom. Equally surprising, these ads, along with other daily ones up to October 14, appeared just as Metropolitan Film was ending production of the *Film Edition*. With these ads, then, was the *Free Press* making one last effort to pressure the company into renewing its contract, or was it more likely giving a "last hurrah" for what it considered the success of its "Visualizing Newspaper"?

This analysis of the *Free Press Film Edition* is particularly valuable for the questions of historiographical methodology it raises. First of all, given the lack of surviving film prints, one has to rely for source material on newspaper ads and

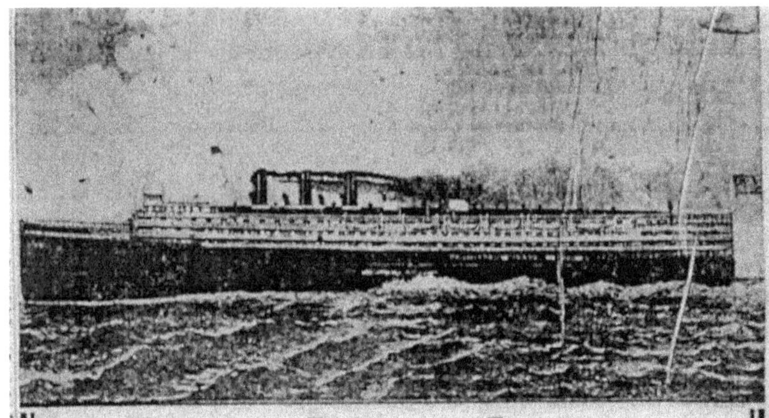

Fig. 3.10. *Detroit Free Press Film Edition* ad, *Detroit Sunday Free Press* (September 23, 1923): Feature 7.

promotional articles to gather a sense of what stories made up each week's issue, what story was most prominent, and even what stories were included, which could differ in each source. The week of April 2, 1922, offers a good example. The ad's headline highlighted the Rotarian banquet for fathers and daughters ("numbering more than 500"), complemented by a photo of one young girl sitting on a father's lap. No other story was mentioned. The article, however—with the headline "Mermaid Reel Shown by Free Press Film"—led off with wintering "Detroit people [of a certain class] doing the Virginia reel in the style of Neptune at the casino" in Miami, Florida. The third story mentioned was "the Rotarians' father and daughter luncheon," not a banquet. Second, the extent of the *Film Edition*'s circulation varied widely, again depending on the sources one consults and the time period referenced during the newsreel's nearly six-year existence. In 1918–1919, a few *Free Press* ads offered a complete listing of as many as seventy theaters showing the *Film Edition*, not only on Sunday but also during the rest of a week. From then until September 1923, the *Free Press* ads listed only which theaters were showing the newsreel on Sundays. During that time, the neighborhood theater columns in the *News* suggest that no more than ten to twenty theaters booked the newsreel during any one week. The same could be said of the *Times*'s neighborhood theater columns, introduced in early 1923. The sudden return, in September 1923, of complete listings of nearly one hundred theaters in the *Free Press* ads reveals that any conclusion about the newsreel's circulation between January 1920 and August 1923 is far from certain.

"Detroit-Made" Local Newsreels from the Metropolitan, II

In the fall of 1923, Metropolitan Film signed a contract with the *Detroit News* to continue producing and distributing the city's local weekly newsreel, now titled the *Pictorial*; this arrangement lasted through the 1920s.[162] Whether or not the *News* outbid the *Free Press* is unclear. Although the claim is impossible to verify, the *News* stated that Metropolitan Film "had enlarged its staff of camera men," so as "to have no less than four events taken at one time," and had also acquired new equipment.[163] A half-page ad in the *News* announced that the *Pictorial* would premiere at the Capitol, would circulate to one hundred theaters in the city (listed alphabetically) and then would show in two dozen more in Michigan, from suburban Royal Oak, Ferndale, Ecorse, and River Rouge to faraway Jackson, Howell, and Lansing.[164] This number of exhibition venues nearly matched those for the last issues of the *Film Edition*, with very slight variation. First released on October 21, 1923, the *Pictorial* also looked little different from its predecessor.[165] The local stories included high-society activities in Grosse Pointe and Bloomfield Hills, where "society debs are rehearsing for a forthcoming theatrical production" in the autumn woods; sports events (from "highlights of the Michigan–Ohio

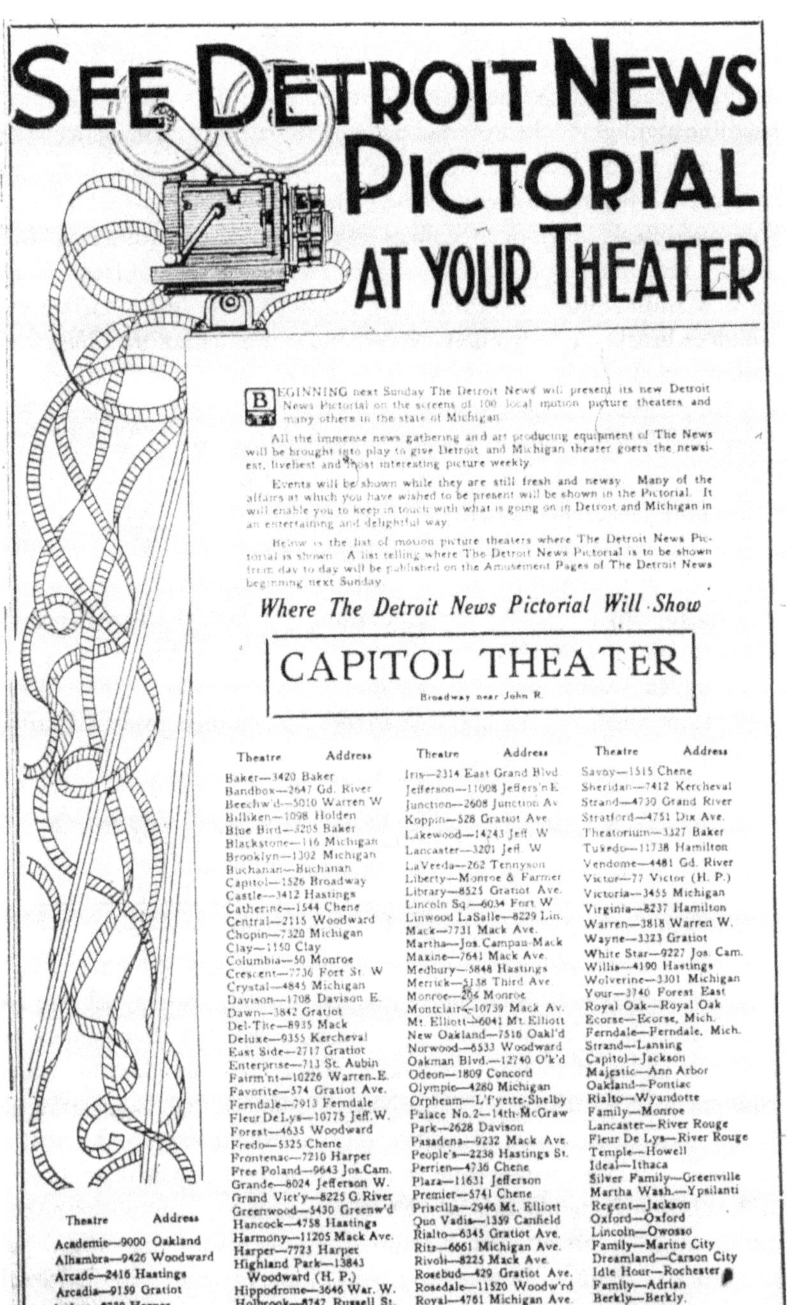

Fig. 3.11. *Detroit News Pictorial* ad, *Detroit Sunday News* (October 14, 1923): 2.7.

football game" to amateur golf champions receiving trophies); Chaplin visiting the city and meeting Henry Ford; the funeral parade for a police "detective hero"; and, in a condescending note, "laughter as the little folks in a great orphan asylum struggle for hundreds of bags of candy."[166] In another short piece that day, reproduced film strips promoted three of those stories: the Chaplin–Ford meeting; a society deb performing a "nature dance"; and one small child, at not just any orphanage, but specifically the "German-American Orphan Asylum"—a rare reference to the city's earlier heritage.[167] A second ad that Sunday confirmed the newsreel's social posturing with a drawing of one of the "Grosse Pointe maidens compet[ing] in the ancient pastime of archery."[168]

Analyzing the *Pictorial*, unlike analyzing the *Film Edition*, involves drawing on different source material—and thus requires a different methodological approach. The *Pictorial* survives not only in weekly ads and occasional articles but also in hundreds of discrete film stories, digitized and made accessible on Wayne State University Library's website. Yet navigating this rare treasure trove is hardly without problems. First, the library has offered little information about when and why the newsreel was cut up into these stories—but very likely that was done for commercial purposes, as was the case with many newsreels. Second, the stories are numbered in puzzling batches (2.1–2.31, 3R1.1–3R1.41, etc.) and are dated by year rather than month and day, with several groups assigned vaguely to the "mid-1920s." Third, the assigned dates as well as the numbers make it difficult to reconstruct a sequence of digital stories into a single newsreel issue. Research on the weekly ads from late 1923 through early 1925[169] reveals that many if not all of those dated 1923 actually should be dated 1924. Moreover, trying to match any of the newspaper ads' list of selected stories with discrete clips on the website can prove daunting—and rarely yields success. For instance, the ad for October 12, 1924, includes the story "U. of M. Plays M.A.C.," numbered 2.5 on the website; the ad for October 19, 1924, however, has "Rotarians Go Balloon Joy Riding," numbered 2.3. Even more puzzling, the ad for November 23, 1924, promotes two stories, "Michigan-Iowa Play Last Game" and "'Gar' Wood Is Made Commodore of the Sea Scouts," but they are numbered 2.6 and 2.29, respectively, on the website.

Despite these discrepancies in classifying and dating the *Pictorial*'s surviving stories, one still can determine what kinds of stories the newsreel favored by drawing examples from selected ads and clips as separate but sometimes linked sources. And those stories compiled a sense of the city's identity very much like that created by the *Film Edition*. Especially prominent were stories that highlighted Detroit's development as a major metropolis in the early 1920s. Some stories involved heavy industry: the "largest ore ship to enter River Rouge"; the Rouge Trolley Line carrying twenty thousand workers to and from the big Ford factory (some from Black Bottom); "the first all-metal plane [to] make an experimental flight"; and the "Mechanical Hen," an incubator that "hatches 25,000 chicks a

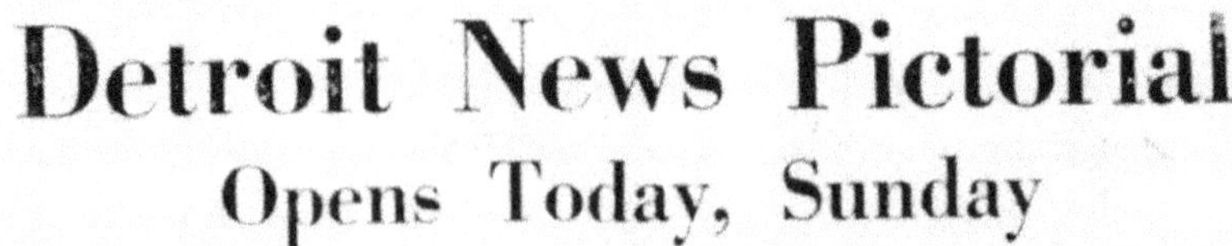

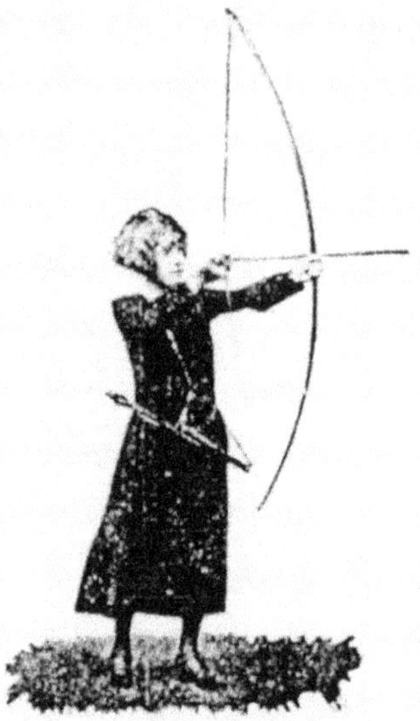

Fig. 3.12. *Detroit News Pictorial* ad, *Detroit Sunday News* (October 21, 1923): M7.

week." Others dealt with new construction: the widening of Woodward Avenue, which decades earlier "farsighted men had envisioned as "Detroit's Grand Boulevard"; and plans for "a municipal landing field" that later became the Ford airport in Dearborn, where "the first automobile ever to be transported by air was carried to Cleveland."[170] This last story suggests that, linked by Lake Erie, Detroit and Cleveland had a close, but competitive, relationship, perhaps stronger than any connection that Detroit had with Chicago.[171] Then there were stories that represented, as had the *Film Edition*, the city's development either spatially, in "Bird's eye views of Detroit," or over time, in a series that looked back "at the Detroit of fifty years ago" and the "past and present" differences in the city's skyline and street traffic.[172] Interestingly, several stories seemed to either repeat or extend those from the last issues of the *Film Edition*: building "the great lake steamer, the Detroiter," and tracing the process of filtration in the new water facility. Because a few other stories involved repetition—"teaching future carpenters at Highland Park" school; "the world's champion mail sorter at work"; and "Eddie Cantor and Flo Ziegfeld train[ing] the beauties in the new show, 'Kid Boots'"—could Metropolitan Film have recycled these during the transition from one newsreel to the other? Finally, in January 1924, the *Pictorial* featured a story similar to Ford's industrial, *De-Light*: "the development of the book from earlier times to the present day shown in a 400 foot reel."[173]

News cameramen continued to film famous visitors who toured the city. Among the entertainment stars other than Cantor and Ziegfeld, the "famous Russian actress" Galena Kopernack appeared at the Madison; Alice Brady and Irene Delroy "thrilled the kiddies" at St. Francis School for [orphan] Boys; the following month Snub Pollard showed off his "prize antics" at the same school, and John Philip Sousa conducted a performance of the touring Marine Band.[174] Later celebrities included Helen Keller, Notre Dame's football coach Knute Rockne, and polar explorer Captain Donald B. MacMillan.[175] Among the foreign dignitaries were the Prince of Wales, filmed by the *News* humorist Straphanger; the Polish general Joseph Haller; ace pilots René Fonck and Eddie Rickenbacker; the German ambassador to the United States; and even a "Danish gym master and his troupe of athletes.[176] Besides filming celebrities, Straphanger contributed pithy versions of his "pungent paragraphs" printed in the newspaper.[177] Indeed, as a measure of the city's growing international status, several stories highlighted delegation exchanges with foreign countries: in one week, the visits of Peace Special members and four rabbis from abroad; in another, the reverse visits of Detroit architects to a conference in England.[178]

For all its attention to metropolitan growth and popular celebrities, the *Pictorial*, again following the *Film Edition*, continued to treat audiences to scenes of important social events. Some appeared as a regular attraction each year, notably from the parades on Armistice Day, Memorial Day, and Arbor Day in Lansing to the annual dog shows as well as flower festivals and winter carnivals on Belle Isle. Others promoted high-society activities, from a Grosse Pointe Hunt Club steeplechase or Detroit Riding and Hunting Club horse show to the Detroit Federation of Women's Clubs' donation of trees to the city or the annual Community Fund Drive, the extended subject of an earlier *Ford Educational Weekly*.[179] But there were singular events as well: Mrs. Henry Ford "breaking ground" at Dearborn for a new library; the Detroit Yacht Club's ball, with members dressed as

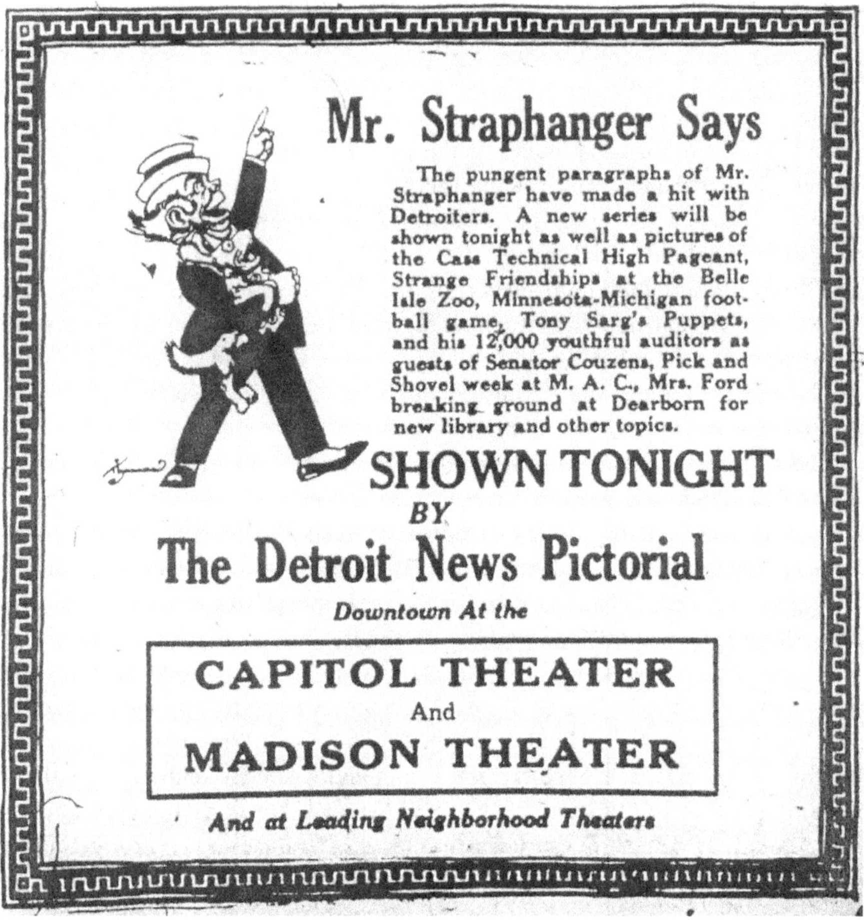

Fig. 3.13. *Detroit News Pictorial* ad, *Detroit Sunday News* (November 25, 1923): 2.7.

pirates "frolicking peacefully"; an East Jefferson merchants parade; Rotarians taking "a ramble in the clouds" in a balloon joyride; the harvest of the burgeoning cherry crop, with the assistance of "local Indians"; and a peculiarly insensitive stunt cryptically entitled "Wedding in Jail."[180] By contrast, the *News* itself sponsored a "hero contest" in which the top prize was a $10,000 furnished model home, which was won by a blind war veteran.[181] As with the *Film Edition*, sporting events like auto and yacht races, regattas, golf tournaments, and swimming contests were a constant feature.[182] And college football clearly was becoming an obsession for more and more fans in southeast Michigan, given weekly coverage of the University of Michigan games each fall."[183] A surprising number of stories were devoted to children of all ages at work and at play. They ranged from Tony

Sarg's Puppets delighting "12,000 youthful auditors," a performance of *Alice in Wonderland* at East High School, a pageant displaying technical advances for the home at Thirkell School, a "Contest of Nations" pageant at Franklin School, and the National Oratorical Contest at Cass Technical High, to a masquerade put on by the Detroit News Young Writers' Clubs, "Keating School boys building a huge slide for children at Farmington Hospital," Linden and Ellis School classmates making toys and dolls for poor kids, and children enjoying little Sheba the elephant newly arrived at the Belle Isle zoo.[184]

Like the *Film Edition*, the *Pictorial* could not ignore stories that did not fit the *News*'s promotion of the city, although such stories were infrequent. Cameramen recorded images of fires that destroyed the downtown dock section at the foot of Woodward and that killed three people in another building just east of downtown.[185] With few stories about the auto industry, the newsreel instead captured footage of motoring accidents like that of a student driver, "a trip through Detroit's auto scrap heap [of] broken down fliv[s]," and "unusual views of . . . congested traffic areas."[186] Besides the scenes of well-off children helping their poorer peers, the newsreel showed footage of a baby left alone on a doorstep, crippled children invited to a special Christmas party, and Ypsilanti coeds blithely modeling "their ability to live on a budget of $3 a week."[187] Rarely did stories of lower-class workers slip in: a street car conductor who had been "on the job for 38 years," Department of Street Railways (DSR) workers removing "disputed tracks" after the transfer from a private to a public streetcar system and then constructing new tracks in record time, and skilled workmen completing the top of the Book Cadillac Hotel.[188] Even more rare were stories of crime or of explicit class or ethnic conflict, and those tended to focus on the city as a hub of bootlegging during Prohibition. One story posed Sheriff Walters surrounded by "his host of captured stills"; another reported on a meeting of National Prohibition chiefs seeking ways to "stop the rum flow" into the city.[189] Perhaps the most intriguing showed "State Troopers conduct[ing a] 'booze' raid in Hamtramck" in May 1924.[190] This story focused on a Polish gang (possibly involving that city's mayor, who was later indicted for bootlegging)—a story that singled out the Polish rather than other criminals like the Purple Gang.[191]

What can one glean from selecting some ten *Pictorial* stories from the surviving film clips to analyze—stories that nearly all were part of particular newsreel issues between late 1923 and early 1925? Most of those, at one point or another, produce the kinds of attraction so characteristic of the earliest *actualités*. A few offer moving images of famous people visiting the city. In a mid-November 1924 clip, there are close shots of "Commander John Philip Sousa" and "Capt. William H. Santelmann, director of the President's own Marine Band" during a local band performance. A week later, similar shots show "Gar" Wood, the "internationally known yachtsman" (and a Detroit native), honored as "commodore of the Sea

Scout Troop No. 31" at a Detroit Yacht Club ceremony. Others address audiences more directly, asking them to identify friends, relatives, and even themselves on the screen. In December 1923, the leaders of the local Goodfellows gather as "Old Newsboys"—in one shot, the camera pans across a line of them as James Brady, founder of the organization, heartily shakes their hands—in an annual campaign to raise funds for the city's poor children. At the same time, the newsreel crams in as many masquerading members of the Yacht Club Barnacles as possible during their "Pirate Ball." There is a close up of Harold Aarons, captain of the Barnacles, as a smiling Captain Kidd and another of Dr. Charles W. Coulter as "one of Capt. Kidd's fiercest," leering evilly over a big knife clutched in his teeth. At least one other member, Miss Mariann Boftwick, appears with Kidd in a "Colonial costume." Others singled out, however, remain unnamed—whether "jolly pirates," "gentle lady pirates," or a young woman tentatively trying to stab a pirate—leaving audiences to try to recognize them. Hardly any of those filmed in any of these clips, of course, seem "ordinary" citizens.

The film clip titled "Old and New Detroit," from November 1924, provides a good example of the *Pictorial*'s boosterism, its promotion of the city's progress. This story is organized as a series of contrasts between photographs of specific sites from 1871 to 1900 and shots of buildings located at the same site in the present. Repeatedly, small wooden or brick structures—the First Baptist Church—give way to imposing light-colored skyscrapers—the Dime Bank, YMCA, and Kresge Building. The last photo of the series shows the Detroit City Hall, built in 1871 on rather empty grounds, followed by a recent shot of the same building dwarfed by looming skyscrapers. Perhaps as a way to maintain interest in this repetitive organization, the newsreel deploys a bevy of transitional filmic devices: fades, irises, dissolves, and blurs in and out. Whether or not this contrast between old and new would have pleased audiences at the time, it has a different effect now, at least for this viewer. The new buildings seem coldly monolithic, almost replicating one another from one shot to another. They may exemplify the "modern," as evidence of Detroit's status as a new metropolis, but they also seem to define the "modern" in terms of size, clean architectural lines, and "heavenly" reach at the expense of actual people, who are nowhere to be seen. Admirable as the new and modern may seem, at a distance, how would one inhabit and work in that world?

Three other film clips deploy different filmic devices. The first, "150-Foot Chimney Is Lowered" (undated, but likely from late 1923), exploits a trick found in early actualités. Basically, it reproduces in long shot the collapse of an "obsolete smoke shaft" just west of downtown on the riverfront. Initially that collapse occurs in real time; then it recurs in slow motion (filmed from a slightly different angle); and lastly, as an intertitle says, "We'll put it together again" through reverse slow motion. The second film clip, "Rogue Trolley Line Is Open," looks incomplete—and also may have been shot later in 1925. It begins as a high-angle long shot panning right across a crowd gathered for the ribbon-cutting ceremony, followed by a closer shot of Fordson mayor Floyd E. Yinger greeting Detroit officials. Resembling early phantom train rides, the remaining long shots, taken from the trolley cab, dolly forward toward a group of workmen before panning left as the rails curve, under a bridge, and then into a tunnel. Half of the visible workmen seem African American (Ford's new River Rouge plant hired a large number), but there is no sense that the trolley will be transporting them for a great distance, back and forth from Black Bottom. The third, "Three Killed, Four Injured in Downtown Fire" (from early December 1924), demonstrates the cameramen's skill in capturing firemen trying to cope with a major fire. This story begins with half a dozen long shots (two from a low angle) of a four-story building on fire in the gray evening mist, firemen carrying hoses up a fire escape, others barely outlined on the roof in the smoke, and four streams of water aimed at one façade wall. An intertitle, "Smoke from explosion of paint and varnish hinder fire fighters' efforts," adds a degree of danger to a tilting-up shot of smoke billowing in the darkness as well as several more of firemen working in the midst of smoke filling the frame. A final long shot shows two DSR linemen (according to an intertitle) trying to cut off the power to a high-tension wire; against a black background lit by the fire's flaring blaze, they come into focus only briefly as silhouettes on a ladder rising through some scaffolding.

Two lengthy film clips are very process-oriented in depicting different aerial events. One, "Six Rotarians Are Guests in Balloon Joy Ride" (from October 1924), includes shots of the balloon pilot, Ralph H. Upton ("chief engineer of Aircraft Development Corp."), and the six Rotary members whom many in a theater audience might identify. Most of the footage, however, focuses on preparations for the balloon launch in a gray misty morning. Those preparations include attaching the gondola to the balloon, checking the balloon's funnel, and collecting sandbags. Several short sequences, without intertitles, deploy well-established editing patterns. A long shot of two men positioning a large metal ring between the balloon and the gondola is followed by a closer low-angle shot of them grappling with the ring. After a shot of one man putting sand bags into the gondola, a high-angle close-up shows a sandbag dropping alongside others; then another, slightly different shot shows the same man putting in more sandbags. The film clip ends with a long shot of the balloon launch, with a tilt-up to follow its ascent and reveal the men clustered in the gondola and Upton perched on the ring above them. The other, "Fourth-Fifth Cities United by Air Line" (from early July 1925), offers to share with moviegoers the experience of a group of unnamed men (audiences likely could identify them) on an airplane flight from Detroit to Cleveland. Again, half a dozen shots show the men boarding, the plane moving forward before take-off, three or four men talking with one another inside the cabin, one looking out a window, the cockpit instrument panel, and a hand pointing at a location on a map. A short sequence deploys a point-of-view editing pattern familiar from fiction films: a mid-close-up of a different man looking out a window, a high-angle long shot of an ore ship that slowly turns in a circling pan, and another shot of the same man looking as before. Other high-angle long shots follow: a train being overtaken as it slices across the landscape, an unidentified cityscape that passes below. After an intertitle, "We encounter fog and rise above it," the plane is seen flying steadily through the gray sky, apparently shot from another plane nearby. The arrival in Cleveland, "one hour and forty minutes from Detroit," ends with another high-angle long shot of the airport landing area, with the plane and camera aligned in a gentle half-circle turn.

Finally, what can one glean from analyzing *News* ads about the *Pictorial*'s distribution and exhibition between late 1923 and early 1925? Most ads simply announced that the newsreel premiered downtown at both the Capitol and the Madison, where it could be seen all week. Apparently, the *News* and Metropolitan Film had an exclusive contract with Kunsky, which excluded the other competitive first-run theaters: the Broadway Strand, Regent, and Majestic. The earliest full-page ads, however, purportedly listed all theaters in the city (in alphabetical order) and in nearby towns where the *Pictorial* was screened.[192] Among those one hundred city venues were twenty located in or near one of three ethnic neighborhoods. The majority catered to Polish communities, but other than the Holbrook, Iris, and Russell, most had relatively small seating capacities. The ads, moreover, excluded two of the largest theaters, the Farnum and New Home in Hamtramck. Smaller ads, moreover, reveal that the theaters showing the *Pictorial* on Sundays, other than the Capitol, initially fluctuated, and distribution after that may have been staggered. In late October, the second issue appeared at the Dawn, De Luxe, and Tuxedo as well as two others in Jackson and Lansing. At the same time, the first issue was reaching the Stratford and the Library as well as a theater in Pontiac. In early November, the third issue screened, as before, at the first three venues; the second, at the Stratford and Library; and the first, at the Columbia, Harper, Jefferson, and Warren. None of those were ethnic neighborhood theaters.

In mid-December 1923, however, another large ad proves invaluable because it listed all of the theaters where the *Pictorial* was screening each specific day of the week.[193] While the newsreel opened at both the Capitol and the Madison for full-week runs, now it also appeared on Sunday at seventeen other theaters, nine of them not mentioned before, suggesting that the newsreel's distribution was becoming more stable. As expected, other Kunsky theaters were prominent: the Liberty also screened the newsreel all week, while the Garden had it only on Sunday; the Alhambra and Strand first showed it on Tuesday, after which it continued through Wednesday at the Strand. Of particular interest are the days when the *Pictorial* reached one or more theaters in ethnic neighborhoods. Two small venues—the Premier (Hamtramck) and the Enterprise (Little Italy)—also

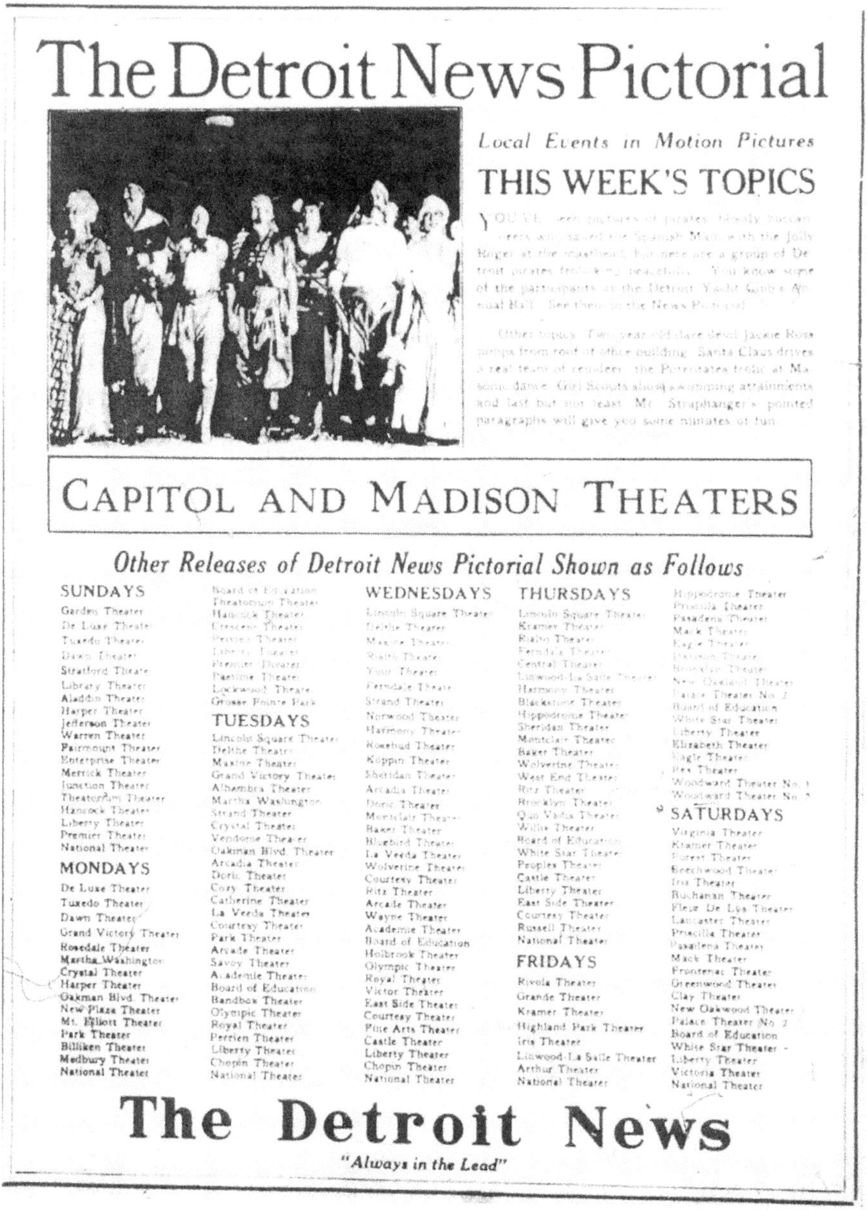

Fig. 3.14. *Detroit News Pictorial* ad, *Detroit Sunday News* (December 16, 1923): 2.12.

played it on Sunday, but for only one day. Seven others showed it on Monday—the Martha Washington, Park, Pastime, Perrien, and Premier (Hamtramck); the Crystal (West Side); and the Crescent (Del Ray)—for one- or two-day runs. Four more had it on Tuesday—the Arcade, Catherine, Savoy (Lower Poletown), and La Veeda (Highland Park)—again, for one- or two-day runs. Another three screened the newsreel on Wednesday—the Holbrook (Hamtramck), the Koppin and Rosebud (Black Bottom). Thursday was the turn of the Russell and White Star (Hamtramck), People's (Lower Poletown), and Quo Vadis (Little Italy). On Friday, the *Pictorial* finally came to the Eagle and Iris (Hamtramck) as well as the Highland Park.

Because the *News* posted no large ads throughout 1924, searching neighborhood theater columns in the Detroit papers results in a very sketchy picture of the *Pictorial*'s circulation. In mid-March, for instance, eight theaters in the *Sunday News*'s "Photoplays Today" column listed the newsreel on their programs: the Dawn, De Luxe, Fairmont, Garden, Harper, Jefferson, Library, and Tuxedo.[194] But two theaters in that column—the Merrick and Stratford—did not, although they were among those named in the *News*'s December ad. Moreover, eight theaters in the earlier ad—the Aladdin, Enterprise, Hancock, Junction, National, Premier, Theatorium, and Warren—did not even appear in the mid-March column. By early August, only five theaters in the *News*'s column—the Dawn, Harper, Jefferson, Library, and Tuxedo—named the newsreel on their programs.[195] A month later, La Veeda replaced the Dawn.[196] Other newspaper sources offer a little more information on the newsreel's circulation during the rest of that mid-March week. According to daily columns in the *Free Press*,[197] the Strand screened the *Pictorial* on Tuesday and Wednesday; the Lincoln Square, on Tuesday through Thursday. The Tuxedo also kept it on-screen from Sunday through Monday. Based on a few *Hamtramck News* ads, the Martha Washington also showed the newsreel on Monday and Tuesday.[198] Finally, in early 1925, while the *Pictorial* continued to screen all week at the Capitol and Madison, a few ads in the *Brightmoor News* suggest that it also was appearing on Monday at the Virginia, one of two theaters in the western suburb of Redford.[199] Despite this incomplete mapping of the *Pictorial*'s circulation between early 1924 and early 1925, especially in ethnic neighborhood theaters (with only brief references to the La Veeda and Martha Washington), the *News* and Metropolitan Film apparently found their local newsreel successful enough to sustain its production and distribution through the remaining years of the decade.

And So . . .

This "case study" of two local newsreels in Detroit undoubtedly raises many questions that involve broader contextualizing, only two of which will be taken up here (see also the afterword). First, assuming that both the *Film Edition* and the *Pictorial* were condensed weekly "magazines" of the previous week's newspaper stories, which stories were selected, and which were excluded, from among all those filling each paper's hundreds of pages? The first issue of the *Film Edition*, together with the past week of *Free Press* daily issues in March 1918, offers one very provisional answer. The initial *Film Edition* ads listed seven or eight stories, five of which received space in the newspaper. Of these five, three were short pieces: the funeral of John Whelan, held at his home by the Knights Templar; the appearance of Lillian Russell, DeWolf Hopper, and Raymond Hitchcock in a "Stage Women's War Relief benefit entertainment"; and new recruits escorting the Camp Custer Army Band in a city parade.[200] Variations on the fourth, Red Cross workers making surgical dressings, appeared almost daily: through lists of the various venues where the work was done, or, once, in the account of a Polish countess at the Central workroom headquarters, reporting on grave conditions in her country.[201] The fifth covered a big fire that destroyed the Monarch Steel Casting Plant in Solvay (on the city's western edge), which cost the company $100,000 and threw two hundred employees out of work.[202] Two stories either did not appear in the paper or perhaps were buried in a column or included within a war-related report: Detroit volunteers going off to their barracks in Columbus, and the ninety-two-year-old woman knitting socks for soldiers. In sum, the *Film Edition* seemed to choose stories of visual interest that demonstrated the city's contribution to the war effort and featured well-known or unusual individuals.[203] A similar question could be asked about the relationship between the stories shown in the *Pictorial* and those broadcast that week or the previous week on the *News*'s pioneering radio station, WWJ, which first began transmitting in August 1920.[204]

Second, related questions have to do with how these newsreels functioned, either implicitly or explicitly, as a form of "boosterism," continually promoting Detroit's industrial growth; the civic-mindedness of its population; and the wide range of social, cultural, and sporting activities on offer. Was the "boosterism" of the *Film Edition* in 1918–1919, stamped by the war and the Americanization movement, different from that of the *Pictorial*'s post-war era of booming manufacturing, rising prosperity, and increasing leisure and consumption? And did that "boosterism," however it was understood, have to serve different communities within the city differently? While both newsreels celebrated Detroit's elite citizens, often at play, both also told stories that modeled social behavior and occupational aspirations for most levels of society. But for whom, specifically? The apparent absence of stories representing the city's black community (except for that distant shot of black workers at River Rouge) seemed to confirm those citizens' persistent invisibility. Moreover, the choice of certain crime stories also betrayed a bias against the Polish and Italian communities, a bias that the distribution/exhibition patterns of the *Pictorial* in particular, at least initially, accentuated. But could those patterns also have set one community off from the other by favoring theaters (even small ones) that catered to each of the Polish neighborhoods while reaching no more than two neighborhoods in either Little Italy or Black Bottom? Furthermore, in the way they covered local social events, sports, politics, crimes, and disasters, might these newsreels have offered a framework for such coverage in later media forms such as radio and television news?

Notes

1. Lee Grieveson, "The Work of Film in the Age of Fordist Mechanization," *Cinema Journal* 51 no. 3 (Spring 2012): 25–51; Katy Peplin, "Ford Films and Ford Viewers: Examining 'Nontheatrical' Film in the Theaters and Beyond," in *The Institutionalization of Educational Cinema*, ed. Marina Dahlquist (Bloomington: Indiana University Press, forthcoming), The latter began as a paper submitted in an Advanced Seminar in Film History, in the Screen Arts & Cultures Department at the University of Michigan, Fall 2012.

2. Hearst had founded his newsreel in early 1916; its war stories, given his political position, largely came from correspondents in Germany after the British denied the International News Service—which Hearst formed in 1909 to coordinate his syndicated material by transmitting reports through its cable service—David Nasaw, *The Chief: The Live of William Randolph Hearst* (Boston: Houghton Mifflin, 2000), 234, 237, 245.

3. The *Hearst-Pathé News* merger ended in late 1918, probably due to Hearst's pro-German sympathies—Louis Pizzitola, *Hearst Over Hollywood: Power, Passion, and Propaganda in the Movies* (New York: Columbia University Press, 2002), 169.

4. Pathé News ad, *DSFP* (November 21, 1920): 4.14. Spot-checking reveals that *Pathé News* appeared at theaters from the De Luxe and Tuxedo to the Martha Washington and La Veeda throughout 1924—"Photoplays Today," *DSN* (January 12, 1924), n.p., and (March 16, 1924): Metropolitan, 6; Tuxedo ad, *HP* (April 25, 1924): 4; and Martha Washington ad, *HN* (July 13, 1924): n.p.

5. "What's Playing at Your Neighborhood Theatre," *DT* (June 3–10, 1923). See also Farnum ads, *HN* (August 22, 1924): n.p., and (October 24, 1924): n.p.

6. "With First Run Theaters," *MPN* (January 10, 1920): 611; and Farnum ads, *HN* (September 28, 1924): n.p., and (December 7, 1924): n.p.

7. "What's Playing at Your Neighborhood Theatre," *DT* (June 3–10, 1923). A year later, *Fox News* also was playing at the Kramer and the Virginia on Sunday—"Photoplays Today," *DSN* (July 6, 1924): Metropolitan, 6.

8. See also the Adams's "Current Events" compilation that included material from the *Universal Weekly* and *Pathé News*.

9. CPI's *The Making of an American Officer* did appear at one other first-run theater—Broadway Strand ad, *DSFP* (April 21, 1918): n.p. See also "Government Use of Motion Pictures," *R&S* (April 1918): 11–12.

10. For a good historical study of these women wireless operators, see Elizabeth Cobbs, *The Hello Girls: America's First Women Soldiers* (Cambridge, MA: Harvard University Press, 2017).

11. "Pathé Handles Army Pictures," *MPN* (September 7, 1918): 1546; and "War Reviews Interesting," *MPN* (January 18, 1919): 402.

12. "Buys Six New 'Italian Battlefront' Prints," *MPW* (January 5, 1918): 118; "'Behind the Lines in Italy'—Kleine," *MPN* (October 5, 1918): 2251; and "Pathé Release 'Alsace Lorraine,'" *R&S* (March 1919): 14. *France in Arms* appeared earlier at the Madison, but its source was

not given—Madison ad, *DSFP* (November 18, 1917): n.p. Other war films, such as *The Field of Flanders*, unidentified except for titles, appeared at the Adams in early 1919.

13. See the Arena Gardens Auditorium ad for *Wartime Europe: Impressions of 1918* in *DJC* (September 20, 1918): 3.

14. The Bray Pictograph allegedly carried stories drawn from *Women's Home Companion, Every Week, Popular Scientific Monthly, Metropolitan, Leslie's,* and *Field and Stream*—Paramount ad, *MPW* (February 9, 1918): 740–741.

15. Bray Studios ad, *MPN* (January 20, 1917): 371.

16. "Bray-Pictograph Drafted by the Government," *MPN* (July 28, 1917): 593; and "Screen Chat," *DFP* (August 25, 1918): 6.

17. Goldwyn Bray Pictograph ads, *MPN* (August 30, 1919): 1779, and (September 27, 1919): 2519.

18. "Ambitious Plans for Paramount Magazine," *MPN* (July 19, 1919): 718; and "Expansion of an Educational Dep't," *MPN* (October 4, 1919): 2791.

19. See the Baker ads, *DN*, from August 15 through November 14, 1920, and the Oakman ads, *DN*, from July 18, 1920, through January 2, 1921.

20. Gaumont produced the films compiled in Mutual's *Reel Life*—see the Gaumont ads, *MPN* (October 21, 1916): 2369, and *MPW* (February 10, 1917): 786.

21. Strand program, *WFN* (November 25, 1917): 15. One film featured in *Reel Life* was *Seeing the Undersea Garden*—see the Strand program, *WFN* (August 26, 1917): n.p.

22. "Topicals," *MPW* (February 2, 1918): 662. During that month, Paramount released five issues. See also the Universal ads, *MPN* (March 23, 1918): 1751, (April 6, 1918): 2085, (April 20, 1918): 2405), and (May 18, 1918): 2990.

23. "Screen Chats," *DFP* (February 2, 1920): 8, and (February 5, 1920): 10.

24. The *Kinogram* series was produced by Kinogram Publishing—"World Releases New Kinograms Series," *MPN* (January 11, 1919): 246; and Kinogram Publishing ad, *MPN* (January 25, 1919): 518. Charles Urban initially headed the company; Ray L. Hall served as editor, and Terry Ramsaye as associate editor.

25. "Screen Chats," *DSFP* (February 23, 1919): n.p.

26. "What's Playing at Your Neighborhood Theatre," *DT* (June 3–10, 1923); and "Photoplays Today," *DSN* (March 16, 1924): Metropolitan, 6. Apparently First National had taken over production of the weekly *Kinograms*, with fifty cameramen around the world, by 1921—Educational Films ad, *MPN* (February 26, 1921): 1595.

27. Kineto ad, *EFM* (February 1920): 3; "Feature Subjects of Short Length," *MPN* (October 2, 1920): 2560, and (November 27, 1920): 4120; and Kineto ad, *MPN* (January 1, 1921): 341.

28. Interestingly, it was in 1922 that "Charles Urban's Library of Films [were] Now Available in the Non-Theatrical Field," *EFM* (January 1922): 2.

29. *Pathé Review* ads, *MPN* (July 5, 1920): 39, and *MPN* (August 26, 1922): 1033. See, for instance, the Virginia ad, *DN* (December 6, 1919): n.p.

30. "What's Playing at Your Neighborhood Theatre," *DT* (June 3–10, 1923). In early 1925, *Pathé Review* also appeared at theaters like the Virginia in Redford—Virginia ad, *BJ* (February 2, 1925): n.p.

31. Making short appearances at the Majestic in 1918–1919 was Prizma's short-lived "natural color" series, with titles such as *Catalina Islands*. In late October 1922, the Broadway Strand screened *The Glorious Adventure*, starring Lady Diana Manners, filmed in "the perfected Prizma process"—Broadway Strand ad, *DSN* (October 22, 1922): Metropolitan, 7.

32. See the Washington, Alhambra, and Strand programs, *WFN* (September 17, 1916): n.p., and the Washington program, *WFN* (April 6, 1919): n.p.

33. "Sell Travel Pictures on Timely News Appeal," *MPW* (August 6, 1921): 603.

34. In 1922, the Koppin, for instance, was playing Burton Holmes Travelogues on Tuesdays and Wednesdays—Paramount ad, *DSFP* (March 12, 1922): 5.17.

35. See the Adams ads in *DSFP*, from July 14 to November 17, 1918.

36. Washington ads, *DSFP* (September 28, 1919): 4.11, (October 5, 1919): 4.17, and (November 2, 1919): 4.20; Lakewood ad, *DSFP* (July 18, 1920): 3.15; and Iris ad, DSFP (December 12, 1920): 5.30. See also the Knickerbocker ad, *DT* (June 4, 1923): n.p.

37. This information comes from the Detroit city directories of 1916–1917 through 1923–1924. In 1919, three other nonfiction film distributors—Community Motion Picture, International Church Film, and Robertson-Cole—also set up branch offices, along with a local firm, Maurice Film, but none remained open beyond 1920.

38. "Ditmar Animal Films Gave Book of Nature to Motion Pictures," *DNT* (March 4, 1917): n.p.

39. See also the Arena Gardens Auditorium ad, *DJC* (September 20, 1918): 3.

40. "Traveler Newman Opens Picture Series Tonight," *DSN* (February 26, 1921): Society, 18.

41. Educational Films ads, *MPN* (August 30, 1919): 1791, and February 26, 1921: 1596. Already by early 1920, eighty Bruce Scenics had been released—Educational Films ad, *MPN* (February 7, 1920): 1427.

42. Educational Films ad, *MPN* (December 20, 1919): inside front cover. See also "Bruce Scenics in Fifty Houses," *MPN* (December 18, 1920): 4617; and Lillian May's praise for the new Bruce Scenics series, in "The Soul of Europe," *MPM* (May 1921): 46–47.

43. A unique feature-length travel film to mention was *Sweden and the Gothenburg Exposition*, screened for one Saturday evening only on December15, 1923—Orchestra Hall ad, *DSN* (December 9, 1923): Metropolitan, 15.

44. "Photoplay Magazine Screen Supplement," *PM* (January 1919): 72; and *Photoplay Magazine Screen Supplement* ad, *PM* (July 1919): 126.

45. Educational Films ad, *MPN* (January 11, 1919): 208. Johnson also served as dramatic critic of the *Los Angeles Times* and, in 1922, was hired as manager of Paramount's Editorial department—"Julian Johnson, Noted Photoplay Authority, Appointed to High Office by Jesse L. Lasky," *Paramount Pep* (February 27, 1922): 13.

46. Educational Films ad, *MPN* (March 8, 1919): 1435.

47. No references appear in *Photoplay* or the trade press after February 1920.

48. *Screen Snapshots* ads, *MPN* (August 26, 1921): 1036, and *ETR* (August 26, 1921): 26. *Screen Snapshots* was edited by Jack Cohn and Louis Lewyn.

49. Roy E. Marcotte, "Close Ups," *DFP* (August 24, 1921): 8.

50. "Screen Snapshots Will Be State Righted by C.B.C." *MPW* (August 18, 1923): 385. Cohn and Lewyn continued to produce the series. See also "More Territories Sold on 'Screen Snapshots,'" *MPN* (September 15, 1923): 1330.

51. Garden and Rex ads, *DT* (April 27, 1923): 27; Arcadia ad, *DT* (April 28, 1923): 5; Globe ad, *DST* (April 29, 1923): 5.9, Park ads, *DT* (June 1, 1923): 25, and (July 6, 1923): 21; Ferry Field ad, *DST* (February 10, 1924). 8.4; and Tuxedo ad, *HP* (March 19, 1924): 5.

52. In early 1922, Dodge Brothers used a film to tell dealers why it was reducing the price of its motor cars—"Dodge Brothers Prices Reduced," *DJC* (January 1922): 3.

53. City directories list two other local firms, Joseph Horowitz and David Hartford, that may have manufactured nonfiction films, but only for a short period.

54. See especially chapter 1, "The Silent Pageant: Municipal Booster Films," in Martin L. Johnson, *Main Street Movies: The History of Local Film in the United States* (Bloomington: Indiana University Press, 2018), 16–55.

55. Daniel L. Lewis, *The Public Image of Henry Ford: An American Folk Hero and His Company* (Detroit: Wayne State University Press, 1976), 114; and Grieveson, "The Work of Film in the Age of Fordist Mechanization," 27.

56. "Make Ford Auto and Start in 2 1/2 Minutes—This Remarkable Record Caught in Moving Pictures at the Factory," *Los Angeles Times* (June 22, 1913)—quoted in Steven Watts, *The People's Tycoon: Henry Ford and the American Century* (New York: Alfred A. Knopf, 2005), 140 and 551, fn. 11.

57. Lewis, *The Public Image of Henry Ford*, 114.

58. "The Silent Celluloid Salesman," *FT* (July 1916): 534. Thanks to Katy Peplin for sharing this research information.

59. "The Silent Celluloid Salesman," 536.

60. Lewis, *The Public Image of Henry Ford*, 115.

61. Grieveson, "The Work of Film in the Age of Fordist Mechanization," 29.

62. Monnot & Sacher ad, *Canton Repository* (June 9, 1915): 7. See also the Temple ad, *Sault Ste. Marie* [Michigan] *News* (August 25, 1914): 1; Temple ad, *Ann Arbor News* (December 31, 1914): 7; Colonial ad, *Jackson* [Michigan] *Citizen Press* (October 9, 1915): 5; and "Theaters [Majestic]," *Council Bluffs* [Iowa] *Daily Nonpareil* (August 6, 1916): 18, and (October 8, 1916): 9.

63. Lewis, *The Public Image of Henry Ford*, 115. See also "Ford Exhibits Popular at San Francisco: Assembly Line, Sociological Displays, and Motion Pictures attract interested throngs," *FT* (July 1915): 455. Thanks again to Peplin for sharing this information.

64. Lewis, *The Public Image of Henry Ford*, 115.

65. A. B. Jewett, "Millions Get Ford Message by 'Educational Weekly' Films," *R&S* (March 1918): 31.

66. "Instructional Productions of the Month," *MPA* (December 1919): 20. *From Mud to Mug* survives at the US Library of Congress—see "De-Light: Making an Electric Light Bulb (1920)," in *More Treasures from American Film Archives, 1894–1931*, ed. Scott Simmon (San Francisco: National Film Preservation Foundation, 2004): 40.

67. Jewett, "Millions Get Ford Message," 31.

68. Ibid.

69. "The Ford Weekly," *R&S* (July 1919): 7; Lewis, *The Public Image of Henry Ford*, 115.

70. See, for instance, "Boys Selling Ford's Weekly Are Warned," *DSFP* (March 20, 1921): 1.18; and "Welsh Bill Would End Ford Attack on Jews," *DFP* (April 13, 1921): 17.

71. Lewis, *The Public Image of Henry Ford*, 116.

72. See the Ferry Field ads in *DSFP*, from August 19 to December 23, 1917.

73. Majestic ads, *DSFP* (June 30, 1918): n.p., (August 25, 1918): n.p., (October 13, 1918): 4.6, and (November 10, 1918); 4.8. Despite the demonstrated inability of Ford's Eagle tank to maneuver across trenches, this *Educational Weekly* continued to screen for another week—Majestic ad, *DSFP* (November 17, 1918): 4.9.

74. Washington ad, *DSFP* (August 11, 1918): n.p.; and Majestic ads, *DSFP* (November 24, 1918): n.p., (December 8, 1918): 4.14, and (January 4, 1919): n.p.

75. "Photoplays at Your Favorite Theater Today," *DN* (September 6, 1921): 22.

76. See the Garden ads in *DSN*, from August 30 to December 27, 1921. One other theater listed a *Ford Weekly* even later—see the Dawn ads, *DSN* (June 10, 1922): n.p., and (November 22, 1922): n.p.

77. *Ford Educational Weekly* ads, *R&S* (June 1919): 30, and *MPA* (November 1919): 41.

78. *Ford Educational Weekly* ads, *MPA* (December 1919): 31, and (February 1920): 7. See also Jerome Lachenbruch, "Industrial Film as an Americanizer," *EFM* (February 1920): 15.

79. With Professor William H. Dudley (University of Wisconsin-Madison), also in 1919, Kleine began planning a "library" that would link up with state university extension divisions and supply features, one-reel comedies, and educational shorts for classroom use. Kleine's library finally emerged in 1921 and lasted into the late 1920s, in spite of his attacks (based on an antisemitism that Ford shared) on the National Non-Theatrical Pictures organization. Joel Frykholm, *George Kleine and American Cinema: The Movie Business and Film Culture in the Silent Era* (London: Palgrave, 2015), 143–158.

80. Jessie Robb, "The Educational and Non-Theatrical Field," *MPW* (January 22, 1921): 451. See also Beatrice Barrett, "Visual Education for Every School Everywhere," *EFM* (February 1921): 8.

81. Lewis, *The Public Image of Henry Ford*, 116.

82. Ford Educational Library ad, *EFM* (January 1922): inside front cover; Ford Motion Picture Laboratories ads, *MPA* (September 1922): 19, (October 1922): 19, (November 1922): 19, and (December 1922): 19.

83. Lewis, *The Public Image of Henry Ford*, 116.

84. Ibid.

85. "Ford Library for Theatres: 40 Subjects to Be Available for Exhibitors as Well as Schools," *MPN* (March 12, 1921): 1946.

86. Lee Grieveson analyzes several films that are available for viewing only at the National Archives: *Democracy in Education* (1919), *The Romance of Making a Modern Newspaper* (1919), *Farm Progress* (1924), and *The Road to Happiness* (1924)—see Grieveson, "The Work of Film in the Age of Fordist Mechanization," 34–37, 41. *The Romance of Making a Modern Newspaper* likely was an alternate title for *When Black Is Read*—see Jerome Lachebruch, "Industrial Film as an Americanizer," *EFM* (February 1920): 15.

87. Scott Simmon, "De-Light: Making an Electric Light Bulb (1920)," *More Treasures from American Film Archives*, 40. Simmon also writes that "drawn filaments made of tungsten," which were essential for electric light bulbs, were invented only in 1910.

88. Ford may have been responsible for several earlier local news films: *B. of C. Americanization Campaign*, shown at the Majestic in September 1916, and *Behind the Scenes in a Big Detroit Hotel*, at the Alhambra in late January 1917—Majestic ad, *DSFP* (September 24, 1916): 4.5; and Alhambra program, *WFN* (January 28, 1917): 11. "B. of C.," or the Board of Commerce, was greatly involved in the Americanization movement.

89. Scott Simmon, "Lights and Shadows in a City of a Million," in *Treasures III: Social Issues in American Film, 1900–1934*, ed. Scott Simmon (San Francisco: National Film Preservation Foundation, 2007): 29.

90. See the Rosedale ad, *DSN* (September 26, 1920): Society, 18; the Norwood ad, *DSN* (October 3, 1920): Society, 22; and the Oakman ad, *DFP* (November 30, 1920): 11.

91. See, for instance, Richard Abel, "The 'Much Vexed Problem' of Nontheatrical Distribution in the Late 1910s," *Moving Image* (Fall 2016): 91–107.

92. The *Northwest Weekly*'s first issue may have appeared as early as April or May 1915, according to "Northwest Movies at Orpheum Weekly," *Bismarck Tribune* (October 15, 1915): 4. In early August, the *Northwest Weekly* did offer footage of the Eastland Disaster, perhaps excerpted from the *Herald Movies*—Ideal Theatre ad, *Grand Rapids Leader* [Wisconsin] (August 2, 1915): n.p. See also "Reel Newspaper for Duluthians," *Duluth News Tribune* (September 5, 1915): 12; and "Tribune's Northwest Weekly," *Albert Lea Evening Tribune* (November 6, 1915): n.p.

93. Ray H. Leek, "Here Are the First 'Herald Movies,'" *Chicago Herald* (July 5, 1914): 5.1.

94. *Animated Weekly* ad, *Chicago Tribune* (June 4, 1915): 9.

95. *Indianapolis Star-Universal Animated Weekly* ad, *Indianapolis Star* (October 19, 1915): 9.

96. "Selig-Tribune Showing Today," *Chicago Tribune* (January 3, 1916): 2.1. For a full menu of each *Selig-Tribune* issue, see the listings that begin in "Stories of the Films," *MPW* (January 22, 1915): 656.

97. "Daily Cleveland to Be On Screen," *CPD* (May 24, 1917): 6. For further information on the *Plain Dealer*'s newsreel, see Richard Abel, "Reading Newspapers and Writing American Silent Cinema History," in Daniel Biltereyst, Richard Maltby, and Philippe Meers, eds., *The Routledge Companion to New Cinema History* (New York: Routledge, 2019), 68-82. The *Cleveland Leader* also was putting out a *News Weekly* that was screening in several theaters in late 1919 and early 1920—see "With the First Run Theatres," *MPN* (December 6, 1919): 4084, and (January 10, 1920): 611.

98. "Detroit Wants Magazine Like Plain Dealer's," *CPD* (July 26, 1917): 6.

99. Advertisements, *DSFP* (March 3, 1918): 4.8, and (March 10, 1918): 4.8.

100. "Free Press Photographer Snaps People and Happenings," *DFP* (May 19, 1918): 18; and "Len H. Roos New A.S.C. Member," *American Cinematographer* (October 1924): 23.

101. "The Free Press Film Edition Attraction at Washington," *DFP* (March 17, 1918): 12; and "Detroit's Life in Pictures to Be Seen on Many Screens," *DFP* (March 18, 1918): 5.

102. "The Free Press Film Edition Shows New Topics This Week," *DFP* (March 24, 1918): 16; "Free Press Film Is Replete with Views of City Events," *DFP* (April 8, 1918): 6; and "Free Press Films Show Big Events," *DFP* (April 25, 1918): 2.

103. "Soldiers Moving to East Seen in Free Press Film," *DFP* (June 9, 1918): 8.

104. "The Free Press Film Edition Shows New Topics This Week," *DFP* (March 24, 1918): 16.

105. "Liberty Loan Is Featured in Free Press Film Edition," *DFP* (April 7, 1918): 8; and "Free Press Film Is Replete with Views of City Events," *DFP* (April 8, 1918): 6.

106. "Liberty Loan Drive Events Shown in Free Press Film," *DFP* (April 14, 1918): 8.

107. "Sunday's Great Parade Seen in Free Press Film Edition," *DFP* (May 20, 1918): 6.

108. "Soldiers Moving to East Seen in Free Press Film," *DFP* (June 9, 1918): 8; "Clemens Harness Races Shown in Free Press Film," *DFP* (June 16, 1918): 3; and "Film Edition Will Show Entry of Tank to City," *DFP* (June 20, 1918): 10.

109. "Michigan Soldiers in France Shown in Free Press Films," *DFP* (July 14, 1918): 8.

110. "Women War Workers Big Feature in Free Press Film," *DFP* (September 22, 1918): 11.

111. "Loan Campaign Big Feature of Free Press Films Edition," *DFP* (October 6, 1918): 11; "Italian Alpine Soldiers Shown in Free Press Film," *DFP* (October 13, 1918): 8; and "Free Press Film Edition Shows Veterans of Italy," *DFP* (October 14, 1918): 8.

112. "Free Press 'Movie' Artist Records 'Peace' Celebration," *DFP* (November 10, 1918): 5. Although a long feature story celebrated the women switchboard operators who linked American and French officers during the last months of the war, no story featured the eight from Detroit in the *Free Press Film Edition*—Bernice Stewart, "Interweaving the Speech of Two Nations," *DSFP* (November 3, 1918): Rotogravure, 3. Three of those Detroit operators are mentioned in Cobbs, *The Hello Girls*.

113. "All Phases of Detroit Life Seen in Free Press 'Movies,'" *DFP* (March 31, 1918): 6.

114. "Sixth Free Press Film Brings Treat to All Baseball Fans," *DFP* (April 22, 1918): 9.

115. "'Teddy' and His Smile Seen in Free Press Film Edition," *DFP* (June 3, 1918): 7.

116. "Week's Big Events Pictured in Free Press Film Edition," *DFP* (May 26, 1918): A3; and Advertisement, *DFP* (May 26, 1918): C10.

117. "Soldiers Moving to East Seen in Free Press Film," *DFP* (June 9, 1918): 8.

118. "Michigan Soldiers in France Shown in Free Press Film," *DFP* (July 14, 1918): 8.

119. "Power Boat Race Just One Event in Free Press Films," *DFP* (September 1, 1918): 4.

120. "Live Happenings in Detroit Shown in Free Press Films," *DFP* (May 6, 1918): 7.

121. "Michigan Soldiers in France Shown in Free Press Films," *DFP* (July 14, 1918): 8; "Marine Pictures Feature Free Press Film Edition," *DFP* (August 18, 1918): 4; and "Building of Big Ship Shown in Free Press Film Edition," *DFP* (September 29, 1918): 16.

122. "Italian Alpine Soldiers Shown in Free Press Film," *DFP* (October 13, 1918): 8.

123. "Tigers Maul the White Sox in Free Press Film Edition," *DFP* (June 30, 1918): 15; "Marine Pictures Feature Free Press Film Edition," *DFP* (August 18, 1918): 4; and "Free Press Film Edition Shows Auto Races at Fair," *DFP* (September 8, 1918): 5.

124. "Marine Pictures Feature Free Press Film Edition," *DFP* (August 18, 1918): 4. Here is the relevant sentence: "This scenic wonderland is shown with the summer sunlight glistening on the waterways and shimmering from the green leaves along the wooded shores and, on the return voyage, dressed in the fairy yellows and greens of a moonlit summer evening."

125. "Free Press Photographer Snaps People and Happenings," *DFP* (May 19, 1918): 18; "Free Press Film Edition Shows Auto Races at Fair," *DFP* (September 8, 1918): 5; and "Free Press Film Edition Is Gladsome Review of Smiles," *DFP* (November 7, 1918): 5.

126. Advertisement, *DFP* (March 21, 1918): 8; "Building of Big Ship Shown in Free Press Film Edition," *DFP* (September 29, 1918): 16; and "Bishop's Installation Seen in Free Press Film Edition," *DFP* (November 24, 1918): 14.

127. "Municipal Cleanup Shown in Free Press Film Edition," *DFP* (August 25, 1918): 22.

128. "Influenza Dangers Shown in Fred Press Film Edition," *DFP* (November 11, 1918): 6.

129. "How to Keep Cool Pictured in Free Press Film Edition," *DFP* (August 12, 1918): 2. See also Harry Barnard, *Independent Man: The Life of Senator James Couzens* (New York: Charles Scribner, 1958), 115.

130. Advertisement, *DFP* (May 26, 1918): C10.

131. Advertisement, *DFP* (August 11, 1918): C6. This ad also listed the Warsaw in Hamtramck, but I have found no other reference to this theater.

132. Advertisement, *DSFP* (November 17, 1918): C3.

133. "Big Film Weeklies Merge with Free Press Edition," *DFP* (November 17, 1918): 8.

134. "Can You See Yourself Shopping in Free Press Film Edition," *DFP* (December 29, 1918): 21; and Advertisement, *DFP* (April 6, 1919): 4.12.

135. "Bishop's Installation Seen in Free Press Film Edition," *DFP* (November 24, 1918): 14; "Ex-President Taft Shown in Free Press Film Edition," *DFP* (December 15, 1918): 5; "Sports and War Are Mingled in Free Press Film Edition," *DFP* (January 19, 1919): 8; and "Sicilians' Feuds Feature Free Press Film Edition," *DFP* (March 9, 1919): 16.

136. "Free Press Film To Show What Big Fire Looks Like," *DFP* (February 16, 1919): 16; "Sicilians' Feuds Feature Free Press Film Edition," *DFP* (March 9, 1919): 16; "Elkdom in Pair of Frolics Shown in Free Press Film," *DFP* (June 1, 1919): 8; "Events of World Interest Shown in Free Press Film," *DFP* (June 15, 1919): 18; and "Plans to Receive Dirigible Shown in Free Press Film," *DFP* (June 22, 1919): 8.

137. "Dogdom's Aristocrats Pose for Free Press Film Edition," *DFP* (December 7, 1919): 18.

138. "Bishop's Installation Seen in Free Press Film Edition," *DFP* (November 24, 1918): 14; and "Events of World Interest Shown in Free Press Film," *DFP* (June 15, 1919): 18; "Sports and War Are Mingled in Free Press Film Edition," *DFP* (January 19, 1919): 8; and "Sicilians' Feuds Feature Free Press Film Edition," *DFP* (March 9, 1919): 16; "Signing of Versailles Pact Shown in Free Press Film," *DFP* (July 13, 1919): 5; and "Inter-Allied Games in Paris Depicted in Free Press Film," *DFP* (July 20, 1919): 5.

139. "Wilson Screened Oversea for Free Press Film Issue," *DFP* (January 26, 1919): 10; and "Events of World Interest Shown in Free Press Film," *DFP* (June 15, 1919): 18.

140. "Beautiful Floral Display Shown in Free Press Film," *DFP* (April 14, 1919): 5; "Inter-Allied Games in Paris Depicted in Free Press Film," *DFP* (July 20, 1920): 5; and "Therapy Work of Red Cross Shown in Free Press Film," *DFP* (January 4, 1920): 22.

141. "Elkdom in Pair of Frolics Shown in Free Press Film," *DFP* (June 1, 1919): 8; and "Golden Gate Yacht Racing Is Shown in Free Press Film," *DFP* (June 29, 1919): 27;

142. "To Show Returned Heroes in *Free Press Film Edition*," *DFP* (December 25, 1918): 2.

143. Advertisement, *DSFP* (January 5, 1919): C10; "Wilson Screened Oversea for Free Press Film Issue," *DFP* (January 26, 1919): 10; and "Army Hospital 36 Pictured in Free Press Film Edition," *DFP* (January 27, 1919): 6.

144. "Red Cross Clothing Drive Is Free Press Film Topic," *DFP* (March 30, 1919): 6; "Signing of Versailles Pact Shown in Free Press Film," *DFP* (July 13, 1919): 5; "Inter-Allied Games in Paris Depicted in Free Press Film," *DFP* (July 20, 1919): 5; and "Gen. Pershing's Visit Shown in Free Press Film Edition," *DFP* (December 23, 1919): 22.

145. "Free Press Films to Show Old Newsboys Back on Job," *DFP* (December 22, 1918): 16; "Wilson Screened Oversea for Free Press Film Issue," *DFP* (January 26, 1919): 10; and "Sicilians' Feud Feature Free Press Film Edition," *DFP* (March 9, 1919): 16.

146. "Sports and War Are Mingled in Free Press Film Edition," *DFP* (January 19, 1919): 8; "Beautiful Floral Display Shown in Free Press Film," *DFP* (April 14, 1919): 5; "Detroit Youngsters at Play Is Shown in Free Press Film," *DFP* (May 26, 1919): 9; "Events of World Interest Shown in Free Press Film," *DFP* (June 14, 1919): 18; "Inter-Allied Games in Paris Depicted in Free Press Film," *DFP* (July 20, 1919): 5; and "Isle Pageant, Boat Races, Police Drill Seen in Film," *DFP* (September 8, 1919): 5.

147. "Movie Man 'Shot' City from Clouds," *DFP* (May 4, 1919): 8; and "Golden Gate Yacht Racing Shown in Free Press Film," *DFP* (June 29, 1919): 27.

148. "Free Press Film to Show What Big Fire Looks Like," *DFP* (February 16, 1919): 16; and "Fire at Wadsworth Plant Is Screened by Free Press," *DFP* (August 10, 1919): 5.

149. "Ex-President Taft Shown in Free Press Film Edition," *DFP* (December 15, 1919): 5; and "How Recent Strike Looked Shown in Free Press Film," *DFP* (June 16, 1919): 5.

150. "Where Penny Buys a Meal; Free Press Film Shows It," *DFP* (March 16, 1919): 4; "Children at Fresh Air Camps Depicted in Free Press Film," *DFP* (July 21, 1919): 5; "Aerial 'Cops' Making Arrest Shown in Free Press Film," *DFP* (July 27, 1919): 5; and "Free Press to Show How Detroit Played Santa," *DFP* (December 28, 1919): 12.

151. "Sicilians' Feuds Feature Free Press Film Edition," *DFP* (March 9, 1919): 16; and "Golden Gate Yacht Racing Is Shown in Free Press Film," *DFP* (June 29, 1919): 27.

152. "Departure of 35 City Reds Depicted in Free Press Film," *DFP* (January 18, 1920): 2.

153. "Majestic to Run Free Press Film," *DFP* (February 23, 1919): 15.

154. "Events of World Interest Shown in Free Press Film," *DFP* (June 15, 1919): 18.

155. Advertisement, *DSFP* (September 19, 1920): 3.18.

156. "Free Press Film to Receive News Pictures from Merged Weeklies," *DSFP* (January 16, 1921): C12.

157. "Local News Only, New Free Press Film Idea," *DSFP* (May 29, 1921): D5.

158. "Free Press Film Moves to Madison," *DSFP* (October 16, 1921): 1.6; and Advertisement, *DSFP* (October 16, 1921): 5.10.

159. "'Good Stories' Are Happening Every Day in Detroit," *DSFP* (January 18, 1920): 4.13.

160. Advertisement, *DSFP* (October 16, 1921): 5.10.

161. Edward G. Guest, nicknamed the "Poet of the Plain People," was a frequent contributor to the *DFP* from 1898 on—Frank Angelo, *On Guard: A History of the Detroit Free Press* (Detroit: Detroit Free Press, 1981), 131–136.

162. "Detroit News Takes Over Free Press Reel," *MPN* (November 10, 1923): 2250. See also Ben Strassfeld, "Local Orphans: Examining Detroit Newsreels of the 1920s," presented at the regional Orphans Film Conference at Indiana University, September 26, 2013. His research showed that the *News Pictorial* ceased in mid-1929, probably because of higher costs involved with sound film, but the *Detroit Times*, in conjunction with Metropolitan, did produce a weekly *Times Topics* for at least a year in 1930–1931.

163. "Filmed News Ready Sunday," *DN* (October 20, 1923): n.p.; and "See the News on the Screen," *DSN* (October 21, 1923): 1.1.

164. *Detroit News Pictorial* ad, *DSN* (October 14, 1923): 2.7.

165. *Detroit News Pictorial* ad, *DSN* (October 21, 1923): 2.7.

166. "Filmed News Ready Sunday," *DN* (October 20, 1923): n.p.; and "See the News on the Screen," *DSN* (October 21, 1923): 1.1.

167. "Clipped From The News Pictorial," *DSN* (October 21, 1923): Metropolitan, 9.

168. *Detroit News Pictorial* ad, *DSN* (October 21, 1923): 2.7.

169. Admittedly, the majority of discrete story clips are dated 1927 and 1928, and I have not examined weekly ads during that period. So, research on those years might let one reconstitute more newsreels, either in full or in part.

170. *Detroit News Pictorial* ads, *DSN* (November 4, 1923): Metropolitan, 8, (November 18, 1923): Metropolitan, 7, (December 2, 1923): Metropolitan, 7, (December 30, 1923): Metropolitan, 7, (August 10, 1924): Metropolitan, 6, (November 16, 1924): n.p, and (July 5, 1925): Metropolitan, 7.

171. The rivalry with Cleveland is evident in "Made in Detroit USA: Detroit So Rich You Can Feel It,' Asserts Manhattan Writer," *DFP* (December 29, 1919): 8; and the athletic competition between two German American social organizations in "the Detroit and Cleveland Socialer Turnverein"—Advertisement, *DN* (July 2, 1925): 37.

172. *Detroit News Pictorial* ad, *DN* (November 9, 1924): 2.7, (November 30, 1924): 2.7, (March 21, 1925): n.p., and (July 2, 1925): 37. See also the newsreel stories 3R1.3 and 3R1.33 on the Wayne State University Library website.

173. Advertisement, *DSN* (January 19, 1924): 3.12.

174. *Detroit News Pictorial* ads, *DN* (December 9, 1923): 2.12, (October 12, 1924): 2.7, (November 2, 1924): 2.9, and (November 16, 1924): 2.6.

175. See the numbered stories 2.15, 2.16, and 2.22 on the Wayne State University Library website.

176. *Detroit News Pictorial* ads, *DN* (October 28, 1918): n.p., (November 18 1923): 2.7, and (October 19 1924): 2.7. See also the newsreel stories 3R1.6 and 3R1.27 on the Wayne State University Library website. Rickenbacker appeared at the Detroit Opera House, along with motion pictures and slides compiled as *The Arena of the Sky*—Detroit Opera House ad, *DJC* (2 May 1919): 6.

177. *Detroit News Pictorial* ad, *DSN* (December 23, 1923): Metropolitan, 7.

178. *Detroit News Pictorial* ads, *DN* (June 8, 1924): n.p., and (July 6, 1924): n.p.

179. *Detroit News Pictorial* ads, *DN* (October 28, 1923): 7, (November 2, 1924): 2.9, (November 9, 1924): 2.7, (November 23, 1924): 2.5, (November 20, 1924): n.p,, and (January 19, 1924): 3.1.

180. *Detroit News Pictorial* ads, *DN* (December 16, 1923): 2.12, (August 3 1924): n.p., and (October 19, 1924): 2.7. See also the newsreel stories 2.12 and 3R1.19 on the Wayne State University Library website.

181. *Detroit News Pictorial* ads, *DN* (December 9, 1923): n.p., and (December 30, 1923): n.p.

182. *Detroit News Pictorial* ads, *DN* (October 19, 1924): 2.7, (July 20, 1924): n.p., (August 31, 1914): n.p., (September 7, 1924): n.p., and (October 19, 1924): n.p. See also the newsreel stories 3R1.7 and 3R1.11 on the Wayne State University Library website.

183. See the football games featured in the *Detroit News Pictorial* ads, *DN*, from (November 11, 1923): 2.7, to (November 20, 1925): n.p.

184. *Detroit News Pictorial* ads, *DN* (November 4, 1923): 2.7, (November 11, 1923): 2.7, (November 25, 1923): 2.7, (December 16, 1923): 2.12, (April 4, 1924): n.p., (May 1, 1924): n.p., and (March 21, 1925): n.p. See also the newsreel stories 3R1.5, 3R1.12, 3R1.20, and 3R1.32 on the Wayne State University Library website.

185. *Detroit News Pictorial* ads, *DN* (December 2, 1923): 2.7, and (September 1, 1925): n.p. See also the newsreel story 2.20 on the Wayne State University Library website.

186. *Detroit News Pictorial* ads, *DN* (November 18, 1923): 2.7, (November 26, 1924): 2.7, and (May 1, 1924): n.p. See also the newsreel story 3R2.2 on the Wayne State University Library website.

187. *Detroit News Pictorial* ads, *DN* (November 11, 1923): 2.7, and (October 26, 1924): 2.7. See also the newsreel stories 2.8 and 2.17 on the Wayne State University Library website.

188. *Detroit New Pictorial* ads, *DN* (June 1, 1924): n.p., (June 25, 1924): n.p., and (August 10, 1924): n.p. See also the newsreel story 2.10 on the Wayne State University Library website.

189. *Detroit News Pictorial* ad, *DN* (December 30, 1923): 2.7; also see the newsreel story 3R1.25 on the Wayne State University Library website.

190. *Detroit News Pictorial* ad, *DN* (May 11, 1924): n.p.

191. Frank Serafino, *West of Warsaw* (Hamtramck, MI: Avenue Publishing, 1983), 40. For the full story of the Purple Gang, see Paul R. Kavieff, *The Purple Gang: Organized Crime in Detroit, 1910–1945* (Fort Lee, NJ: Barricade Books, 2000).

192. *Detroit News Pictorial* ads, *DN* (October 14, 1923): 7, and (November 18, 1923): 2.7.

193. *Detroit News Pictorial* ad, *DN* (December 2, 1923): 2.7.

194. "Photoplays Today," *DSN* (March 16, 1924): 6.

195. "Photoplays Today," *DSN* (August 3, 1924): 6.

196. "Photoplays Today," *DSN* (September 7, 1924): 6.

197. "Today's Best from Filmland," *DFP* (March 17, 1924): 11, (March 18, 1924): 11, (March 19, 1924): 24, and (March 20, 1924): 8. A month earlier, the *Pictorial* appeared at the Crystal on Tuesday and the Harmony on Wednesday—"Today's Best from Filmland," *DFP* (February 12, 1924): n.p., and (February 13, 1924): n.p.

198. Martha Washington ad, *HN* (August 31, 1924): n.p.

199. Virginia ads, *BJ* (January 22, 1925): n.p., and (May 21, 1925): n.p.

200. "Troops Escorting Custer Band in Parade," *DN* (March 10, 1918): 1.2; "Whelan Funeral Conducted by K.T." *DN* (March 12, 1918): 5; and "Lillian Russell Heads Noted Cast," *DN* (March 15, 1918): 15.

201. "160 Girls Enroll in New Branch of Detroit Red Cross," *DN* (March 10, 1918): 1.11; "Red Cross Meetings," *DN* (March 12, 1918): 6; and "Polish Countess Tells of Country," *DN* (March 14, 1918): 6.

202. "Fire Destroys Steel Foundry," *DN* (March 10, 1918): 1.2.

203. Surprisingly, one disaster that could have produced sensational images apparently was not filmed: a flood that swept away a dam and bridge in Ypsilanti; admittedly, it was fifty miles west of Detroit—"Ypsilanti Bridge and Dam Swept Away by Flooded Huron," *DN* (March 15, 1918): 2. This story included two photos.

204. William W. Lutz, *The News in Detroit: How a Newspaper and a City Grew Together* (Boston: Little, Brown, 1973), 80–92. Thanks to Ben Strassfeld for alerting me to the *News*'s pioneering radio station.

ENTR'ACTE 6

Star Gazing

THIS DRAWING TAKES UP AT LEAST HALF OF the *Detroit News-Tribune*'s Sunday photoplay page in early October 1916.[1] Occupying a prominent central position, it is framed by a dozen articles and short items that offer information on movies in production and gossip about stars, from Geraldine Farrar, Mary Pickford, Lillian Gish, and Victor Potel at Keystone to "This Week's Favorite" (chosen by readers): Anna Little. The drawing is reminiscent of the influential "In the Frame of Public Favor" star portrait featured each week on the "Right Off the Reel" page edited by Mae Tinee in the *Chicago Sunday Tribune*. But in this close-up, a young woman in profile gazes slightly upward, as if mesmerized by a distant movie screen. Filling the space of her head, as though the reader can see through her stylish, short curls of dark hair, are a dozen small faces of current movie stars.[2] Seven of them are men: J. Warren Kerrigan, William S. Hart, Douglas Fairbanks, Henry Walthall, Francis X. Bushman, William Farnum, and one other who is now less easy to identify. The rest are women: Mary Pickford, Theda Bara, Geraldine Farrar, Norma Talmadge, and Blanche Sweet. The drawing obviously can be read as the newspaper's idea of a movie fan, a "little dream-girl" whose fascination is focused exclusively on stars.[3] That this movie fan is a young woman aligns with many observations of the time, in newspapers as well as fan magazines and the trade press. That she is white and at least middle class gives the portrait a certain racial/ethnic, social, and economic dimension.

What is the meaning of this image of a "dreaming" moviegoer in Detroit in late 1916? First, it suggests that the industry, abetted by newspaper coverage of the movies, has succeeded in its efforts to achieve legitimacy as a new entertainment form by attracting a "respectable" middle-class audience. Second, it also suggests that young female fans are most interested in male stars, especially "manly" ones. And might that be the result, contra the evidence found in fan magazines and scrapbooks, of the assumptions and fantasies of the newspaper's male editors and writers? Third, the image even could be read as a warning of the dangers of movie fandom, which certain elite authorities and organizations had long claimed. From this perspective, movie fandom was a degenerating addiction that threatened to undermine or "hollow out" the norms and values of American society.

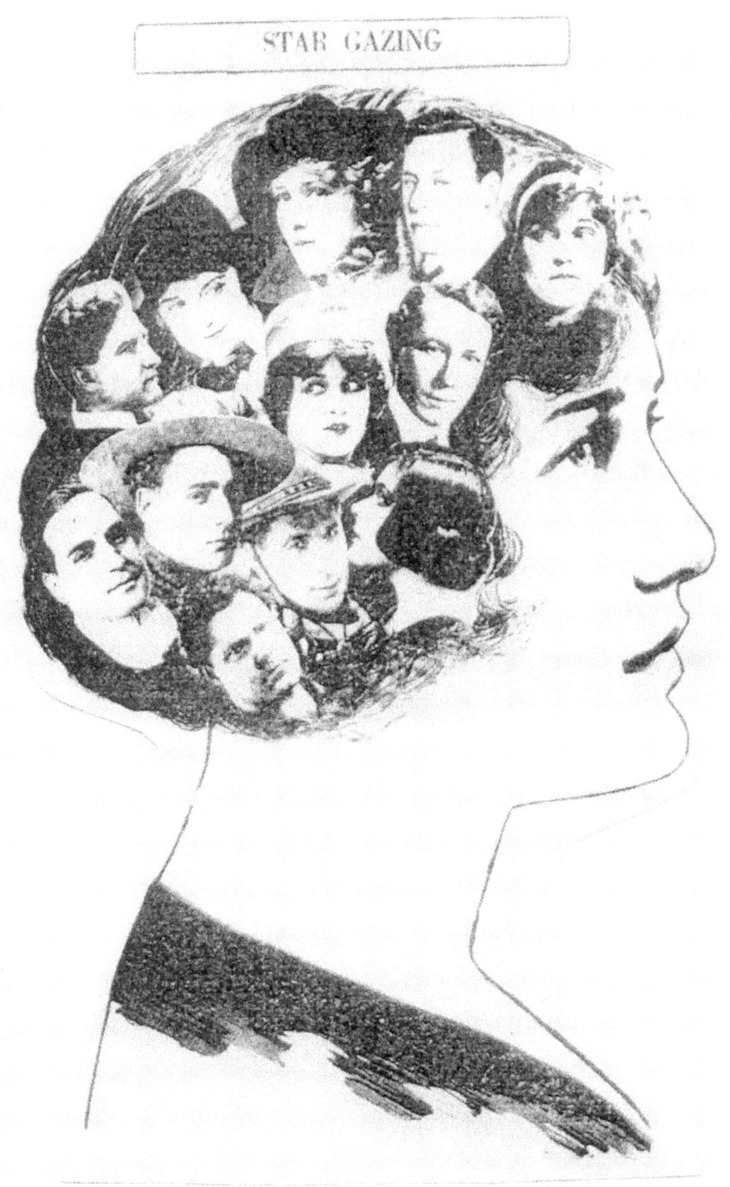

Fig. EA6.1. "Star Gazing," *Detroit News-Tribune* (October 1, 1916): 8.

In the end, the drawing serves as a kind of Rorschach test that invites different readings, depending on the specific positioning of the *News-Tribune*'s readers—whether male or female, young or old, middle class or working class, "native white" (according to the US Census), an immigrant from Eastern or Southern Europe, or a black migrant from the South. How, then, will chapter 4 confirm, modify, or contradict the import of this drawing?

Notes

1. "News and Views of the Photo Play World," *DNT* (October 1, 1916): 8.

2. A possible model for this collage of movie star faces appears in the "'Beauty and Brains' Contest," *PM* (January 1916): 48–49.

3. One year after the *Detroit News-Tribune* printed this image, B. E. Walker of Pasadena named herself "the little dream-girl" in describing how she created a "Happy Memories" scrapbook of movie stars, who, at her request, sent her signed photographs—"Letter to the Editor," *MPM* (September 1917): 158–159. See also the description of such a "dream-girl" in Gladys Hall, "A Girl's Folly," *Motion Picture Magazine* (April 1917): 49.

4

MOTOR CITY MENUS FOR MOVIE FANS

More Financial Advertising Than All Other . . . Detroit Newspapers Combined

Detroit Free Press (June 6, 1922)

A *News* in Every Home

Detroit News (July 22, 1923)

Women say that the *Journal* is as interesting as the best women's magazines

Detroit Journal (September 25, 1919)

MOVIE STAR IDENTIFICATION TEST

Detroit Times (June 21, 1923)

IN THE EARLY TWENTIETH CENTURY, THE PRIMARY FUNCTION of a newspaper was to offer "menus," or maps by which readers could make sense of the complexity of modern urban life.[1] Among those menus, by the mid-1910s, were weekly pages and daily columns devoted to the movies that mediated the interests of the rapidly expanding audience of fans, local exhibitors, producers, and rental exchanges. Arguably, the widespread circulation of this newspaper discourse played a significant role in creating a popular movie culture, including Detroit's—that is, shaping audiences' ephemeral experience of moviegoing, their repeated encounters with the fantasy worlds of "movieland," and their attraction to certain stories and stars. This chapter aims to analyze the movie pages and columns in the four major Detroit newspapers—the *Free Press*, the *News*, the *Journal*, and the *Times*—for how they shaped, often implicitly, their readers' sense of the movies, broadly defined, as a more or less routine part of daily life. What did the newspapers highlight in their menus and menu items that, according to the *Free Press*, "promise[d] much in the way of entertainment"?[2] How did they differ in their choices, and how, if at all, did those choices change over the course of the decade? Given a regular diet of information and gossip that fed fans' desires and longings, whom did the newspapers assume their moviegoing readers to be, and how might those readers have differed from one paper to another? At any time did their movie pages also offer fans some sort of "interactive" forum for voicing their pleasures and displeasures, their questions and anxieties? One more thing: as these pages of columns, photos, and ads accumulate in this chapter, they produce the "thick description" of a tantalizing, ever-changing palimpsest of that magical space and time of "movieland."

In the newspapers of many large and mid-sized cities during this period, women writers often edited pages and wrote columns and reviews devoted to the movies.[3] This was particularly the case in Chicago, where half a dozen women were featured at the *Tribune, Examiner, News, Post,* and *Journal* from the mid-1910s to the early 1920s.[4] Detroit was decidedly different. Among the writers assigned to the movie pages and columns of the *Free Press, News,* and *Times,* not one woman was named or, except for a few syndicated writers and a local reporter or two, even visible. In fact, three of the four newspapers, despite the fact that Mary Humphrey served as the *Free Press*'s Sunday editor,[5] may not have employed many women writers;[6] nor, except for the *News* and the *Journal,* did they give much coverage to broad women's issues, although Michigan, for instance, was the third state to ratify the nineteenth amendment to the Constitution that granted women the right to vote.[7] Still, one of the *News*'s most popular daily features was a column titled "Experience," in which Mrs. J. E. Leslie, as "Nancy Brown," answered readers' questions, for the most part about their domestic problems.[8] The *Journal,* however, proves an exception. For different lengthy periods in 1919–1920, as this chapter will explore, two women signed photoplay columns that appeared almost daily, and they likely edited the paper's Saturday and then Sunday movie pages. Yet this lack of women writers and editors in the other newspapers creates a crucial context for any analysis of Detroit's movie culture, for it is one more telling sign that the city's cultural, social, and political landscape at the time was predominantly masculine.

Detroit Free Press

Detroit newspapers were slow to show much interest in either movies or moviegoers. Only in late 1915 did the *Detroit Sunday Free Press* begin to devote a weekly page to motion pictures, and it adopted a format already established in other newspapers. Much like its "Stage" and "Music" pages, the Sunday "Screen" page surrounded short synopses of the films being featured at nine or more picture theaters with half a dozen star photos and production stills, several large theater ads, and a column of compiled gossip, "Flickers from Film Land" (the title poached from Kitty Kelly's column in the *Chicago Tribune*).[9] For two years, this format remained largely unchanged.[10] Occasional short pieces appeared as filler, such as "Bessie Barriscale Wants to Be Vampire."[11] In January 1917, however, the *Free Press* introduced a daily column, "The Reel Players," that imitated Mae Tinee's "In the Frame of Public Favor" star profiles in the *Chicago Sunday Tribune*, but on a smaller scale. One of the first recounted Viola Dana's rescue, during a Metro film shoot, from drifting out to sea in a canoe.[12] Running as a regular feature for several years, "The Reel Players" gradually accumulated more and more studio publicity on movie stars and their upcoming films.[13]

As the Great War ended and the influenza epidemic waned in November 1918, the *Free Press* ramped up its coverage of the movies. The Sunday edition soon was devoting three pages to ads, photos, theater program summaries, news, and gossip. The January 5, 1919, issue can serve as a template.[14] Still headed "The Screen," the top half of the first page was filled with a collage of nearly a dozen publicity star photos, each in a differently shaped frame. In the bottom half were program summaries for the first-run theaters that placed ads on the following page. As a regular column, "Screen Chat" ran across two pages,[15] supplemented by a few discrete stories such as "'In Love? Pooh!' Said Star—Three Months Later She Married" and other filler items. Most of this material likely came from press agents, without attribution, and whoever edited these pages remained unnamed. In October 1919, the paper's Sunday coverage shrank to two pages, and the discrete stories and filler items disappeared.[16] Yet the paper kept offering the daily "Reel Players" column (also unattributed), looking like a condensed version of the Sunday pages, with program summaries, a shorter "Screen Chat," and the publicity photo of a profiled star.[17]

Beginning in early April 1919, a *Free Press* column written by Karl K. Kitchen and syndicated by the *New York Sunday World* gave Detroit moviegoers an informative, if lightly jaundiced, sense of Hollywood culture.[18] Kitchen's first column described his introduction to "the City of Gelatine Stars": dressed in evening clothes one evening, he found himself mistaken for a waiter.[19] Less personally, he assumed that figures would impress his readers: while the industry employed thirty thousand people annually to produce "films worth between $150,000,000 to $200,000,000," the leading Hollywood grocer did a thriving business each day cashing studio paychecks worth "between $50,000 and $100,000." But he was most interested in studio work and after-hours play. He was amazed by how efficiently and cost-effectively Goldwyn's manager ran the production of multiple films.[20] When D. W. Griffith complained about the "poor quality of stories," Marc Robbins, head of the Fox Scenario department, cited several reasons: stories often were chosen to "fit" a star or else were revised, especially for a new star that Robbins slightingly dubbed "Miss Marybelle Meringue."[21] John W. Semler summarized what he thought were audience tastes: they now wanted "heart kicks . . . good, clean stories with both laughter and tears"; as an example, he cited the 278 prints of Chaplin's *Shoulder Arms* set for release, when "even a very successful

Saturday Night at Vernon's

BY KARL K. KITCHEN.

Reel III. of the Wonders of the Western Film World, Movie Folk and Sporty Los Angelenes Can Dissipate. With a Close Up of the Only Place Where the

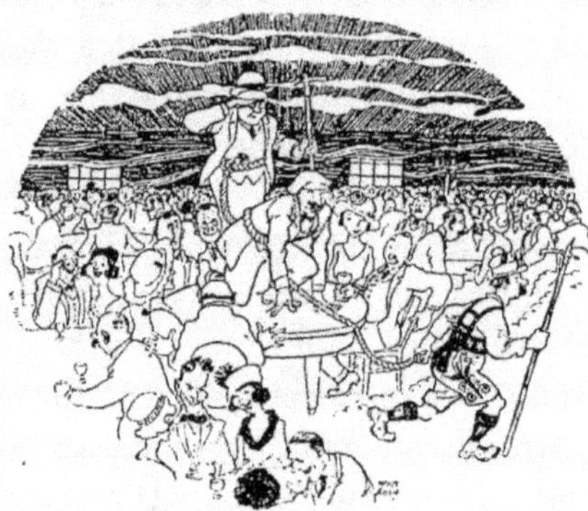

"A midnight supper with near beer is not conducive to early morning hours."

Fig. 4.1. Karl K. Kitchen's column, *Detroit Sunday Free Press* (April 20, 1919): 4.14.

picture rarely ran more than 100 prints."[22] Finally, Kitchen followed movie people one Saturday night to a dance hall called Vernon's Country Club (just outside the city limits) where "fifteen hundred" were dancing and a thousand more were drinking at clusters of tables—and a doorman called it an "off night."[23] Within three years, scandals would have scotched or at least reframed this kind of story.

Given the steady array of photos on "The Screen" page, the *Free Press* highlighted one or more stories about stars each Sunday, in addition to the daily "Reel Players" photo profiles.[24] Intriguingly, the favored subject was Alla Nazimova. One profile described how she learned English; another touted her skill as a violinist; yet many served as advance publicity for her company's *Out of the Fog* and *The Brat*.[25] She allegedly adapted the latter film's scenario, stopped traffic during its filming, and in one scene performed a "wonderful rabbit dance" (sadly, that has not survived).[26] Slightly less favored was Fatty Arbuckle, who claimed that the most successful comic ideas came from sudden suggestions, only to admit that "there are only a limited number of gags."[27] After him came Mabel Normand, who kept actors and crew in stiches by reading from an old etiquette book for *Sis Hopkins*.[28] A similar number featured Charles Ray, whose career trajectory swerved from business school student to theater usher, stage "super," and his current release, *Bill Henry*, in which he proved skillful in a fistfight.[29] More generally, the *Free Press* printed a piece that celebrated the power of "screen personality," with Blanche Sweet its effulgent example.[30] Particularly surprising was an interview with the famous French actor Charles Dullin that celebrated the "craftsmanship" of William S. Hart, whose consistent "calm and sangfroid" struck Dullin as worthy of a "great actor."[31]

Less prominent were stories about the industry's production of features and shorts. Many of the stories lured fans to take knowing looks "behind the scenes." One showed off Lady Duff-Gordon's extravagant gowns designed for Clara Kimball Young; another lauded Metro's largesse in building a small town's church during location shooting.[32] In a third, Cecil B. DeMille explained why, in order to register properly on film stock, the color of costumes, furnishings, and facial make-up could seem so strange under the lights of a studio set—warm yellows, for instance, were used to register shades of white.[33] For an aerial chase in one comedy, Henry Lehrman turned Billie Ritchie and Hugh Fay into daredevils forced onto the wings of their two planes to engage in some thrilling antics.[34] Interviewed afterwards, Lehrman blithely dismissed any danger to either. Finally, an unusual story credited Hugh Ford and Albert E. Davis of Paramount-Artcraft with devising a file card system that catalogued statistics for six thousand movie actors, which allowed a casting director to quickly and easily "suit" appropriate players to a film's character roles.[35] Turning actors into parts ready to be inserted into an assembly line would have resonated with readers in a city filled with automobile manufacturing.

A miscellany of stories tantalized readers with other industry interests and concerns. Several focused on Hollywood's relations with Europe. Metro's general manager claimed that American filmmakers were exploiting "the foreigners' bag of tricks" to produce painterly compositions,[36] but others savored opportunities overseas. Samuel Goldwyn envisioned the widespread export of American films to uplift millions of Europeans "scarred by the ravages of war"; one such film was the eight-reel *Made in America*, which showed how the military draft system transformed civilians so quickly into effective fighting men.[37] There were opportunities at home as well. Disabled veterans could find work in the industry as film cutters and inspectors;[38] Department of Agriculture films promoted new technologies and techniques to American farmers; the YMCA screened films in factories as "an aid in Americanizing foreign workers."[39] A rare syndicated column by Margaret C. Getchell related her experience of sitting beside a deaf woman whose lipreading revealed a frustrating discrepancy between a film's intertitles and what actors were actually saying: in a romantic scene, one actress complained, "I hope we won't have to go over all this a third time. It's getting late, and I'm hungry."[40]

This comic dissonance likely was familiar to Detroit moviegoers, but other stories had a more explicitly local angle. Griffith praised how Arthur S. Hyman enhanced the Opera House's stage frame for *Hearts of the World* and how the augmented orchestra perfectly rendered the requisite musical score and sound effects.[41] In late January 1919, as part of a health campaign in "almost every shop and factory," posters, heralds, and even shop superintendents admonished workers to see *Fit to Win* at the Washington.[42] During a "safety crusade" months later, 125 theaters screened *Dangerous Exploits*, a locally produced film that warned jaywalkers about careless motorists.[43] More restricted, in March and April 1920, were "the best and cleanest movies" screened each Saturday morning for Women's City Club children in the Hudson's department store auditorium.[44] Most intriguing was a "cinema dictionary" that listed useful technical terms then beginning to solidify: *fade*, *iris*, *mask*, and *insert* as well as acronyms for *long shot*, *medium shot*, and *close up*.[45] This "dictionary" also could have given fans more precise lingo for talking knowledgeably about the movies.

During the post-war economic recession, the *Free Press* reduced its standardized pages devoted to the movies, but it also began to offer moviegoers a series of puzzle contests. In November 1919, the Broadway Strand, along with ten local advertisers, sponsored a contest in which readers could win tickets to its premiere of DeMille's *Male and Female*.[46] Matching the film's "civilized" versus "primitive" settings, the ads ranged from furs and "distinctive furniture" to sales of used phonographs and surplus clothing.[47] Two months later, another contest asked readers to make "the name 'Pinto' as many times as possible" from letters in six ads to win tickets to Normand's film of the same name at the Fox Washington.[48] Here the ads varied widely, from electrical appliance companies to the Business Institute, which solicited "young men and young women" to attend classes.

In September 1920, the *Free Press* joined with a host of local companies, all of them upscale, to sponsor seven similar contests for tickets to first-run films at the Adams, Madison, Broadway Strand, Miles, Regent, and Fox Washington.[49] Here each contestant had to "make up the title" of one theater's specific film "from all the letters" found in from six to eleven ads. Unique to each contest, the companies ranged from bankers, builders, real estate developers, furniture stores, and movers to furriers, tailors, shoe stores, restaurants, and cafes. Ads even tended to sync up with particular films: Kimball's piano store with *Humoresque*, Peerless Dentists and Ivory's Suburban Moving with a grinning Fairbanks in *The Mollycoddle*, and washing machine makers with Pickford's *Suds*. In early 1921, Paramount sponsored its own contest for tickets to the Broadway Strand, urging readers to

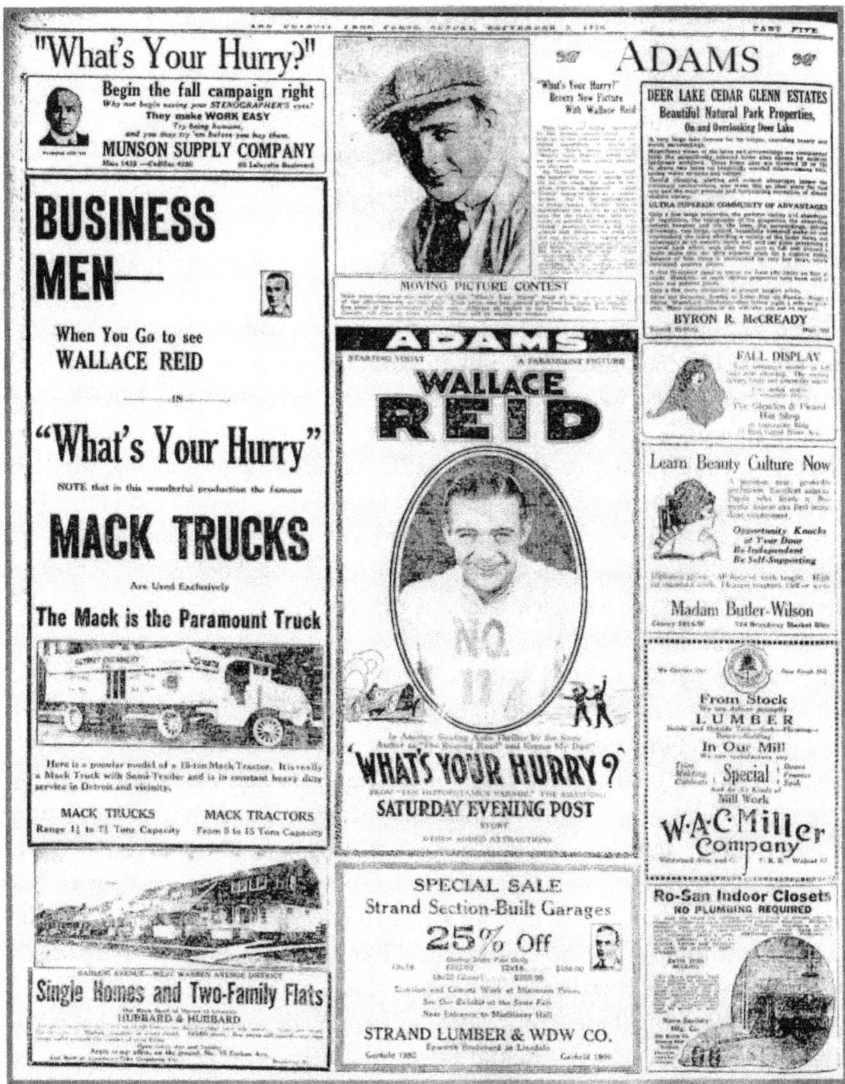

Fig. 4.2. "Moving Picture Contest," *Detroit Sunday Free Press* (September 5, 1920): 5.6.

"count the number of times the word 'Paramount' can be formed from the letters appearing in each advertisement on this page."[50] These ads appealed to readers young and old, male and female: the Business Institute again, Detroit Business University, an appliance manufacturer, a maker of coaster wagons, an outlet for fine luggage, a florist, a commercial laundry, and a coal seller. All of these contests likely had several aims. Theaters aligned themselves with businesses that targeted the city's upper and middle classes; at the same time, they appealed to others who were adept at simple puzzle word games but could not afford the tickets to see their favorite stars in first-run films.

Coinciding with that Paramount contest, the *Free Press* resumed a fuller, three-page coverage of the movies that remained relatively standardized during the next few years. Continually prominent were industry stories of all kinds. Among the stars interviewed were Mae Murray, who repeated the corrective that stars had to work hard,[51] and Anna Q. Nilsson, who believed a woman could attain standing in "any line of business or any field of endeavor."[52] If "experts" claimed Valentino's "elevation to stardom [was] the result of feminine demand," Mix proved his masculine mettle by inviting fans to make up the crowd for a circus scene in *The Rough Diamond*—no hired extras needed.[53] Along with familiar figures like D. W. Griffith, Cecil B. DeMille, and Lois Weber, other directors included Maurice Tourneur as "a master of lights and shadows" and Frank Borzage, who decried the threatened impact of morbid, cynical films from Europe.[54] And what exactly was a director? An anonymous questionnaire had Will Rogers dismissively quip that a good picture needed only a good story and director—"You don't have to worry about anybody else."[55] Economic uncertainty may have contributed to a "lull in production" and a decline in stars' salaries as well as film exports, but profits allegedly kept flowing in from picture theaters;[56] and several industry men agreed that American filmmakers had nothing to fear from a "foreign film invasion."[57] As an example of "uplift" efforts, George Loane Tucker found, in January 1921, that "5,000 American and Canadian Churches" were screening movies regularly, including his own *The Miracle Man*, "shown in 3,987 schools and churches during the last two years."[58] Still troubling were the unremitting efforts to censor films, as when the Ohio chief censor claimed that people were "not fit to judge for themselves."[59] Harassed industry notables included "Jewish movie men" attacked by the antisemitic Lord's Day Alliance and even Watterson R. Rothacker, a Chicago producer of nonfiction films.[60]

Complementing these industry stories were syndicated columns that ran for extended lengths of time. From March 1921 on, "Secrets of the Movies Revealed" appeared on Sundays, Mondays, and Thursdays, with short "back stage" answers to moviegoers' questions about their favorite stars.[61] At the same time, there was "How a Young Girl Broke into the Movies," written by Carolina Jewett, a Cleveland girl who was a stenographer, sales clerk, and reporter before getting studio work in New York.[62] In late November 1921 came "Inside Moves of Movies," signed by Inez Wallace, whose "years of actual experience in all branches of motion picture work" led her to set up a correspondence school in screen acting in Cleveland.[63] For anyone set on an acting career, she warned that there were "four salient requirements": health, talent, "a camera face," and determination. Only once did she define that "anyone" as a man.[64] And what did companies expect of potential actors? Some stage experience and an understanding of the difference between stage acting and film acting; a good sense of their character type ("flappers" were out); knowledge of the "market" for choosing when and where to apply; careful attention to costuming, hairstyle, and makeup; and familiarity with the "cinema dictionary" of specialized terms used by script writers and directors."[65]

Less frequent, a year later, was another column, written by Donald H. Clarke, that took up subjects ranging from advice for those seeking entry into the industry to questionable claims that directors were not interested in box office results.[66] More prominent, beginning in late February 1923, was "Hollywood Film Letter," written by Paul "Scoop" Conlon, which ran nearly every Sunday well into 1925.[67] Published simultaneously in the *San Francisco Sunday Chronicle*,[68] "Hollywood Film Letter" collected news items about new film productions like a remake of *The Spoilers* and directors like James Kirkwood, plus gossip about minor as well as major stars.[69] The most unusual was "What Does Your Face Reveal?," written by Ernest H. Thayer, a self-described "psychoanalyst and character expert."[70] From a publicity photo, he concluded that Colleen Moore is "a warm lovable type of personality, a type that will generally act first and think later."[71] Given such dubious readings, akin to those of a phrenologist, his claim of helping a movie fan "to know yourself" was so unacceptable that the column lasted only three issues.

During the next few years, the *Free Press* maintained the format, columns, and story choices that were already well established—with a few caveats. From September 1922 on, a cluster of nearly ten star photos filled the top half of the page, increasing in size to two-thirds or even three-fourths of the space in late 1923 and early 1924. This emphasis on stars reduced the ads to no more than two or three small ones, accompanied by the major theater synopses and a short column of neighborhood theater programs. On the following two pages, a dozen or more stories and articles complemented the much larger ads for first-run theaters. Although the Sunday pages had no attributed editor, starting in the summer of 1922 the daily "Reel Players" column was signed by Roy E. Marcotte.[72] It's likely that Marcotte also edited the Sunday pages, for, in late October 1922, a large ad for *Robin Hood* included testimonial quotes from the three Detroit papers, among them Marcotte's.[73]

Industry news and gossip dominated the dozen or more stories sprinkled through the *Free Press*'s Sunday pages. Most, of course, centered on stars: from Davies and her "newest gown" or Valentino (whom "all women want to 'mother'"), to Norma Talmadge warning girls that only one in six hundred could hope to make it in films, or Negri's publicity agent penning a fictionalized life story.[74] Flappers and vamps kept stars like Barthelmess and Jetta Goudal (newly arrived from France) busy with contradictory comments: for Colleen Moore, a *flapper* was simply "a little girl trying to grow up."[75] Just as many stories focused

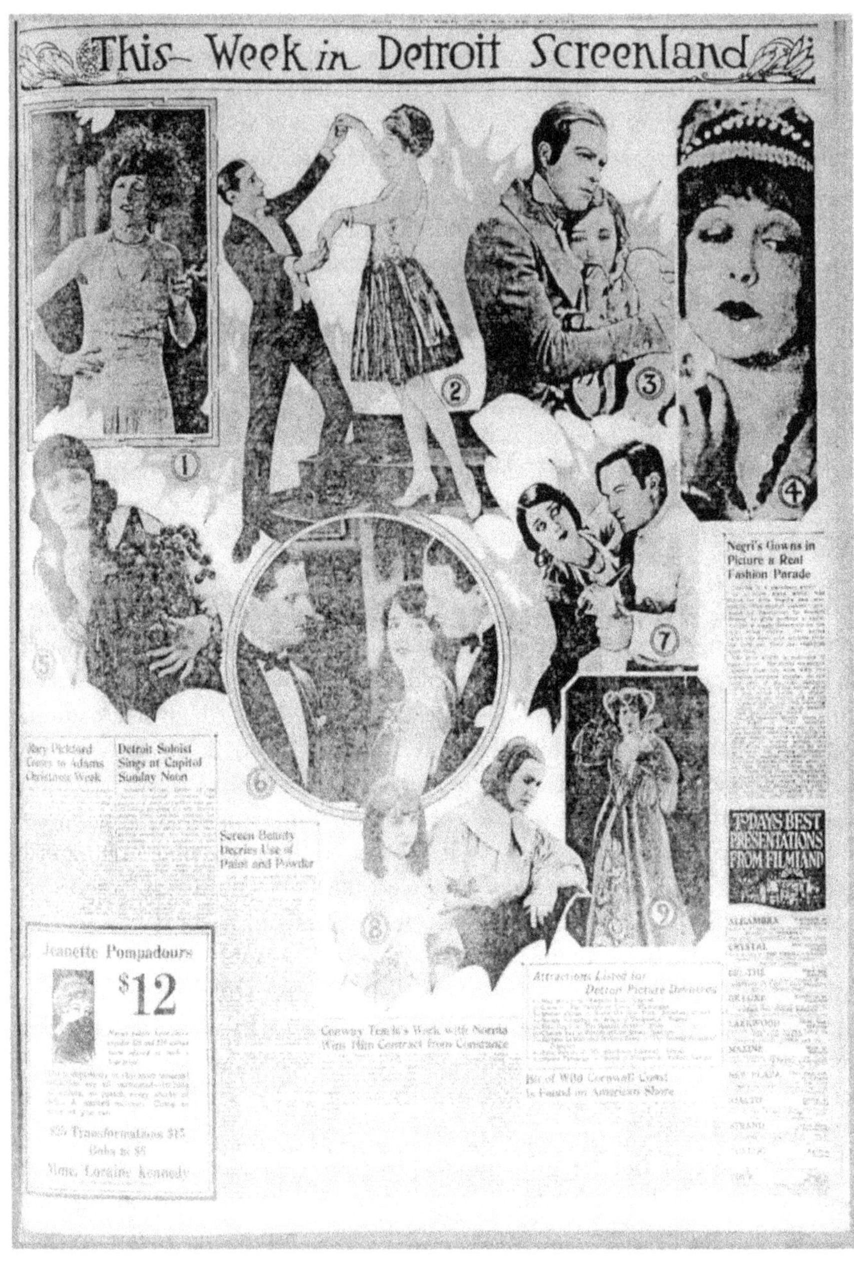

Fig. 4.3. "This Week in Detroit Screenland," *Detroit Sunday Free Press* (December 2, 1923): Feature 5.

on directors. Half a dozen stories featured DeMille; others highlighted "headliners" like Niblo, Dwan, and Lloyd or introduced Mrs. Luis Warrenton, head of a new San Diego production company "composed entirely of women."[76] A few came from scenario writers such as Elinor Glyn and Clara Beranger, who insisted that movie fans wanted to see "real people, true to real life" onscreen.[77] An equal number highlighted set design and fashion: the imposing cathedral façade for *The Hunchback of Notre Dame*, the Vitagraph studio sets on display in Fox's *Behold the Woman*, costume designer Clare West's claim that the movies now set current fashion styles, and Carmel Myers's wonder if male fans really liked "daring clothes" on women.[78] In October 1923, an article reported that banks were wary of investing in the industry, yet other stories seemed to question that statement, touting the aid that Mussolini's government gave to filming *The Eternal City*, the European stars being lured to Hollywood, all the advances being made in lighting and camera work, and the increasing popularity of American films in other countries.[79]

Although it now printed far fewer local stories, the *Free Press* favored certain subjects. It closely followed Kunsky's construction of the Capitol[80] and then his plans to erect a fourth downtown palace cinema, eventually named The State.[81] Marcotte praised the latter theater's three innovations: a set of elevators, "an elevated orchestra pit," and a curtain constructed of gold mirrors designed like a series of French doors.[82] For adult moviegoers in December 1921, the Miles Theater followed its screenings of *Carnival* with a special event each night: patrons could dance in the lobby surrounded by carnival decorations and buoyed by musicians from theaters across the city.[83] The newspaper acted as a publicity agent for the Detroit Motion Picture Company, from stories of constructing a studio and hiring a director and cameraman to photos of a studio set being readied for filming and of the "snake charmer dance" at the film's climax.[84] Less insistently, it credited the scenario of *The Silent Call* (starring Strongheart, Rin-Tin-Tin's rival) to Jane Murfin, implying that she might not be the only Detroit-area woman who could succeed in the industry.[85] The *Free Press* itself displayed photos of usherettes at the Adams and Broadway Strand—costumed, respectively, in "natty new suits, of white satin, trimmed in turkey red," and "quaint garb" like grandma's to demurely match those in that week's feature, *Little Old New York*.[86]

Particularly unique to the *Free Press*, however, was its promotion of the musical or dance performances on first-run theater stages. Scarcely a week went by without at least one short piece, often a photo profile, even when a theater ad made a performer's name prominent. In August 1922, Henry Santrey returned with his orchestra to the Capitol; a month later, Edouard Werner resumed conducting the theater's "popular Sunday concerts."[87] Stories in November featured Fred Waring and his dance orchestra at the Madison and then at the Capitol; weeks later, Cameron McLean joined them as a singer.[88] The following April, the marimba band of seven Soli brothers played at the Broadway Strand; the "musical prodigy" Little Sousa led the Capitol orchestra; and Bobbie Arnst, with "many friends in the city's exclusive north end residential section," performed as a soloist at the Broadway Strand.[89] In September 1923, mezzo-soprano Suzanne Clough "toured" several Kunsky houses and one week performed a new song written by Richard Whiting and Raymond Eagan of Detroit; a "Detroit vocalist," Mme Homer DuBard, sang at the Capitol; and the Quixie Trio of Clevelanders amused Madison audiences.[90] In March 1924, Chief Caupolican, the noted Indian baritone, agreed to a rare engagement at the Capitol; and the vaudeville star Nellie V. Nichols appeared in "Songs," a "unique novelty" act, at the Capitol.[91] In June, the Polish tenor Joseph E. Slazinski was featured at the Broadway Strand; and the Variety Four of singing comedians accepted a summer season at the Cinderella.[92] In early 1925, Finzel's Arcadia orchestra "that all Detroit dances to" came to the Madison; at the same time, Ernie Young's Oriole Terrace Beauty Ballet celebrated the Capitol's third anniversary; and the Capitol featured premier dancer Queenie Chambers in Ned Wayburn's Symphonie Jazz Revue.[93] In so persistently singling out musical and dance performances, the *Free Press* seemed to assume, as a newspaper devoted to the traditional arts, that the performers onstage mattered as much to many of its readers as did those on-screen.

Detroit News

Beginning also in September 1915, the *News-Tribune* offered a greater variety of menu items on Sunday than did the *Free Press*. Its single page of movie-related material had half a dozen downtown ads, half a dozen star photos, short pieces about the films and stars at those advertised theaters, several industry items, and a column of "Close-Ups."[94] The banner soon upgraded from "The Movies" to "Photoplays"; more and more theaters placed ads; and George W. Stark signed a "Motion Picture Comment" column that included synopses of selected theater programs.[95] Within weeks, this coverage (with Stark probably its editor) expanded to two pages—"News and Views of the Photo Play World" on Saturday; "With the Film Stars" on Sunday—with more industry news, photo profiles of stars, and up to sixteen theater ads.[96] Stark weighed in on national and local issues, adopting an explicitly moral tone: the Detroit women's campaign supporting censorship policies, praise for an actress who rejected scenarios she thought immoral, and the overblown language of movie press agents.[97] Like the *Free Press*, the *News-Tribune* believed stars were the main attraction for moviegoers. In May 1916, Edward Stone, who took over Stark's column, wrote this: "Today the movie patron generally looks first to see who is starred at a theater. If the star of the day is a favorite . . . he next learns in what play he or she is appearing. If it is a play he cares to see, he pays the price of admission."[98] Movie fans then likely read the

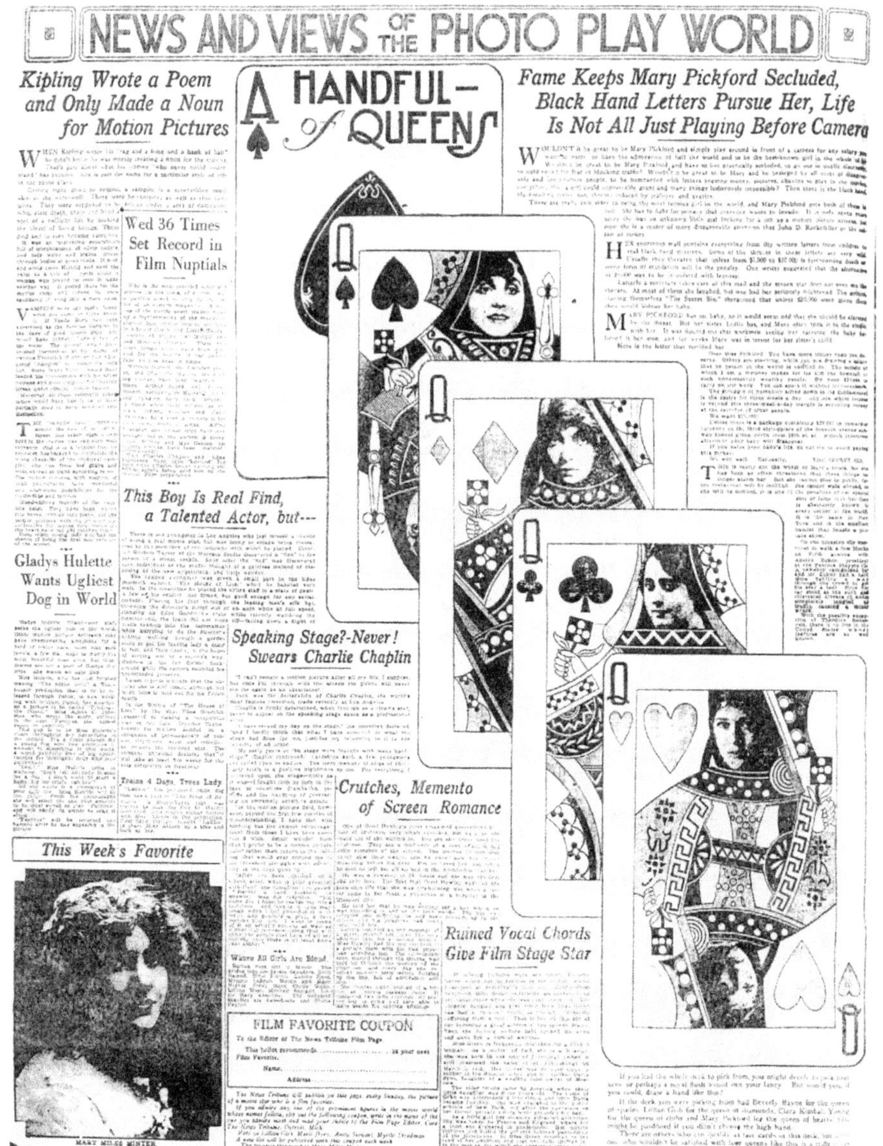

Fig. 4.4. "A Handful of Queens," *Detroit News-Tribune* (September 3, 1916): 8.

News-Tribune rather than the *Free Press*, whether those fans were male, as Stone assumed, or female, as the paper imagined months later in its close-up of a "Star Gazing" young woman.[99]

For more than a year, the *News-Tribune*'s fascination with "star gazing" never wavered. In early September 1916, the Saturday page dealt readers a large five-card playing hand with an ace and four queens representing Beverly Bayne, Lillian Gish, Clara Kimball Young, and Mary Pickford.[100] Singular stories of female stars proliferated: Norma Talmadge's "Little Autobiography," and Miriam Cooper warning girls about entering the motion picture field—"Don't." [101] Especially striking was a series of full-page photos in the Sunday "Rotogravure" section. In mid-January 1917, Mary Pickford, Geraldine Farrar, and Anna Pavlova were among nine "Superwomen"; in mid-March, movie stars filled all fifteen photos typifying the "Perfect Woman."[102] Another series took up the debate over movie "vampires." In November 1916, Madeline Traverse quipped, "All the heroine has to do is be a sweetly, simple boob, while a vampire has to be attractive, devilish, repellent, beautiful, admirable, brave, clever, wicked, loyal, traitorous, and a few other things at one and the same time."[103] On a smaller scale, the *News-Tribune* adopted a contest like that initiated years earlier in the *Chicago Tribune*: Each week, readers could fill out and mail in a "Film Favorite Coupon" (the choices were all women), and the newspaper subsequently would print a photo of the chosen star as "This Week's Favorite."[104]

Among other items, the *News-Tribune* highlighted the new production companies founded by major actresses like Kimball Young, Talmadge, and Pickford.[105] It also singled out Kimball Young's conception of the movies: "The motion picture is not a play or drama but a narrative," which led her to favor novels as the source of movie stories.[106] Anticipating Louis Delluc in France, she argued that the motion picture "will never attain its highest form of expression" until it has no need of intertitles.[107] In contrast, a "behind-the-scenes" piece (as if to dissuade wannabe stars) revealed how unappetizing food looked under Cooper-Hewitt lights: "The wine was made to look like dirty dish-water; the catsup took on the aspect of brown ooze; the meat began to resemble green leather, and bread assumed the appearance of mildewed dough."[108] For several months, Edward Speyer, now the movie page editor, contributed columns unlike Stark's. On censorship, he argued that it would always be "either idiotically restrictive or lax in some respects."[109] As for standing when the organ or orchestra played the national anthem, a sign of the country's preparedness campaign, he lampooned it as "nonsense."[110]

In October 1917, just as the *News*'s big office building opened, the *News-Tribune* turned into the *Sunday News*. Perhaps disruptions from the US entry into the war reduced the paper's movie coverage to a half-page column on Saturday and Sunday: respectively, "Next Week's Stars" and "This Week's Film Stars."[111] By May

1918, however, that coverage again expanded to two pages, highlighted by publicity photos of eight to ten stars and a dozen press agent stories such as "Heavens! Norma 'Gassed' in Film."[112] In late September, the *Sunday News* finally introduced a column signed by a new writer, Harold Hefferman, who likely edited the "Week in Filmdom" page.[113] Once the influenza epidemic abated, Hefferman resumed his column to cover both industry matters and local issues.[114] Among them were Pickford's role as a producer as well as an actress, Goldwyn's contract to distribute Ford's *Educational Weekly*, and the first "Detroit-Made" film.[115] Overall, the paper's menu items ranged even wider than before. Star stories still predominated: a dozen stars promoted the fourth Liberty Loan campaign; Fairbanks and Dustin Farnum aided influenza victims; and Bessie Love was growing out of adolescent roles.[116] Other stories included Paramount's effort to release a film each day, the impact that "punchy" titles had on a film's success, and Italian moviegoers' practice of reading intertitles out loud.[117] Short gossip columns increased: "Close Ups," "Kweries," "Memories," "Short Reels," and "The Movie Grouch." Yet perhaps what attracted moviegoers most was a contest that, each week, asked readers to submit a concise review of one of two named films (all at first-run theaters); winning reviews were published the following Sunday.[118] Most praised films such as *Salome* (with Bara), *Out of a Clear Sky* (with Clark), and *Johanna Enlists* (with Pickford); but one called stage actor Fred Stone "lost" in *The Goat*, and another faulted the "poor lighting and camera work" in *A Hoosier Romance*.[119]

Do these reviews offer further clues about the city's movie culture and its devoted movie fans? Several boys or men gave their full names, but most writers signed only their initials, so some of those may have been women. Those who listed addresses seem to have resided in middle-class and skilled working-class areas to the east of Belle Isle Bridge, south of the Regent on North Woodward, and on the near west side—all with streetcar access to first-run theaters. The exception was a reviewer with the initials L. L. D. from Hamtramck's Polish community. Obviously, one cannot draw preliminary conclusions from so small a sample. Unfortunately, moreover, the influenza epidemic halted this contest, minimizing its effect.

In early 1919, readers of the *News* still could peruse three weekend pages devoted to the movies, one on Saturday and two on Sunday, the latter bannered "Film Fare" in the "Photoplay and Society" section. Hefferman filled these pages with so many different stories (nearly twice as many as did the *Free Press*) that every kind of reader had something to feast on. The wealth of industry stories makes it difficult to choose what was representative, but some patterns emerged. Many, as before, featured stars and directors,[120] but others taking readers "behind the scenes" were unique. Now that Los Angeles reigned as the world's motion picture capital, the paper reproduced a stereoscopic photo of one of its biggest

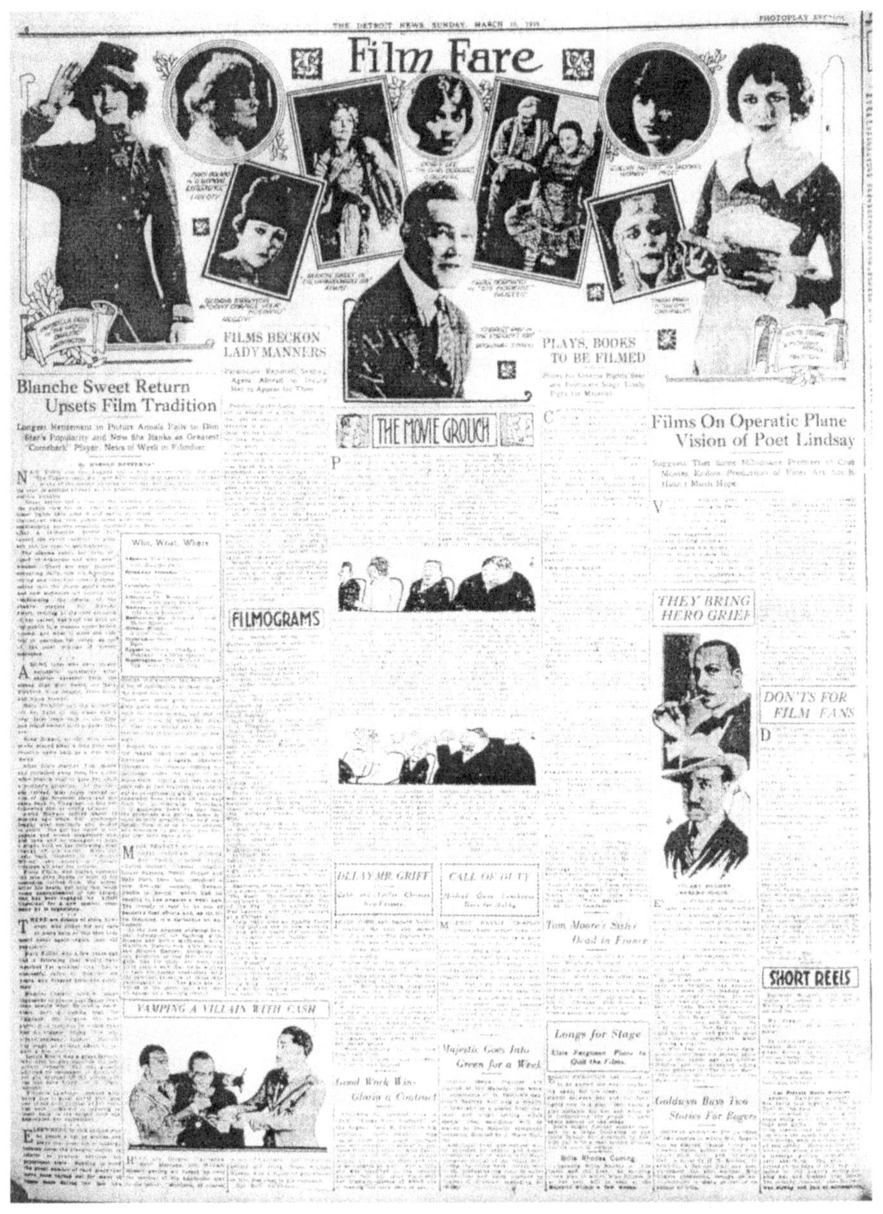

Fig. 4.5. "Film Fare," *Detroit Sunday News* (March 16, 1919): Photoplay, 6.

studios, Universal City.[121] Numerous stories revealed details of the production process and its effects: why onlookers typically were barred from studio sets so as not to disturb the actors, and how new camera lenses were educating the public about the "beauty of soft effects in modern photography."[122] Others expressed an assumed interest in music: Pickford and Kitty Gordon insisted on having an orchestra on set; Farnum banned music during his "scenes of emotion"; at Universal, the director, "music master," and his assistant scored or wrote cue sheets for a feature during the projection of a final print.[123] The most unusual story focused on the technical process of fixing the film negative, inspecting frames for imperfections, assembling selected shots into scenes and then a "trial print," and projecting that to find what more editing was needed—without mentioning that women often did much of the inspecting and editing.[124]

Censorship remained timely. After the state board objected to a film title, a Baltimore theater manager cleverly plastered all of his posters with "Theda Bara in 'Banned by the Censors.'"[125] If the National Association of the Motion Picture Industry discouraged sensational film titles, fearing more scrutiny from censors, others worried that, because titling was so important to a film's success, poor spelling and grammar in intertitles reflected badly on the industry as a whole.[126] Other industry stories took up film distribution, from First National's growing influence to the difficulties that schools had in booking the "right films," fiction or nonfiction.[127] And what of the international market? After revealing German plans to "flood the world with propaganda stories" (had Germany won the war), the *News* printed many stories promoting America's own "film invasion" abroad.[128] Particularly intriguing was Georgette Le Blanc's article, translated from *Mercure de France*, arguing that cinema was a new form of art and praising the "youthfulness of American films."[129] While the National Council of Women was shipping nonfiction films about sanitation, hygiene, home building, and civic beautification, "primarily for the benefit of foreign women," the Jewish Relief Committee specifically targeted Polish children with public health films.[130] In March 1920, Jackson D. Haag summed up the sheer number of exported films as evidence of the American invasion's success.[131]

Unsurprisingly, the *News* bested the *Free Press* in local coverage. Here, too, were stories of censorship. In January 1919, an unnamed theater cut out "incidental scenes" in Griffith's *The Greatest Thing in Life*; months later, the Recreation Commission took over local censorship from the police department, but with the same reassigned police officers.[132] Although George Beban's personal appearance was a big story,[133] local industry figures received more attention. Jacob Smith, publisher of the *Michigan Film Review*, left to found an *International Film Review* in Chicago; Harry Guest, former editor of Kunsky's *Weekly Film News*, became the chief scenario writer for H. N. Nelson; Harry Garson, part owner of the Broadway Strand, planned to premiere Sweet's new film, *The Hushed Hour*, there;

and, in a rare interview, Kunsky explained why the "independents" were forming the First National Exhibitors Circuit.[134] Unexpected was a story about Charles Boni's plans to produce films with an "all Negro cast,"[135] which suggests that migrants flooding into Black Bottom read the *News* rather than any other paper besides the *Detroit Leader.*[136] Supporting this hypothesis was a rare ad for boxer Jack Johnson's personal appearance at the Koppin in December 1922.[137]

To the *News*, local exhibition was a big part of the city's movie culture. While some stories voiced exhibitor concerns about dealing with lost articles or problems in programming,[138] most were full of praise. In late March 1919, the *News* singled out the Adams's new stage setting, an "elaborate woodland scene with waterfall and rustic bridge," and the special lights that created "artistic effects" during the opening overture.[139] In July, Griffith praised the music accompanying *Hearts of the World*, especially when children sang "Nearer My God to Thee" backstage during the mother's burial.[140] The paper hoped that Santrey, now performing at the Majestic, would revive the Community Sing that audiences had enjoyed earlier at the Regent.[141] The Majestic also sponsored a dance party for its female ushers, with five of the twenty-two "goils" performing as a jazz band.[142] Similarly, for one night the De Luxe hosted a special midnight screening of *A Midnight Romance*, preceded by a dance in the foyer decorated to resemble the film's key ballroom scene.[143] The *News* thought movie fans favored not only "clean, light comedy drama productions" like *Mickey*, but also "scenics and the external locations in feature productions" that appealed, in the cliché, to those who could only take a "vacation through the eyes."[144]

Beginning in February 1919, the *News* introduced a syndicated column from Imogene Devore (a gossip columnist in Los Angeles) that first appeared sporadically and later frequently as "Fugitive Flashes."[145] When Hefferman became the regional director for First National's distribution network in July,[146] Stanley Rushton, the *Detroit Journal*'s former assistant city editor,[147] took over his Sunday column for several months, followed briefly by Edward Speyer and Robert Kelly, the latter through January 1920. Each stuck closely to the format already established, except that Hefferman and Rushton often included a short review—actually more like a "promo"—of at least one weekly feature film. In January 1919, Hefferman found Lillian Gish especially "delightful" in *The Greatest Thing in Life*: "In close ups—and there are many—she never appeared to better advantage."[148] In March, despite her alleged fading reputation, he admired the way Weber had directed *A Midnight Romance*: "She is an artist at injecting little original touches."[149] In September, without a hint of irony about Pickford's real life, Rushton raved about *The Hoodlum*, in which she plays "a spoiled heiress who dropped through a mail chute... discovers," among other things, "that robbing one's own $1,000,000 mansion is a most thrilling experience."[150] There, too, he lauded Nazimova's skill in *The Brat* at portraying "humor, pathos, longing, vixenish anger and wistfulness" and noted how "her boyish little figure is ever alert and vital." In November, he gushed over the luxuriousness, spectacular beauty, and dramatic strength of *Male and Female*.[151] Rushton even praised Pathé's *Bound and Gagged*, bowing to fans' interests so different from his own: "There is in this city an exceedingly large element of motion picture devotees who find an especial appeal to the serial."[152]

In spring 1920, perhaps due to the recession, the *News* scaled back its movie coverage to a single page and dropped its "Screen Topics" banner. For two months that page was housed in the Sunday "Feature" section; then, for nearly a year, in the women's "Society" section. During this period, the editor and chief columnist was Jackson D. Haag, whose interests differed from Hefferman's. Typically, Haag's columns ignored local news in favor of more general matters. Subjects ranged from Gaumont's new color film process or filmmaking in Italy, reprinted from the *Chicago News*, to studio departments' new dependency on electricity, from *The Electric Journal*.[153] Another was a (translated) survey from *Le Film* that asked well-known French writers to foresee the future of film.[154] He also reprinted stories with industry insiders: a sardonic piece on stars by Tod Browning, and a plug for film editing as a profession for women.[155] Haag also focused on technical details involving film prints and their projection: the gamble that *The Old Swimmin' Hole* (starring Ray) would succeed with no intertitles; the intricacies of an unusually specific cue sheet for *Down Home*.[156]

More in line with local stories that might address women, Haag reported on the "News Beauty Contest" that selected, from a hundred girls who submitted photographs and letters, potential performers for Paramount's upcoming production of *Beauty*.[157] Supporting the industry's "house cleaning,"[158] Haag also seized on local movie regulation. Two columns promoted Baker's role as the city's chief censor: one described him as a proponent of viewing a serial in its entirety rather than episode by episode; the other claimed that he and his new assistant Stephen A. Geitz were less "ruthless" than censors in cities like Chicago.[159] Yet they did ban fourteen films (unnamed) and ordered extensive cuts and intertitle deletions in 240 others, including "three serials [that] were virtually rebuilt." The *News* also praised the Junior Cinema Committee of the Women's City Club for organizing Saturday morning screenings for children at five neighborhood theaters,[160] where serials featured and "young folk" made up their audience.

In March 1921, the *Sunday News* resumed two or three pages of movie coverage, with Haag's column bannered simply "Motion Pictures."[161] Industry news again loomed large. "Big films," from *Way Down East* to *The Queen of Sheba*, required a strange mix of studio sets depicting different countries, all on view in a tour of Paramount's Hollywood studio—like that tracked later for laughs in *Singin' in the Rain*.[162] A short series of stories paid tribute to earlier stars such as Kathlyn Williams, but now Arbuckle had joined them; and the Arbuckle–Rappe affair, Haag argued, should lead to a "cleaning up of the Aegean Stables of the motion picture world."[163] Yet earlier he had admired Universal's clever stunt in which censors, seemingly invited to assist in editing *Foolish Wives*, elicited "a tremendous amount of the finest kind of publicity."[164] With the success of German films such as *Passion* and *Deception*, some in the industry called for protective tariffs; yet more and more American films were deluging theaters in countries from Argentina and Brazil to China and Japan.[165]

Finally, a long column on feature film distribution and the publicity it required led Haag to describe the rental exchanges in the city: while the smallest might have only a manager, two salesmen, and [as an afterthought] an office girl, the largest had as many as sixty personnel.[166] But distribution included educational films and nontheatrical venues as well, and Haag praised the National Board of Review for approving many educational films on the sciences: 354 on geography, 233 on zoology, 52 on biology, and 25 on botany.[167] Despite his interest in technical issues, Haag dismissed the "synchronization of phonograph and motion picture" with the prescient "theory" that silence constituted the movies' chief fascination: "The average spectator at a motion picture show wants to do his own talking to himself, just as a man in deep reverie is likely to do so."[168]

In December 1921, after Haag left the *News* for New York,[169] Hefferman returned; soon the *News*'s movie coverage was integrated into a series of pages bannered "Plays and Photoplays."[170] Hefferman's writings now became a little more critical. He bemoaned the National Board of Review's choice of the five "best films" of 1921 (three of which were "foreign-made"), ignoring such favorites as *Way Down East* and *The Four Horsemen of the Apocalypse*.[171] Despite the industry's recent downturn,[172] things were looking up. Hefferman cited an exhibitors' campaign to eliminate "indirect advertising" in feature films—that is, product placement, including "automobiles, cigarettes, soap, phonographs, tires."[173] After years of limited investment, "costume films" were back in vogue, especially with the success of *The Three Musketeers* and *Passion*.[174] On a very different note, a talk by screen writers John Emerson and Anita Loos at Smith College prompted many students (all young women) to plan on pursuing careers in the industry, from writing scenarios or designing sets to producing films.[175]

The *News* still assumed that its readers could not get enough of their favorite stars. A doubly promotional photo profile showed the "reigning he-flapper of film," Valentino, intently reading a copy of the *Detroit News*.[176] The paper echoed the *Free Press* in concluding that fears of a "foreign invasion" had lessened.[177] Reciprocally, the US Department of Commerce joined the National Association of Manufacturers to plan using motion pictures "in boosting American trade abroad."[178] Although Hefferman rarely showed any concern for technical issues, he did share Haag's interest in educational films and their distribution, but he tended to single out individuals. Bruce was integrating stories into his scenics; Newman had a new nature film series; and Charles Urban was preparing a new catalogue of his "Living Book of Knowledge."[179] Unlike the *Free Press*, however, Hefferman gave scant attention to the opening of the Capitol Theater and the Detroit-Made Film Company.[180] He found the complaint that movies had caused a drop in reading to be false when the Detroit Public Library revealed that "picturized book[s]" like *The Three Musketeers*, *Humoresque*, or *The Four Horsemen of the Apocalypse* often were "in constant circulation."[181]

As its coverage of the movies expanded, the *News* subscribed to several syndicated columns. In October 1921, it picked up one written by James W. Dean from New York. Typical were Dean's gossipy interviews with stars like Chaplin and Fairbanks and filmmakers like Lubitsch; with the partners Emerson and Loos; and with Rex Ingram, who labeled Valentino "the new heart palpitator."[182] In February 1922, the *News* introduced a second, more prominent column, written by H. G. Salsinger from Hollywood. An early column reported that reducing costs was de rigueur everywhere, from building exterior studio sets to controlling stars' behavior: "We used to be afraid to spank the players, but now," boasted one director, "we spank them good and hard."[183] More surprising was a third, short-lived column sent from Berlin, in which Miriam Teicher described conditions in the German film industry. One column painted a vivid picture of the girl extras thronging a "monster café," called the "Film Bourse," as they waited to be hired.[184] In the last column, she was struck by Pola Negri's "valiant and almost boyish youthfulness"; her "wide, spontaneous, happy smile"; and her "amazing light blue eyes" that on-screen registered as "deep, glowing pools of infinite darkness."[185]

From summer 1922 on, the *News*'s coverage was no less standardized than that of the *Free Press*. Each Sunday's "Metropolitan" section had a page bannered "Plays and Photoplays," with one-half devoted to the theater and the other to the movies, suggesting their equivalence in status. Typically, this half page included two relatively small photo profiles (usually of stars); anywhere from four to ten brief industry stories; and a weekly column by Hefferman, who remained editor. Half a dozen ads filled two-thirds of the latter pages, with very large ads for the Capitol, Adams, Madison, and Broadway Strand. Within the restricted space left were several photo profiles and a dozen industry stories; after March 1924, those on the third page ran under a new headline: "Film News and Gossip Gathered by Special Correspondents"—although the correspondents were never named. What the *News* offered its readers thus differed from the *Free Press* in several crucial ways. No cluster of star photos dominated the first page; a named editor was responsible for the paper's coverage; and there were more industry stories, sometimes even local ones. Not only did the "Photoplays Today" column of fifty neighborhood theater programs run along the edge of the second or third Sunday page, it also consistently skirted the daily Society page—whose readers were chiefly women.

Besides Hefferman's Sunday column, several others became fixtures. In August 1922, "Shadowgraphs" began collating dozens of gossip items on the stars.[186] Soon after that column vanished, Monroe Lathrop's syndicated "Tales from Filmland" replaced it with equally brief gossip and ran regularly thereafter.[187] Through fall 1923, Dean's column continued with subjects like these: charges that costly "atmospheric" footage slowed a film's action; Negri "clamoring for close ups" or "beeg heads" in her films; and Naldi's take on Valentino that "hundreds are better looking."[188] In March 1923, the *News* added a column by Jack Jungmeyer on a trade war pitting "independents" against "the big producing corporations."[189] By the following July Jungmeyer, too, was a regular contributor. His subjects ranged from the efforts by Little Theater Films to counter the public's desire for "sex appeal and hokum" to the use of rehearsals in filmmaking, "fitting players for roles," and interviews with Buster Keaton and Louise Fazenda.[190] In summer 1924, a fourth column signed by Harry Carr appeared, following the jokey, cigar-chomping Lubitsch on a shoot; by early 1925 it, too, was a regular feature.[191] In a revealing shift, the *News* phased out one column from New York and regularized the three others, all with bylines from Hollywood—a sign of the latter's increasing "mythic" centrality to the industry.

Star stories remained a staple for moviegoers. In summer 1922, several had Bara hoping to return to the screen but as a "motivated vampire . . . who encoils the victim for love's sweet sake, which makes it all right."[192] Very different stories featured Wallace Reid and Ruth Roland. In late 1922, two stories described Reid's seclusion after several nervous breakdowns, but none reported his death months later from a drug overdose.[193] A third story admired Roland's financial savvy for putting her money into securities and a valuable business corner in the city.[194] By contrast, half a dozen stories followed the Arbuckle scandal and his attempts at reinstatement in the industry.[195] Such scandals led Hefferman, in November 1924, to lampoon the many books that "sugar-coated" notable stars and others.[196] New stars also emerged: Will Rogers, who sent up "the illuminati of Hollywood" in *All for Art*; Lon Chaney, the "champion movie contortionist"; Wallace Beery as a "drink-crazed sea captain" in *The Devil's Cargo*; and Ramon Navarro, whom Carr's "flapper friends" mooned over and who "unhorsed Valentino from the favored position on all the boarding house dressing tables."[197] The *News* also took note of forgotten and fading stars. In July 1924, Florence Turner, Maurice Costello, and Lillian Walker met in New York to reminisce over tea.[198] At the same time, Normand and Bara slipped into "the shadow of [their] fame."[199]

The *News* continued to make much of other leading figures and kept readers abreast of the industry's amazing growth. While Sweet and other "alumni" honored their mentor with a "Griffith Day" in early 1924, the "master" himself pooh-poohed the records set by *The Covered Wagon*.[200] What may have provoked Griffith's ire was the press story heralding James Cruze as the "movie genius of

1922"—confirmed by having four movie hits in a row by early 1924.[201] While Jungmeyer admired Pickford's skill as an actor and producer, her distaste for "dealing" led the *News*'s headline writer to dismiss her stereotypically as "no business woman."[202] After financial setbacks and a production slump in 1923, studios reportedly were again operating at "full speed" by early 1924,[203] and the industry overall now ranked eighth nationwide in capital investment.[204] This growth was evident in exterior sets that showed off Hollywood's superiority: several city blocks of a Midwestern town for Warner Brothers's *Main Street*; DeMille's "colossal set" for *The Ten Commandments*; an entire Paris square erected for *The Hunchback of Notre Dame*.[205] Besides the turmoil caused by Griffith leaving United Artists, major changes were in process: companies were establishing studios back East; others were leaving Hollywood for the Los Angeles suburbs; Goldwyn and Metro were merging into a single company.[206]

The *News* also kept taking readers "behind the scenes," for both the initial and final stages of filmmaking. Hefferman complained that the "careless editing" of release prints often irritated audiences, but Jungmeyer breezily defended the "film cutter" who sometimes found it impossible to piece together an acceptable continuity.[207] In a debate over happy versus tragic endings, Ingram asked exhibitors to poll audiences and then screen one of two different prints of *Where the Pavement Ends*.[208] As for the initial stage, C. Gardner Sullivan and Frances Marion used different lenses to observe how scenario writing had changed over the past decade.[209] Contrasting stories now targeted would-be writers. While Hefferman promoted the Palmer Photoplay Corporation as a legitimate "school," the Screen Writers Guild and the Authors League of America railed against "irresponsible correspondence schools."[210] In early 1923, a noteworthy series celebrated three top scriptwriters, all women: Frances Marion, a model for feminists; "DeMille's scenario chief" Jeannie Macpherson, "vacationing" in New York City; and June Mathis, recently hired as "editorial director" for what was still Goldwyn Pictures.[211] Capping this series was a survey of many others, not only scenarists but also editors and wardrobe managers.[212] Whatever their impact on young women, all of these created an image of Hollywood to counter the salacious one filled with star scandals.

Comparatively few stories dealt with distribution and exhibition, dubbed the "uninteresting" ends of the business. Yet Hefferman argued that a film's success often depended on the strength of its distribution, which favored the large corporations at the expense of smaller companies.[213] As for exhibition, in early 1923 the *News* printed a useful set of statistics from the Motion Picture Theater Owners of America about the country's theaters—their number, seating capacity, and weekly attendance.[214] If, according to a survey, daily movie attendance really had shrunk by one-fourth between 1915 and 1924,[215] what were exhibitors doing to attract moviegoers? On the one hand, the Motion Picture Theater Owners

Fig. 4.6. "Hefferman's Best of 1922," *Detroit Sunday News* (December 24, 1922): M3.

organization adopted a "clean up" program pressuring producers and distributors to eliminate salacious film titles and advertising.[216] On the other, several Los Angeles exhibitors were sponsoring film "previews" for invited guests drawn from "the Social Bluebook, . . . the Bench and Bar Association, and Who's Who in Hollywood, " which turned "first night" moviegoing into an elaborate social event.[217] A syndicated story about how New York City palace cinemas dressed their usherettes to match a feature film attraction suggested why young women might seek a local job in the industry.[218] An usherette earned "$17.00 a week," and her tips could run "from $10 to $16 a week more."

Complementing what can only be called industry boosterism, critics started to judge the "best films" of a particular year or season. In August 1922, the *News* summarized *Life* critic Robert E. Sherwood's top twenty-four titles for the first half of the year.[219] In December, Sherwood cut that number to eleven for the year, from *Robin Hood* to *Blood and Sand* and *Nanook of the North*.[220] While Hefferman came up with his own list of 1922's "quality 10," largely agreeing with Sherwood,[221] he also separated out comedies, starting with Lloyd's *Grandma's Boy*, Chaplin's *Pay Day*, and Keaton's *My Wife's Relations*.[222] In September, he summed up a different survey in which MPPDA chair Will Hays asked critics every three months to choose their "best" and "worst" recent films.[223] Despite great disagreement, they voted William DeMille's *Only 38* as "the best," and then turned moralistic, choosing *The Rustle of Silk* and *Souls for Sale* as "the worst." In December, the *News* printed Sherwood's tally of "best films" (from June 1922 to August 1923), which now included *Safety Last*, *The Covered Wagon*, *When Knighthood Was in Flower*, and *The Eternal Flame*—and excluded *Nanook*.[224] Finally, in early 1925, the *News* reprinted the 1924 "best films" list of the Los Angeles critics, led by *The Thief of Bagdad* and, surprisingly, *Greed*—with the caveat that several "extraordinary films" had yet to screen in Detroit.[225]

The *News* now showed much less interest in local stories, and weeks often passed without a single one. Unlike the *Free Press*, which touted musical performers almost weekly, the *News* devoted only a few short photo profiles or brief items to them.[226] Likewise, only one big stage production rated mention: Ned Wayburn's prologue for the Capitol's third-anniversary program.[227] The same lack of stories marked personal appearances: in May 1923, a tiny insert announced Bushman and Bayne's visit to the Capitol; one month later, Bebe Daniels would be dancing at the same theater.[228] By contrast, the *News* paid more attention to theater owners: in July 1922, Gleichman and Kunsky battled in court over who could screen Paramount films; in June, a "war" broke out within the Motion Picture Theater Owners of America, leading the state's four hundred members to withdraw.[229] After First National's annual October convention, Kunsky and Trendle floated plans to counter the "road show menace," in which big first-run films bypassed their theaters.[230] In summer 1924, brief stories noted these theater

Are You a Real Movie Fan? Answer These and Qualify

WHAT is a movie fan? Often we read of this and that star receiving so many hundreds of letters daily from movie fans, but no one has given much thought to what a movie fan really is. What are his or her qualifications for being placed in that category? Thinking along these same lines, Marshall Neilan, the director, has figured out a questionaire. If you can answer these questions, says Mr. Neilan, you qualify as a regular "dyed-in-the-wool fan." Here they are:

1. What pictures made D. W. Griffith famous?
2. Who wrote the scenario for "The Four Horsemen of the Apocalypse?"
3. What two foreign directors have just come to America?
4. In what two pictures did Mary Pickford play dual roles?
5. Who played the lead in "The River's End?"
6. Who directed "Foolish Wives?"
7. Who played the leading role in "Passion?"
8. What is a close-up?
9. What is the length of a reel?
10. Who writes his own stories, adapts them, directs them and writes all the titles?

Fig. 4.7. "Movie Fan Contest," *Detroit Sunday News* (April 15, 1923): M6.

changes: Kunsky named his new downtown palace cinema The State; Gleichman redecorated the Broadway Strand; Miles acquired the Ferry Field; and Kunsky sold the De Luxe to James Robertson, owner of the Cinderella.[231]

Perhaps readers most appreciated the *News*'s promotion of half a dozen prize contests. Like the *Free Press*, the *News* highlighted Universal's 1923 student essay contest, won by Edward Mable of Central High School.[232] But it also noted a second Universal contest that year, awarding college scholarships to encourage scenario writing.[233] For its part, in June the Authors League of America sponsored a national contest, for submitting the best ideas for "better pictures"—and the winner was a Detroit youth, Laverne Caron.[234] But there was more. In April 1923, Marshall Neilan challenged readers to answer a series of "trivia" questions—In what two pictures did Mary Pickford play dual roles? What is the length of a reel? What is a close-up?—to qualify as "real movie fans."[235] No prizes were given, only confirmation that one was a "dyed-in-the-wool fan." Although these contests implied that fans could interact with and even influence the industry, undoubtedly their primary aim was to burnish Hollywood's image.

One final note: In February 1922, Hefferman printed an unusual story about the preservation of motion pictures for the future.[236] Would films really "show the important events and personalities of today for centuries," as many believed?

How long could film negatives last? Could those of Biograph and Keystone pictures "in their prime" be in good enough condition to strike new prints? Hefferman added, "What about our war pictures and the news libraries?" Preservation was something for "the Society of Motion Picture Engineers to work out," and solutions gradually would emerge—and continue to this day. In July 1922, a *News* story wondered whether someone would begin collecting film prints, and offered a neologism, "kineophile," to describe such collectors.[237] Even Will Hays proposed installing vaults in the White House cellars "for the scientific storage of films"—until a "proper building" could be constructed.[238] In late 1924, as Hollywood was celebrating its thirteenth anniversary as the "movie capital," industry leaders began to contemplate an annual fiesta to honor the movies, which several years later would become the first Academy Awards ceremony.[239] Ironically, that celebration ignored the industry's general reluctance to give either the time or the money needed for preserving its films, which too often were viewed as scrap; this attitude and inaction would compromise the cultural heritage of the movies for years.

Detroit Journal

For several years after the Great War, the *Detroit Journal* became a third news source for moviegoers. Subscription figures kept it from being a strong rival to either the *Free Press* or the *News*, but the *Journal* would take a different perspective on the movies. In early January 1918, its coverage consisted of a single Saturday page edited by Charles G. Steinhauer, with the usual cluster of star photos, eight first-run picture theater ads, their weekly program synopses, and fewer than a dozen short news and gossip items.[240] By the end of the year, little on this page had changed. In parallel with the *Free Press*, the *Journal* printed a "Motion Picture Directory" of weekly programs for nine neighborhood theaters, four of which—the Gladwin Park, Grande, Montclair, and Rosedale—were not in the *Free Press*.[241] In early January, the *Journal*, too, bannered its Saturday page "The Screen."[242] Within weeks, the "Motion Picture Directory" turned into a daily column of twelve neighborhood theaters, titled "Go to the Movies To Day at Your Favorite Theater."[243] For months, under movie page editor Charles C. Reed, the paper's coverage continued as before.[244] Theater ads increased to a dozen, and those in the "Go to the Movies" column also grew slightly.[245] That fall, despite the economic downturn, the *Journal* initiated several significant changes.

First, the Saturday coverage expanded to three pages.[246] Besides the dozen star photos, dozen picture theater ads, weekly program synopses, and "Go to the Movies" column of twenty neighborhood theaters, there were filler stories such as a US Bureau of Commerce plan to send eight mobile projection units into rural communities to show educational films.[247] Second, the paper introduced a

"Today" page that included "A Daily Review of Photo-Play" section with a star photo or cartoon, a "Movie Programs" column, and half a dozen short pieces like the tongue-in-cheek "How Joyous Is the Life of a Screen Actor."[248] Third, and most important, Marjorie Daw signed on as editor of both the Saturday and daily pages. From September 1918 through September 1919, Daw had served as photoplay editor of the *Cleveland Sunday Plain Dealer* (which had the largest circulation in the city), where she sometimes chatted cheerfully with readers.[249] In one June 1919 column she wrote, "In the words of Kipling, [some may] exclaim 'it's pretty, but is it art?' The real movie fan doesn't care about anything so banal."[250] This playful tone, reminiscent of Kitty Kelly, would carry over into the *Journal*.

Besides her own column, Daw introduced other gossipy tidbits: "Our Daily Worse Than Verse" doggerel; "Things Young People Ought to Know," mostly about stars; and "Right Off the Reel," repurposed from the *Chicago Tribune*.[251] She printed occasional short star profiles as well as a few serious pieces: Red Cross staff in Baltimore summarized current "Topics of the Day" films for blind soldiers; a Sing Sing inmate wrote a prize-winning composition about *The Miracle Man*.[252] Yet most of her selected stories had a local angle: Fairbanks's *His Majesty, the American* broke the Majestic's attendance record on its first day; a clever ten-year-old boy, with the manager's permission, raked in 30¢ a day selling gum in the Broadway Strand lobby.[253] She also held a contest for fans to explain, in three hundred words or less, why Eugene O'Brien was a "perfect lover" in the film of that title, with the prize displayed in Salton's jewelry store.[254] The *Journal* itself sponsored two series of "Movie Puzzle Contests." The first, in conjunction with the downtown Colonial, offered one thousand tickets to entrants who correctly named the stars "hidden" in two different cartoon pictures printed each day.[255] The second also offered one thousand tickets to the Adams or the Madison, with winners having to unscramble two sets of letters to form the names of stars.[256] These contests, like those in the *Free Press* and the *News*, likely served a double purpose: on the one hand, they promoted downtown moviegoing attendance; on the other, they sought to increase the newspaper's readership.

Typically, Daw seemed to address women, whom the *Journal* assumed were its main readers.[257] The best evidence came in two columns. In one, Daw repeated the advice of several columnists before her: that motion pictures were an exciting new professional field for women. Specifically, she encouraged young women to take up writing scenarios, at which, said a Universal editor, women excelled.[258] In a second, Daw singled out Nellie M. Scott, "the president and directing head of a million dollar . . . plant," which made industrial films.[259] Still, Daw likely appealed to any reader attracted by her colloquial, humorous style.[260] She once described Chaplin and Fairbanks going to the circus: "Seems sorta odd, though, to think of the two funniest stars in the movies traipsing off to the sideshow, doesn't it? That's the nicest thing about those two fellows. They just can't seem to

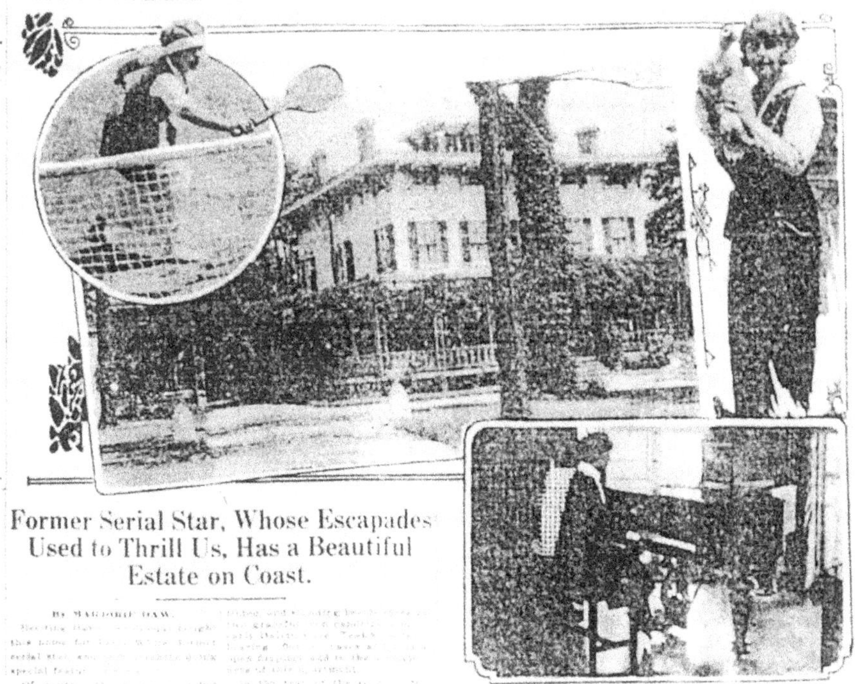

Fig. 4.8. Marjorie Daw's column, *Detroit Journal* (December 27, 1919): Today, 1.

grow up."[261] In another, she pretended concern about Prohibition's effect on the movies: "How is Bill Hart ever going to get up the gumption enough on a couple of chocolate sodas to walk right up to the sheriff and hit his nose and take his guns and his nice shiny star away from him? Where's the punch in the scene?"[262] Even given the heavy promotion of *Male and Female*,[263] Daw could not be completely serious. Her caption for a photo ad, in which Meighan's huge helmet looms over Swanson's feathered headdress, came close to parody, as he seemed to bellow, 'I Was a King in Babylon, and You Were a Christian Slave.'"[264]

Some characteristics of Daw's work continued during early 1920—"The Year of the Women."[265] Leap year gave her license to prod "girls" to keep on sending in all those marriage proposals that torment "the handsome actor."[266] A bit more seriously, she tried to placate a reader ("Now we know I have a reader") who feared that "some naughty producer" might steal her scenario's plot.[267] After warning "Mildred and Beulah, Julia and Bobbie" not "to think of" becoming a movie star, she rattled off all the difficulties of trying to be a minor actress.[268] She also reprinted an interview with Neilan, who advised her readers, "Shop for your movies as you do for shoes . . . by shopping in the newspapers," but especially in the *Journal*.[269] Beginning with Pearl White in late December 1919, Daw introduced a series of stories that gave readers virtual tours of stars' splendid homes.[270] Accompanied by photos—of exteriors, interiors, and relaxing stars—each "little journey" resembled the kind of "good life" story found in fan magazines. The roster of stars included Ethel Clayton, Eugene O'Brien, Billie Burke, Wesley Barry, Charlie Chaplin, Charles Ray, and Enid Bennett.[271]

From January through February 1920, Daw also collected more industry news. The topics ranged widely, from Loew purchasing Metro Pictures and the return of Bara, "she of the come-hither eyes and the heaving and hectic emotions," to the Community Motion Picture Bureau library's extensive data on films marketed since 1915.[272] Two columns of particular interest were Metro's experiment testing two different endings (happy and sad) to *The Right of Way* and Daw's own dismay at the "ubiquitous closeup" that reveals "the wrinkles and blemishes of our favorite stars."[273] Her choice of local news often focused on personnel: Tom Moule, manager of the Adams and Madison; "Sid" Lawrence, the "boy manager" of the Fox Washington; or Watterson Rothacker, who promoted "celluloid advertising" to the Detroit Board of Commerce.[274] Finally, each Monday, until the "Today" page disappeared in late February, Daw offered synopses of the week's feature films, sometimes adding a sentence of praise or disdain. In mid-January she dismissed *Six Feet Four*: "a melodramatic western . . . with ranches and stage coaches, bandits and cowboys distributed generously, one might almost say recklessly throughout."[275] This dismissal also mildly slammed the taste of the Liberty's relatively downscale audience.

Two months after Daw left the *Journal*, in early March 1920, Ann Greene became the paper's chief movie editor.[276] Greene's columns and selected stories often followed Daw's lead. She added a tour of Olive Thomas's home to Daw's series, this one inadvertently poignant, given the star's death months later.[277] Greene also abhorred close-ups, especially of a weeping heroine like Katherine MacDonald, whom she rather nastily claimed had "no more expression than a wax doll."[278] But she edged away from Daw on several counts. Two early columns showed a rather censorial streak. If "lurid photoplays" like *Six Feet Four* were no better than "dime novels,"[279] the worst among the "human nuisances who infest the moving picture houses" were the "female buzzers"; and she printed a series of cartoons of such "Movie Pests."[280] If the caption for an early cluster of star photos read "Every Good 'Movie' Fan is a Star-Gazer," Greene later qualified that statement: while men may like the Hart, Farnum, and Mix types, "women simply adore the Wally Reids, and the Thomas Meighans, and the Earl Williams" who are "diplomatic" in their courting.[281] As a further example, she added a photo profile of DeMille, "the popular producer with the ladies" supposedly "because he understands the feminine nature."[282] Implicit was the assumption that such "ladies" were the *Journal*'s targeted class of readers.

During her last months as editor, ending in early January 1921, Greene did not stint on industry news, some of it familiar. Following a story about William Fox's origins, she added one stressing how important women were as "directors and scenario writers," from Weber to Marion, Macpherson, Loos, and Alice [Guy] Blaché.[283] Others introduced new interests. For nearly ten years projectors had been sold for school, church, and even home use, but now Greene wondered if Urban would develop a better machine.[284] A photo profile showed how artistic titles and intertitles were made; another story promoted slow-motion filmmaking as so beneficial for scientific experiments.[285] Yet Greene could take contradictory positions—or pretend to. In one column, she decried the reformed hero (the product of Prohibition) who no longer was ruthless enough to dispose of the villain.[286] In another, she let the "Movie Crab" gripe about how audiences loved speed, as in "a corking bit of an automobile race," but yawned at a fleet of slow-moving motor trucks, even in a climactic scene where they toiled through a rainy night with supplies to repair a threatened dam.[287]

During this time, the *Journal* also foregrounded several local initiatives. The publicity director of the Madison and Adams, Howard O. Pierce, twice contributed articles about programming first-run theaters. One described the detailed operation of six daily performances, timed "to the very minute," like a train schedule.[288] This depended on the "limited working hours of the orchestra" and required "a system of signals connecting the operating booth with the musical director." The other explained the exhibitor's job of choosing which films to program in any given week.[289] He had to know his audience and the current conditions that might affect them, which led Pierce to claim that it took "more discretion and skill to pick a good comedy" than a feature. In late 1920, along with (ironically?) the Hubris Company in Chicago, the *Journal* chanced to produce its own short film, *A Romance of Detroit,* which screened for one week at the Adams.[290] Unlike the newsreels of the *Free Press* and *News*, this venture had no follow up. Finally, the *Journal* teamed up with *Moving Picture World* and thousands of First National exhibitors to sponsor a contest that had readers "pick the most popular film stars" of the day.[291] From mid-December on, each ballot asked contestants to name a favorite actor and actress and submit that name to one of a hundred city theaters or mail it to the paper's Photoplay Editor.[292] The *Journal* promised to post the ballot tallies daily, with Pickford, Ray, Reid, and Norma Talmadge early favorites.[293] By the contest's conclusion in early March 1921, joining them were Constance Talmadge and Meighan.[294]

Once Greene left the *Journal*, only a few weeks went by before, on February 1, 1921, Charles Richard Laurence became the new editor, and he continued in that post up to the *Journal*'s demise.[295] Like those of Daw and Greene, Laurence's columns headed not only the three-page Saturday coverage of the movies but also a daily page supported by picture theater ads. Within weeks, a block ad almost plaintively invited readers to "Write to Me!" asking questions and suggesting subjects, but rarely did Laurence seem to respond to them.[296] Instead, his presence seemed to mark some change in the subjects of columns, in the assumptions about fans, and perhaps in the *Journal*'s overall editorial slant.

One sign was that stories of local matters waned. Some might have been expected, such as coverage of the January opening of the downtown Capitol, where Laurence spoke briefly with Marcus Loew.[297] Yet others were unusual. A local reporter, Sarah Maybury, penned a breezy interview with Bara as a "changed vampire": "Gosh, when she used to turn her eyes on a caller, she would drop her special eyelid and just look ice cold. [Now] She smiles. She laughs. She has dimples."[298] On a different note, a YMCA secretary in Grand Rapids insisted that high school boys now "want girl pals," not vamps and flappers—supposedly confirming the cliché that vamps were out of favor.[299] Laurence also could address fans directly. In September he reprinted a pen-and-ink drawing of Fairbanks "for your scrap book of stars"; the following January, he asked readers if they agreed with the previous year's "best films" chosen by the National Board of Review.[300] Of the seventeen listed, six were "foreign-made," and he was curious why *Little Lord Fauntleroy* was relegated to a list of runners-up.[301] Even in the Monday synopses of the week's films, he added local touches: appearing in *Experience* was "pretty Miss Juliette of this city."[302] In perhaps the most startling story, the Michigan branch of the Motion Picture Theater Owners of America voted not to screen *The Lonely Trail*, a film already passed by Detroit's censors, because the main actor was an "Indian guide" somehow involved in a "notorious" divorce case in the state.[303]

By contrast, Laurence deluged readers with industry stories. Many assumed a fascination with stars, including those who were not making personal appearances in the city. Particularly favored was Marion Davies, whom an English artist judged "the most beautiful blonde in America," and whom a publicity photo portrayed in a sumptuous costume for *The Young Diana*.[304] But so was Cleo Ridgley, making a comeback after having twins and now playing "heavy" roles because "loving mothers make [the] best villains."[305] Others included Nazimova, who was taking on "highbrow" roles in *A Doll's House* and *Salome*; Colleen Moore, who believed that "the face is a mirror for the thoughts and emotions"; Anna May Wong, branded with the moniker "Oriental Cinderella"; and even western heroes like Tom Mix, Harry Carey, Hoot Gibson, and Buck Jones.[306] Industry bigwigs also caught Laurence's eye.[307] After resigning as President Harding's US Postmaster General, Will Hays accepted an extremely generous offer to join the industry and eventually to head the new MPPDA.[308]

Among the miscellany of other industry stories, Laurence revealed his special interest in France: while he highlighted the innovative portable studio of director Louis Mercanton, he reported the anti-Red hysteria in Paris, when Communists provoked violent protests at a screening of *La Russie Rouge*.[309] In several columns on exhibition, he bemoaned the adverse effect of superfluous intertitles and assumed the stereotypical claim that "bachelors and women [were] the readiest weepers" at the movies.[310] In a different column, he took New York censors to task for trying to banish "Sennett's bathing beauties" from the stage."[311] Yet, in two strongly worded columns, Laurence fumed about "fake schools for movie actors," decrying the effort and money that amateurs lost by answering disreputable ads.[312] Instead, he endorsed the spread of movies into schools across the country, as "part of regular scholastic instruction."[313]

From the beginning of his tenure, Laurence signaled that he was partial to taking readers "behind the scenes." He described the lengthy, specialized process of film developing from negative to positive prints and later described the task of the film editor in reducing all the footage shot by one-sixth to construct the final print.[314] He singled out the dangerous work of a *Pathé News* cameraman in filming a volcano eruption and the trick effects of Virgil E. Miller, "Director of Cinematography Research at Universal."[315] If he laid the responsibility for a film's success on the shoulders of the director, he also noted differences between "old and new school directors," between those who exploited action and those who preferred subtle emotion.[316] Elaborate exterior sets were being constructed on studio lots—for example, a country home built for *The Young Diana*, with a photo of a night scene, shot under klieg lights.[317] Accuracy in sets, costumes, and props demanded research, and here Laurence relied on Elizabeth McCaffey, head of Famous Players-Lasky's research bureau.[318] Shortly thereafter, he also promoted *A Trip to Paramountown*, which included some "clever trick photography" by Karl Brown.[319] In the end he returned to his anger at fake acting schools and lauded what he considered the "real thing": a Paramount school whose aim was to create "a perpetual reservoir of talent from which can be drawn the stars of tomorrow."

One last tactic the *Journal* used to attract and hold readers revived a practice much more prevalent in the 1910s: a story unfolding in serial episodes over several weeks or even months. Introduced as a daily feature in September 1921, "Love Story of a Movie Star" posed this teasing question: "Can You Guess Who Wrote It?"[320] "The End" came in late October,[321] but, apparently, no answer was forthcoming. Did the tactic work? Perhaps not, for a second movie story never appeared, just as no other film followed *A Romance of Detroit*.

Detroit Times

Before Hearst bought the *Detroit Times* in October 1921, the newspaper offered little to interest moviegoers. Only in early 1919 did a half page appear in the Saturday edition, under the heading "Screen," with half a dozen star photos, three or four theater ads, and a few of the week's program synopses.[322] Two years later, the coverage had expanded to a full page, much of it taken up with theater ads, and only four of the nine theaters screened movies.[323] The principal addition was a "Real News of Reel People" column, with bits of information and gossip, some penned as comic asides. Each Tuesday edition and Thursday edition now also had an "Amusements" page that included a star photo, one or more stories, and a column of theater ads, among them for Kunsky's three downtown theaters. In June came several one-off stories: an interview with Negri, in which she claimed that her pantomime performance as the Black Dancer in Reinhardt's *Sumurun* (in Warsaw before the war) eased her path into the movies; a parody of a fictional actress working for Dunkem and then Floosey Films; and a cheeky claim that recent costume pictures rendered "America . . . no longer the Land of Jazz."[324] By late 1921, the *Times*'s coverage of the movies looked very different.

One change followed the practice of the *News* and the *Journal*. In December, Ralph Holmes began editing separate "Stage" and "Screen" pages on Saturdays (each topped by a strip of star photos) and a daily page that combined the two. He also wrote a Saturday column summing up the next week's first-run theater programs and a Monday film review. His first praised Barthelmess for the "wistfulness" of his starring role in *Tol'able David*.[325] A week later came his take on *The Iron Trail*, a "two-fisted action" adaptation of a Rex Beach novel.[326] That same Monday, as he would thereafter on occasion, A. F. Munroe added a second review: *What Do Men Want?*, a "sex picture" that director Lois Weber handled with her usual "consummate . . . artistry."[327] Later, if Munroe fawned over *The Lotus Eater*, starring John Barrymore, Holmes described William DeMille's *Miss Lulu Bett* as only "a more than passably good movie."[328] During his early tenure, Holmes sometimes inserted one or more industry stories. In January 1922, one reported that *Foolish Wives* was released before the censors finished their work; another had 12,000 theaters celebrating the tenth anniversary of *Queen Elizabeth* as the earliest multiple-reel film.[329] At the Capitol's opening, he highlighted the theater's "pre-set switchboard" that created "wonderful color effects," described the throng of 4,500 people that besieged the first night show, and profiled Kunsky himself.[330]

In early December 1921, the *Times* used the movies as a scheme for luring new readers to become subscribers. A heavily promoted "movie title test" asked readers to guess what film a cartoon drawing represented.[331] Until just before Christmas, a different cartoon appeared each day, followed by a coupon to fill out and a long list of possible movie titles from which to draw an answer.[332] The awards offered were unusually large: $1,000 for first prize, $250 for second, $150 for third, $100 for fourth, and lesser amounts for the remaining 134—totaling $2,500 in all. While most contest ads ran one-half to one-third of a page, at the end of the first week the *Times* used a full page to summarize each day's earlier cartoons, coupons, rules, awards, and list of movie titles.[333] Finally announced on February 1, 1922, first prize went to Otto Lee, described as a "paralytic"; second prize, to Mrs. Anna Rogers; third prize, to Miss Carrie Gray; and fourth prize,

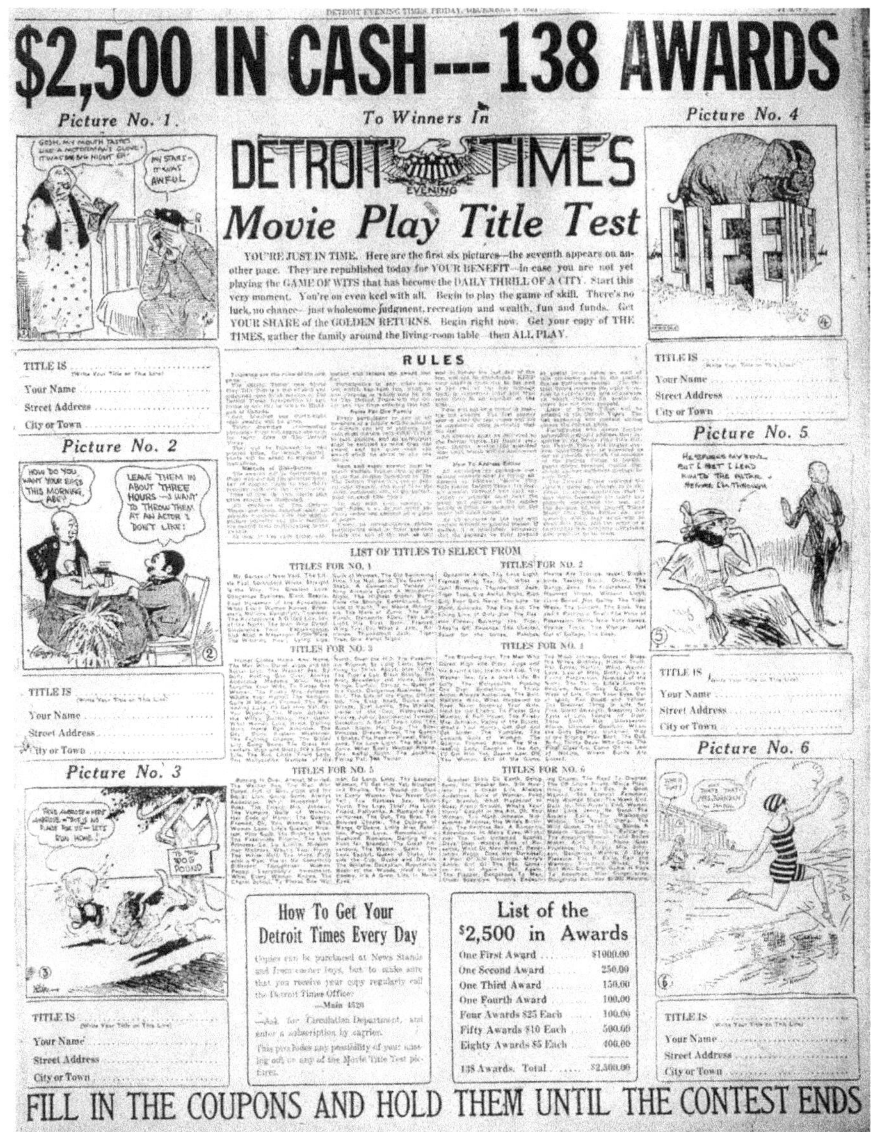

Fig. 4.9. "Movie Play Title Test," *Detroit Times* (December 12, 1921): n.p.

to William D. Duckett.[334] Of the remaining winners, receiving $5 or $10 each, nearly half were women, as many married as single. The only other woman to win $25 was Delphine Sproule, who lived in East River Rouge. Further analysis of the winners and their addresses (listed in tiny print) could reveal their specific locations and whether they came from middle-class, working-class, or ethnic communities (and which ones) in the city.

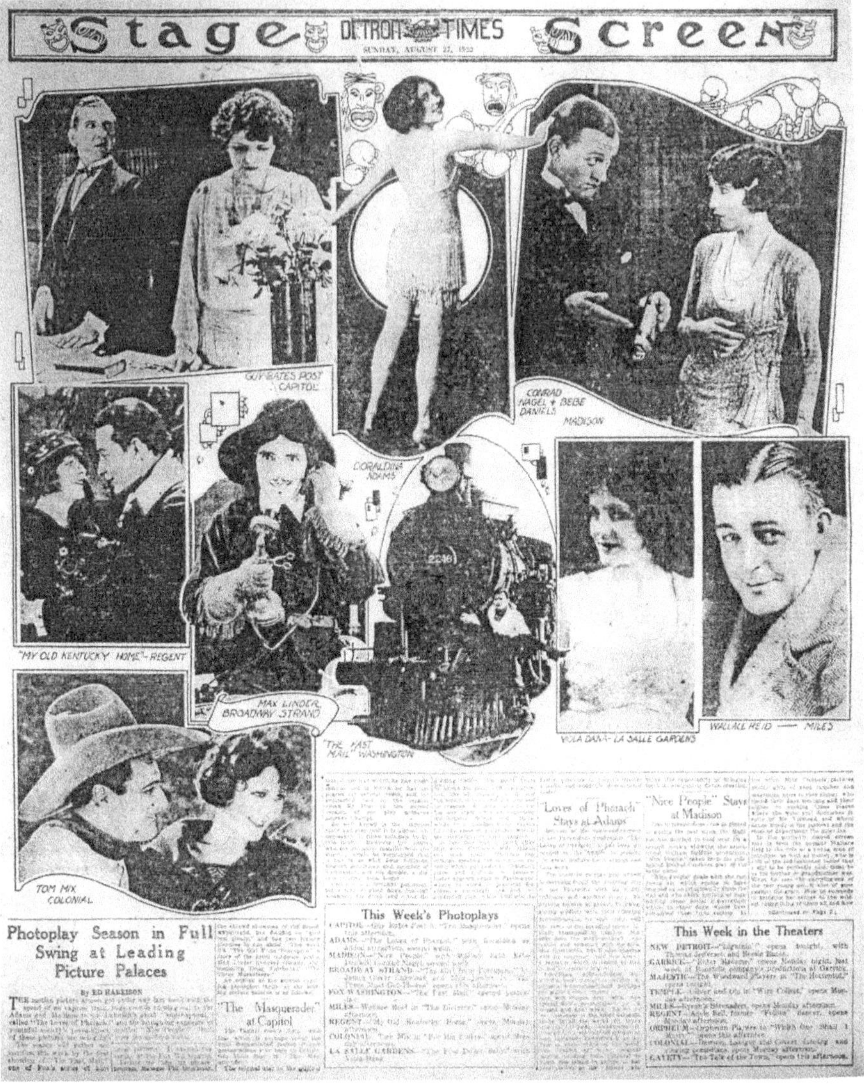

Fig. 4.10. Stage/Screen, *Detroit Sunday Times* (August 27, 1922): 4.1.

In early August 1922, the *Times* began publishing a Sunday edition and initially combined "Stage" and "Screen" on the first of four pages, with the following two pages devoted to the movies and the fourth devoted to the theater.[335] Within weeks, "Screen" took over the first page entirely, and as many as ten movie star photos filled two-thirds of its space, leaving room for little more than one or two columns and brief story items.[336] The prominence of this gallery may have spurred the *Free Press* the following month to initiate a very similar collage of photos. By early summer 1923, the "Screen" and "Stage" pages became a major part of the Sunday "Society" section, implying that, despite the paper's overall rhetoric of "yellow journalism," the targeted movie readership may have been a certain class of women.[337] By early 1924, a new banner, "Motion Picture Reviews and News," headed one page each weekday, although the "reviews" read like publicity material.[338] During these few years, then, the *Times* established a relatively standardized weekly coverage to match that of the *Free Press* and *News*, one that the paper kept current through early 1925.

Within this standardized format, the *Times* assigned a series of writers to edit the "Screen" pages and come up with at least one weekly column. In early March 1922, Holmes resumed writing only about the theater, and Ed Harrison took over coverage of the movies, which soon included a recurring column of gossip, "News of Filmland."[339] In May 1922, Harrison singled out "careers for girls in movies"—like Lucita Squier, who went from a mere typist to a scenario writer for Neilan, or "Mme Violet," who honed her sewing skills as Sennett's costume designer.[340] While promoting the Detroit-Made Company's *The First Woman*, he offered short reviews that ranged from citing Marie Prevost as the only thing worth seeing in the "absurd tale" of *The Married Flapper* to expropriating Nanook's survival skills to describe *Nanook of the North* as "a slice right off the flanks of life."[341] During Harrison's tenure, Allan Jenkins wrote a few similar reviews: *Beyond the Rocks* was little more than a "silly story," despite Swanson and Valentino's "fine acting."[342] Replacing "News of Filmland" were occasional gossip columns such as Guy Price's "Screen Notes" and Ray H. Leek's "Film Talk at Hollywood" and more sustained stories from *Cosmopolitan* writer William Talbot that included stars shopping for new fashions.[343] In March, when Griffith and the Gish sisters were in town, Harrison interviewed the "master," allowing reporter Madelyn Miller to write a lengthy story in which the Gish stars freely discussed matrimony, their mother, and the value of self-control.[344]

Starting in late November 1922, Joseph L. Kelley took a turn as the *Times*'s film editor. Like his predecessor, Kelley surrounded the Sunday cluster of star photos with first-run theater program summaries[345] and signed his name to the daily pages. His daily stories focused on stars like Pearl White returning to the screen or Mary Miles Minter disappearing, after the Taylor scandal, and on surveys which concluded that audiences preferred films of mixed lengths on theater programs.[346] From early January 1923 through April 1924, he essentially selected a slew of stories from publicity material and added the frequent column of a writer tagged "The Rambler."[347] Early on, The Rambler profiled the generosity of a star like Pickford, summarized the career of a director like Neilan, reviewed current films like *Dr. Jack* and *The Hottentot*, and ballyhooed the personal appearance at the Capitol of Dr. Katherine M. H. Blackford—a famous "character reader" and consultant for "the big financiers."[348] Later columns ranged from a relatively long story of Viola Dana's "life history" to Ince's challenge in choosing to film *Anna Christie* with Blanche Sweet.[349] From mid-April to early May 1924, the first Sunday page of "Stage / Screen" paired Kelley's and The Rambler's columns. In their last ones, Kelley merely summarized that week's feature films, while The Rambler singled out the experimental short film *Plastigrams*, which sought to create the illusion of three dimensions on the Capitol's screen.[350]

In mid-May 1924, a fourth writer, Lee J. Smith, took over as editor.[351] Nothing more was heard from The Rambler, suggesting that Smith may have been the real author behind the pseudonym. His role apparently was to maintain the kind of formats, columns, and stories now well established for both the Sunday and daily pages. While Smith's Sunday columns breezily described the features at first-run theaters and supplemented that coverage with unsigned brief items during the week, he sometimes offered more, even if tongue-in-cheek, as in a mid-June column of "Don'ts": "If you are a bootlegger," don't go see the Madison's Prohibition film, *Those Who Dance*.[352] More seriously, he warned "little girl moths" and would-be "flappers" about what to avoid when producers come searching for new faces.[353] Unsurprisingly, Smith assumed the period's gender norms: if women favored films of what "might have been," the really successful films were "tales of rugged adventure."[354] In early 1925, the *Times* introduced a Los Angeles writer for *Cosmopolitan*, Chandler Sprague, who penned a weekly Sunday column usually devoted to notable Hollywood figures such as former star Louise Glaum, who was seeking a comeback; scenarist Marion, whom Fox was tempting with a fabulous salary offer; and DeMille, who was joining the Producers Distributing Corporation.[355] Sprague also interviewed Valentino at the height of his masculine posturing: a man, he declared, is the "master of his family" and his "wife is only [a] helpmate."[356]

Much like the *Free Press* and the *News*, the *Times* tantalized readers with stories about the stars, likely written by press agents. Only a few of the longer pieces were about men. In May 1922, Valentino praised American women for their dancing skills and faulted their male partners, who, he said, typically lacked the grace he displayed on the dance floor.[357] In January 1923, a publicity piece hyped Meighan's popularity, claiming he "holds the record for having towns renamed"—that is, streets, parks, and businesses.[358] Among women, the *Times* often kept Negri in the news: on her arrival in Hollywood in late 1922, Leek wondered whether she would become a "feminine Valentino"; if Famous Players soon "tamed" her exotic European look, one intriguing sign was that she needed no makeup in public because her complexion was so flawlessly, transparently "white."[359] Pickford, too, initially remained prominent: in January 1923, a story named her one of the "twelve greatest women in the United States."[360] In late June 1924, the *Times* summarized box office reports from five thousand theater managers: while Valentino, Chaplin, Talmadge, and Pickford remained popular, the "Screen Idol" of most fans turned out to be Meighan.[361]

Other featured industry figures were familiar directors like Tourneur and Cruze, as well as Edwin Carewe in a headlined story about his Native American heritage and his financial aid to the Chickasaw tribe.[362] The *Times* also singled out several on the fringes of the industry. When Coolidge became US president, Hollywood heaved a sigh of relief—for, as governor of Massachusetts, he had vetoed a movie censorship bill, and he later supported efforts to rescind the tax on theater admissions.[363] Yet the preponderance of stories promoted scenario writers, all of them women. In a photo profile, Loos was exploring radio as a way to teach photoplay writing; in her "old home town" of Detroit, Macpherson got herself jailed to give some "local color" to her script for *Manslaughter*; and the most lauded of all, Marion, founded her own production company in alliance with the Producers Distributing Corporation.[364] A related piece even suggested that any "clever woman" had another career option: working as a continuity writer.[365] One more headlined story offered a long interview with Osa (Mrs. Martin) Johnson—a mere "slip" of a girl, in one male writer's words—who, with her husband, endured a two-year expedition to make *Trailing African Wild Animals*, then playing at the Miles and Regent.[366] If, according to a prominent ad, the *Times* thought its women readers wanted to know "what is going on in [the] women's realm," that realm ranged far beyond the usual domestic borders.[367]

Readers who wanted to follow broader industry developments could pursue a variety of major stories, some of which tracked the financial health of film production and distribution.[368] Like the other papers, the *Times* took readers "behind the scenes": Cedric Gibbons, Goldwyn's art director, claimed to use color on a movie set to create an appropriate mood for the actors.[369] Because naming the year's best film had become a "popular pastime," the *Times* also relayed *Photoplay*'s pick for 1922: King's *Tol'able David*.[370] Two years later, the paper agreed with *Photoplay*'s choice of *The Covered Wagon* as best film of 1924,[371] yet it also confronted fans with the *New York Sun*'s insistence that *Greed* and *He Who Gets Slapped* were among the year's "five worthiest films."[372] Although there were fewer stories now dealing with foreign film industries, all signaled Hollywood's dominance vis-à-vis Europe.[373] By contrast, the *Times*, perhaps more than the *News*, showed increasing interest in the movies' relationship with the new medium of radio. Several stories broached the idea of broadcasting motion pictures through radio's "ether waves"[374] As an experimental advertising ploy in early 1924, Hollywood notables lent their voices to radio listeners, with Valentino's suave words as the "Sheik" aimed at swooning "American girls."[375] Whereas Louis B. Mayer and director John Stahl believed that radio would not cut into movie attendance, Kunsky feared that it loomed as a "menace."[376] That is, until he entered the radio business at the end of the decade.

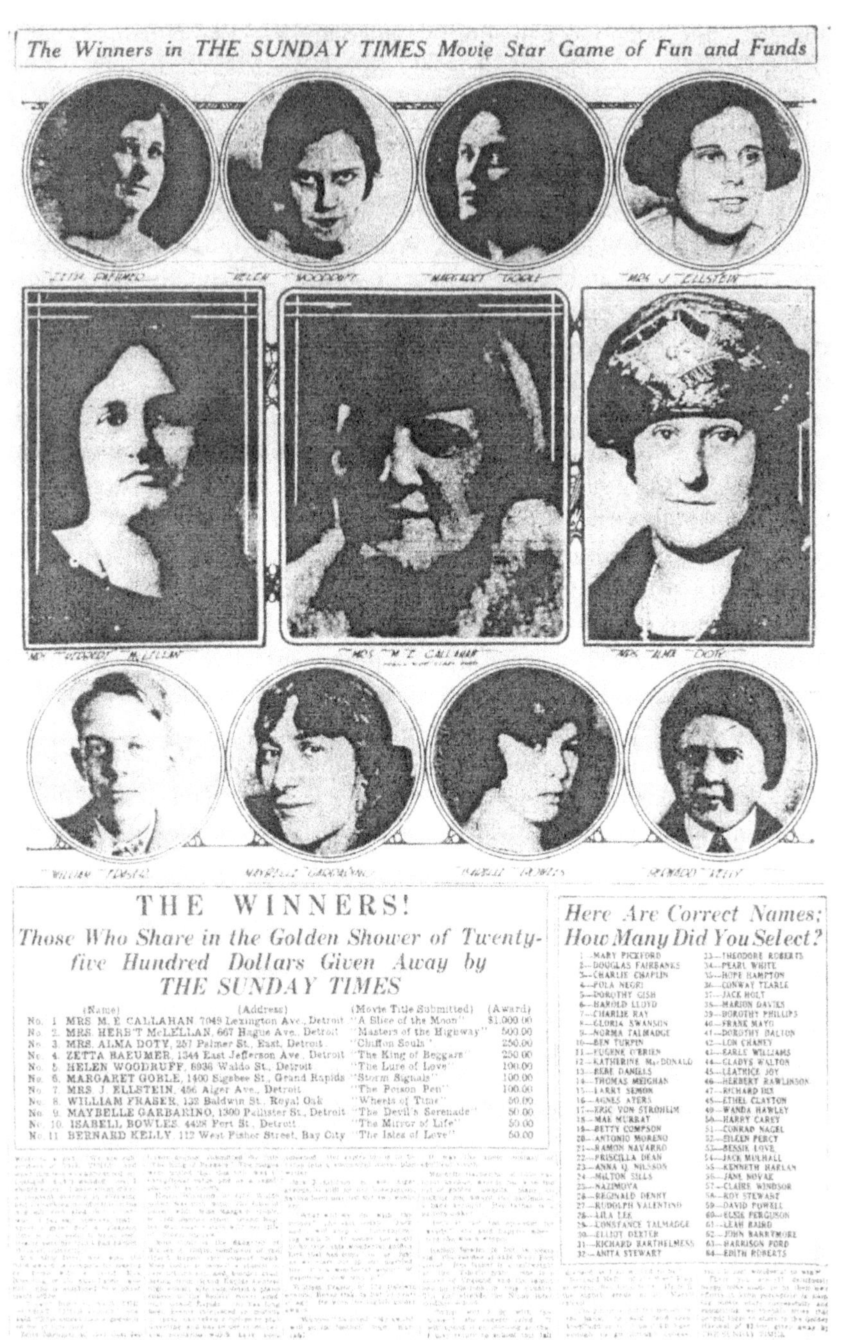

Fig. 4.11. "Movie Star Game Winners," *Detroit Sunday Times* (August 26, 1923): 1.12.

The *Times* did not neglect local news events, but its coverage was hardly extensive. The only exhibitor to merit stories was Kunsky: in December 1922, he set a new policy of return engagements at his first-run theaters; a year later, he negotiated with Paramount to make the Madison a key theater for premieres.[377] Much like the *Free Press*, the *Times* printed many stories about musical performances. Singers were a particular favorite: Emmons and Colvin, the "Siamese Twins of Song," at the Broadway Strand; the "big time" baritone Wade Booth at the La Salle Garden; and the stage "prima donna" Eileen Van Biene at the Madison.[378] Likewise, orchestras: Ray Miller's "Kings of Syncopation" at the Fox Washington; Sunday concerts conducted by Edward Warner, as well as Ned Wayburn's jazz revue, at the Capitol.[379] In late September 1922, during its showing of *The Light in the Dark*, the Capitol arranged a special Wednesday matinee for "red-haired girls" to attend free and meet the "auburn-haired" star Hope Hampton, who was making a personal appearance.[380]

In September 1924, the *Times* asked readers whether or not they read a story before they saw its rendition in a picture.[381] This kind of direct appeal was one of three crucial ways that the *Times*'s coverage differed from that of the *Free Press* and the *News*. The most consistent appeal came in the extensive daily column, "What's Playing at Your Neighborhood Theatre" (see fig. 1.13) that shared the Saturday page with "Daily Happenings in Detroit Society."[382] Beginning in early January 1923, it would have been the "go to" site for movie fans to find program snapshots for their nearby picture theaters.[383] Within weeks, the column was listing more than seventy theaters, or nearly half of those operating in Detroit.[384] Although it included theaters ranging from the large and prestigious—the Alhambra, Lincoln Square, Oakman—to smaller ones in ethnic communities—the Arcade, Catherine, Park—excluded were others like the Del Ray, Quo Vadis, and Koppin. Less consistent, yet much ballyhooed, were the contests giving added incentives to moviegoers. In late June 1923, the *Times* launched a "Movie Star Identification Test."[385] Like the earlier "movie title test," this one offered $2,500 in prizes, distributed among eleven winners. For the next eight weeks, each Sunday edition printed publicity photos of eight stars, along with a list of rules and an answer form to complete and submit.[386] When the winners were announced in late August, nine of the eleven were women—four were married, three of whom won the top prizes; the others were single—and the two men were from out of town.[387] According to interviews with the winners, nearly all of the women were in white, skilled working-class families, and one, from Grand Rapids, already had written and sold several film scenarios.

The *Times* also differed in a second, hardly unexpected way. In February 1922, sensational front-page stories and photos about the shooting death of film director William Desmond Taylor ran for no less than two weeks.[388] Although the chief suspect was Taylor's valet, the *Times* kept circulating photos and stories of well-known Hollywood figures possibly involved—Mabel Normand, in particular—and rumors of a "drug orgy."[389] As this coverage went on, Taylor's life turned into a lurid tale that "reads like fiction."[390] After a "love note" and "nightie" were found in Taylor's home, Normand, Mary Miles Minter, and Claire Windsor became his "intimate friends."[391] Once the murder weapon was found and the arrested valet confessed, the paper quickly lost interest.[392] For a whole year, such sensational stories proliferated. In late February, following Taylor's death, Normand suffered a collapse and went into hiding.[393] The *Times* kept the Arbuckle scandal alive, and Kelley asked Detroiters to render a verdict on his status when he told his story onstage at the Capitol.[394] In August 1922, Valentino countered salacious charges[395] with his "own life story," which appeared in a two-page spread, published in conjunction with Hearst's Sunday magazine, *The American Weekly.*[396] From Mrs. Wallace Reid (Dorothy Davenport) came the most sustained story, which the *Times* reprinted in a series of five parts, from Hearst's *Los Angeles Examiner*, in early January 1923.[397] This series had a double objective. On the one hand, it presented the popular star Wallace Reid as a heroic figure battling against his drug addiction, struggling to recover only to repeatedly relapse. On the other hand, as another "lurid tale," it excoriated a Hollywood culture that indulged in wild parties and allowed "parasites" to exploit Reid's generosity. The real scandal of Reid's death, consequently, was a morally corrupt movie industry that required a thorough stable cleaning—and that became the task of Will Hays.

Finally, the *Times* engaged in an unusually explicit promotional campaign for Marion Davies and her feature films with Heart's Cosmopolitan Film Company.[398] As Hearst increasingly sought to advance Davies's career, his re-negotiated distribution contract with Paramount turned the *Times*, like other Hearst papers, into a singular medium of publicity.[399] The promotional campaign was relatively limited at first, with a large ad and a short review, in March 1922, for *The Bride's Play* and another large ad and a longer review, months later, for Davies's "gleaming beauty" in *Beauty's Worth.*[400] It intensified with prominent advance notices for the historical spectacular *When Knighthood Was in Flower.*[401] In late August 1922, a full-page article hyped the film's production, from the scenario and direction to the large cast and thousands of extras.[402] Among the props were genuine Gothic tapestries, ancient armor, and antique jewelry—the jewelry on display in a high headdress crowning a publicity photo of Davies.[403] All of this advance publicity culminated, in October, in a large ad for the film, which was then "playing to capacity" at New York's Criterion Theatre.[404] On Saturday, November 4, a full-page ad announced the Sunday opening at the Adams, with Victor Herbert conducting a doubled orchestra; on Monday, another headlined story claimed that crowds were besieging the theater.[405]

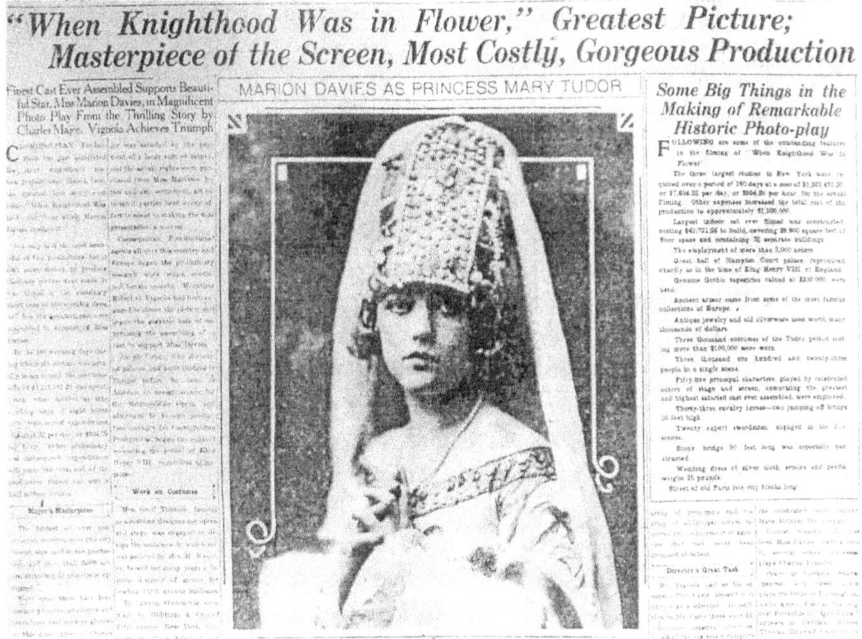

Fig. 4.12. "When Knighthood Was in Flower," *Detroit Times* (August 27, 1922): 4.

The *Times* mounted a similar publicity campaign for Davies's next feature, *Little Old New York*. In July 1923, a special wire story reported that the film was first shown on the ocean liner SS *Leviathan*, and a later story quoted testimonies from those on board.[406] Once again, a full-page article ballyhooed the film's official premiere at New York's Cosmopolitan Theatre, reprinting laudatory reviews by critics such as Quinn Martin, Robert Sherwood, Harriet Underhill, and Louella Parsons.[407] When, in November, the film finally opened at Detroit's Broadway Strand, the *Times* ran photos of the exterior sets that duplicated the city of a hundred years ago and sketches of the cartoon characters Toots and Casper admiring a cross-dressed Davies.[408] The *Times* gave less attention to her next film, *Yolanda*,[409] but the hype returned in late 1924 for *Janice Meredith*, also premiering at the New York Cosmopolitan. Among the testimonials, boxing champion Jack Dempsey declared Davies a "real knockout."[410] In a December lead-up to the film's opening at the Adams, a headlined story named the stage stars supporting Davies, along with thousands of extras.[411] Once again, moviegoers supposedly thronged the theater, perhaps encouraged by a "vivid" review, and another big story lured fans to its third-week run by enumerating all the challenges facing the film's production.[412] Moreover, a large ad printed more testimonials from local figures like Kunsky and the mayor.[413] Upping the overall hype that lured all those throngs into theaters was Pola Negri, who had honored her friend as the "one and only real beauty" of the movies.[414]

And So . . .

Despite having a number of menu categories in common, including large ads for first-run theaters, were these four newspapers distinctive enough in how they envisioned Detroit's movie culture? Most generally, were industry stories or local news more important to that culture? Did that focus change over time, and if yes, how? Of what kinds were those industry stories, and how did each paper rank them? All made the profiles of stars and other figures such as directors and scenario writers (especially women) particularly prominent, from the *Journal*'s tours of stars' homes to the *Times*'s unique scandalmongering and promotional publicity for Marion Davies. The *Free Press* and the *News* tracked studio developments in production, from companies' growth and/or mergers to the building of extravagant exterior sets; also, both papers sometimes revealed unusual work practices "behind the scenes," from what went into taking shots to how the lengthy preparation and editing of release prints was accomplished. The *News*, in particular, supplemented its own coverage with syndicated columns, most notably from Hollywood, and asked its readers to agree or disagree with the emerging annual lists of "best" films. While each newspaper made sure that moviegoers followed export and import conditions in the international market, which greatly favored American films, the *Free Press* and *News*, to a lesser extent, also apprised viewers of "educational" film production and distribution.

Likewise, what kinds of local stories were reported, and how did each paper rank them? The *Free Press*, far more than the others, hyped musical stage performances and prologues as much as, or even more than, the programmed films. Together with the *News*, the *Times* published lengthy daily columns that advertised the programs of nearly half of the city's neighborhood theaters; while some listings were generic, many were at least briefly informative, if cryptic. Although the columns' placement suggests that the people most often looking for neighborhood theater programs were women, perhaps especially of a certain class, other signs supported that hypothesis. Both the *News* and the *Times* gave lots of attention to women scenario writers and also urged young women to explore employment opportunities in the industry, from script writing and continuity writing to film editing, costuming, and other professional or semiprofessional positions. With its two women editors/columnists, notably Daw, the *Journal* was unique in making direct appeals to its women readers. Along with the *Free Press*, the *Times* conducted heavily promoted movie puzzle contests, often sponsored by local businesses, which solicited readers' engagement in testing the limits of their fandom. Winners seemed rather evenly divided between men and women, young and old, until the *Times* ran its 1923 "Movie Star Identification Test," which was won mainly by women. Generally, then, the four papers assumed or imagined that moviegoing readers were rather different from the *News*'s early drawing of a "star-struck" young woman.

In the end, this extensive newspaper coverage of the movies, however diverse and layered as in a palimpsest, merged into a more or less steady stream of public discourse that cut through Detroit's overtly masculinized landscape to produce a kind of parallel fantasy universe, an ever-changing variety show of the city's effervescent "movieland" culture.

Notes

1. See certain key essays from the Chicago School of Sociology: Robert E. Park," The Natural History of the Newspaper," *American Journal of Sociology* 29, no. 3 (1923): 273–289; and Ernest W. Burgess, "The Growth of the City," in R. E. Park, E. W. Burgess, and R. D. MacKenzie, eds., *The City* (Chicago: University of Chicago Press, 1925), 47–62.

2. "Menu for Screen Fans," *DSFP* (January 19, 1919): 4.9.

3. Richard Abel, *Menus for Movieland: Newspapers and the Emergence of American Film Culture, 1913–1916* (Oakland: University of California Press, 2015).

4. For a survey of Chicago women writers in the late 1910s, see Richard Abel, "'My Goodness Gracious, Girls': Women Writers on the Movies in US Newspapers, 1911–1920," in *Presence and Representation of Women in the Early Years of Cinema, 1895–1920*, ed. Angel Quintana and Jordi Pons (Girona: Fundacio Museu. del Cinema, 2019), 45–60.

5. Edgar A. Guest, "Breakfast Table Talk," *DFP* (July 30, 1918): 4; and "How the Journal Is Made: Miss Mary Humphrey Speaks at Opening of Library," *DFP* (January 17, 1924): 3. In late 1922, Humphrey began editing the Sunday "Book Review Section."

6. Frank Angelo names a dozen or more women who were working at the *Free Press* during this period, but he singles out Elizabeth Johnston, who edited the "Household" page—Frank Angelo, *On Guard: A History of the Detroit Free Press* (Detroit: Detroit Free Press, 1981), 139.

7. "Michigan Third to Put O.K. on Suffrage Act," *DFP* (June 11, 1919): 1; and "Women Seek Prompt Action on Suffrage," *DFP* (June 13, 1919): 4. Only days before, Michigan voted to support the Nineteenth Amendment, Detroit chartered a Women's City Club—"Detroit Will Have Women's City Club," *DFP* (May 30, 1919): 5. Despite having Mary Humphrey as its Sunday editor, the *Free Press* allegedly was contemptuous of Detroit Women's Club activities—Jayne Morris-Crowther, "Municipal Housekeeping: The Political Activities of the Detroit Federation of Women's Clubs in the 1920s," *Michigan Historical Review* 30, no. 1 (2004): 96.

8. "Experience," and Mrs. J. E. Leslie, "Out of Darkness, Dawn," *DN* (April 19, 1919): 15. Leslie had been signing columns as early as "Home or College for Happiness," *DN* (January 18, 1919); n.p. See also Lutz, *The News in Detroit*, 110–124.

9. "The Screen," *DSFP* (December 19, 1915): 3.10. No editor was named. "Flickers from Filmland" soon turned into "Screenland Chatter," "Screen Chatter," and finally "Screen Chat."

10. Early on, the "Rotogravure" section did include photos of "stage beauties" such as Marion Davies and production stills of Metro's *Romeo and Juliet*, with Bushman and Bayne—"Some of the Stage Beauties Who Grace the Ziegfeld Follies," *DSFP* (September 10,

1916): Rotogravure, 1; "For Never Was a Story of More Woe Than This of Juliet and Her Romeo," *DSFP* (September 24, 1916): Rotogravure, 1.

11. "Bessie Barriscale Wants to Be Vampire," *DSFP* (October 29, 1916): 4.3. See also "Submarine Gave Him a Bad Shock," *DSFP* (February 4, 1917): C2.

12. "The Reel Players," *DFP* (January 8, 1917): 6.

13. "The Reel Players," *DFP* (August 1, 1918): 6, (November 24, 1918): and (December 30, 1918): 6.

14. "The Screen," *DSFP* (January 5, 1919): 4.8-10.

15. The "Filmland" column of weekly neighborhood theater programs also continued through May 16, 1919.

16. For a month in late 1919 and early 1920, the first page's header turned into a series of generic banners before reverting to "The Screen"—"Screen Play Offerings in Detroit Houses for the Holidays," *DSFP* (December 21, 1919): 4.15, and "Screen Attractions to Be Seen at Detroit Theaters This Week," *DSFP* (January 11, 1920): 4.11–12.

17. These star profiles included Lillian Gish, Robert Harron, Charles Ray, Wallace Reid, Douglas Fairbanks, Clara Kimball Young, Mary Pickford, Mabel Normand, and Norma Talmadge—see "The Reel Players" columns in the *Detroit Free Press* between (January 6, 1919): 8, and (January 8, 1920): 12.

18. Although unacknowledged by the Detroit paper, Kitchen was a "special writer for the Sunday World"—"To Write Human Interest Series," *FD* (February 7, 1919): 2.

19. Karl K. Kitchen, "Behind the Screen—The True Story of the Movies," *DSFP* (April 6, 1919): 4.10.

20. Karl K. Kitchen, "Interesting Glimpses of Filmland When It's Running at Full Blast," *DSFP* (May 4, 1919): 4.12, 14.

21. Karl K. Kitchen, "Now Comes the Question—'What About the Future of the Movies?,'" *DSFP* (May 25, 1919): 4.14, 16; Kitchen, "Why Movie Scenarios Are What They Are," *DSFP* (June 22, 1919): 4.10, 12.

22. Karl K. Kitchen, "Heart Kicks Are Trumps, Says Movie Scout," *DSFP* (July 27, 1919): 4.9. A week later, vamps again were dismissed in "Flirts and Vampires . . . There's a Difference," *DSFP* (August 3, 1919): 4.9.

23. Karl K. Kitchen, "Saturday Night at Vernon's," *DSFP* (April 20, 1919): 4.14, 16. At the time, Los Angeles prohibited restaurants from serving liquor after 9:00 p.m.

24. See, also, Vivian Martin, "Why I Went Into the Movies," *DSFP* (June 15, 1919): 4. 10; and Dorothy Dalton, "Why I Went Into the Movies," *DSFP* (July 6, 1919): 4.9.

25. "Versatile Nazimova—Violinist, Actress," *DSFP* (August 31, 1919): 4.14; "How Nazimova Learned the English Language," *DSFP* (September 28, 1919): 4.14; "Nazimova Deserts Stage to Devote Time to Films," *DSFP* (February 2, 1919): 411; "Nazimova's New Play Filmed Off Gloucester," *DSFP* (February 23, 1919): 4.10.

26. "Nazimova Adapts Her New Play, 'The Brat,'" *DSFP* (July 20, 1919): 4.9; "Nazimova Is Wonderful in 'The Rabbit Dance,'" *DSFP* (August 10, 1919): 4.10; and "Traffic Ceased While Nazimova Acted Scene," *DSFP* (October 19, 1919): 4.18.

27. "Real Comedy Must Be Spontaneous, Says Star," *DSFP* (January 26, 1919): 4.9; "'There's Nothing New Under the Sun,' Repeats Arbuckle," *DSFP* (April 20, 1919): 4.10. See also Keene Thompson, "Yelping Dogs Drove Arbuckle to His Fame," *DSFP* (May 4, 1919): 4.14.

28. "Mabel Normand's Etiquette Book Gave Friends Much Amusement," *DSFP* (March 30, 1919): 4.10. See also "It's Lots of Fun When Mabel Is on Location," *DSFP* (June 8, 1919): 4.11.

29. "A Circus Changed Charles Ray's Career," *DSFP* (July 6, 1919): 4.10; "Charles Ray Wasn't Proud of His Acting," *DSFP* (July 13, 1919): 4.10; and "Charles Ray Holds His Own in a Fist Fight," *DFP* (August 10, 1919): 4.10.

30. "Elusive Power of Screen Personality," *DSFP* (September 14, 1919): 4.10.

31. "Charles Dullin French Actor, Admires W. S. Hart," *DSFP* (February 9, 1919): 4.10. This column, surprisingly, appeared several months later as "Hart's Art," in the *New York Times* (May 18, 1919): 51. Dullin was then performing onstage in New York. Thanks to Richard Koszarski for sharing the *New York Times* piece.

32. "Film Company Presents Quaint Town with Church," *DSFP* (January 19, 1919): 4.10; "Clara Kimball Young's Gowns Are by Lady Duff Gordon," *DSFP* (February 16, 1919): 4.10.

33. "Expert Discusses Lighting of the Modern Photoplay," *DSFP* (February 23, 1919): 4.13.

34. "Pioneer in the Field of Aerial Screen Thrills," *DSFP* (October 12, 1919): 4.19.

35. John Doe, "Card-Cataloguing the Screen Folk," *DSFP* (May 9, 1919): 4.11.

36. "Advance in Screen Art Is Discussed by Director," *DSFP* (February 2, 1919): 4.11.

37. "Use Films for Promotion of Good Will Between Nations," *DSFP* (March 23, 1919): 4.14; "'Made in America' to Be Shown Overseas," *DSFP* (March 30, 1919): 4.10. See also "Value of the Film in the Training of Soldiers," *DSFP* (January 26, 1919): 4.9.

38. "New Occupation for Wounded," *DSFP* (January 5, 1919): 4.8; "Work Available for Disabled Soldiers in Inspecting Films," *DSFP* (January 19, 1919): 4.11. A series of "Stage Women's War Relief films . . . depicted stage and screen stars doing volunteer work in New York"—"Stage and Screen Stars Filmed in War Relief Work," *DSFP* (August 3, 1919): 4.12.

39. "Films to Help the Farmer," *DSFP* (January 26, 1919): 4.9; "Americanizing Effect of Movies in Factories," *DSFP* (October 19, 1919): 4.20. Interestingly, none of these mentioned well-known Ford films.

40. Margaret C. Getchell, "Side-Lights on the Movie Art," *DSFP* (February 8, 1920): 4.10.

41. "Setting and Music Play Important Part," *DSFP* (July 27, 1919): 4.11. See also several personal appearances—"George Beban to Be in Detroit in Person" and "Story of Aurora Mardiganian, Who Is Appearing in Detroit," *DSFP* (May 25, 1919): 4: 15, 17; Local Screen House Has New Soloist," *DSFP* (September 14, 1919): 4.11.

42. "'Fit to Win' Shown to the Police Forces," *DSFP* (January 26, 1919): 4.10.

43. "Many Detroit Houses Showing Safety Film," *DSFP* (June 8, 1919): 4.12.

44. "Children of City Club Members See Best Movies," *DSFP* (February 29, 1920): 3.1.

45. "A Cinema Dictionary," *DSFP* (January 19, 1919): 4.11.

46. A notable exception was the promotional piece, "'Male and Female' Unusual Story, Production, and Cast," *DSFP* (November 30, 1919): 4.12–13.

47. Several months earlier, readers had been asked to identify items mentioned in six ads that "could contribute to the regeneration of Tom Moore" in *The City of Comrades*, then playing at the Adams. "Making a Man in 'The City of Comrades,'" *DSFP* (August 17, 1919): 4.8.

48. "Mabel Normand in 'Pinto' at the Washington," *DSFP* (February 8, 1920): 4.13.

49. These full-page contests ran in the *DSFP* (September 5, 1920): 5.6–12.

50. "Paramount Pictures—Famous Players!" *DSFP* (January 9, 1921): 4.15.

51. "Hard Work Took Place of Romance and Adventure," *DSFP* (February 20, 1921): 5.9. See also Karl Kitchen, "'Fatty' Arbuckle—What He Saw in Europe," *DSFP* (January 16, 1921): 5.12.

52. "No Limit To What Women Can Attain, Believes Anna Q. Nilsson," *DSFP* (April 17, 1921): 5.8.

53. "Feminine Appeal Leads to Stardom," *DSFP* (November 13, 1921): 5.9; "Tom Mix's Popularity Draws Big 'Atmosphere' Crowd," *DSFP* (December 11, 1921): 5.10. In that crowd supposedly were "tourists, business men, actors and actress from other studios, society people, Chinamen, Indians, ranchers and nearly every branch of activity in and around Los Angeles." See also Norma Talmadge's admission that she was still puzzled by her popularity— "Norma Talmadge Puzzled Over Her Success Before the Camera," *DSFP* (November 27, 1921): 5.11.

54. "American Director Is 'All Het up' Over Naughty Pictures from Europe," *DSFP* (July 3, 1921): 4.8; "Master of Lights and Shadows is Maurice Tourneur," *DSFP* (August 28, 1921): 5.6.

55. "What Is a Director? Picture Men Try to Answer Question," *DSFP* (October 23, 1921): 5.12.

56. "Lull in Picture Production Said Not to Be to Reduce Salaries," *DSFP* (February 6, 1921): 5.9; "Motion Picture Theaters Not Hit by Existing Stringent Conditions," *DSFP* (April 3, 1921): 5.9; "Screen Star Salaries Take Big Drop Because of Business Slump," *DSFP* (July 24, 1921): 5.7; and "Rentals Cut to Small Exhibitors," *DSFP* (February 12, 1922): 5.12. Whether Detroit exhibitors enjoyed those "rental cuts" is unclear.

57. "Film Imports Grow Fast: Exports Show Big Decline," *DSFP* (March 22, 1921): 5.11; "Foreign Films to Return This Season After Absence of Years," *DSFP* (September 4, 1921): 5.3; "Rupert Hughes Has No Fear of Foreign Screen Invasion," *DSFP* (October 2, 1921): 5.7; "American Picture Makers Need Not Fear Europeans, Says Robertson," *DSFP* (April 9, 1922): 5.10.

58. "Thousands of American and Canadian Churches Showing Photoplays," *DSFP* (April 10, 1921): 5.9. Among those thousands were "Catholic, Protestant, and Jewish" congregations.

59. "American People Not Fit to Judge for Themselves, Says Woman Censor," *DSFP* (April 23, 1922): 5.9.

60. "Charge on Jewish Movie Men Denied," *DJC* (March 11, 1921): 1; "Who Puts Sense in Censorship? Asks Harassed Screen Producer," *DSFP* (May 15, 1921): 5.9; "Censor Advocates Aim at Death of Pictures, Claims Producer," *DSFP* (May 22, 1921): 5.10; "Film Censorship Worries Nazimova," *DSFP* (August 7, 1921): 5.7; and "Declares Censorship Will Kill Photoplay Industry if Continued," *DSFP* (September 25, 1921): 5.8.

61. "Secrets of the Movies Revealed," *DSFP* (March 13, 1921): 5.9. This column was still running well into 1922.

62. Advertisement, *Baltimore Sunday Sun* (March 27, 1921): 1.17; Carolina Jewett, "How I Broke into the Movies," *Fort Wayne News and Sentinel* (May 27, 1921): Magazine, 1. Jewett's column was syndicated by the Thompson Feature Service.

63. Inez Wallace, "Inside Moves of Movies," *DSFP* (November 13, 1921): 5.10. See also "Inez Wallace Will Take Film to Coast," *MPN* (July 24, 1915): 54; "Correspondence Course in Screen Acting is Formed," *CPD* (July 2, 1922): Amusement, 5; and Inez Wallace Institute of Screen Acting ad, *CPD* (September 7, 1922): 12. Later Wallace would become a regular writer for the Sunday Magazine—"Inez Wallace, Long Film Writer, Dies," *CPD* (June 30, 1966): 67.

64. Inez Wallace, "Inside Moves in the Movies," *DSFP* (January 29, 1922): 5.10.

65. Inez Wallace, "Inside Moves in the Movies: Language of the Studios," *DSFP* (March 28, 1922): 5.10; and "Inside Moves of Movies," *CLD* (December 5, 1922): Amusement, 5. The subjects of later columns included "Foreigners in Our Films," Personality in Pictures," "Matrimony—or Movies?," and "Professional Photographs."

66. Donald H. Clarke, "Twenty-Five Is Deadline for Women Who Aspire to Screen Success," *DSFP* (July 16, 1922): 5.9; Clarke, "Box Office Not Considered in Picture-Making, Directors Claim," *DSFP* (October 22, 1922): 5.11; Clarke, "Movie Language a Strange Dialect to Studio Visitors," *DSFP* (November 26, 1922): 3.17; Clarke, "How to Get Into Moving Pictures," *DSFP* (May 13, 1923): 3.10.

67. A publicity agent, Conlon had worked for Selig, served as dramatic editor of the *Los Angeles Times*, and then hired on as manager and publicity director for William S. Hart. "Conlon Forms Own Business," *FD* (April 8, 1922): 4; "Four Years Ago in Hollywood," *Camera!* (November 18, 1922): 14; "Coast Brevities," *FD* (September 25, 1923): 2; "Who's Who and What's What in Filmland this Week," *Camera!* (October 25, 1923): 13. Conlon also was a member of the United Studio Club—see "Meetingless Club Is Quite Meet," *Camera!* (March 17, 1923): 13.

68. See, for instance, Scoop Conlon, "Movie Director Is Cook Book Student," *San Francisco Sunday Chronicle* (March 4, 1923): D6; and Scoop Conlon, "Busy Days in Hollywood Movie Land," *San Francisco Sunday Chronicle* (September 30, 1923): D4.

69. Scoop Conlon, "Hollywood Letter," *DSFP* (February 25, 1923): 3.13, (March 11, 1923): 3.15, (June 10, 1923): Feature, 11, (December 9, 1923): 4.14, (November 2, 1924): Feature, 5.

70. Dr. Ernest H. Thayer, "What Does Your Face Reveal?," *DSFP* (December 9, 1923): 4.15.

71. Dr. Ernest H. Thayer, "What Does Your Face Reveal?," *DSFP* (December 23, 1923): 4.6.

72. "The Reel Players by Roy E. Marcotte," *DFP* (July 16, 1922): 10; Roy E. Marcotte, "The Reel Players," *DFP* (January 2, 1923): 17.

73. Orpheum ad, *DSFP* (November 12, 1922): 5.10.

74. "Marion Davies in Newest Gown," *DSFP* (October 8, 1922): 5.11; "Says All Women Want to 'Mother' Valentino," *DSFP* (October 29, 1922): 5.10; "One Girl in 600 Has Chance in Films, Noted Star Claims," *DSFP* (June 3, 1923): 3.17; Norma Talmadge, "Why I Prefer Moving Pictures to the Stage," *DSFP* (June 1, 1924): Feature, 9; Pola Negri, "Milestones in Life of Motion Picture Actress," *DSFP* (December 14, 1924): Feature, 6. See also William Cohill, "The Search for New Faces for the Screen Never Ceases," *DSFP* (May 25, 1924): Feature, 7; and "European Director Loud in Praise of Pola Negri," *DSFP* (December 21, 1924): 4.14.

75. Richard Barthelmess, "Barthelmess Says 'Flapper' Represents Finest Womanhood," *DSFP* (August 6, 1922): 5.11; "Colleen Moore Answers Question—'What Is a Flapper?,'" *DSFP* (August 20, 1922): 5.8; "French Film Star Discusses Vamps of Both Sexes," *DSFP* (June 24, 1923): 5.14.

76. "Fred Niblo, Lecturer and Actor, Becomes Famous as Director," *DSFP* (October 1, 1922): 5.9; "Allan Dwan, Famous Director, Explains Theory of Picture-Making," *DSFP* (May 6, 1923): 3.11; "Cecil B. DeMille Discusses the Photoplay of the Future," *DSFP* (May 13, 1923): 3.11; "Women Launch New Photoplay-Making Company," *DSFP* (July 1, 1923): 5.18; DeMille, "The Drama Is Greater Than Picture Values, Declares Director," *DSFP* (August 5, 1924): 3.10; DeMille, "Be Brief, Is Director's Advice," *DSFP* (April 13, 1924): Feature, 7; Frank Lloyd, "What Is the Future of the Motion Picture? Director Answers," *DSFP* (May 25, 1924): Feature, 6.

77. Jack Gardner, "Scenario Writers Blaze New Trails in Search for Realism and Sincerity," *DSFP* (April 1, 1923): 3.12; Clara Beranger, "Real People Now Demand of Screen Fans, Writer Says," *DSFP* (October 14, 1923): Feature, 6; Elinor Glyn, "Aileen Pringle in 'Three Weeks,'" *DSFP* (April 20, 1924): Feature, 7.

78. "'Hunchback of Notre Dame' One of Season's Notable Productions," *DSFP* (August 12, 1923): Feature, 9; "Says Screen Sets Style for Entire Nation," *DSFP* (August 10, 1924): Feature, 10; "Screen to Show How Movies Are Made," *DSFP* (August 24, 1924): Feature, 8; Claire Myers, "Do Men Like Daring Clothes Upon Women," *DSFP* (October 5, 1924): Feature, 8. After designing costumes for *Intolerance*, West worked for Cecil B. DeMille, the Talmadge sisters, and MGM's production of *The Merry Widow*.

79. "Foreign Stars Make American Film International in Character," *DSFP* (July 22, 1923): 5.1; "Banks Still Frown on Moving Picture Business—Refuse Aid," *DSFP* (October 14, 1923): Feature, 5; "Italy's Premier Rewarded for Aid in Producing 'The Eternal City,'" *DSFP* (November 4, 1923): 3.1; "Italian Officials Aid Filming of 'Eternal City,'" *DSFP* (February 17, 1924): 5.10; "Film Directing and Lighting Show Big Advances in Year," *DSFP* (August 3, 1924): Feature, 11; "American Films Popular in Japan Despite Boycott," *DSFP* (August 31, 1924): Feature, 7.

80. "Promenade One Block Long Feature of New Capitol Theater," *DSFP* (December 25, 1921): 5.7; "Wonderful Lighting Installed to Illuminate Detroit's Finest Theater," *DSFP* (January 1, 1922): 5.9; "Tremendous Development of Cinema Shown in City's Newest Picture Palace," *DSFP* (January 8, 1922): 5.9; and "Capitol Switchboard a Marvel of Electrical Engineering Skill," *DSFP* (January 15, 1922): 5.10.

81. "John H. Kunsky Plans Fourth Theater for Downtown District," *DSFP* (December 9, 1923): 4.15; "Detroit's New Theater to Be One of World's Finest Picture Palaces," *DSFP* (March 2, 1924): 5.14; "'The State' Selected as Name of John H. Kunsky's New Theater," *DSFP* (May 18, 1924): Feature, 5.

82. Roy E. Marcotte, "The Reel Players," *DFP* (November 15, 1924): 12. See also "Theater Men Seek Aid of Public in Removal of Amusement Tax," *DSFP* (January 6, 1924): Feature, 5; "Many Towns Lose Picture Theaters Because of Admission Tax Burden," *DSFP* (January 27, 1924): Feature, 9.

83. "Miles Patrons Will Dance in Theater Lobby," *DSFP* (October 30, 1921): 5.9.

84. "Detroit Company Will Be Making Motion Pictures in Few Weeks," *DSFP* (October 22, 1922): 5.10; "Skilled Photographer Is Signed by Detroit's New Motion Picture Company," *DSFP* (April 29, 1923): 4.13; "Detroit Motion Picture Company Engages Director and Writers," *DSFP* (July 22, 1923): 5.10: "Sets Erected for First Play by City's New Producing Company," *DSFP* (September 30, 1923): Feature, 6; "Stars in City, Filming Starts at Detroit Studio," *DSFP* (November 4, 1923): 3.1; "Snake Charmer Dance Features Closing Scene of Detroit Film," *DSFP* (December 23, 1923): 4.6.

85. "World's Most Famous Dog in Photoplay Written by Detroit Woman," *DSFP* (February 19, 1922): 5.11. Murfin was a successful scenario writer and founding member of the Screen Writers Guild. See also stories that singled out Claire Anderson and Virginia Caldwell as "Detroit girls" who had made it as actresses, if only for a short time—"Of Interest to Movie Devotees," *DSFP* (February 20, 1921): 5.9; "Another Detroit Girl of Great Beauty Makes Good in Picture," *DSFP* (May 29, 1921): 5.5; "Rare Beauty of Detroit Girl Wins Promising Screen Career," *DSFP* (July 10, 1921): 5.6.

86. "It Is Now a Real Pleasure to Be Escorted to Seat in Adams Theater," *DSFP* (August 6, 1922): 5.11; "Theater Girls in Quaint Garb," *DSFP* (December 16, 1923): 5.12.

87. "Santrey to Become Detroit Citizen," *DSFP* (August 13, 1922): 5.11; "Capitol Will Resume Popular Sunday Concerts" *DSFP* (September 17, 1922): 5.9. That month the Broadway Strand staged its own Sunday concerts to compete with the Capitol.

88. "Waring's Dance Orchestra Will Play at Madison," *DSFP* (November 12, 1922): 5.11; "Waring's Syncopators to Remain at Capitol," *DSFP* (November 26, 1922): 5.16; "Cameron McLean Sings at Capitol," *DSFP* (December 3, 1922): 3.19. See also "Drummer Beats Time More Ways Than One," *DSFP* (November 19, 1922): 5.9.

89. "One of the Unique Organizations in the Musical World Comes to Broadway Strand for Engagement," *DSFP* (April 8, 1923): 3.11; "Musical Prodigy Leads Orchestra," *DSFP* (April 22, 1923): 3.9; "Detroit Girl Returns a Star," *DSFP* (April 29, 1923): 3.10.

90. "Singer Pleases Movie Audiences," *DSFP* (September 2, 1923): Feature, 10; "Detroit Vocalist Sings at Capitol," *DSFP* (September 9, 1923): Feature, 9; "Detroiters Write New Song Hit," *DSFP* (September 23, 1923): Feature, 5; "Clevelanders to Amuse Detroiters," *DSFP* (September 30, 1923): Feature, 7.

91. "Capitol Presents Famous Vocalist," *DSFP* (March 23, 1924): 4.9; "Vaudeville Star Comes to Capitol," *DSFP* (March 30, 1924): Feature, 8.

92. "New Tenor at the Broadway Strand," *DSFP* (June 22, 1924): Feature, 7; "Variety Four, Comedy Quartet, Opens Summer Engagement at Cinderella," *DSFP* (June 29, 1924): Feature, 7.

93. "Finzel's Artists on Madison Program," *DSFP* (January 11, 1925): Feature, 6; "Musical Comedy Girls Aid Capitol Celebrate Third Anniversary Week," *DSFP* (January 11, 1925): Feature, 8; "Versatile Dancers Offer Sprightly Steps in Broadway Strand Theater," *DSFP* (February 8, 1925): Feature, 7; "New Wayburn Sends His Pretty Dancers to Cavort at Capitol," *DSFP* (February 22, 1925): Feature, 8.

94. "The Movies," *DNT* (September 5, 1915): 11.

95. "Photoplays," *DNT* (September 12, 1915): 13. Stark later became president of the Detroit Historical Society and a founder of its Historical Museum—Lochbiler, *Detroit's Coming of Age, 1873–1973* (Detroit: Wayne State University Press, 1973), 258.

96. "Photoplays," *DNT* (September 26, 1915): 17.

97. George W. Stark, "Motion Picture Comments," *DNT* (November 7, 1915): 18, (November 14, 1915): 18, and (December 29, 1915): 16.

98. Edward Stone, "Motion Picture Comment," *DNY* (May 7, 1916): Photoplay, 3. Another writer sometimes signed this column—Arthur Hathaway, "Motion Picture Comment," *DNT* (May 21, 1916): Photoplay, 6, and (May 28, 1916): Photoplay, 6.

99. News and Views of the Photo Play World," *DNT* (October 1, 1916): 8.

100. "A Handful of Queens," *DNT* (September 3, 1916): 8.

101. Norma Talmadge, "A Little Autobiography," *DNT* (February 18, 1917): Society, n.p.; "Warns Girls Away from the Films," *DNT* (March 11, 1917): Society, n.p.

102. "Superwomen," *DNT* (January 14, 1917: Rotogravure, 1; "A Perfect Woman Nobly Planned," *DNT* (March 18, 1917): Rotogravure, 1. Among the other "Superwomen" were Helen Keller, Marie Curie, and Sarah Bernhardt. By contrast, Chaplin was the only movie star among ten "Supermen"—"Supermen," *DNT* (January 21, 1917): n.p.

103. "Wicked Vampire Ladies Have Edge on Heroines," *DNT* (November 12 1916): 8. Theda Bara proudly claimed that her screen roles were based on the vampire's "most vital characteristic . . . her eyes"—"Rosebud Mouth Sometimes Hides Tongue of Vampire," *DNT* (January 21, 1917): n.p. See also "Pauline Frederick Declares She Is a Different Vampire," *DNT* (March 11, 1917): n.p.; and "The Original Vampire," *DNT* (April 22, 1917): n.p.

104. See the "Film Favorite Coupon" and "This Week's Favorite" in the *Detroit News-Tribune*, from September 3, 1916, to November 12, 1916. Within those limits, Detroit fans' favorites ranged widely: Mary Miles Minter, Lillian Gish, Marie Doro, Anna Little, June Caprice, Bessie Love, May Allison, Louise Glaum, Mary Maclaren, Juanita Hanson.

105. "Soon to Be Seen in First Play Produced by Her Own Company," *DNT* (September 24, 1916): Photoplays, 6; "Norma Talmadge to Head Own Company," *DNT* (October 15, 1916): n.p.; Edward Speyer, "Mary Pickford Reappears on the Screen in Her Own Company, a Little Waif of Orient, to Add New Chapter to History of Movies," *DNT* (November 5, 1916): n.p.; and "Clara Young Fairly Busy This Winter," *DNT* (December 31, 1916: n.p.

106. "Movies Narrative, Says Clara Kimball Young," *DNT* (September 3, 1916): n.p.

107. "Titles Must Go, Declares Miss Young," *DNT* (October 29, 1916): n.p.

108. "Ill as Food Looks Queer Under Lights," *DNT* (October 1, 1916); 8. See also "Music Stimulated Actors Working in 'Civilization,'" *DNT* (March 18, 1917): Photo Plays, 6; and Rex Beach, "How Beach Found a Man to Write 'Barrier' Music," *DNT* (March 25, 1917): n.p.

109. Edward Speyer, "With the Film Stars," *DNT* (September 10, 1916): n.p.

110. Edward Speyer, "With the Film Stars," *DNT* (October 1, 1916): Photo Plays, 3.

111. "Next Week's Film Stars," *DSN* (December 22, 1917): 12; and "This Week's Film Stars," *DSN* (December 23, 1917): Photo Plays, 11. See, for instance, the profile of Pavlova that complemented her film at the Madison, *Daughter of Destiny*—"The Career of Pavlova," *DSN* (January 13, 1918): Photo Plays, 12.

112. "Heavens! Gloria 'Gassed' in Film," *DSN* (May 26, 1918): 5.1.

113. Harold Hefferman, "Here's Goltz Spying Again," *DSN* (September 22, 1918): 5.1.

114. Harold Hefferman, "Films Regain Old Footing," *DSN* (November 10, 1918): Feature, 9.

115. "Harold Hefferman, "Pickford Now Own Producer," *DSN* (November 17, 1918): Feature, 10; "Goldwyn Service Gets Ford Weekly," *DSN* (December 8, 1918): Feature, 9; and "Detroit-Made Picture on Screen This Week," *DSN* (December 15, 1918): 5.1.

116. "Fairbanks Gives Blood to Save Employee's [*sic*] Life," *DSN* (November 24, 1918): Feature, 8; "Farnum Aids Flu Orphans," *DSN* (December 1, 1918): Feature, 9; "Bessie's Hair Up, Skirts Long; She's Growing Up," *DSN* (December 22, 1918): Photoplay, 9.

117. "Photoplay a Day Paramount's Task," *DSN* (October 5, 1918): Feature, 9; "Title Punch Makes Film," *DSN* (November 17, 1918): Feature, 10; and "Italian Fans Shout Titles," *DSN* (September 22, 1918): 5.1.

118. "You Are to Decide Merit of Photoplay," *DSN* (September 22, 1918): 5.1.

119. "Fans Critical in Reviewing," *DSN* (September 29, 1918): Feature, 9; "Critics Rap Stone, Like Clark Picture," *DSN* (October 5, 1918): Feature, 9; and "Detroit Critics Pick Flaws in New Films," *DSN* (October 12, 1918): n.p.

120. The most featured stars were Chaplin, Pickford, Nazimova, Swanson, the Talmadge sisters, and Gish. Griffith now was idolized as "the father of the close up"; after the record-breaking release of *The Miracle Man*, Tucker was proclaimed a genius; the Johnsons were returning to the South Sea Islands to film cannibal life. Loos was urging writers to compose their own scripts and serve apprenticeships, as in other professions.

121. "Films Know Los Angeles as City of Gelatine Stats," *DSN* (May 4, 1919): Feature, 16; "Birdseye View of an Entire City Devoted to Making of Motion Pictures," *DSN* (June 1, 1919): Photoplay, 16.

122. "Bar Visitors; Here's Reason," *DSN* (July 27, 1919): Photoplay, 14; "Films Better Portrait Art," *DSN* (November 16, 1919): Photoplay, 14. See also Jerome Laucenbruck, "Trick of Making Animated Cartoons," *DSN* (February 15, 1920): Photoplay, 10.

123. "Actors Demand Music While They Act," *DSN* (April 20, 1919): Photoplay, 15; "Movie Music Cues Big Job," *DSN* (May 18, 1919): Photoplay, 4; "Music Ban Is Asked in Studio," *DSN* (January 11, 1920): Photoplay, 10.

124. "Anatomy of Photoplay Probed in Laboratory," *DSN* (August 31, 1919): Photoplay, 15. See also "There's a Long Jump Twixt Studio and Screen," *DSN* (June 22, 1919): Photoplay, 14; and "Expense of Films Reaches Millions," *DSN* (February 8, 1920): Photoplay, 10.

125. "Beating the Censors," *DSN* (April 13, 1919): Photoplay, 14.

126. Harold Hefferman, "Film Titling Grows to Be Job in Itself," *DSN* (March 30, 1919): Photoplay, 6; "Little Slips Real Menace," *DSN* (April 27, 1919): Photoplay, 14; Hefferman, "Sordid Captions Endanger Films," *DSN* (May 4, 1919): Photoplay, 14.

127. Stanley Rushton, "Film Industry Waits Next Move in Battle," *DSN* (November 30, 1919): Photoplay, 19. "Getting Right Films, School Movie Problem," *DSN* (December 7, 1919): Photoplay, 3.

128. "Germans Saw Movie Value," *DSN* (January 26, 1919): Photoplay, 5; "Pictures to Push U.S. Trade in Other Lands," *DSN* (April 13, 1919): Photoplay, 15; E. A. Batchelor, "Movies Serials Bring Vivas of Parisians," *DSN* (June 15, 1919): Photoplay, 14; "Plan Foreign Film Invasion" and "Putting the Razz on American Made Films in Britain," *DSN* (July 20, 1919): Photoplay, 16. "U.S. Prepares Film Rush on Former Enemy," *DSN* (July 27, 1919): Photoplay, 13; "Chinese Like Our Features and Comedies," *DSN* (August 31, 1919): Photoplay, 15; "Brazil Movie Fans Demand Yankee Films," *DSN* (November 9, 1919): Photoplay, 16. See also Louis I. Goodnow, "Social Disaster Looms for England in Barring U.S. Films," *DSN* (July 13, 1919): Photoplay, n.p.

129. "Links Life with Art of Cinema," *DSN* (January 11, 1920): Photoplay, 10. Le Blanc was a well-known stage actress, singer, and former wife of Maurice Maeterlinck, who later starred in Marcel L'Herbier's *L'Inhumaine* (1924).

130. "Overseas Films Teach Women," *DSN* (January 26, 1919): Photoplay, 12; "Movies Help Fight Disease in Poland," *DJC* (September 9, 1921): 5. See also "Movies Go on Mission in Far East," *DSN* (January 18, 1920): Photoplay, 9; and the "exclusive motion pictures of the National Conference of American Jewish Relief" in the Adams ad, *DJC* (April 14, 1922): 8.

131. Jackson D. Haag, "Great Quantities of Film Exported," *DSN* (March 28, 1920): Feature, 15.

132. "Slashed Film Hits Griffith," *DSN* (January 18, 1919): Photoplay, 7; "Detroit Film Censors Under New Direction," *DSN* (July 13, 1919): Photoplay, n.p. The Recreation Commission already was inspecting films from 'the angle of child morality'—"Pictures Made Safe for Detroit Children," *DJ* (January 18, 1919): 6.

133. "Beban's Act to Play Here with New Film," *DSN* (April 27, 1919): Photoplay, 14.

134. Harold Hefferman, "Holy Week's Screen Bill Pretentious," *DSN* (April 13, 1919): Photoplay, 14; Hefferman, "Sordid Captions Endanger Films," *DSN* (May 4, 1919): Photoplay, 14; "Picks Detroit for Premier," *DSN* (May 11, 1919): Photoplay, 16; "Independents Form to Fight Combines," *DSN* (December 28, 1919): Photoplay, 7.

135. "All Negro Cast Seen on Screen," *DSN* (April 22, 1920): Photoplay, 12. Boni hoped to set up a studio in the South and persuade comic Bert Williams to join him.

136. Unfortunately, the Detroit Public Library has surviving copies of the city's major black newspaper, the weekly *Detroit Leader*, only through April 1914. Whether other work by black filmmakers screened in Detroit remains to be discovered.

137. Koppin ad, *DSN* (December 3, 1922): 8.

138. "Patrons' Notes Often Guide Movie Manager—To Despair," *DSN* (March 2, 1919): Photoplay, 1; Edward Speyer, "New Pictures Late Reaching Detroit," *DSN* (December 21, 1919): Photoplay, 10. Among those lost articles were false teeth!

139. "New Stage Setting At Adams Surprises," *DSN* (March 30, 1919): Photoplay, 6.

140. "Griffith Praises Showing Here," *DSN* (July 27, 1919): Photoplay, 11. See also Harold Hefferman, "Fitting Music to Photoplay Artistic Job," *DSN* (June 15, 1919): Photoplay, 14; and "Music Helps in Creating Story's Mood," *DSN* (January 25, 1920): Photoplay, 10.

141. Harold Hefferman, "Houdini, Star Episode Hero, Foils 'Em All," *DSN* (March 9, 1919): Photoplay, 6.

142. "Ah! 'Twas de Ushers! Goils Give 'Em a Hop," *DSN* (April 20, 1919): Photoplay, 14.

143. "Theater Gives Midnight Ball," *DSN* (April 27, 1919): Photoplay, 14.

144. "Crowds Still Pursue Mabel Normand Film," *DSN* (March 30, 1919): Photoplay, 6; Stanley Rushton, "Local Film Fans Grow 'Screenwise,'" *DSN* (August 10, 1919): Photoplay, 13.

145. Imogene Devore, "Keeping Fit Keeps Movie Folk Active," *DSN* (February 2, 1919): Photoplay, 5; Imogene Devore, "Fugitive Flashes," *DSN* (November 30 1919): Photoplay, 9. The only other brief references to Devore that I have found are in "Polly Perkins Says," *FD* (March 24, 1919): 21; and "Pretty Face and Straight Legs Don't Make Screen Stars," *Dubuque Times Journal* (May 14, 1919): 20.

146. "Hefferman With First National," *FD* (July 25, 1919): 1.

147. "Hodkison's Detroit Manager Stages Big Midnight Trade Screening of 'Sex,'" *MPW* (April 10, 1920): 283.

148. Harold Hefferman, "Griffith Treats Love Theme in New Manner," *DSN* (January 12, 1919): Photoplay, 9. See also his review of *The Romance of Happy Valley*—"Happy Valley Charms with Simple Story," *DSN* (February 16, 1919): Photoplay, 9.

149. "Harold Hefferman, "Star Combine Ranks Opened to Four More," *DSN* (March 23, 1919): Photoplay, 6.

150. Stanley Rushton, "'Hoodlum' Is Best Pickford Film Yet," *DSN* (September 7, 1919): Photoplay, 11. See also Harold Hefferman, "Chaplin 'Pan' Dance Rouses New Comedy," *DSN* (June 22, 1919): Photoplay, 14. In hindsight, Chaplin's own predatory attitude towards young women at the time comes close to being unmasked in this scene.

151. Stanley Rushton, "'Male and Female' Is De Mille's Best," *DSN* (November 23, 1919): Photoplay, 16.

152. Stanley Rushton, "Serial Thrillers Have Their Inning," *DSN* (October 26, 1919): Photoplay, 16.

153. Jackson D. Haag, "Pictures in Colors New French Scheme," *DSN* (February 8, 1920): Society, 10; Edgar Ansel Mowrer, "Making Films in Italy" and "Electricity in Picture Making," *DSN* (August 1, 1920): Society, 18.

154. Jackson D. Haag, "Future of Film Being Forecast," *DSN* (April 11, 1920): Feature, 12. See also W. Somerset Maugham, "Novelist Sees Picture Future," *DSN* (March 6, 1921): Society, 18.

155. Tod Browning, "Seven Ages Seen on Silver Screen," *DSN* (November 14, 1920): Society 22; "Film Editing, Profession for Women," *DSN* (January 22, 1921): Society, n.p.

156. Jackson D. Haag, "Intricate Music Cues for Cinema Orchestras," *DSN* (November 7, 1920): Society, 22; "Told Without Titles," *DSN* (March 6, 1921): Society, 18.

157. "Hundreds Enter Beauty Contest," *DSN* (February 20, 1921): Society, 14.

158. Jackson D. Haag, "House Cleaning Time for Motion Pictures," *DSN* (March 13, 1921): Society, 18.

159. Jackson D. Haag, "Fixing Serials for General Consumption," *DSN* (February 6, 1921): Society, 14; Haag, "What a Censor Does in the Course of a Year," *DSN* (March 20, 1921): Society, 16.

160. "Women Working to Help Pictures," *DSN* (March 27, 1921): Society, 15.

161. Jackson D. Haag, "Motion Pictures," *DSN* (March 27, 1921): Society, 14.

162. Jackson D. Haag, "Motion Pictures," *DSN* (May 1, 1921): Society, 8; "Around the World in Thirty Minutes," *DSN* (October 30, 1921): Society, 8.

163. Jackson D. Haag, "Motion Pictures," *DSN* (September 18, 1921): Society, 8. "Was a Serial Star," *DSN* (October 30, 1921): Society, 9; Haag, "Taking a Change Only Just Part of the Game," *DSN* (November 6, 1921): Society, 8.

164. Jackson D. Haag, "Motion Pictures," *DSN* (August 28, 1921): Society, 6. See also "Way Films Are Fixed for Public," *DSN* (September 11, 1921): Society, 6.

165. Percy Monteith, "Tariff Demanded as a Protection," *DSN* (April 24, 1921): Society, 10; "American Films in Far-Off Places," *DSN* (October 2, 1921): Society, 8; Jackson D. Haag, "Danes and Swedes Join Film Invasion of U.S.A.," *DSN* (November 20, 1921): Society, 8.

166. Jackson D. Haag, "Motion Pictures," *DSN* (June 19, 1921): Society, 10. Early photos of Universal's rental exchange showed women working in the Examining department—"The Detroit Universal Company's Offices," *Universal Weekly* (January 23, 1915): 28. Paramount later singled out Violet Dodd and Annetta Wilder in its Detroit exchange—"A Detroiter," *Paramount Pep* (December 26, 1921): 3; and "A Fair Detroiter," *Paramount Pep* (February 27, 1922): 10.

167. "Films for the Non-Theatrical," *DSN* (May 29, 1921): Society, 8; Haag, "Motion Pictures," *DSN* (September 11, 1921): Society, 8; Haag, "Motion Pictures," *DSN* (September 25, 1921): Society, 8. See, for instance, Richard Abel, "The 'Much Vexed Problem' of Non-Theatrical Distribution in the Late 1910s," *Moving Image* 16, no. 2 (Fall 2016): 91–107.

168. Jackson D. Haag, "Motion Pictures," *DSN* (April 3, 1921): Society, 10.

169. Jackson D. Haag, "When Writers Go a Hunting," *DSN* (November 20, 1921): Society, 10. Once more, Edward Speyer stepped in to edit the *News*'s Sunday pages during late November and early December.

170. "Plays and Photoplays," *DSN* (January 29, 1922): Society, 6–8.

171. Harold Hefferman, "Debates on Year's Best Pictures Now in Order," *DSN* (December 25, 1921): Society, 10. The three foreign films were *All for a Woman*, *The Cabinet of Dr. Caligari*, and *The Golem*.

172. Harold Hefferman, "Readjustments Foretell Better Pictures in 1922," *DSN* (January 1, 1922): Society, 10. See also Hefferman, "Hollywood Under Fire as Seat of Production," *DSN* (February 12, 1922): Society, 9; and "Axe Swings on Star Salaries," *DSN* (April 2, 1922): Society, 11.

173. Harold Hefferman, "Film Drama Ads Nearing End as Exhibitors Fight," *DSN* (March 12, 1922): Society, 7.

174. Harold Hefferman, "Hail, the Costume Film! It's On the Way Back," *DSN* (February 19, 1922): Society, 7.

175. "Smith College Girls Plan Courses for Film Careers," *DSN* (December 25, 1921): Society, 11.

176. "The Francis X. of '22," *DSN* (March 26, 1922): Society, 7. See also "Norma Owns Dolls and a Tiny Theater," *DSN* (February 19, 1922): Society, 7; and Hefferman, "Film Players in Person Shatter Old Illusions," *DSN* (March 26, 1922): Society, 7.

177. James W, Dean, "Doug Ridicules Studios Abroad," *DSN* (December 18, 1921): Society, 7.

178. James W. Dean, "Films Aid U.S. in Trade Drive," *DSN* (March 26, 1922): Society, 11. See also James W. Dean, "'Film League' European Plan," *DSN* (February 26, 1922): Society, 18; and "French Seek U.S. Stars," *DSN* (April 2, 1922): Society, 15.

179. "William Fox Inaugurates Education Department," *DSN* (January 15, 1922): Society, 5; James W. Dean, "Scenic-Drama Newest Treat," *DSN* (February 19, 1922): Society, 12; "Traveler Newman Opens Picture Series Tonight," *DSN* (February 26, 1922): Society, 18; "Now We'll Have Film Circulating Libraries," *DSN* (April 2, 1922): Society, 14.

180. Harold Hefferman, "New Capitol Theater Opens to Record Crowd," *DSN* (January 13, 1922): 26; "Detroit-Made Film to Open Here Soon," *DSN* (February 19, 1922): Society, 7; Harold Hefferman, "Cameras to Grind Here With Coming of Spring," *DSN* (March 5, 1922): Society, 13.

181. Harold Hefferman, "Pictured Books Awake Interest in Libraries," *DSN* (February 26, 1922): Society, 15.

182. James W. Dean, "Back to Custard Pie," *DSN* (October 30, 1921): Society, 8; Dean, "Lubitsch Acts Like Diplomat," *DSN* (January 1, 1922): Society, 11; Dean, "Emerson-Loos Producing Now," *DSN* (January 29, 1922): Society, 6; Dean, "Shift in Hero Type Foreseen," *DSN* (March 12, 1922): Society, 11. Dean was the Newspaper Enterprise Association's Motion Picture editor.

183. H. G. Salsinger, "Cost Comes First with Dawn of New Film Day," *DSN* (February 26, 1922): Society, 19.

184. Miriam Teicher, "75 Marks Day Pay in 'Bourse,'" *DSN* (January 22, 1922): Society, 10. See also her interview with Albert Kaufman, European manager for Famous-Players Lasky, in Teicher, "Most German Films Failures," *DSN* (February 5, 1922): Society, 8.

185. Miriam Teicher, "Negri a Fiery Human Figure," *DSN* (February 12, 1922): Society, 8.

186. "Shadowgraphs," *DSN* (August 5, 1922): Metropolitan, 6.

187. "Shadowgraphs," *DSN* (September 17, 1922): Metropolitan, 7; Monroe Lathrop, "Tales from Filmland," *DSN* (October 8, 1922): Metropolitan, 3.

188. James W. Dean, "Film 'Footage' Hinders Action," *DSN* (July 9, 1922): Metropolitan, 9; Dean, "Negri Clamors for Close-Ups," *DSN* (February 18, 1923): Metropolitan, 3; Dean, "Ruddy Didn't Impress Nita," *DSB* (October 1, 1922): Metropolitan, 3.

189. Jack Jungermeyer, "Hays, Doug Line Up Theaters Join in War," *DSN* (March 4, 1923): Metropolitan, 3. See also "United Artists War on Chains" on the same page.

190. Jack Jungmeyer, "Films Favoring Rehearsal Idea," *DSN* (July 8, 1923): Metropolitan, 3; Jungmeyer, "Buried Movie Art Will Thrive," *DSN* (July 15, 1923): Metropolitan, 3; Jungmeyer, "He Laughs—But Not For the Movies," *DSN* (July 22, 1923): Metropolitan, 4; Jungmeyer, "Film Buffoon Now a Butterfly," *DSN* (August 5 1923): Metropolitan, 3. See also Harold Hefferman, "Public Taste Stifles Artistry in Pictures," *DSN* (September 17, 1922): Metropolitan, 3.

191. Harry Carr, "Smiles Follow Herr Lubitsch," *DSN* (May 25, 1924): Metropolitan, 4; Carr, "Player-Ruled Efforts Fail," *DSN* (February 8, 1925): Metropolitan, 13.

192. Edward Speyer, "Idol Makers of Movies Can't Get Worshippers," *DSN* (July 16, 1922): Metropolitan 8; Westbrook Pegler, "Film Vamp Is 'Motivated,'" *DSN* (September 10, 1922): Metropolitan, 4.

193. "Reid Secluded in Mountains," *DSN* (November 5, 1922): Metropolitan, 8; "Reid Is Forced to Health Camp," *DSN* (December 10, 1922): Metropolitan, 4.

194. "Few in Movies Are Financiers," *DSN* (January 7, 1923): Metropolitan, 3.

195. "Hays to Hear Arbuckle Plea," *DSN* (July 30, 1922): Metropolitan, 8; James W. Dean, "Think of Fatty and Have Care!," *DSN* (October 1, 1922): Metropolitan, 6; Harold Hefferman, "Unseen Forces Help Arbuckle," *DSN* (October 15, 1922): Metropolitan, 3; "Three Roscoe Film Scrapped," *DSN* (November 26, 1922): Metropolitan, 5; Jack Jungmeyer, "Fatty Back But Not in Person," *DSN* (April 8, 1923): Metropolitan, 3. Because Arbuckle helped develop his performances in the late 1910s, another story claimed Keaton would hire him as a director under a tongue-in-cheek pseudonym, Will B. Good—"'Fatty' Directs Buster Keaton," *DSN* (January 27, 1924): Metropolitan, 4.

196. Harold Hefferman, "Books on the Movies," *DSN* (November 16, 1924): Metropolitan, 5.

197. "Champion Movie Contortionist," *DSN* (February 24, 1924): Metropolitan, 4; "Rogers Bites Films, Drama," *DSN* (March 2, 1924): Metropolitan, 4; Harry Carr, "Ramon Speeds to Front Rank," *DSN* (August 31, 1924): Metropolitan, 6; "The Latest Beery Villainy," *DSN* (February 22, 1925): Metropolitan, 15. Yet Valentino was not "unhorsed"—"Swarthy He-Men Still the Rage," *DSN* (November 16, 1924): Metropolitan, 6.

198. "Fame One Day, Oblivion Next!," *DSN* (July 20, 1924): Metropolitan, 3. Others mentioned included Flora Finch, Mary Fuller, and Helen Holmes.

199. "Theda's Ready for a Come-Back," *DSN* (May 25, 1924): Metropolitan, 7; "Mabel Slips Into Shadow of Her Fame," *DSN* (July 20, 1924): Metropolitan, 3.

200. "Players Start 'Griffith Day,'" *DSN* (January 27, 1924): Metropolitan, 8; "'Covered Wagon' Record Is Scorned by Griffith," *DSN* (February 3, 1924): Metropolitan, 3; Harold Hefferman, "Griffith Sells Himself Away/Will United Artists Disband?," *DSN* (July 20, 1924): Metropolitan, 3; "Griffith Move a War Signal," *DSN* (October 5, 1924): Metropolitan, 9.

201. "A Movie Genius of 1922" and Jack Jungmeyer, "Jimmy Cruze Makes Good in Movies and Hollywood Rejoices," *DSN* (September 16, 1923): Metropolitan, 7; Harold Hefferman, "Cruze Tops 'Em All," *DSN* (March 9, 1924): Metropolitan, 4.

202. Jack Jungmeyer, "Mary Pickford May Be No Business Woman—But She's Clever," *DSN* (February 3, 1924): Metropolitan, 7.

203. "Studios Going at Full Speed," *DSN* (January 27, 1924): Metropolitan, 7; Monroe Lathrop, "Movie Camps Must Speed Up to Prevent Shortage in Fall," *DSN* (March 23, 1924): Metropolitan, 7.

204. Harold Hefferman, "Movies Eighth of Industries," *DSN* (February 17, 1924): Metropolitan, 4; Hefferman, "Banks Turn to Movies," *DSN* (September 14, 1924): Metropolitan, 3. Hefferman also quoted the National Bank of Commerce describing the industry, with its total of "14,000 players," as "a safe bet"—Hefferman, "14,000 Players Now in Movies," *DSN* (March 23, 1924): Metropolitan, 4.

205. "Gopher Prairie Main Street Rises on Hollywood Lot," *DSN* (April 8, 1923): Metropolitan, 7; "Film's Biggest Sets Planned," *DSN* (April 22, 1923): Metropolitan, 3; "A Remarkable Achievement in Set Construction," *DSN* (February 10, 1924): Metropolitan, 7. But ballooning costs, like those for *Ben Hur*, were "curing [this] foreign fever"—Harold Hefferman, "Movies Still Showering Gold in Waste Basket," *DSN* (June 15, 1924): Metropolitan, 5; Monroe Lathrop, "Foreign Fever Cured by Costs," *DSN* (February 1, 1925): Metropolitan, 15.

206. "Movie Capital Back to East," *DSN* (September 23, 1923): Metropolitan, 5; "Hollywood Putting Up Hard Fight to Hold Movie Leadership," *DSN* (March 9, 1924): Metropolitan, 9;

Harold Hefferman, "Waste and Extravagance Brings a New Film Merger," *DSN* (April 27, 1924): Metropolitan, 4; "Hollywood Slips as Movie Capital," *DSN* (July 6, 1924): Metropolitan, 5; "Eastward Ho! Is First National Cry," *DSN* (October 12, 1924): Metropolitan, 9.

207. Harold Hefferman, "Careless Editing Clouds Many Current Features," *DSN* (May 20, 1923): Metropolitan, 4; Jack Jungmeyer, "Screenland Hath No Fury Like a Film Cutter Peeved," *DSN* (July 15, 1923): 4; James W. Dean, "Bad Continuity Seen by Critics," *DSN* (September 16, 1923): Metropolitan, 8.

208. Harold Hefferman, "Tragic vs. Happy Endings: Take Choice—Ingram," *DSN* (May 27, 1923): Metropolitan, 4. Lasky later condemned any "tragic ending"—Jack Jungmeyer, "Happy Ending in Pictures Here for a Long Stay, Says Lasky," *DSN* (February 24, 1924): Metropolitan, 7. See also the preview of *The Hunchback of Notre Dame* that asked a group of exhibitors and critics to vote on which of three different endings would serve as its finale—"Three Endings for This Film," *DSN* (January 18, 1925): Metropolitan, 16.

209. "Film Fame for a Copy Reader," *DSN* (April 6, 1924): Metropolitan, 4; "Story Prices Still Soaring," *DSN* (April 13, 1924): Metropolitan, 4.

210. Harold Hefferman, "New Production Factor to Stake All on Story," *DSN* (February 18, 1923): Metropolitan, 3; "Untried Film Authors Hit," *DSN* (July 9, 1923: Metropolitan, 8; "Film 'Courses' Bait for Many," *DSN* (June 29, 1924): Metropolitan, 6. For an excellent analysis of the Palmer Photoplay Corporation, see Anne Morey, *Hollywood Outsiders: The Adaptation of the Film Industry, 1913–1934* (Minneapolis: University of Minnesota Press, 2003), 70–111.

211. "Women Pluck Rich Plums as Writers and Directors," *DSN* (January 7, 1923): Metropolitan, 7; James W. Dean, "Jeanie M'Pherson Rests," *DSN* (January 21, 1923): Metropolitan, 5; "Film Job Others Scorned Gives June Mathis Wealth," *DSN* (February 4, 1923): Metropolitan, 9. For an excellent analysis of women screen writers during this period, including these three prominent figures, see Giuliana Muscio, "Clara, Ouida, Beulah, et al.," in *Reclaiming the Archive: Feminism and Film History*, ed. Vicki Callahan (Detroit: Wayne State University Press, 2010), 289–308.

212. According to costume designer Clare West, Europe now was dependent on American films "for ideas on women's fashions"—"Claims Our Movies Set Styles Abroad," *DSN* (March 4, 1923): Metropolitan, 7. For a further example of women working "behind the scenes," see the photos of the perforating, printing, and assembling rooms in Rothacker's "Moving Pictures" catalog (1919), available as a digitized file on the Margaret Herrick Library website. See also the column listing a score of "college girls" working in the industry—Jungmeyer, "College Girls in the Movies," *DSN* (November 2, 1924): Metropolitan, 6.

213. Harold Hefferman, "Distribution Dominant Factor in Film's Career," *DSN* (February 24, 1924): Metropolitan, 4.

214. "Movie Facts Boiled Down," *DSN* (February 18, 1923): Metropolitan, 3. The statistics came from the Motion Picture Theater Owners of America.

215. Harold Hefferman, "Survey Shows Movie Attendance Shrinks 400 Per Cent," *DSN* (August 3, 1924): Metropolitan, 5.

216. Harold Hefferman, "Exhibitors Clean Up," and "Juvenile Film Houses Coming," *DSN* (June 22, 1924): Metropolitan, 5.

217. "Film 'Preview' a Social Event," *DSN* (October 7, 1923): Metropolitan, 8.

218. L. L. Stevenson, "Usherettes Dressing Up Broadway Film Palaces," *DSN* (September 16, 1923): Metropolitan, 7.

219. "'Best of '22' Again Picked," *DSN* (August 6, 1922): Metropolitan, 3.

220. "'The 11 Best' by Sherwood," *DSN* (December 31, 1922): Metropolitan, 3. Sherwood also was motion picture editor of the *New York Herald*.

221. Harold Hefferman, "The Season's Quality 10," *DSN* (December 24, 1922): Metropolitan, 3.

222. *Grandma's Boy* had a record 19-week run at the Symphony theater in Los Angeles—"Lloyd Smashes Comedy Record," *DSN* (October 1, 1922): Metropolitan, 6. Later he predicted *The Covered Wagon* would be "the picture of the year"—Harold Hefferman, "Year of Few Big Ones," *DSN* (April 8, 1923): Metropolitan, 3.

223. Harold Hefferman, "Critics Disagree in Vote on Best, Worst Pictures," *DSN* (September 30, 1923): Metropolitan, 4.

224. "Mr. Sherwood Picks Them Over," *DSN* (December 2, 1923): Metropolitan, 9. See also Hefferman's list—"The Ten Best Pictures," *DSN* (December 30, 1923): Metropolitan, 4.

225. Jack Jungmeyer, "'10 Best' Lists Keeping It Up," *DSN* (January 11, 1925): Metropolitan, n.p. See also a summary of *Photoplay*'s survey of audience favorite stars and directors, according to five thousand exhibitors—"Exhibitor Vote Packs Surprises," *DSN* (May 18, 1924): Metropolitan, 4.

226. "Entertainers Return to the Movie Fields," *DSN* (July 30, 1922): Metropolitan, 11; "Henry Starts Out," *DSN* (August 5, 1922): Metropolitan, 3; "Bandman Simons," *DSN* (October 15, 1922): Metropolitan, 6; "Scotch Baritone Is Soloist at Capitol," *DSN* (December 3, 1922): Metropolitan, 9; "Michigan Girls Feature in Capitol Musical Act," *DSN* (October 28, 1923): Metropolitan, 5.

227. "Movie Theatre Prolog from Ned Wayburn," *DSN* (January 4, 1925): Metropolitan, 12.

228. "Bushman and Bayne at Capitol Next Week," *DSN* (April 29, 1923): Metropolitan, 3; "Bebe to Dance at the Capitol," *DSN* (June 17, 1923): Metropolitan, 6.

229. Edward Speyer, "Who'll Have Paramount Spoils of Court Battle," *DSN* (July 23, 1922): Metropolitan 8; "Film Men War, Michigan Quits," *DSN* (June 10, 1923): Metropolitan, 4.

230. "First National Meeting Calls Kunsky and Trendle," *DSN* (October 21, 1923): Metropolitan, 5; "Movie Managers Fight Road Show Menace," *DSN* (December 9, 1923): Metropolitan, 15.

231. "Kunsky'a New Theater Name," *DSN* (May 18, 1924): Metropolitan, 6; "Many Changes Made in Broadway Strand," *DSN* (July 27, 1924): Metropolitan, 4; "Ferry Field Bought by Charles Miles," *DSN* (August 10, 1924): Metropolitan, 6; "East Side Theater Changes Ownership," *DSN* (August 17, 1924): Metropolitan, 6.

232. "Essay Contest Time Extended," *DSN* (April 22, 1923): Metropolitan, 6; "Central Pupil Essay Winner," *DSN* (June 17, 1923): Metropolitan, 6.

233. "Producer Offers Film Scholarship," *DSN* (February 25, 1923): Metropolitan, 3; Jack Jungmeyer, "Colleges Aid Infant Movie," *DSN* (November 25, 1923): Metropolitan, 5. "Here's a Chance to Win $500," *DSN* (October 7, 1923): Metropolitan, 5.

234. "Here's Your Chance to Help the Movies Grow Better," *DSN* (June 3, 1923): Metropolitan, 7; "Detroit Youth Qualifies as the Most Constructive Movie Critic in America," *DSN* (July 1, 1923): Metropolitan, 3. A year later, the Authors League held another contest offering $10,000 to the winning author "whose story or play makes the best picture"—"Judges Seek $10,000 Movie," *DSN* (September 7, 1924): Metropolitan, 7. See also the prize for the best "comedy sketch," which would be performed at the industry's "annual Naked Truth" dinner in New York—"$100 Reward For a Sketch," *DSN* (February 17, 1924): Metropolitan, 7.

235. "Are You a Real Movie Fan? Answer These and Qualify," *DSN* (April 15, 1923): Metropolitan, 6.

236. "How Long Does the Film Last?," *DSN* (February 19, 1922): Society, 7.

237. "Kineophile, Film Fancier, May Be Collecting Factor," *DSN* (July 16, 1922): Metropolitan, 10. See also "Historical Film for Smithsonian Institution," *DSN* (February 18, 1923): Metropolitan, 6.

238. "U.S. Government May Adopt Plan for Memorial Movie Hall," *DSN* (March 2, 1924): Metropolitan, 7.

239. "Hollywood Is 13 Years Old," *DSN* (November 23, 1924): Metropolitan, 5; "Films Propose Annual Fiesta," *DSN* (December 1, 1924): Metropolitan, 15.

240. Charles G. Steinhauer, "Screen Stars to be Seen in Themes from Speaking Stage," and "Popular Plays Are Dramatized for Week's Photoplay List," *DJ* (January 5, 1918): 7; Steinhauer, "Comedy and Fist Fights Afford Screen Diversion," and "Spy Plots and Heart Interest Dramas Are Made Film Topics," *DJ* (January 12, 1918): 7.

241. "Motion Picture Directory," *DJ* (December 21, 1918): 5.

242. "The Screen," *DJ* (January 11, 1919): 6.

243. "Go to the Movies To Day at Your Favorite Theater," *DJ* (January 28, 1919): 6.

244. Charles C. Reed, "New Features in Pictures," *DJ* (July 19, 1919): 7.

245. "Go to the Movies To Day," *DJ* (July 31, 1919): 7; "The Screen," *DJ* (August 2, 1919): 7.

246. "The Screen," *DJ* (September 6, 1919): 7–9.

247. "Moving Picture Theaters That Really Do Move," *DJ* (September 6, 1919): 7.

248. "A Daily Review of Photo Play," *DJ* (September 10, 1919): n.p.

249. Marjorie Daw, "Players of Shadow World Undimmed by Autumn Days," *CPD* (September 1, 1918): Editorial/Dramatic, 4. Why Daw left the *Plain Dealer* to work as photoplay editor for the *Journal* is unclear.

250. Marjorie Daw, "Every Cinema Has Its Day During Sultry Months," *CPD* (June 1, 1919): Editorial/Dramatic, 4.

251. "Our Daily Worse Than Verse" and "Things the Young People Ought to Know," *DJ* (September 16, 1919): n.p.

252. "Mixing Up with Tom Mix Cowboy Actor," *DJ* (September 18, 1919): n.p.; "Constance Danced Her Way into Stardom in Pictures," *DJ* (December 11, 1919): n.p.; Marjorie Daw, "Blind-Soldiers Are Amused by Film Topics," *DJ* (December 12, 1919): 1; "What '66460' Thinks of 'The Miracle Man,'" *DJ* (December 20, 1919): 8.

253. "Doug Breaks House Record at Majestic," *DJ* (September 11, 1919): n.p.; Marjorie Daw, "Told of Billy a Gum Merchant," *DJ* (November 28, 1919): n.p.

254. "What Do You Know About a Perfect Lover?" and Marjorie Daw, "'Perfect Lover' Letters Pour In," *DJ* (September 10, 1919): n.p.

255. "A New Series of Journal Movie Puzzle Pictures," *DJ* (September 15, 1919): 6.

256. "Third Big Week in the Journal's Movie Contest," *DJ* (November 24, 1919): 6.

257. "Women—and the newspaper" ad, *DJ* (September 25, 1919): n.p.

258. Marjorie Daw, "Still Another Field For Girls," *DJ* (November 14, 1919): n.p. See also the reference to Ince's scenario contest in Daw, "If You Are a Student of Photoplay Writing at Columbia University You Are Eligible," *DJ* (March 4, 1920): 10.

259. Marjorie Daw, "How a Woman With an Idea Built a Business With a Soul," *DJ* (December 24, 1919): n.p. Scott's first film was being shot at Bantam Ball Bearing in Connecticut.

260. See also the unsigned column, shortly before Daw's name appeared, about the script-writing course at Columbia University—"Goodbye, Cicero! Hello Charley Chaplin! College Now Teaches the Movies," *DJ* (August 25, 1919): n.p.—as well as the stereotypical dialogue in which a wife bribes her husband to go with her to the movies one night—Marjorie Daw, "The Week in Photoplay," *DJ* (November 15, 1919): 7.

261. Marjorie Daw, "Doug and Chas. at the Circus," *DJ* (November 11, 1919): n.p.

262. Margorie Daw, "Prohibition Must Answer for This," *DJ* (November 20, 1919): n.p.

263. The *Journal* printed a one-page version of the two-page spread in the *Free Press*—"C.B. DeMille's 'Male and Female,'" *DJ* (December 6, 1919): 9.

264. "Says Tom: 'I Was a King in Babylon, And You Were a Christian Slave,'" *DJ* (November 15, 1919): 8.

265. "1920—The Year of the Women, God Bless 'Em—1920," *DJ* (January 2, 1920): n.p.

266. Marjorie Daw, "Don't Hesitate, Girls—Leap Year Is Pop Year," *DJ* (January 27, 1920): n.p.

267. Marjorie Daw, "Have You a Little Photoplay Scenario in Your Head?," *DJ* (January 28, 1920): n.p.

268. Marjorie Daw, "Answering the Cry—'How Shall I Get in the Movies?,'" *DJ* (February 11, 1920): n.p.

269. Marjorie Daw, "Shop for Your Movies As You Do for Shoes," *DJ* (January 20, 1920): n.p. Almost as a sop to boys, Daw printed her own bit of doggerel—Marjorie Daw, "It's Nice to Be a Movie Star But It's Nicer to Turn the Crank," *DJ* (March 3, 1920): 12.

270. Marjorie Daw, "This Little Journey Takes Us to the Home of Pearl White," *DJ* (December 27, 1919): n.p.

271. Marjorie Daw, "This Is a Little Journey to the Home of Ethel Clayton," *DJ* (January 3, 1920): n.p.; Daw, "Our Fourth Little Journey—The Home of Eugene O'Brien," *DJ* (January 10, 1920): n.p.; Daw, "This Little Journey Takes Us to the Home of Billie Burke," *DJ* (January 17, 1920): n.p.; Daw, "This Is a Little Journey to the Home of Wesley Barry," *DJ* (January 24, 1920): n.p.; Daw, "A Little Journey to the Home of Mr. and Mrs. Charles Chaplin," *DJ* (January 31, 1920): n.p.; Daw, "This Little Journey Takes Us to the Home of Charles Ray," *DJ* (February 7, 1920): n.p.; Daw, "This Little Journey Takes Us to the Home of Enid Bennett," *DJ* (February 14, 1920): n.p.; and Daw, "This Time We Journey to the Home of Mr. and Mrs. Thomas H. Ince," *DJ* (March 6, 1920): 5.

272. Marjorie Daw, "Loew Purchases Metro Pictures," *DJ* (January 8, 1920): n.p.; Daw, "Bara Returns—The Most Famous Vamp of All!," *DJ* (January 9, 1920): n.p.; "Largest Library of Motion Pictures," *DJ* (January 13, 1920): n.p.; "Movies Invade World's Most Ancient Cities," *DJ* (February 4, 1920): n.p.; "Regulate Films by Federal Law," *DJ* (February 20, 1920): n.p.

273. Marjorie Daw, "Do You Like Unhappy Endings to Pictures?," *DJ* (February 24, 1920): n.p.; Daw, "A Wail About the Ubiquitous Closeup," *DJ* (February 25, 1920): n.p.

274. "Film Advertiser Talks at Board of Commerce," *DJ* (January 6, 1920): n.p.; "Sees More Movies Than Anybody in Town," *DJ* (January 21, 1920): n.p.; "'Boy Manager' Comes to Fox's Washington," *DJ* (February 6, 1920): n.p.

275. Marjorie Daw, "What to See This Week at Photo Play Theaters," *DJ* (January 12, 1920): n.p.

276. Ann Greene, "Film Versions of Popular Novels Will Be Featured Next Week," *DJ* (May 1, 1920): 7.

277. Ann Greene, "Olive Is Proud of Her Long Island Home," *DJ* (May 15, 1920): 9; "Film Fans Mourn Death of One of Their Favorites," *DJ* (September 11, 1920): 7.

278. "Let Heroine Weep in Peace to Avoid the 'Close-Up,'" *DJ* (May 17, 1920): 12.

279. Ann Greene, "A Lurid Photoplay Is Logical Successor of Dime Novel," *DJ* (May 12, 1920): 7.

280. Ann Greene, "News of the Screen and Its Players" and "'Movie' Pests: Reel 1," *DJ* (May 20, 1920): 10. These cartoons lasted at least into early June.

281. "Every Good 'Movie' Fan Is a Star-Gazer," *DJ* (May 1, 1920): 8; "The 'Treat 'Em Rough' Movie Hero Doesn't Appeal to Ladies," *DJ* (June 9, 1920): 16.

282. "Cecile De Mille Will Solve Your Problems for You," *DJ* (June 12, 1920): 9.

283. "William Fox Started in the Cloth-Sponging Business," *DJ* (September 5, 192)): 6; "Women Help Develop Movies as Writers, Directors, Players," *DJ* (November 21, 1920): 23. See also Mary S. O'Connor, "Advice to Writers of Photo-Drama," *DJ* (September 5, 1920): 6; and "Drama Is Essential to Movie, Is Creed of Scenario Chief," *DJ* (December 21, 1920): 17.

284. "Will Every Home Have a Photo-Play Outfit Soon?," *DJ* (September 25, 1920): 6.

285. "They're Dishing Up a Movie Title," *DJ* (December 7, 1920): 14; "Slow Motion Movie Useful in Solving Science Problems," *DJ* (December 17, 1920): 18. See also Greene's reprint of an interview with Henry King in "'Clever Subtitles Add to Enjoyment of Picture' Says Director," *DJ* (May 7, 1920): 15.

286. Ann Greene, "News of the Screen and Its Players," *DJ* (September 3, 1920): 5.

287. "American Public Likes Speed—Movies Prove It," *DJ* (September 11, 1920): 6.

288. Howard O. Pierce, "How a Big Theater Arranges and Times Its Programs," *DJ* (September 18, 1920): 6.

289. "Putting Movie Show Together a Problem for Skilled Buyer," *DJ* (December 9, 1920): 6.

290. "Couzens to Play Mayor's Part in Journal's Movie," *DJ* (November 23, 1920): 1; "Here Are Leading Figures in Journal's Movie Play, 'A Romance of Detroit,'" *DJ* (December 6, 1920): 1; "'Romance of Detroit' Ready for Showing," *DJ* (December 10, 1920): 1; Adams ad, *DJ* (December 11, 1920): 5; "Journal Film Play Full of Fun and Real Talent," *DJ* (December 14, 1920): 10; "Fun Loving Film Crowd," *DJ* (December 15, 1920): n.p.

291. "You Can Help Pick Most Popular Film Stars of America," *DJ* (December 4, 1920): 7; "What Star Rules the Screen Today?," *MPW* (December 4, 1920): 568; "Who, Really, Is the Popular One?," *MPW* (December 4, 1920): 569. See also "Star Contest Will Have Nation-Wide Co-operation," *MPW* (December 11, 1920): 698–699. The *Detroit Journal* announcement was reprinted as a prominent example in *MPW* (December 18, 1920): 834.

292. "Who Do You Say Are King and Queen of Filmdom? Cast Your Ballot Today," *DJ* (December 14, 1920): 1.

293. "Mary Pickford Jumps Two, Lands Right in Queen Row," *DJ* (December 18, 1920): 1; "Pearl Leaps to Queen Row; Little Mary Has a Tumble," *DJ* (December 21, 1920): 1.

294. "Norma Talmadge and Wallace Reid Win National Star Popularity Contest," *MPW* (March 19, 1921): 247.

295. Charles Richard Laurence, "Movies in School Becoming Part of Regular Studies," *DJ* (February 1, 1921): 4.

296. "Write to Me!," *DJ* (February 25, 1921): 19.

297. Charles Richard Laurence, "Now's the Season When Film Stars Make Personal Appearances," *DJ* (October 28, 1921): 22; Laurence, "Jan. 10 Set Aside for Social Program," *DJ* (January 7, 1922): 3; Laurence, "Capitol, Movie House, Has 4,500 Seats, Cost Million," *DJ* (January 12, 1922): 6.

298. Sarah Maybury, "Well, Well! Theda's Getting Too Pretty to Be a Horrid Vampire," *DJ* (October 12, 1921): 22.

299. "'Vamps' and 'Flappers' Are Barred by Grand Rapids Boys," *DJ* (February 28, 1922): 11. See also Charles Richard Laurence, "Film Vamps Wink and Shake Out of Filmdom's Favor," *DJ* (February 10, 1921): 18.

300. "For Your Scrap Book of Stars," *DJ* (September 6, 1921): 18; Charles Richard Laurence, "Are the Movie Plays You Thought Best Listed by C.R.L.?," *DJ* (January 20, 1922): 20.

301. Among this second list, intriguingly, was a French import, Abel Gance's *J'Accuse*.

302. C.R.L., "Experience at the Broadway Strand" and "Theda Bara Doesn't Shock Us," *DJ* (October 10, 1921): 10.

303. "Michigan Theater Owners Bar Indian Guide's Film," *DJ* (January 21, 1922): 5.

304. "Blonde Scores As Most Beautiful," *DJ* (February 24, 1921): 18; "It's Her Own Idea of Smilin' Through," *DJ* (May 26, 1922): 6.

305. "Can They Come Back? Well, Here's Cleo Ridgley," *DJ* (August 31, 1921): 6; Constance Calumet, "Loving Mothers Make Best Villains," *DJ* (January 31, 1922): 20.

306. Peter Gridley Smith, "Movieland's Oriental Cinderella," *DJ* (September 3, 1921): 6; Charles Richard Laurence, "Host of Derringer Devils Still Spread Cowboy Fame," *DJ* (October 21, 1921): 18; "Turning to Pictures of Higher Sort, Says Star," *DJ* (May 3, 1922): 14; Laurence, "Screen Player Can't Hide Behind Part or Face, Says Colleen," *DJ* (June 23, 1922): 16. See also "The Father," "Dorothy Dalton's a Nice Girl—And an Actress," *DJ* (October 10, 1921): 7; and "She's [Negri] Presumed to Typify 'Passion,'" *DJ* (May 16, 1922): 16.

307. "Meet Carl Laemmle, One of the Pioneers of Movies," *DJ* (August 27, 1921): 5; Charles Richard Laurence, "Something About the Men Whose Names Follow 'Produced By' Line," *DJ* (October 7, 1921): 18; Laurence, "Producer of 'Passion' Here to Study American Movie Methods," *DJ* (January 4, 1922): 16; Laurence, " 'Passion' Producer Tells How He Manages Mobs in Movie Plays," *DJ* (January 11, 1922): 14; Elder Small, " 'Doll Face' and Matinee Idol Losing Out in Films," *DJ* (May 16, 1922): 16.

308. "Hays to Quit Cabinet for Movie Post," *DJ* (January 14, 1922): 2; Charles Richard Laurence, "Exhibitors Wonder If Will Hays Will Cut the Cost of Pictures," *DJ* (January 25, 1922): 10. See also "Will Hays Is Injured in Rail Wreck," *DJ* (October 28, 1921): 2.

309. Charles Richard Laurence, "'Griffith of France' Picks His Settings as He Tours with Picture Crew," *DJ* (September 8, 1921): 20; Laurence, "Reds in Paris Riot Over Unflattering Movie Film," *DJ* (January 5, 1922): 16.

310. Charles Richard Laurence, "Movie Subtitles Are Quite Superfluous If Play Is Right," *DJ* (February 23, 1921): 5; Laurence, "Movie Theater Greatest Tear Factory in World for Man and Maid," *DJ* (May 1, 1921): 18. See also C. C. McIntyre, "All New York Shows Interest in Movies," *DJ* (May 20, 1922): 5.

311. Charles Richard Laurence, "Sennett's Bathing Beauties Would Be Banished by New Yorkers," *DJ* (September 6, 1921): 18.

312. Charles Richard Laurence, "Fake Schools for Movie Actors Lure Ambitious Amateurs," *DJ* (February 7, 1921): 16; Laurence, "Embryo Stars Tumble to Fraud When Fake Movies Schools Are Raided," *DJ* (February 21, 1921): 9.

313. Charles Richard Laurence, "Movies in School Becoming Part of Regular Studies," *DJ* (February 1, 1921): 4.

314. Charles Richard Laurence, "Thousands of Feet of Film Developed for One Photoplay," *DJ* (February 4, 1921): 10; Laurence, "Barely Sixth of Film Footage Taken Appears in Final Picture," *DJ* (October 5 1921): 16.

315. "The Movies News Man Gambles With His Life," *DJ* (September 1 1921): 20; Charles Richard Laurence, "Trick Movie Camera Man Is Past Master of Art of Legerdemain," *DJ* (October 10, 1921): 10. See also Laurence, "Metronome Times Double Film Exposure to Fraction of Second," *DJ* (October 3, 1921): 10.

316. "Maze of Lights Vital in Making of Modern Movie," *DJ* (January 26, 1921): 4; Charles Richard Laurence, "Success of Picture Rests on Shoulders of Movie Director," *DJ* (February 2, 1921): 10; Laurence, "Old and New School Movie Directors Clash in Battle of Opinions," *DJ* (October 10, 1921): 16; "Even Film Kiss Is Changed, Sighs Clara Kimball Young," *DJ* (October 20, 1921): 16.

317. Joseph A. Jackson, "A Country Home Built in the Studio," *DJ* (October 1, 1921): 7. See also "Here's Whole Village Being Built to Stage Photoplay," *DJ* (January 25, 1921): 12.

318. "Movie Research Bureau a Mine of Information," *DJ* (January 4, 1922): 16. McCaffey did much of the original research for Cecil B. DeMille's films.

319. "New Film Gives Glimpse of Life in Movie Studio," *DJ* (May 24, 1922): 10.

320. "Love Story of a Movie Star," *DJ* (September 9, 1921): 14.

321. "Love Story of a Movie Star," *DJ* (October 29, 1921): 7.

322. "Screen," *DT* (March 16, 1919): 7, and (March 23, 1919): 7. The coverage expanded ever so slightly through the rest of that year—"Screen," *DT* (August 10, 1919): 9, and (November 29, 1919): 7.

323. "The Screen," *DT* (April 2, 1921): 16.

324. Milton Bronner, "Fall of Warsaw Made Star of Negri," *DT* (June 7, 1921): n.p.; Neal R. O'Hara, "The New Film Stars," *DT* (June 9, 1921): n.p.; "Goodbye, Jazz! Howdydo, to the Costume Plays," *DT* (June 30, 1921): n.p.

325. Ralph Holmes, "Barthelmess Pleases in First Star Role," *DT* (December 12, 1921): 4. See also his stage column that day—"'Thumbs Up' Is Verdict on the Follies."

326. Ralph Holmes, "Two-Fisted Action Fills Film at Madison," *DT* (December 19, 1921): 4.

327. A. F. Monroe, "Shattered Romance Is Theme of Film at Adams," *DT* (December 19, 1921): 4. Two other reviews were unsigned: "'The Call of the North' Is Hudson Bay Story" and "Mix in Glory in Wild West Thriller." Some scenes in *What Do Men Want?* were thought too risqué and cut—see Emma-Lindsay Squier, "What Do Men Need?" *Picture-Play Magazine* (May 1921), reprinted in *Lois Weber Interviews*, ed. Martin F. Norden (Jackson: University of Mississippi Press, 2019), 124–126.

328. Ralph Holmes, "'Miss Lulu Bett' Done Well in DeMille Film," *DT* (January 9, 1922): 4; A. F. Munroe, "'The Lotus Eater,' Capitol Film, Is Superb," *DT* (January 16, 1922): 4.

329. "Censorship After Exhibition Is the Latest," *DT* (January 21, 1922): 5; "Multiple Reel to Be 10 Years Old in March," *DT* (January 27, 1922): 7.

330. Ralph Holmes, "Wonderful Color Effects at New Capitol," *DT* (January 9, 1922): 4; "Capitol Theater Opens; 4,500 Enjoy Big Show," and "Kunsky Has Dramatic Rise to Fame," *DT* (January 13, 1922): 4.

331. "Here Is the Opening Picture in Times Movie Play Title Test," *DT* (December 2, 1921): 3. The *Times* sponsored a later subscription contest for boys and girls, offering prizes of two thousand bicycles worth $50 each—Advertisement, *DT* (May 11, 1922): 12.

332. "Times' $2,500 Golden Movie Title Test Thrills City," *DT* (December 5, 1921): 3; "Great Interest Manifested in Times' $2,500 Movie Title Test," *DT* (December 8, 1921): 3; "Here Is Movie Play Title Test No. 19," *DT* (December 24, 1921): 43. The *Times* also arranged to have promotional "movie title slides" shown in nearly every one of the city's picture theaters except the big first-run theaters—"Theaters Aid Movie Fans in Times' Title Play Test," *DT* (December 7, 1921): 3.

333. "$2,500 in Cash—138 Awards," *DT* (December 9, 1921): n.p.

334. "Times Awards $2,500 to Winners of Movie Title Test," *DT* (February 1, 1922): 7. For a photo of Otto Lee (with his cane) receiving his award, see "Winners of Times Movie Title Test Receive Their Awards," *DT* (February 2, 1922): 9.

335. "Stage / Screen," *DST* (August 6, 1922): 4.1–4.

336. "Stage / Screen," *DST* (August 20, 1922): 4.1.

337. "Society News / Stage and Screen," *DST* (June 10, 1923): 2.1.

338. "Motion Picture Review and Notes," *DT* (January 7, 1924): 8, and (January 12, 1924): 5.

339. Ed Harrison, "News of Filmland," *DT* (March 15, 1922): 4.

340. Ed Harrison, "'Mme Violet's' Brains Helped Her Needle" and "Hollywood Typists Graduate into Writing Scenarios," *DT* (May 15, 1922): 15; and Harrison, "Anita Stewart Warns Girls Who Seek Fame in Movies," *DT* (July 14, 1922): n.p. See also Eric von Stroheim, "Movie Villain Tells Girls How to Avoid 'Bad Men' in Life," *DT* (June 7, 1922): 5; and "Continuity Writer Is Movie Career for Clever Woman," *DT* (June 7, 1922): 11.

341. Ed Harrison, "Detroit-Made Film in Week's Attractions," *DT* (June 3, 1922): 4; Harrison, "The First Woman Puts Detroit in Films," *DT* (June 5, 1922): 4; Harrison, "Marie Prevost

Charms Despite Absurd Tale," *DT* (July 31, 1922): 11; Harrison, "Nanook, Rare and Novel Entertainment," *DT* (September 18, 1922): 9.

342. Allan Jenkins, "Beyond the Rocks Has Fine Acting in Silly Story," *DT* (May 8, 1922): n.p.

343. William Talbot, "Film Folk," *DT* (April 19, 1922): 15; Talbot, "Anita Stewart's Style Dazzles Girl Scribe," *DT* (May 3, 1922): 15; Talbot, "Film Celebrities Display Latest Fashions," *DT* (May 4, 1922): 15; Guy Price, "Screen Notes," *DT* (July 23, 1922): 11; Ray H. Leek, "Film Talk at Hollywood," *DST* (September 17, 1922): 4.4; Talbot, "News of the Movies," *DT* (October 13, 1922): 26. Leek's column was syndicated in other papers—see "New Claire Windsor Kidnaping; Why Film Titles Are Changed," *Oakland Tribune* (October 1, 1922): Amusements, 1.

344. Ed Harrison, "D. W. Griffith Almost Eclipses Own Film," *DT* (March 13, 1922): 4; and Madelynne Miller, "Gish Sisters Discuss Marriage, Mothers, and Temperament," *DT* (March 14, 1922): 5.

345. Joseph L. Kelley, "All-Star Films Open with Much Promise to Detroiters," *DST* (December 3, 1922): 4.1.

346. Joseph L. Kelley, "Pearl White Back in 'Thrillers' After Turn on Stage," *DT* (November 29, 1922): n.p; Kelley, "Film Fans Regulate Type and Length of Cinema Drama," *DT* (December 1, 1922): 22; Kelley, "Mary Miles Minter Drops from Stardom," *DT* (December 14, 1922): 10.

347. At least one column interviewing C. Sullivan Gardner appeared earlier: The Rambler, "Promised Writer for the Screen Takes Stand Against 'Dope Evil,'" *DST* (June 10, 1922): 2.3.

348. The Rambler, "'Dr. Jack' Guarantees Cure for All Cases of the Blues," *DT* (January 4, 1923): 16; Rambler, "Melodramatic Photoplays Returning to Own on Silver Sheet," *DST* (January 14, 1923): 4.2, 4.3, 4.4; Rambler, "Woman Character Reader Promises to You All About Yourself," *DST* (April 15, 1923): 6.5.

349. The Rambler, "Here's Life History of Viola Dana, Screen's Flappiest Flapper," *DST* (September 16, 1923): 6.4; Rambler, "Tom Ince Had 'Nerve' With Him When He 'Shot' *Anna Christie*," *DST* (November 25, 1923): 6.2.

350. Rambler, "Third Dimension on Silver Screen," *DST* (April 27, 1924): 4.1.

351. Lee J. Smith, "Busy Week for Film Fanatics," *DST* (May 11, 1924): 4.1. Smith's name was missing from the Sunday pages through much of October and November, and Kelley subbed for him at the end of December.

352. Lee J. Smith, "Some Timely 'Don'ts' for Film Viewers Picking Their Show," *DST* (June 15, 1924): n.p.

353. Helen Fox, "Little Girl Moths Flutter Toward Bright Hollywood," *DST* (May 11, 1924): 4.2; "Mothers of America, Hide Your Flapper Daughters," *DST* (June 22, 1924): n.p.

354. Lee J. Smith, "Every Woman Dreams of 'Might Have Beens,' One Lesson of Films," *DST* (August 10, 1924): 5.1; Smith, "Biggest Successes on Screen Are Tales of Rugged Adventure," *DST* (February 22, 1925): 5.2.

355. Chandler Sprague, "Louise Glaum Returns to Screen After Two Years Absence," *DST* (January 18, 1925): 7.11; Sprague, "Fox Offers Woman Scenario Writer Yearly Salary of $150,000," *DST* (January 25, 1925): 7.2; Sprague, "Cecil B. De Mille Joins Powerful Western Film Combine," *DST* (February 1, 1925): 7.4.

356. Chandler Sprague, "Rudolph Valentino Declares He Is Master of His Family," *DST* (February 8, 1925): 7.4. See Giorgio Bertellini, *The Divo and the Duce: Promoting Film Stardom and Political Leadership in 1920s America* (Oakland: University of California Press, 2019).

357. Rudolf Valentino, "Valentino Finds Women of U.S. Dance Well," *DT* (May 6, 1922): n.p.

358. "Meighan Holds Record for 'Making Over' Movie Towns," *DST* (January 28, 1923): 8.2.

359. Ray H, Leek, "Will "2,000 Per Week Keep Pola Negri Happy?," *DST* (October 15, 1922): 4.4; "No 'Make-up' for Pola in Public," *DST* (November 2, 1924): n.p.

360. "Mary Pickford Named as One of 12 Greatest American Women," *DST* (January 7, 1923): 8.8; "Chatter from Hollywood Says Mary's 'Dorothy Vernon' Flops," *DST* (April 20, 1924): 8.4. See also The Rambler, "Our Mary Has Figured in Rise of Many Screen Stars," *DT* (January 6, 1923): 4.

361. "Who Is America's Screen Idol? See If You Can Guess," *DST* (June 29, 1924): 5.12.

362. "Director Tells of Why His Sea Drama Holds with Tense Interest," *DT* (June 1, 1923): 25; "James Cruze Production Declared Beet Film of Last Year," *DST* (November 16, 1924): 8.2; "Director Declines to Become Chief of His Worried Tribe," *DST* (November 30, 1924): 7.3.

363. Joseph J. Kelley, "Picture People Believe They Have a Friend in President Coolidge," *DST* (August 12, 1923): 2.5; "President Coolidge Favors Abolishment of Tax on Admissions," *DST* (December 23, 1923): 8.3.

364. "Teaching Photoplay Writing by Radio," *DT* (March 21, 1922): n.p.; "Author Gets 'Color' for Movie in Detroit Jail," *DST* (October 8, 1922): 4.3; "Film Director's Wife Aids in Making Photoplays," *DST* (October 15, 1922): 4.2; "Screen's Most Successful Woman Writer to Become Producer," *DST* (March 1, 1925): 7.3. See also the Cinderella story of Auria Yezierska, a former Polish Jewish immigrant and sweatshop worker, who published the book adapted into the Goldwyn film, *Hungry Hearts*, which appealed to Jewish audiences when shown at the Broadway Strand—"'Hungry Hearts' at the Broadway Strand," *DJC* (December 8, 1922): 3; and Joseph J. Kelley, "Girl Sweatshop Worker Writes Classic in Film Drama," *DT* (December 15, 1922): 24.

365. "Continuity Writer Is Movie Career for Clever Woman," *DT* (June 7, 1922): 11.

366. Robert Campbell, "'Slip' of a Girl Tells of Hunting Big Game in Africa," *DT* (April 27, 1923): 26.

367. Advertisement, *DST* (October 26, 1924): n.p.

368. "What Do You Know About Distribution of Motion Pictures?," *DST* (April 13, 1924): 8.2; J. Boynton, "Profit in the Movie Production Is Fifteen Per Cent," *DST* (June 15, 1924): 8.12.

369. "Film Cutter Has Screen's Hardest Work," *DT* (June 26, 1923): 15; Goldwyn's Cutter, "Film Doctor Explains Technique of Cutting Pictures," *DST* (February 10, 1924): 8.3; "Did You Know, That Colors Had No Effect on Movie Settings," *DST* (April 27, 1924): 8.3; "Orchestra Music Made to Fit Films Plan of Altschuler," *DST* (June 22, 1924): 8.12. Gibbons must have assumed that tinting would "correct" any spectrum discrepancies on orthochromatic film stock.

370. "Picking Year's Best Photoplay Popular Pastime Now," *DT* (November 17, 1922): 24. The same article reprinted Sherwood's list of titles in a "Hall of Film Fame," from *The Birth of a Nation* and *Intolerance* to several Chaplin and Fairbanks films as well as *Nanook of the North*.

371. "James Cruze Production Declared Best Film of Last Year," *DST* (November 16, 1924): 8.2.

372. "'He Who Gets Slapped' Listed Among Best Films of Last Year," *DST* (January 25, 1925): 7.1.

373. "American Photoplays Dominate Europe, Says Producer," *DST* (March 22, 1925): 7.3.

374. "Broadcasting of Motion Pictures Is Possible," *DT* (June 30, 1923): n.p.; "Scientists Promise Films by Radio," *DST* (November 9, 1924): 8.4.

375. "Rudolph Valentino Radios 'Sheik' Voice to American Girls," *DST* (March 6, 1924): 8.4.

376. "Radio Will Not Interfere with Photoplays, Says Producer," *DST* (February 8, 1925): 7.1; Chandler Sprague, "Radio Looms as Menace to Screen, Says Kunsky in Questionnaire," *DST* (March 15, 1925): 7.1.

377. Joseph L. Kelley, "Picture's Return Engagement Establishes Theater Policy," *DT* (December 12, 1922): 16; "Detroit Chosen as Key City, Madison as Key Theater for New Movies," *DST* (October 14, 19243): 8.4.

378. "Emmons and Colvin Ten-Year Partners," *DT* (August 6, 1922): 5; Joseph L. Kelley, "Big Time Voice Heard by Detroiters," *DT* (August 4, 1923): 5; "Madison Soloist Was Prima Donna With Shubert's Hit 'Maytime,'" *DST* (December 9, 1923): 8.2.

379. "Ray Miller's Famous Orchestra Here," *DST* (October 22, 1922): 4.3; "Capitol Symphony Concert Resumes Today Under Werner's Baton," *DST* (November 18, 1923): 8.4; "Many Unusual Attractions Listed for Showing at Capitol," *DST* (January 18, 1925): 7.10.

380. "Matinee for Redhead Girls at Capitol Today," *DT* (September 20, 1922): 14.

381. "Do You Read Story Before Seeing Picture?" *DST* (September 21, 1924): 8.3.

382. "What's Playing at Your Neighborhood Theatre," *DT* (January 13, 1923): 5.

383. "What's Playing at Your Neighborhood Theatre," *DT* (January 7, 1923): 4.

384. "What's Playing at Your Neighborhood Theatre," *DST* (April 15, 1923): 8.4.

385. Full page ad, *DT* (June 21, 1923): 14; "Times' $2,500 Movie Star Identification Test Opens Sunday," *DT* (June 22, 1923): 5; "Sunday Times' Movie Star Identification Test Opens" and "You Know Them—Name Them," *DST* (June 24, 1923): 1.5. At the same time, Grinnell Brothers sponsored its own "Movie Star Identification Test," with player pianos as prizes—Grinnell Bros. ad, *DST* (June 24, 1923): 1.7. This kind of movie star contest had long been a staple of fan magazines—see, for instance, "'Beauty and Brains' Contest," *PM* (January 1916): 47–51.

386. "Last Installment in Movie Star Identification Test" and two-page ad, *DST* (August 12, 1923): n.p.

387. "Winners of Times' Movie Star Identification Test Are Announced," *DT* (August 26, 1923): 1.12. Isabell Boyles, whose father was a millwright at Timken Axle, was just sixteen years old; Maybelle Garbarino's father was an Italian American pattern maker.

388. "Drug Orgy Taylor Slaying Clue; Detectives Close in on Suspect," *DT* (February 3, 1922): 1; "Taylor Tragedy Re-Enacted in Home," *DT* (February 16, 1922): 1.

389. "Film Stars, Friends of W. D. Taylor, Slain Director" and "Star Tells of Taylor Death Threat," *DT* (February 4, 1922): 1; "Movie Stars Names in Taylor Slaying Mystery," *DT* (February 6, 1922): 3; "Star's Love Note to Taylor Found," *DT* (February 7, 1922): 1; "Beauty of Films Believed by Police to Be Assassin," *DT* (February 8, 1922): 2.

390. "Career of Slain Moving Picture Director Reads Like Fiction," *DT* (February 4, 1922): 3.

391. "Jealous Ex-Husband Sought in Taylor Murder Mystery," *DT* (February 6, 1922): 3; "Girl Film Star Suspected in Taylor Murder Mystery," *DT* (February 7, 1922): 2; "Intimate Friends of Slain Movie Director" and "'Jealousy or Drugs Taylor Motive,' Says 'Craig Kennedy,'" *DT* (February 9, 1922): 3.

392. "Taylor Death Weapon Found" and "Police Give Description of Missing Valet," *DT* (February 9, 1922): 3; "Taylor Valet Breaking Down Under Severe Questions," *DT* (February 14, 1922): 2.

393. "Seeks Refuge While Suffering Collapse," *DT* (February 20, 1922): 3; "Press Agent Sues Mabel Normand," *DT* (September 20, 1922): 11.

394. "'Fatty' Arbuckle Issue Still Agitates Film World," *DT* (November 3, 1922): 14; A Theater Owner, "Motion Picture Theater Owners Comment on Arbuckle," *DST* (December 24, 1922): 4.2; Joseph L. Kelley, "'Powder' River Proves War Films Are Not 'Dead' Movie Entertainment," *DST* (August 5, 1923): 2.5.

395. Rudolph Valentino, "Valentino Charges There Is a Plot to Discredit Him," *DT* (July 5, 1922): n.p.

396. Advertisement, *DT* (August 11, 1922): 16; "Rudolph Valentino's Sadly Interrupted Honeymoon," *DST* (August 13, 1923): n.p. See also "Mary Pickford on Witness Stand in Suit," *DT* (March 1, 1922): 4; "Divorce Granted to Constance Talmadge," *DT* (June 2, 1922): 15; "Gloria Swanson Leaves Wealthy Husband," *DT* (August 10, 1922): 1; "Screen 'Vamp' Finds Legal Entanglement When Divorce Pends," *DST* (December 2, 1923): 5.3.

397. Mrs. Dorothy Davenport Reid, "Hollywood Movie Colony Cleared in Mrs. Reid's Story of Death," *DT* (December 31, 1922): 1.4; "Mrs. Reid Relates Struggles of Film Star with Dope Habit," *DT* (January 1, 1923): n.p; Mrs. Reid, "Hollywood Parasites Preyed on Wallace Reid, Says Wife," *DT* (January 2, 1923): 3; Mrs. Reid, "Heroic Dope Battle of Wallace Reid Described by Wife," *DT* (January 3, 1923): 3; Mrs. Reid, "Mrs. Reid Ends Tragic Story of 'Wally's' Dope Battle," *DT* (January 4, 1923): 3.

398. Fred Lawrence Guiles, *Marion Davies: A Biography* (New York: McGraw-Hill, 1972), 45–73, 79–82; David Nasaw, *The Chief: The Life of William Randolph Hearst* (Boston: Houghton Mifflin, 2000), 257–258; Louis Pizzitola, *Hearst Over Hollywood: Power, Passion, and Propaganda in the Movies* (New York: Columbia University Press, 2002), 185–187.

399. In 1919, Cosmopolitan Productions replaced Hearst's Graphic Film Company (founded in 1917)—Guiles, *Marion Davies*, 89–90; Nasaw, *The Chief*, 280, 306; Pizzitola, *Hearst Over Hollywood*, 112, 175.

400. Madison ad, *DT* (March 18, 1922): 4; "Marion Davies Is Liked in Film at Madison," *DT* (March 20, 1922): 4; Ed Harrison, "Marion Davies' Beauty Gleams at Capitol," *DT* (July 17, 1922): 4; Capitol ad, *DT* (July 18, 1922): 4.

401. A London art dealer praised the accuracy of the film's sets and costumes, and a large production photo offered evidence in one scene—Robert J. Prew, "Duveen Praises Marion Davies' Picture," *DT* (July 31, 1922): 11; "Scene From 'When Knighthood Was in Flower,'" *DST* (August 6, 1922): 4.

402. "'When Knighthood Was in Flower,' Greatest Picture; Masterpiece of the Screen, Most Costly, Gorgeous Production," *DST* (August 27, 1922): 4. Much of this detail was repeated in "How Easy to Make a Big Motion Picture," *DT* (September 6, 1922): 12.

403. Ed Harrison, "Marion Davies Charms in 'The Young Diana.'" *DT* (September 4, 1922): 9; Alan Dale, "Marion Davies Sets New Pace for Pictures," *DST* (September 17, 1922): 4.4; "Marion Davies' Advice to Blondes," *DST* (October 15, 1922): 7.4.

404. Advertisement, *DST* (October 8, 1922): 7.4. See also "'When Knighthood Was in Flower' Booked for Detroit," *DT* (October 19, 1922): 15.

405. Advertisement, *DT* (November 4, 1922): 6; "William J. McGrath, "Crowds Besiege Adams Theatre at 'Knighthood' Premiere," *DT* (November 6, 1922): 6. Davies received "glowing notices for her acting," especially for her moments of brilliant comedy, not only in the Hearst papers but also *"the non-Hearst press"*—Guiles, *Marion Davies*, 111.

406. John MacMahon, "'Little Old New York' With Marion Davies Shows Aboard Leviathan," *DST* (July 8, 1923); 2.6; "'Little Old New York' Wins Ovation at Its Premiere Aboard Liner Leviathan," *DST* (July 22, 1923): 2.6. Testimonies came from the shipping board chairman, a congressman, the secretary of labor, the general manager of the Ritz Carlton, and others.

407. "Critic's Praise of 'Little Old New York' Breaks All Film Records," *DST* (August 5, 1923): 1.12.

408. "Little Old New York, 100 Years Ago, Duplicated for Film," *DST* (November 25, 1923): 8.3; "Noted Artist Sketches High Lights from 'Little Old New York,'" *DST* (December 2, 1923): 8.3; "It Made a Hit with 'Toots and Casper,'" *DST* (December 9, 1923): 8.2; "Boston Acclaims 'Little Old New York,'" *DST* (January 28, 1924); 8.3. In the cartoon, Davies is dressed as a boy, in the male guise of her dead brother; she wears this disguise for at least one-third of the film—Guiles, *Marion Davies*, 123.

409. Lee J. Smith, "Love and War Were Full of Romance in the Days of 'Yolanda,'" *DST* (September 7, 1924): 8.1.

410. "Magazine Writer Pays Tribute to Marion Davies as 'Janice,'" *DT* (September 16, 1924): 18; Jack Dempsey, "'Janice Meredith' Ideal Picture, Says Jack Dempsey," *DST* (October 26, 1924): 8.2.

411. "Thousands of Players Appear in New Cosmopolitan Film," *DST* (December 14, 1924): 7.3; Adams ad, *DST* (December 21, 1924): 7.4. Almost lost in this publicity was a story of Davies's

generosity, however minimal, when she opened a bank account for a quartet of babies born in Baltimore or rather, the ones named after her—"Marion Davies Opens Bank Account for Quartette of Bouncing Babies," *DST* (December 2, 1924): 8.2.

412. "Throngs Acclaim 'Janice Meredith' in Second Week at Adams," *DST* (January 4, 1925): 7.2; "Marion Davies Film Vivid," *Detroit Times* (January 5, 1925): 4; "Many Obstacles Encountered in Producing 'Janice Meredith,'" *DST* (January 11, 1925): 7.2.

413. Adams ad, *DST* (January 11, 1925): 7.4.

414. "Pola Negri Selects Marion Davies as Beauty," *DT* (September 29, 1922): 18.

AFTERWORD

To take Pooh's question, "What do we do next?" more seriously than A. A. Milne probably intended, let me prompt further research by positing, however briefly, a series of questions derived from the previous four chapters that could extend, modify, or complicate this book's "thick description" and analysis of Detroit's "movieland" culture.

In chapter 1, the *Michigan Film Review* suggests that rental exchanges played perhaps the most crucial role in the circulation of films in Detroit and the surrounding region. Most generally, what would other metropolitan areas and even smaller cities reveal about the role of such exchanges, especially if one could research any other regional surviving trade journals, such as those listed in a 1927 Associated Publications ad[1] or the one (unlisted) that Matthew Bernstein has found in Atlanta. More specifically, how were local exchanges—from Kunsky's Madison Film Exchange to Standard Film Service—related to those of the major companies, and how did those relations change over time? Together with a closer examination of the trade press and with historical studies of other cities' economic, political, social, and cultural parameters, research in regional trade journals could also lead to a much needed, more nuanced understanding of that "least interesting" sector of the movie industry, overall film distribution, during this period—and beyond. In terms of exhibition, what would further research on zoning policies, class and ethnic/racial demographics, commercial and manufacturing sites, and transportation systems reveal about their influence on motion picture theater locations in Detroit as well as in other cities? How did the economic recession of late 1919 to early 1921 and the exclusionary federal immigration laws of the early 1920s also affect film exhibition as well as audience attendance, especially in neighborhood theaters, and how might that effect have differed in cities other than Detroit?

Chapter 2 demonstrates that Detroit movie theaters nearly always programmed variety shows that offered patrons a smorgasbord of features, short comedies, newsreels, other nonfiction films, and live performances. And sometimes a theater, especially a first-run theater, promoted a musical performance, rather than a feature film, as the headliner. Would research on other cities' theaters confirm this programming practice or lead to any significant differences? Together with the spatial spread of theaters in the city described and analyzed in chapter 1, these practices raise questions about audience demographics. If first-run theaters were probably easily accessible for well-to-do patrons, as Kunsky's *Weekly Film News* suggests, to what degree were they also accessible for working-class people, especially in ethnic communities? Could some moviegoers, especially African Americans, have been segregated within first-run theaters and even some neighborhood theaters? More specifically, would Black Bottom residents attend certain downtown theaters like the Liberty and even the Fox Washington, but perhaps not the major Kunsky palace cinemas?[2] Moreover, what effect did spatial shifts in ethnic/racial neighborhoods—that is, the expanding black population moved east and north of Black Bottom[3]—have on the programming in and audience attendance at various theaters? How crucial for ethnic communities was the city's transit system: its routes, its cost, and its scheduled runs on particular days and times of day? Could neighborhood theaters really assume that their patrons came from within walking distance, or did some—especially the larger ones outside ethnic communities—rely more on automobile traffic and the major arteries of the transit system? These kinds of questions, of course, also should be asked of other cities, whether large or small, in other regions of the country; and research on their programming practices could reveal either many parallels to those in Detroit or else striking differences.

Chapter 3 raises a question that could also provoke further research far beyond Detroit. Were the city's two local newsweeklies so unique, as the *Free Press* once claimed, or did newspapers produce their own newsreels in other cities across the country? As late as 1926, a Bell & Howell ad for its "automatic professional motion picture camera," the Eyemo, suggests that they did.[4] Among those "putting the neighborhood in the movies" with the Eyemo, the ad cited the *Chicago News* and the *Detroit News* for their "local screen service"—but added that "other newspapers and independent exhibitors" were doing likewise. Two not mentioned were the *Cleveland Plain Dealer*'s weekly newsreel, the *Motion Picture Magazine*, which ran through 1919 and perhaps beyond, and the *Cleveland Leader News*, also screening at several first-run theaters.[5] In early 1919, moreover, a large Gaumont ad in *Moving Picture World* lists two dozen "independent exchanges" that distribute the company's "news reels of *real* news."[6] Could at least some of the companies other than the Metropolitan in this ad—Savini Films in Atlanta, Eltabran Film in Charlotte, Doll-Van Film in Indianapolis, Pearce Films in New Orleans, or Doo-Lee Film in Syracuse—also have been producing and distributing local newsreels? Given the Bell & Howell ad and the two newsreels in Cleveland, the Gaumont ad should provoke further research on the newspapers in its listed cities, as well as others not cited, research that likely would reveal that the *Detroit Free Press Film Edition* and *Detroit News Pictorial* were hardly unique.

If chapter 4 offers an extensive analysis of Detroit's movie culture envisioned by the city's four newspapers, what would more research reveal about the city's economic, political, social, and cultural context within which each paper operated? What links were forged between any one newspaper and either press agents or studio publicity departments, through rental exchanges, and how did those affect the newspaper's coverage? What links existed between any one newspaper and others through "news brokers" and wire services, and how did those also affect that coverage? What could be said about any one editor or columnist drawing on further biographical information? Would studies of newspapers in other cities produce similar patterns—that is, an emphasis on music and other live acts, the prevalence of puzzle contests, an advocacy for women's employment in the industry? Or would different patterns emerge—and of what kind? Obviously, more research is needed on the question of who went to the movies, where, when, how often, and what they thought and felt about their moviegoing experiences. The Detroit newspapers offer hints in where they placed movie pages and columns, in who were the winners of their frequent puzzle contests, and in often implicit and sometimes explicit direct appeals. Those hints either assumed that women made up a large part of the city's movie audiences, or else sought, within the city's dominant masculine culture, to lure women into movie theaters of one kind or another. Would research on other cities' newspapers and even fan magazines yield similar results, or different ones? There also could be rich material in surviving scrapbooks[7] and in the movie marginalia in school "memory books"—as Leslie Midkiff DeBauche has found in scrapbooks put together by young women in the 1910s and 1920s, including from the prestigious Liggett High School in Grosse Pointe, Michigan.[8]

Finally, extant issues of the *Weekly Film News* also offer hints. From early October 1916 through December 1917, the movie fan who collected these issues cut out very particular snippets from certain pages.[9] Those snippets, which likely were intended for a scrapbook,[10] included small photos of stars and blocks or strips from the programs of specific Kunsky theaters' weekly or daily film listings. Numerous cutouts come from the downtown Washington, Madison, and Liberty theaters as well as the midtown Garden and fewer from the Alhambra and Strand to the north and west, respectively. The cutout daily strips suggest the prominence of certain stars. The most frequent is Pickford, and this fan may have seen many of her films exhibited over the course of a year, including *A Poor Little Rich Girl*, featured during the Madison's opening week in March 1917. Slightly less frequent are young Marguerite Clark; the older stage star Ethel Barrymore; Clara Kimball Young; Pauline Frederick; and the only male actor, Sessue Hayakawa. At least two serials stand out: *The Great Secret* (with Francis X. Bushman and Beverly Bayne), whose first episode appeared at the Liberty in February and later repeated one day at the Strand; and *Patria* (with Irene Castle), whose first episode opened at the Washington in February, with subsequent episodes circulating to the Garden and Alhambra in March. Surprisingly, several big films at the Washington escaped this fan's scissors—*Daughter of the Gods* and *Civilization*—as did

Intolerance in its reappearance at the Madison. But so did other films, such as *Her Double Life* (with Theda Bara), and many starring either Charlie Chaplin or Douglas Fairbanks. Do these choices of what was cut out versus what was not suggest, very tentatively, that this fan may have been a single, middle-class woman whose tastes were relatively eclectic but who could afford to go to Kunsky theaters quite frequently, often a few times each week?[11]

In the end, the variety-show appeals to movie fans were so varied that Detroit movie theaters overall seemed intent on offering—usually on the same, tightly organized programs—a smorgasbord to satisfy every taste. There was something for everyone, from those fascinated chiefly by feature films, to those attracted by big musical and dance stage numbers in first-run theaters, to those interested in local newsreels' sports coverage, to those lured by the "burlesque" performances in Polish neighborhood theaters, to the "star gazing" young woman in the 1916 *News-Tribune* drawing. They included the hypothetical single, middle-class woman snipping strips and photos from the 1916–1917 *Weekly Film News*; the winners (nearly all women in white, skilled, working-class families) of the 1923 *Times* "movie star identification test"; and the newspaper writers promoting all kinds of career opportunities for women in the industry (not to "make it" on the screen but rather to enjoy working behind the scenes).[12]

What's next? "History allows us to see patterns and make judgments," Timothy Snyder writes. "It reveals moments, each one of them different, none entirely unique. To understand one moment is to see the possibility of being the cocreator of another."[13] Much of that which we often think of as old, overly familiar, and so widely assumed can always be excavated, reexamined, and viewed anew. Is the past ever really past?

Notes

1. Associated Publications ad, *FD* (August 16, 1927): n.p.

2. Further research in police records and court documents could determine whether Detroit had or instituted any laws that segregated or even excluded black residents from picture theaters, as they did from many dance halls until after midnight.

3. See the 1925 map, "with percentage density of black population," in David Allan Levine, *Internal Combustion: The Races in Detroit, 1915–1926* (Westport, CT: Greenwood Press, 1976), frontpiece.

4. Bell & Howell Col. ad, *MPN* (September 18, 1926): 1069.

5. Sometime in the summer of 1918, the *Plain Dealer* changed the newsreel's title to *Screen Magazine*. For the *Leader*'s newsreel, see "With First Run Theatres," *MPN* (December 6, 1919): 4084, and (January 10, 1920): 611.

6. Gaumont ad, *MPW* (January 4, 1919): 38.

7. See, for instance, Edna Vercoe's six scrapbooks compiled in 1914–1915—Richard Abel, *Menus for Movieland: Newspapers and the Emergence of American Film Culture, 1913–1916* (Berkeley: University of California Press, 2015), 257–273.

8. Leslie Midkiff DeBauche, "Memory Books, the Movies, and Aspiring Vamps," Observations on Film Art, http://davidbordwell.net/blog/2015/02/08/memory-books-the -movies-and-aspiring-vamps. For references to 1917–1918 Liggitt School "memory books," see Leslie Midkiff DeBauche and Sally Key DeBauche, "American Girls' Memory Books: Accessing a Personal Archive, Revealing a Vernacular Movie Fan Culture" (presentation, Doing Women's Film and Television History Conference, University of East Anglia, Norwich, England, April 10–12, 2014). Despite DeBauche's urging, unfortunately, I have yet to research those and other "memory books."

9. That there may have been only one fan collecting these issues is complicated. Michael Hauser purchased his collection in two batches on eBay, so the issues may have come from two different fans. However, that does not explain why cutouts sometimes come from two different theaters on the same day or, in July 1917, from the Garden on three or four consecutive days or even once over a whole week.

10. See the model of how to create such a scrapbook offered by one of six teenage girls, members of a "Motion Picture Club" in Anderson, South Carolina—"Concerning Cut-Outs and Covers," *MPM* (June 1917): 154–155. See also Esther Hoffman, "My Movie Scrap Book," *The Daily Book*, 2nd ed. (May 7, 1916): 4.

11. Admittedly, the many issues of the *Weekly Film News* that no longer survive could complicate this hypothesis as well.

12. See, for instance, the *Omaha World-Herald*'s weekly series "Opportunities for Women in the Movies," from August 6 to November 19, 1922. Each of the seventeen columns focused on a single industry position and one exemplary woman. Positions ranged from secretary, hairdresser, artist, and musician to publicity writer, scenario writer, continuity writer, continuity clerk, location scout, film editor, production manager, assistant director—and, surprisingly, even director. Some of these columns are reprinted in Richard Abel, "Opportunities for Women in the Movies," *Film History* 30, no. 3 (2019): 179–196.

13. Timothy Snyder, *On Tyranny: Twenty Lessons from the Twentieth Century* (New York: Tim Duggan Books, 2017), 125.

BIBLIOGRAPHY

Historical and Theoretical Contexts

Baldasty, Gerald. *E. W. Scripps and the Business of Newspapers*. Urbana: University of Illinois Press, 1999.

Boutros, Alexandra, and Will Straw, "Introduction." In *Circulation and the City: Essays on Urban Culture*, edited by Alexandra Boutros and Will Straw, 3–36. Montreal: McGill-Queen's University Press, 2010.

Campbell, W. Joseph. *Yellow Journalism: Puncturing the Myth Defining the Legacies*. Westport, CT: Praeger, 2001.

Cooper, Patricia A. *Once a Cigar Maker: Men, Women, and Work Culture in American Cigar Factories. 1900–1919*. Urbana: University of Illinois Press, 1987.

Fourteenth Census of the United States. Washington, DC: US Government Printing Office, 1923.

Gabriele, Sandra, and Paul S. Moore. "The Globe on Saturday, the World on Sunday: Toronto Weekend Editions and the Influence of the American Sunday Paper, 1886–1895." *Canadian Journal of Communication* 34, no. 3 (2009): 337–358.

Henri, Florette. *Black Migration: Movement North, 1900–1920*. Garden City, NY: Anchor/Doubleday, 1975.

Jacobson, Matthew Frye. *Special Sorrows: The Diasporic Imagination of Irish, Polish, and Jewish Immigrants in the United States*. Cambridge, MA: Harvard University Press, 1995.

Kaplan, Richard L. *Politics and the American Press: The Rise of Objectivity, 1865–1920*. Cambridge, UK: Cambridge University Press, 2002.

Lee, Benjamin. "The Subjects of Circulation." In *The Postnational Self: Becoming and Identity*, edited by Ulf Hedetoft and Mette Hjort, 233–249. Minneapolis: University of Minnesota Press, 2002.

Massey, Doreen. *Space, Place, and Gender*. Minneapolis: University of Minnesota Press, 1994.

Nasaw, David. *The Chief: The Live of William Randolph Hearst*. Boston: Houghton Mifflin, 2000.

Nord, David Paul. *Communities of Journalism: A History of American Newspapers and Their Readers*. Urbana: University of Illinois Press, 2001.

Park, Robert E. *The Immigrant Press and Its Control*. New York: Harper, 1922.

———. "Natural History of the Newspaper." *American Journal of Sociology* 29, no. 3 (1923): 273–289.

Peterson, Joyce Shaw. *American Automobile Workers, 1900–1933*. Albany: State University of New York Press, 1987.

Pizzitola, Louis. *Hearst Over Hollywood: Power, Passion, and Propaganda in the Movies*. New York: Columbia University Press, 2002.

Zunz, Olivier. *Making America Corporate, 1870–1920*. Chicago: University of Chicago Press, 1990.

Early Twentieth-Century History of Detroit

Abonyi, Malvina Hauk. *Hungarians in Detroit*. Detroit: Wayne State University Press, 1977.

———. *Touring Ethnic Del Ray*. Detroit: Southeast Michigan Regional Ethnic Heritage Studies Center, 1975.

"A Motto Wrought into Education." *Ford Times* (April 1916): 406–409.

Angelo, Frank. *On Guard: A History of the Detroit Free Press*. Detroit: Detroit Free Press, 1981.

Barnard, Harry. *Independent Man: The Life of Senator James Couzens*. New York: Charles Scribner, 1958.

Bates, Beth Tompkins. *The Making of Black Detroit in the Age of Henry Ford*. Chapel Hill: University of North Carolina Press, 2012.

Beynon, Erdmann Doane. "The Hungarians of Michigan." *Michigan History* 21 (Winter 1937): 89–102.

Björn, Lars. *Before Motown: A History of Jazz in Detroit, 1920–1960*. Ann Arbor: University of Michigan Press, 2001.

———. "Black Men in a White World: The Development of the Black Jazz Community in Detroit, 1917–1940." *Detroit in Perspective* 5, no. 1 (Fall 1980): 1–19.

Boles, Frank. "Michigan Newspapers: A Two-Hundred-Year Review." *Michigan Historical Review* 36, no. 1 (Spring 2011): 31–69.

Boyle, Kevin, and Victoria Getis, eds. *Muddy Boots and Ragged Aprons: Images of Working-Class Detroit, 1900–1930*. Detroit: Wayne State University Press, 1997.

Brophy, Anne. "'The Committee . . . has stood against coercion': The Reinvention of Detroit Americanization." *Michigan Historical Review* 29, no. 2 (Fall 2003): 1–39.

Collier, Peter, and David Horowitz. *The Fords: An American Epic*. New York: Summit, 1987.

Conot, Robert. *American Odyssey: A History of a Great City*. New York: Morrow, 1974.

Davis, Donald F. "The Price of Conspicuous Production: The Detroit Elite and the Automobile Industry, 1900–1933." *Journal of Social History* 16, no. 1 (1982): 21–46.

Detroit City Directory. R.L. Polk & Co., 1916–1926.

Fragnoli, Raymond B. *The Transformation of Reform: Progressivism in Detroit—And After, 1912–1933*. New York: Garland, 1982.

Hamtramck Public Schools, 1923–1924. Hamtramck, MI: Board of Education, 1924.

Henrickson, William. *Detroit Perspectives: Crossroads and Turning Points*. Detroit: Wayne State University Press, 1991.

Holli, Melvin G., ed. "Part Three: Dynamic Detroit." In *Detroit*, 117–158. New York: New Viewpoints, 1976.

Hooker, Clarence. *Life in the Shadows of the Crystal Palace, 1910–1927: Ford Workers in the Model T Era*. Bowling Green, OH: Bowling Green State University Press, 1997.

Hyde, Charles K. "'Dodge Main' and Detroit's Automobile Industry, 1910–1980." *Detroit in Perspective* 6, no. 1 (Spring 1982): 49–82.

Jackson, Kenneth T. *The Ku Klux Klan in the City, 1915–1930*. New York: Oxford University Press, 1967.

Johnson, Christopher H. *Maurice Sugar: Law, Labor, and the Left in Detroit, 1912–1950*. Detroit: Wayne State University, 1988.

Kowalski, Greg. *Hamtramck: The Driven City*. Charleston, SC: Arcadia, 2002.

Levine, David Allen. *Internal Combustion: The Races in Detroit, 1915–1926*. Westport, CT: Greenwood Press, 1976.

Lewis, David. *The Public Image of Henry Ford: An American Folk Hero and His Company*. Detroit: Wayne State University Press, 1976.

Lochbiler, Don. *Detroit's Coming of Age, 1873–1973*. Detroit: Wayne State University Press, 1973.

Lutz, William W. *The News of Detroit: How a Newspaper and a City Grew Together*. Boston: Little, Brown, 1973.

Maloney, Thomas, and Warren Whatley. "Making the Effort: The Contours of Racial Discrimination in Detroit's Labor Market, 1920–1940." *Journal of Economic History* 55, no. 3 (1995): 465–493.

Mayer, Albert J. *Ethnic Groups in Detroit.* Detroit: Wayne State University Press, 1951.

Meyer, Stephen. "Adapting the Immigrant to the Line: Americanization in the Ford Factory, 1914–1921." *Journal of Social History* 14, no. 1 (Fall 1980): 67–82.

———. *The Five Dollar Day: Labor, Management and Social Control in the Ford Motor Company, 1908–1921.* Albany: SUNY Press, 1981.

Moon, Elaine Latzman. *Untold Tales, Unsung Heroes: An Oral History of Detroit's African American Community, 1918–1967.* Detroit: Wayne State University Press, 1994.

Morris-Crowther, Jayne. "Municipal Housekeeping: The Political Activities of the Detroit Federation of Women's Clubs in the 1920s." *Michigan Historical Review* 30, no. 1 (2004): 31–57.

Napolski, Sister Mary Remigia. *The Polish Immigrant in Detroit to 1914.* Chicago: Polish Roman Catholic Union of America, 1946.

O'Geran, Graeme. *A History of the Detroit Street Railways.* Detroit: Conover Press, 1931.

Radzialowski, Thaddeus C. "Ethnic Conflict and the Polish Americans of Detroit, 1921–1942." In *The Polish Presence in Canada and America*, edited by Frank Renkiewicz, 195–207. Toronto: Multicultural History Society of Ontario, 1982.

Rankin, Lois. "Detroit's Nationality Groups." *Michigan History* 23 (Spring 1939): 129–211.

Serafino, Frank. *West of Warsaw.* Hamtramck, MI: Hamtramck Avenue Publishing, 1983.

Street, Julian. "Detroit the Dynamic, Chapter IV of 'Abroad at Home,' American Ramblings, Observations, and Adventures." *Collier's* (July 4, 1914): 8–9, 23–27.

Swastek, Joseph. *Detroit's Oldest Polish Parish: St. Albertus, 1872–1973.* Detroit: St. Albertus Centennial, 1974.

Thomas, Richard. *Life for Us Is What We Make It: Building Black Community in Detroit, 1915–1945.* Bloomington: Indiana University Press, 1992.

Watts, Steven. *The People's Tycoon: Henry Ford and the American Century.* New York: Knopf, 2005.

White, Lee H. *The Detroit News: Eighteen Hundred and Seventy-Three–Nineteen Hundred and Seventeen—A Record of Progress.* Detroit: Evening News Association, 1918.

Wilson, Brian. "The Spirit of the Motor City: Three Hundred Years of Religious History in Detroit." *Michigan Historical Review* 27, no. 1 (2001): 21–56.

Woodward, Frank. *All Our Yesterdays: A Brief History of Detroit.* Detroit: Wayne State University Press, 1969.

Wytrwal, Joseph A. *The Polish Experience in Detroit.* Detroit: Endurance Press, 1992.

Zunz, Olivier. *The Changing Face of Inequality: Urbanization, Industrial Development, and Immigrants in Detroit, 1880–1920.* Chicago: University of Chicago Press, 1982.

Early Twentieth-Century Cinema History

Abel, Richard. *Americanizing the Movies and "Movie-Mad" Audiences, 1910–1914.* Berkeley: University of California Press, 2006.

———. "The Circulation of Local Newsreels in the Silent Period: The Case of Detroit." In *Rediscovering U.S. Newsfilm: Cinema, Television, and the Archive*, edited by Mark Garrett Cooper, Sarah Beth Levavy, Ross Melnick, and Mark Williams, 133–154. New York: Routledge, 2018.

———. "House Organs and the Detroit *Weekly Film News* in the 1910s." *Film History* 27, no. 3 (2015): 137–179.

———. *Menus for Movieland: Newspapers and the Emergence of American Film Culture, 1913–1916.* Oakland: University of California Press, 2015.

Afra, Kia. *The Hollywood Trust: Trade Associations and the Rise of the Studio System*. Lanham, MD: Rowan & Littlefield, 2016.

Aldridge, Henry Belden. "Live Musical and Theatrical Presentations in Detroit Moving Picture Theatres, 1896–1930." Ph.D. diss., University of Michigan, 1973.

Allen, Robert C. "Relocating American Film History: The 'Problem' of the Empirical." *Cultural Studies* 20, no. 1 (2006): 48–88.

Anderson, Mark Lynn. *Twilight of the Idols: Hollywood and the Human Sciences in 1920s America*. Berkeley: University of California Press, 2011.

Aronson, Michael. *Nickelodeon City: Pittsburgh at the Movies, 1905–1929*. Pittsburgh, PA: University of Pittsburgh Press, 2008.

Askari, Kavah, et al., eds. *Performing New Media, 1890–1915*. New Barnet, UK: John Libbey, 2014.

Bertellini, Giorgio. *The Divo and the Duce: Promoting Film Stardom and Political Leadership in 1920s America*. Oakland, CA: University of California Press, 2019.

———. "DUCE/DIVO: Displaced Rhetorics of Masculinity, Racial Identity, and Politics among Italian-Americans in 1920's New York City." *Journal of Urban History* 31, no. 5 (2005): 685–726.

———. "Sovereign Consumption: Italian American's Film Culture in 1920s New York City." In *Making Italian America: Consumer Culture and the Production of Ethnic Identities*, edited by Simone Cinottto, 83–99, 270–273. New York: Fordham University Press, 2014.

Collins, Sue. "Star Testimonials and Trailers: Mobilizing during World War I." *Cinema Journal* 57, no. 1 (Fall 2017): 46–70.

DeBauche, Leslie Midkiff. *Reel Patriotism: The Movies and World War I*. Madison: University of Wisconsin Press, 1997.

Everett, Anna. *Returning the Gaze: A Genealogy of Black Film Criticism, 1909–1949*. Durham, NC: Duke University Press, 2001.

Frykholm, Joel. *George Kleine and American Cinema: The Movie Business and Film Culture in the Silent Era*. London: Palgrave, 2015.

Fuller-Seeley, Kathryn, ed. *Hollywood in the Neighborhood: Historical Case Studies of Local Moviegoing*. Berkeley: University of California Press, 2008.

Grieveson, Lee. "The Work of Film in the Age of Fordist Mechanization." *Cinema Journal* 51, no. 3 (2012): 25–51.

Hallum, Julia, and Les Roberts, eds. *Locating the Moving Image: New Approaches to Film and Place*. Bloomington: Indiana University Press, 2014.

Hauser, Michael, and Marianne Weldon. *Detroit's Downtown Movie Palaces*. Chicago: Arcadia, 2006.

Johnson, Martin L. *Main Street Movies: The History of Local Film in the United States*. Bloomington: Indiana University Press, 2018.

King, Rob. "'Made for the Masses with an Appeal to the Classes': The Triangle Film Corporation and the Failure of Highbrow Film Culture." *Cinema Journal* 44, no. 2 (2003): 3–33.

Klenotic, Jeffrey. "Putting Cinema History on the Map: Using GIS to Explore the Spatiality of Cinema." In *Explorations in New Cinema History*, edited by Richard Maltby, Daniel Blitereyst, and Philippe Meers, 58–84. Malden, MA: Blackwell, 2011.

Köhler, Kristina. "Moving the Spectator, Dancing with the Screen: Early Dance Instruction Films and Reconfigurations of Film Spectatorship in the 1910s." In *Corporeality in Early Cinema: Viscera, Skin, and Physical Form*, edited by Marina Dahlquist et al., 275–288. Bloomington: Indiana University Press, 2018.

Koszarski, Richard. *History of the American Cinema: An Evening's Entertainment, 1915–1928*. New York: Charles Scribner, 1990.

Lescarboura, Austin C. *Behind the Motion Picture Screen.* New York: Benjamin Blom, 1971 [1919].

Lindstrom, J. A. "Where Development Has Just Begun: Nickelodeon Location, Moving Picture Audiences, and Neighborhood Development in Chicago." In *American Cinema's Transitional Era: Audiences, Institutions, Practices*, edited by Charlie Keil and Shelley Stamp, 217–238. Berkeley: University of California Press, 2004.

Luckett, Moya. *Cinema and Community: Progressivism, Exhibition, and Film Culture in Chicago, 1907–1917.* Detroit: Wayne State University Press, 2014.

Maltby, Richard, et al., eds. *Going to the Movies: Hollywood and the Social Experience of the Cinema.* Exeter, UK: University of Exeter Press, 2008.

———. *Explorations in New Cinema History: Approaches and Case Studies.* Chichester, UK: Wiley-Blackwell, 2011.

Moore, Paul S. *Now Playing: Early Moviegoing and the Regulation of Fun.* Albany: SUNY Press, 2008.

Moore, Paul S. "Space, Place, and Case: Surveying the Grounds of Cinema History." *Early Popular Visual Culture* 13, no. 4 (November 2015): 336–343.

Negra, Diane. "Immigrant Stardom in Imperial America: Pola Negri and the Problem of Typology." In *A Feminist Reader in Early Cinema*, edited by Jennifer Bean and Diane Negra, 374–404. Durham, NC: Duke University Press, 2002.

Norden, Martin F. *Lois Weber Interviews.* Jackson, MS: University of Mississippi Press, 2019.

Orgeron, Devin, et al., eds. *Learning with the Lights Off: Educational Film in the United States.* New York: Oxford University Press, 2012.

Peplin, Katy. "Ford Films and Ford Viewers: Examining 'Nontheatrical' Film in the Theaters and Beyond." In *The Institutionalization of Educational Cinema: North America and Europe in the 1910s and 1920s*, edited by Marina Dahlquist and Joel Frykholm, chapter 9. Bloomington: Indiana University Press, on press.

Quinn, Michael. "Paramount and Early Film Distribution, 1914–1921." *Film History* 11, no. 1 (1999): 98–113.

Rosenzweig, Roy. *Eight Hours for What We Will: Workers and Leisure in an Industrial City, 1870–1920.* Cambridge, UK: Cambridge University Press, 1998.

Singer, Ben. "Manhattan Nickelodeons: New Data on Audiences and Exhibition." *Cinema Journal* 34, no. 3 (1995): 5–35.

Stewart, Jacqueline. *Migrating to the Movies: Cinema and Black Urban Modernity.* Berkeley: University of California Press, 2005.

Stokes, Melvyn, et al., eds. *American Movie Audiences: From the Turn of Century to the Early Sound Era.* London: British Film Institute, 1999.

Waller, Gregory. *Main Street Amusements: Movies and Commercial Entertainments in a Southern City, 1896–1930.* Washington, DC: Smithsonian Institution, 1995.

Detroit Movie Theaters

Hauser, Michael. "Detroit's Growing Theatre District: The Rebirth of Grand Circus Park." *Marquee* 24, no. 3 (January 1992): 12–25.

Hauser, Michael, and Marianne Weldon. *Detroit's Downtown Movie Palaces.* Chicago: Arcadia Publishing, 2006.

Galbraith, Stuart IV. *Motor City Marquees, 1906–1992.* Jefferson, NC: McFarland, 1994.

Michigan Film Review, 1917–1918.

Morrison, Andrew Craig. *Opera House, Nickel Show, and* Palace. Dearborn, MI: Greenfield
     Village and Henry Ford Museum, 1974.
Photoplay Weekly, 1924–1925.
Weekly Film News, 1916–1919.

Detroit Area Newspapers

Brightmoor Journal
Dearborn Press
Detroit Free Press
Detroit Jewish Chronicle
Detroit News
Detroit Times
Dziennik Polski
Ferndale News
Hamtramck News
Highland Parker
Tribuna Italiana d'America

Early Twentieth-Century Trade Press

Educational Film Magazine
Educational Screen
Exhibitors Herald
Film Daily
Motion Picture Magazine
Motion Picture News
Moving Picture World
Photoplay Magazine
Reel and Slide/Moving Picture Age
Variety

INDEX

Page numbers in *italics* indicate figures.

Academy Awards, 225
advertising films: *The B. of C. Americanization Campaign* (1916), 89; *Behind the Scenes in a Big Detroit Hotel* (1917), 91; *Liberty Bonds—How and Why They Are Made* (1918), 32; *Lights and Shadows in a City of a Million* (1920), 157; *Majestic Baby Show* (1919), 97; *Parisian Style Show* (1921), 97; *Shoe Fashion Revue* (1921), 97
American Social Hygiene Association, 43
Americanization Movement, 8–9, 16n50, *154*, 155, 164, 185, 190n88; Ford English School, 8, 155; Ford Sociological Department, 8; YMCA, 8, 16n49, 155, 158, 180, 203, 230
archives and libraries: Bentley Historical Library, 3, 17n77, 18; Detroit Historical Society, 249n95; National Archives, 155, 158, 190n86; Wayne State University Library, 3, 175
Argentina, 218
Associated Publications, 18, 267
Authors League of America, 221, 224, 256n234
automobile companies: American Car, 7; Buick, 140, 142n8; Cadillac Motor, 7, 140; Chrysler, 140; Dodge Brothers, 5, 7, 13n17, 16n49, 52, 188n52; Ford Motor Company, 5, 8, 11, 32, 102, 143, 150–158; General Motors, 60n4; Hudson, 140; Lincoln Motor, 5; Maxwell Motor, 7; Packard Motor, 5, 7

Better Photoplay League, 43

Coolidge, Calvin, 237
censorship, 32–34, 61n16, 63n61, 74n260, 82, 210, 212, 215, 237; Detroit Police Commission, 33; Detroit Recreation Commission, 215, 251n132; National Board of Review, 218, 230
cinema historians, 2; Afra, Kia, 37; Allen, Robert C., 2; Bernstein, Matthew, 267;

DeBauche, Leslie Midkiff, 269, 271n8; Frykholm, Joel, 190n79; Grieveson, Lee, 151, 190n86; Hauser, Michael, ix, 126n19, 271n9; Johnson, Martin L., 126n18; Klenotic, Jeffrey, 2; Koszarski, Richard, 10; Melnick, Ross, 99; Moore, Paul S., ix; Reich, Jacqueline, 62n51; Simmon, Scott, 157
comic shorts: *Bees in His Bonnet* (1918), 107; *The Big Show* (1920), 104; *The Boat* (1921), 96; *Capt. Kidd's Kids* (1920), 96; *Charlie Chaplin Review* (1920), 70n184; *A Desert Hero* (1919), 108; *A Dog's Life* (1918), 35; *Fatty the Aviator* (1918), 108; *Fatty's Wash Day* (1918), 108; *The Foolish Age* (1919), 96; *Four Times Foiled* (1920), 104; *His Day Out* (1918), 108; *"Katzenjammer Kids"* (1918), 102; *Ladies First* (1918), 95; *Love and Doughnuts* (1921), 96; *Merry Jailbirds* (1919), 104; *Mutt and Jeff* (1920), 104; *My Wife's Relations* (1922), 223; *Never Weaken* (1921), 96; *Number, Please* (1920), 96; *The Orderly* (1918), 107; *The Other Man* (1916), 89; *Pay Day* (1922), 223; *The Playhouse* (1921), 96; *Roaring Lions on the Midnight Express* (1918), 107; *She Sighed by the Seaside* (1921), 96; *Shoulder Arms* (1919), 201; *The Village Smith* (1920), 102

dancers and dance acts: Barry & Milton and Their 8 Dancing Dolls, 112; Bessie Bright and Her "Flappers," 120; Blackbirds, 67n143; Brown Skinned Models, 67n143; Budrow, Manuela V., 99; Bunke's 15 Peppy Youngsters, 119; By Jingo Girls, 120, 134n222; Cliff Nichol's "Klever Kiddies," 114, 119; Dancing Maidens of the Orient, 100; Doraldina, *117*, 118; Ernie Young's Oriole Terrace Beauty Ballet, 210; Espinosa, Senor and Senora, 99; Frazier's Girl Follies, 124; Harold Brow's Yankeeland Girls, 111, 120, 124; Houkelani, Lily (Samoan Hula Dancer), 99; Klown

RICHARD ABEL is professor emeritus of International Cinema and Media Studies at the University of Michigan. He is author of *Americanizing the Movies and "Movie-Mad" Audiences, 1910–1914* (University of California Press, 2006) and *Menus for Movieland: Newspapers and the Emergence of American Film Culture, 1913–1916* (University of California Press, 2015); editor of the *Encyclopedia of Early Cinema* (Routledge, 2005/2010); and coeditor of *Early Cinema and the "National"* (Indiana University Press, 2008) and *The Sounds of Early Cinema* (Indiana University Press, 2001). Currently he is editing the forthcoming *Movie Mavens: Writing US Newspaperwomen Back into Cinema History, 1914–1923*.

CPSIA information can be obtained
at www.ICGtesting.com
Printed in the USA
BVHW030936030220
571269BV00002B/157